# THE EUROPEAN MUSICAL HERITAGE
## 800–1750

Revised Edition

# THE EUROPEAN MUSICAL HERITAGE
## 800–1750

Revised Edition

## Sarah Fuller

The State University of New York at Stony Brook

Consulting Editor in Music

## Allan W. Schindler

Eastman School of Music

Boston   Burr Ridge, IL   Dubuque, IA   Madison, WI   New York   San Francisco   St. Louis
Bangkok   Bogotá   Caracas   Kuala Lumpur   Lisbon   London   Madrid   Mexico City
Milan   Montreal   New Delhi   Santiago   Seoul   Singapore   Sydney   Taipei   Toronto

 **Higher Education**

THE EUROPEAN MUSICAL HERITAGE: 800–1750, REVISED EDITION
Published by McGraw-Hill, a business unit of The McGraw-Hill Companies, Inc., 1221 Avenue of the Americas, New York, NY,
10020. Copyright © 2006 by The McGraw-Hill Companies, Inc. All rights reserved. No part of this publication may be reproduced
or distributed in any form or by any means, or stored in a database or retrieval system, without the prior written consent of The
McGraw-Hill Companies, Inc., including, but not limited to, in any network or other electronic storage or transmission, or
broadcast for distance learning.
Some ancillaries, including electronic and print components, may not be available to customers outside the United States.

This book is printed on acid-free paper.

1 2 3 4 5 6 7 8 9 0 QPD/QPD 0 9 8 7 6 5 4

ISBN 0-07-232452-X

Editor in Chief:   *Emily Barrosse*
Publisher:   *Lyn Uhl*
Senior Sponsoring Editor:   *Melody Marcus*
Executive Marketing Manager:   *Suzanna Ellison*
Editorial Assistant:   *Beth Ebenstein*
Managing Editor:   *Jean Dal Porto*
Project Manager:   *Cathy Iammartino*
Associate Designer:   *Marianna Kinigakis*
Cover Designer:   *Marianna Kinigakis*
Cover Credit:   *Print Collection, Miriam and Ira D. Wallach Division of Art, Prints and Photographs, The New York Public Library, Astor,
    Lenox and Tilden Foundations*
Associate Production Supervisor:   *Jason I. Huls*
Media Project Manager:   *Kate Boylan*
Composition:   *Interactive Composition Corporation*
Printing:   *45# Scholarly Matte, Quebecor Dubuque*

Library of Congress Control Number: 2004115452

www.mhhe.com

To

R. P. F.

and

J. L. F.

# PREFACE TO THE REVISED EDITION

A five-CD set of recordings (ISBN: 0-07-232453-8) is now available with the revised edition of *The European Musical Heritage.* There are a total of 91 tracks included.

A star appears before each piece listed in the Table of Contents that is represented on the CD set. Throughout the anthology, for each piece where a recording is provided, a small, rectangular box with a CD icon directs the reader to the appropriate CD and track number.

Inevitably, with a project like this, questions arise over why some pieces are included on the CDs and others excluded. Clearing licensing for music is a complex process. Difficult choices must be made based upon availability of high quality recordings, the accommodation of the individual labels, and cost. Every effort was made to give you the highest quality package possible at a reasonable price. We hope that you will find this CD set a valuable companion to *The European Musical Heritage.*

This volume is intended as a treasury of great music from the past and a guide to the formative millennium of Western musical culture. It begins with the monophonic chant of the Western church and concludes with the intricate tonal polyphony of Johann Sebastian Bach and George Frideric Handel. The compositions have been chosen for their representative qualities as well as for their beauty. They compass the major genres of the European musical tradition as interpreted by its most imaginative composers (some of them anonymous) and illustrate primary compositional techniques adopted in various epochs. The selections are perforce limited to the written remains of the tradition. These, through the fifteenth century, emanate mainly from the prime centers of literacy: rich cathedrals, major monasteries, and princely courts. The myriad songs, dances, instrumental *pièces d'occasion,* and other musics that must have been transmitted orally or extemporized as required have left little or no physical trace. With the spread of music printing in the sixteenth century, the scope of written music becomes somewhat more diversified, and the field of representation broadens as well.

The anthology is organized chronologically, under subheadings that reflect the shifting dichotomies of modern convention. The distinction is first between monophony and polyphony, then between sacred and secular, and finally between vocal and instrumental. Arrangements within these headings sometimes convey significant messages. Presentation of chant in two separate sections is intended to underscore that chant composition and settings of new sacred texts took place over many centuries and coexisted with the development of polyphony. The grouping of a Petronian motet (No. 15d) with other types of late thirteenth-century motet signals the diverse background from which the *ars nova* motet emerged.

Many factors have entered into the choice of content. Care has been taken to seek out works with clearly profiled stylistic features, pieces that both possess individual artistic merit and represent a historically significant genre, style, or technique. Some attention has been given to the availability of good recordings that can serve to demonstrate performance practices and to provide concrete sound images of the scores. Practical space limitations limit the coverage to the generally acknowledged mainstream of achievements and developments, but a certain depth of perspective on processes of stylistic change is offered by substantial representation of the thirteenth-century motet and the late Renaissance Italian madrigal, and by favoring Guillaume Dufay and Claudio Monteverdi with varied cross-sections of work. Currents of tradition and continuity are suggested through coordination of selections. Some of the *ars antiqua* polyphony (Nos. 10a, 10b, 11, 13f, and 14) is based on chants from the Easter Mass (Nos. 1e, 1f). Several motets (Nos. 24b, 28, 41) take the plainsong antiphon *Ave regina caelorum* as their point of departure. Two settings of Guarini's *Cruda Amarilli* (Nos. 53 and 56) and parts of two dramatizations of the Orpheus legend (Nos. 62 and 63) illustrate diverse contemporary responses to common literary material.

Commentaries accompany each work included. The purpose of these is to supply a rudimentary historical context and to draw attention to notable features of style, technique, and expression. They are not intended to take the place of a detailed music history text. Since the historically noteworthy features of a composition depend on its genre, position within a tradition, and authorship, the commentary follows no standard formula but responds to individual conditions. The reader should actively relate observations made about one composition to others and should compare salient features of neighboring works. By means of the index, the user can trace the development of individual genres (such as polyphonic Mass, opera, trio sonata), compare approaches to specific techniques (such as canon, variation), and locate primary definitions. In matters such as the spelling of terms and of composers' names and the (often uncertain) birth and death dates of individuals, the commentary follows the conventions of *The New Grove Dictionary of Music and Musicians,* edited by Stanley Sadie (London, Washington, Hong Kong: Macmillan Publishers Ltd., 1980). The reader should consult that monument of modern scholarship on alternate spellings, evidence for dating, lists of works, and the like, as well as for additional information on particular genres, individual composers, and basic bibliography for further research.

Once the choice of content has been made, the most difficult aspect of an anthology such as this is how to present the music itself. Many early pieces exist in a number of legitimate versions and cannot be considered to have (or ever to have had) a single "authoritative" reading (compare, for example, Nos. 7a and 24c). The solution adopted here is to present either the text of a single representative manuscript or the consensus of a group of central sources (the standard "critical edition"). The list of sources (p. 610) provides information on each edition and references to publications with critical notes.

Many diverse conventions and techniques of notation were employed over the thousand years spanned in this collection, and no single modern system can adequately render them all. Moreover, modern notations of early music, far from being straightforward, unambiguous rewritings, are in reality translations involving much choice and interpretation on the editor's part. The modes of renotation presented here vary according to the nature of the original and the choice of modern conventions. For instance, some of the fifteenth- and sixteenth-century pieces are measured in conventional common-practice style (making them seem more metrical than they are), while others are marked off between staves with the prevailing mensural unit (the *tempus*) or are barred to show large rhythmic groupings. The user should understand that the resultant differences in appearance pertain only to the surface, not to the musical substance. In some instances where bar lines have not seemed appropriate the poetic line is the unit of measure. In others, figures analogous to rehearsal numbers have been provided to facilitate reference to specific spots within the piece. The plainchant, drawn from sources in several different styles of notation, has been largely translated into late twelfth-century square notation without extraneous editorial markings. A few examples appear in a neutral point notation to facilitate comparison with a polyphonic work based on the chant melody.

The degree to which the printed score might be said to represent or dictate a performance also fluctuates markedly from piece to piece. In some cases, rhythms are indeterminate in the original notation. In others, the musicians are called on to supply harmonic background, to modify intervallic progressions, to ornament melodic lines at their discretion. In most of the works collected here, tempo, instrumentation, vocal production, and dynamic nuance are left unspecified. The living performance traditions that supplied these and other essential musical elements faded away over the course of centuries, but in recent decades a number of skilled individuals and groups have dedicated themselves to reviving early music and exploring appropriate modes of performance. Some of the results have been more felicitous, some more well-informed, than others, but all have helped to sensitize contemporary listeners to varied possibilities of realizing older music. In recognition of the fact that any music takes on life only when realized in actual sound, I have, whenever possible, provided references to recordings of the works presented (see Selective Discography, p. 602). These recordings should be viewed not as definitive renditions, but as concrete instances of interpretation in which specific performance decisions have had to be made for better or for worse. The recorded performances may often differ legitimately from the printed score, and this in itself may engender thoughtful consideration of what constitutes the essential qualities of a particular piece. Some of the recordings cited are quite recent, while others were issued some years ago and will be available only in libraries. The reader should refer to current catalogues for up-to-date listings. *Early Music Discography* by Trevor Croucher (2 vols., Phoenix, Arizona: Oryx Press, 1981) is also an invaluable reference.

Live and recorded interpretations are important adjuncts to the printed score, but the music should also be experienced through personal performance. Singing and playing the compositions presented in this anthology will not only aid development of a sure stylistic sense but will also force direct confrontation with fundamental issues of restoration and interpretation. First-hand involvement through performance will, moreover, enable the student better to cope with the divorce of early music from its original context. This music was not intended to be passively absorbed in a public concert hall or transmitted impersonally through loudspeakers or headphones. The sacred works are in a real sense "service" music and functioned to embellish and exalt the worship of God. Those secular works known to us were primarily ornaments of court and civic life. They served both as entertainment and as graceful expressions of the social values and aesthetic sensibilities of the aristocracy (and, eventually, of the bourgeoisie). The

music needs to be perceived as an element within the fabric of European civilization, in a concrete social and institutional environment and within an appropriate architectural setting. A full richness of context is hard to recreate even in imagination, but in endeavoring to perform individual compositions, the student can at least draw nearer to the vital substance of early music. Such direct engagement will bring its own lasting rewards of pleasure, enrichment, and understanding.

This volume owes its existence to the cooperation and toil of many people, whose contributions I acknowledge here with real gratitude. My thanks extend to the staffs of the Music Library at the State University of New York at Stony Brook and of the music and manuscript reading rooms at the Bibliothèque nationale in Paris, who provided access to materials, and especially to Judith Kaufman, music librarian at Stony Brook, who expedited special orders and resolved many difficulties; to Leslie Morgan and Elias Rivers of the State University of New York at Stony Brook and Michael J. Freeman of the University of Leicester, who supplied translations; and to former colleagues Eric Chafe and Eva Linfield, who gave informed advice.

I am indebted besides to the following individuals, who reviewed the manuscript in its various stages: Professors C. T. Barr, State University of New York College at New Paltz; Paul W. Cherry, University of South Dakota; John Hill, University of Illinois, Urbana; D. Kern Holoman, University of California, Davis; Edward L. Kottick, University of Iowa; James W. McKinnon, State University of New York at Buffalo; David Poultney, Illinois State University; Wallace J. Rave, Arizona State University; Robert L. Smith, Florida State University; and Brownlee Waschek, Dekalb Community College, Clarkston, Georgia.

Cordial thanks go also to the staff of Music-Book Associates, particularly to George Chien, John Davis, and Claudette Hickman; and to the staff of Random House, especially to Roth Wilkofsky, who guided the project from its inception, to Carolyn Viola-John, who skillfully shepherded the manuscript into print, and to Della Mancuso, who handled the production. I am grateful too to Barbara Gerr, who scrutinized manuscript and proofs, suggesting countless improvements, and to Marianne Richert, who meticulously prepared the index.

A special debt is due to those teachers who initiated me to the splendors of early Western music, particularly Richard Crocker of the University of California at Berkeley, Nino Pirrotta and John M. Ward of Harvard University, and James Haar of the University of North Carolina at Chapel Hill. May this volume convey a measure of their spirited enthusiasm and kindle in new generations of students genuine appreciation for the art works of a grand and amazingly diverse musical heritage.

Sarah Fuller

# CONTENTS

PREFACE    ix

A Note on Square Notation    xvii

## 8TH–11TH CENTURY: SACRED MONOPHONY

1. Easter Mass Proper and Ordinary    2
   - *1a. *Resurrexi* (Introit)    2
   - 1b. *Quem queritis in sepulchro* (Introit trope 1)    3
     - *Ecce pater cunctis* (Introit trope 2)    4
   - *1c. Kyrie *Cunctipotens genitor* (melismatic and Latin versions)    5
   - *1d. Gloria    7
   - *1e. *Haec dies* (Gradual)    8
   - *1f. Alleluia *Pascha nostrum*    9
   - 1g. *Fulgens praeclara* (prose)    11
   - 1h. Credo    14
   - 1i. *Terra tremuit* (Offertory)    17
   - 1j. Sanctus    19
   - *1k. Agnus Dei    19
   - 1l. *Pascha nostrum* (Communion)    20
   - 1m. Ite, missa est    20
2. First Vespers on the Feast of the Nativity of the Lord (excerpts)    23
   - 2a. *Deus in adjutorium* (opening versicle)    23
   - 2b. *Rex pacificus* (antiphon and Psalm 112)    24
   - 2c. *Magnificatus est* (antiphon and Psalm 124)    26
   - 2d. *Veni redemptor gentium* (hymn)    27
   - 2e. *Benedicamus Domino* (closing versicle)    28
3. Modal Formulas    29
   - 3a. 9th-Century Series (from *Commemoratio brevis de tonis et psalmis modulandis*)    29
   - 3b. 12th-Century Series (from *De Musica* by John of Afflighem)    29

## 8TH–11TH CENTURY: POLYPHONY

### Theorists' Examples

- *4a. *Rex caeli Domine* (organum at the fourth, from *Musica Enchiriadis*)    32
  - *Rex caeli Domine* (sacred song, principal melody of No. 4a)    32
- *4b. *Sit gloria Domini* (organum at the fifth with octave doubling, from *Musica Enchiriadis*)    33
  - *Sit gloria Domini* (Psalm 103, verse 31, principal melody of No. 4b)    33
- 4c. Guido of Arezzo, *Ipsi soli* (organum, from *Micrologus*)    33
  - *Ipsi soli* (antiphon, principal melody of No. 4c)    34
- 4d. Kyrie *Cunctipotens genitor* (from *Ad organum faciendum*)    34
- 4e. Alleluia in 5th performance mode (from *Ad organum faciendum*)    34
  - Alleluia *Justus ut palma* (principal melody of No. 4e)    35
- *5. Wulfstan of Winchester (?), Alleluia *Te martyrum*    35

## 12TH-13TH CENTURY: SACRED MONOPHONY

6. *Castitatis lilium effloruit* (versus)                                                    37

### Liturgical chant

7a. *Ave regina caelorum* (votive antiphon)                                                  38
★7b. *Veni sancte spiritus* (prose)                                                          38
7c. *Pange lingua gloriosi corporis* (hymn)                                                  40
7d. *Aeterna Christi munera* (hymn)                                                          40

## 12TH-13TH CENTURY: SECULAR MONOPHONY

### Troubadour and Trouvère Songs

★8a. Bernart de Ventadorn, *Can vei la lauzeta mover*                                         42
8b. Peire Vidal, *Baros de mon dan covit*                                                    44
8c. Gaucelm Faidit, *Fortz chausa es* (1199)                                                 45
8d. *Chevalier mult estes guariz* (Crusaders' song, 1147)                                    47
8e. Gace Brulé, *Biaus m'est estez*                                                          49
8f. Guillaume d'Amiens, *Prendes i garde* (rondeau)                                          51

## 12TH-13TH CENTURY: POLYPHONY

9a. *Viderunt Emmanuel* (Aquitanian versus)                                                  54
9b. Kyrie *Cunctipotens genitor* (from *Codex Calixtinus*)                                   55
★10a. Leonin, Alleluia *Pascha nostrum* (organum duplum)                                      58
10b. Alleluia *Pascha nostrum* (organum duplum, later revision of verse)                     60
11. Perotin (?), Alleluia *Pascha nostrum* (organum triplum)                                 67
12. Conductus                                                                                74
    12a. *Deus in adjutorium* (conductus sine cauda)                                         74
    12b. *O tocius Asie* (conductus cum cauda)                                               75

### 13th-Century Motets (to c. 1250)

13a. Discant clausula on *Regnat* (from Alleluia *Hodie Maria virgo*)                        78
13b. *Ad solitum vomitum/Regnat* (two-voice motet)                                           78
13c. *Ad solitum vomitum/Regnat* (three-voice conductus motet)                               78
13d. *Depositum creditum/Ad solitum vomitum/Regnat* (Latin double motet)                     80
13e. Alleluia *Hodie Maria virgo* (source chant for *Regnat* clausula)                       82
★13f. *L'autre jour/Au tens pascour/In seculum* (French double motet)                         83
★14. "A certain Spaniard," *In seculum breve* (instrumental hocket)                           86

### 13th-Century Motets (after c. 1250)

★15a. *El mois de mai/De se debent bigami/Kyrie* (French double motet)                        87
★15b. *On parole de batre/A Paris/Frese nouvele* (French double motet on secular tenor)       89
★15c. *Alle psallite cum luya/Alle psallite cum luya/Alleluya* (Latin voice-exchange motet)   91
★15d. Petrus de Cruce, *Aucun ont trouvé/Lonc tans/Annuntiantes* (French double motet)        93

## 14TH CENTURY: *ARS NOVA*

*16.  Philippe de Vitry, *Tribum que/Quoniam secta/Merito hec patimur* (isorhythmic motet)   99
17.  Guillaume de Machaut, *Bone pastor Guillerme/Bone pastor qui pastores/Bone pastor*
    (isorhythmic motet)   104
18.  Guillaume de Machaut, secular songs
  18a.  *Nes que on porroit* (ballade)   109
  *18b.  *Quant j'ay l'espart* (rondeau)   112
  18c.  *Dame a vous sans retollir* (virelai)   113

## 14TH CENTURY: *TRECENTO*

*19.  Jacopo da Bologna, *Non al suo amante* (madrigale)   116
*20.  Gherardello da Firenze, *Tosto che l'alba* (caccia)   118
*21.  Francesco Landini, *Questa fanciull'amor* (ballata)   122

## LATE 14TH CENTURY: *ARS SUBTILIOR*

22.  Borlet (?), *Ma trédol rosignol joly* (virelai)   125
*23.  Johannes Ciconia, *Sus un' fontayne* (virelai)   128

## 15TH CENTURY: SACRED POLYPHONY

24.  Leonel Power
  24a.  Credo (*Opem nobis*)   132
  *24b.  *Ave regina caelorum* (motet)   138
  24c.  *Ave regina caelorum* (melody of Sarum tradition)   140
*25.  John Dunstable, *Beata mater* (motet)   141
*26.  Guillaume Dufay, *Christe, redemptor omnium* (hymn)   143
27.  Guillaume Dufay
  *27a.  Agnus Dei from *Missa Se la face ay pale*   146
  27b.  *Se la face ay pale* (tenor of three-voice song)   151
*28.  Guillaume Dufay, *Ave regina caelorum* (III) (motet)   153
29.  Johannes Ockeghem, Agnus Dei from *Missa Mi-mi*   161

## 15TH CENTURY: SECULAR SONG

30.  Guillaume Dufay
  30a.  *Ce moys de may soyons lies et joyeux* (rondeau)   168
  *30b.  *Adieu m'amour, adieu ma joye* (rondeau)   169
31.  Hayne van Ghizeghem, *De tous biens plaine* (rondeau)   171

## LATE 15TH-EARLY 16TH CENTURY: SACRED

*32.  Josquin Desprez, *Ave Maria gratia plena . . . virgo serena* (motet)   175
*33.  Josquin Desprez, Agnus Dei II from *Missa L'homme armé super voces musicales*   182
34.  Josquin Desprez
  *34a.  Kyrie from *Missa Pange lingua*   185
  *34b.  Agnus Dei from *Missa Pange lingua*   188

## LATE 15TH–EARLY 16TH CENTURY: SECULAR

*35a. Josquin Desprez, *Faulte d'argent* (chanson a 5)  195

35b. Antoine de Févin, *Faulte d'argent* (chanson a 3)  199

36. Heinrich Isaac, *La mi la sol* (instrumental piece)  202

37. Juan del Encina

    37a. *Señora de hermosura* (villancico)  205

    *37b. *Triste España* (romance)  206

38. *Orsù orsù car'signori* (Italian carnival song)  208

*39. Marchetto Cara, *Io non compro più speranza* (frottola with introductory recercare by
Franciscus Bossinensis)  210


## 16TH CENTURY (from c. 1520): SACRED

40a. Martin Luther, *Aus tiefer Not* (chorale melody, 1524)  213

40b. Johann Walter, *Aus tiefer Not* (four-part setting, 1524)  214

40c. Arnold von Bruck, *Aus tiefer Not* (four-part setting, 1544)  215

*40d. Johann Sebastian Bach, *Aus tiefer Not* (four-part setting, 1724)  216

*41. Nicholas Gombert, *Ave regina caelorum* (motet)  218

*42a. Giovanni Pierluigi da Palestrina, *Veni sponsa Christi* (motet)  224

42b. *Veni sponsa Christi* (antiphon)  227

*43. Giovanni Pierluigi da Palestrina, Kyrie from *Missa Veni sponsa Christi*  228

*44. Orlande de Lassus, *Tristis est anima mea* (motet)  233

*45. Orlande de Lassus, *In teneris annis* (*Sibylla cimmeria*), Section IV of *Prophetiae Sibyllarum*  236

46a. William Byrd, *Miserere mihi, Domine* (motet from *Cantiones Sacrae*)  239

46b. *Miserere mihi, Domine* (antiphon)  245

*47. Giovanni Gabrieli, *Canzona Septimi Toni a 8* (from *Sacrae Symphoniae*, 1597)  246


## 16TH CENTURY (from c. 1520): SECULAR

48. Clément Janequin, *Ou mettra l'on ung baiser* (Parisian chanson)  254

49a. Luis de Milán, Pavan 1 (from *El maestro*)  259

49b. Diego Ortiz, *Recercada settima* (from *Tratado de glosas*)  260

*50. Jacques Arcadelt, *Il bianco e dolce cigno* (madrigal)  263

*51. Cipriano de Rore, *Da le belle contrade d'oriente* (madrigal)  266

52. Luca Marenzio, *Scaldava il sol* (madrigal)  272

*53. Claudio Monteverdi, *Cruda Amarilli* (madrigal)  278

*54. Carlo Gesualdo, *Moro, lasso, al mio duolo* (madrigal)  282


## 17TH CENTURY: VOCAL

*55. Giulio Caccini, *Perfidissimo volto* (solo madrigal from *Le nuove musiche*)  287

*56. Sigismondo d'India, *Cruda Amarilli* (solo madrigal)  292

57. John Dowland

    *57a. *Flow my teares* (lute song)  295

    57b. *Lachrimae Gementes* (instrumental pavane)  297

58. Claudio Monteverdi, *Zefiro torna* (continuo madrigal from *Scherzi musicali*)  300

*59. Giovanni Gabrieli, *In ecclesiis* (concertato motet from *Symphoniae sacrae* II)  313

60. Heinrich Schütz, *O quam tu pulchra es* (from *Symphoniae sacrae* I)  326

*61. Heinrich Schütz, *Saul, Saul was verfolgst du mich?* (from *Symphoniarum sacrarum tertia pars*)  336

62. Jacopo Peri, *Euridice* (excerpt from scene 2) 349
63. Claudio Monteverdi, *Orfeo* (excerpts from Act II)
     ★63a.  *Vi ricordi* through *Ahi caso acerbo* ✓ 355
     ★63b.  *A l'amara novella* through *Ahi caso acerbo* 359
★64. Claudio Monteverdi, *L'incoronazione di Poppea* (Act I, scene 3) 364
65. Giacomo Carissimi, *Jephte* (oratorio)
     65a.  *Cum autem victor* through *Cantate mecum* 373
     65b.  *Cum vidisset Jephte* through *Heu mihi! filia mea* 380
66. Francesco Cavalli, *Scipione Africano* (Act II, scene 8) 385
67. Antonio Cesti, *Alpi nevose e dure* (cantata) 388
★68. Jean-Baptiste Lully, *Alceste* (Act II, scenes 7-8) 393
★69. Henry Purcell, *Dido and Aeneas* (concluding scene) ✗ 400

## 17TH CENTURY: INSTRUMENTAL

★70. William Byrd, *John come kiss me now* (from *The Fitzwilliam Virginal Book*) 407
71a. Samuel Scheidt, *Jesus Christus unser Heiland, der von uns* (from *Tabulatura Nova*, Part III) 413
71b. *Jesus Christus unser Heiland, der von uns* (chorale melody) 420
72. Girolamo Frescobaldi, Toccata No. 8 (from *Toccate e partite . . . libro primo*) 421
73. Girolamo Frescobaldi, *Canzona dopo l'epistola* (from *La Messa della Domenica, Fiori musicale*) 426
★74. Johann Jacob Froberger, Suite VI 428
★75. Louis Couperin, *Prélude a l'imitation de Mr. Froberger* (unmeasured prelude) 434
76. Salamone Rossi, *Sonata in dialogo,* "La Viena" 441
77. Giovanni Battista Vitali, *Sonata a due Violini col suo basso continuo per l'organo* 446
78. Arcangelo Corelli, *Sonata da camera a tre*, Opus 4, No. 5 450
79. Heinrich Ignaz Franz von Biber, *Rosary Sonata X* (*The Crucifixion of Christ*) 454
★80. Arcangelo Corelli, *Sonata for violin and violone or cembalo*, Opus 5, No. 1 459

## 18TH CENTURY: VOCAL

★81. Alessandro Scarlatti, *Su le sponde del Tebro* (cantata, Arias 3 and 4 and recitative) 472
82. George Frideric Handel, *Admeto*
     ★82a.  Act II, scenes 7 and 8 481
     82b.  Act III, scene 6 493
83. Jean-Philippe Rameau, *Hippolyte et Aricie* (Act I, scene 2) 499
★84. Giovanni Battista Pergolesi, *La serva padrona* (intermezzo primo, excerpt) 507
★85. Johann Sebastian Bach, *Jesu, der du meine Seele*, BWV 78
     (cantata for the 14th Sunday after Trinity) 514

## 18TH CENTURY: INSTRUMENTAL

★86. François Couperin, *Pièces de clavecin, Premier livre* (*Premier ordre*, excerpts) 548
★87. Johann Sebastian Bach, Prelude and Fugue in D minor, BWV 851-852
     (from *Das wohltemperirte Clavier* I) 555
88. Domenico Scarlatti
     ★88a.  Sonata in D minor, K. 120 (L. 215) 560
     ★88b.  Sonata in D major, K. 119 (L. 415) 564
★89. Antonio Vivaldi, Violin Concerto in G minor, Opus 8, No. 8, RV 332
     (from *Il cimento dell'armonia e dell'inventione*) 571

90. Johann Sebastian Bach, *Musikalisches Opfer*, BWV 1079
    *90a. *Canon 1. a 2 cancrizans*     593
    *90b. *Canon 2. a 2 violini in unisono*     594
    *90c. *Canon 3. a 2 per Motum contrarium*     595
    *90d. *Canon 4. a 2 per Augmentationem, contrario Motu*     596
    *90e. *Canon perpetuus*     597

## PLATES

1. *Resurrexi* (No. 1a), Montpellier, Bibliothèque de l'École de Médecine, MS H 159, page 47.     1
2. Alleluia *Pascha nostrum* (No. 10b), opening, Florence, Biblioteca medicea-laurenziana Pluteo 29. 1, f. 109r.     57
3. Agnus Dei of *Missa Mi-mi* (No. 29), by Johannes Ockeghem. Rome, Biblioteca Apostolica Vaticana, Chigi Codex C VIII.234, ff. 13´-14     167
4. Agnus Dei II from *Missa L'homme armé super voces musicales* (No. 33), by Josquin Desprez. *Dodecachordon* (1547), p. 442.     184
5. "Non piango e non sospiro" from *Euridice* (No. 62), by Jacopo Peri (Florence: 1600), page 17.     348
6. "Explanation of Ornaments and Signs" from *Pièces de clavecin, Premier livre* (see No. 86), by François Couperin.     547

## FIGURES

1. Comparison between early and revised versions of Alleluia *Pascha nostrum* (Nos. 10a and 10b).     65
2. Design of de Vitry's *Tribum que/Quoniam secta/Merito hec patimur* (No. 16).     103
3. Design of Dufay's *Ave regina caelorum* [III] (No. 28).     160

## MAPS

Europe in the Mid-Fourteenth Century     600
Europe in the Late Sixteenth Century     601

## SELECTIVE DISCOGRAPHY

    602

## SOURCES AND ACKNOWLEDGMENTS

    610

## INDEX

    617

* Indicates pieces/songs available on the audio CD set

# A NOTE ON SQUARE NOTATION

Square chant notation was developed in northern France during the late twelfth century, some three hundred years after singers began to notate the music of the Christian ritual. This notational system soon spread to other regions and eventually became the standard method for writing or printing chant. In order to have access to the contents of modern chant collections such as the *Liber Usualis,* some fluency in reading square notation is necessary. The symbols used in this volume largely follow the convention of the modern Vatican plainsong editions (but without the additional editorial markings). However, since many of the sources used for this edition were written in earlier plainsong notations, some modifications have been necessary in order to represent the original versions more faithfully.

In square notation, the notational figures, or *neumes,* are written on a four-line staff with either a C-clef on one of the upper three lines

or, less frequently, an F-clef.

Single pitches are represented by simple figures, a *punctum*

A

or a *virga.* The virga indicates a rise in pitch relative to the tone immediately preceding.

B

Groups of pitches are shown by compound neumes called *ligatures.* Ligatures are read from left to right. When one element is above another (as in *b*), the lower note is sung first. (The one exception to this rule is a descending liquescent, shown below.) An oblique stroke (as in *c*) denotes only two pitches, located at the beginning and end points of the stroke. A descending scale figure is usually represented as in *d*. The diamond-shaped notes have the same significance as square *puncta.*

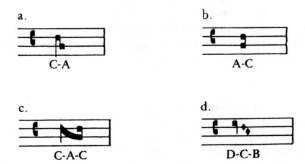

a. C-A   b. A-C   c. C-A-C   d. D-C-B

Several notational symbols indicate special qualities of timbre or vocal production. The exact results intended are subject to dispute, but plausible interpretations are indicated here.

**Quilisma.** The middle pitch, written as a jagged line, is sung lightly, perhaps delivered with a slight tremolo. This figure mainly occurs in approaching F or C from the half step below.

A-qB-C

**Liquescent.** A liquescent is indicated by a small note head and is always produced *after* the main pitch. This second tone is "liquid," colored by the text syllable, not produced with full voice. Liquescents tend to occur on the semivocal consonants *l, m, n, r* and *f, s, v.*

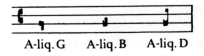

A-liq. G   A-liq. B   A-liq. D

**Oriscus.** The oriscus is indicated here by the symbol ⌐ over the note concerned. It always occurs as the second of two unison pitches and usually marks the end of a phrase or a neume group. It may involve an ornamental fluctuation in pitch.

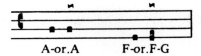

A-or.A   F-or.F-G

Unlike later square notation, the neume-letter notation of the manuscript on which the following edition of the Easter propers (No. 1) is based employs alternative symbols for those pitches that have a half step above them (See Plate I, line 4 on *mirabilis*).

These symbols apparently designate an interval smaller than a half step (i.e., a microtone). In this edition, such an intonation is indicated by a + over the inflected pitch. If the + occurs above two superimposed notes, it applies to the lower one. The "high" E or B normally occurs within a neighboring motion to the adjacent upper pitch.

D-F-raised E-F-F    F-raised E-F

Tables of neumes giving the names of the most common figures may be found in the *Liber Usualis* (Tournai: Desclée, numerous editions), pp. xix-xxii, and in R. Hoppin, *Medieval Music* (New York: Norton, 1978), p. 61.

The neumes of square notation are rhythmically neutral and do not indicate duration of individual pitches or pitch groups. In fact, considerable controversy attends the rhythmic interpretation of chant. Some specialists advocate relatively equal duration for each note, with some accents and lengthenings prompted by the text. Others advocate irregular rhythms governed variously by proportional relationships, by interpretation of rhythmic signs in specific early manuscripts, by judgments on decorative and structural melodic elements in conjunction with text delivery. In modern times, the smoothflowing "equalist" interpretation developed by the Benedictine monks at Solesmes and promulgated in the official Vatican chant books has been widely influential. Medieval documents indicate that chant rhythm was not set and invariable but differed between locales and changed over the centuries.

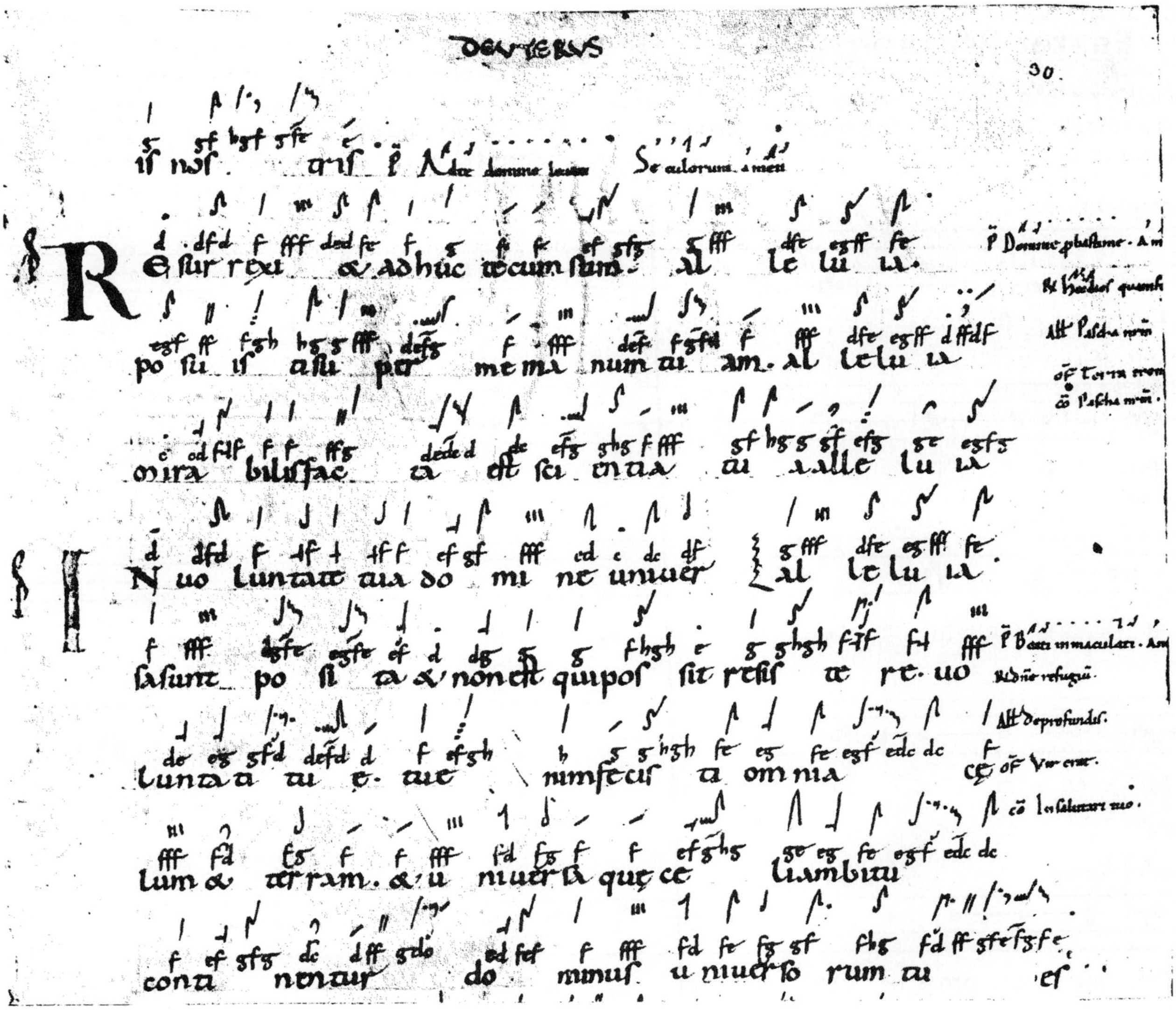

**Plate 1.** Montpellier, Bibliothèque de l'École de Médecine, MS H 159, in *Paléographie musicale* VIII, p. 47. Original notation of No. 1a.

## 1. Easter Mass Proper and Ordinary

[ 1 ] Track 1

### 1a. Resurrexi

Introit

**Antiphon**

Re - sur - re - xi    et ad - huc te - cum sum al - le - lu - ia.

Po - su - i - sti su - per me ma - num tu - am

al - le - lu - ia.    Mi - ra - bi - lis fac - ta    est

sci - en - ti - a    tu - a    al - le - lu - ia    al - le - lu - ia.

**Psalm Verse**

Do - mi - ne pro - ba - sti me    et cog - no - vi - sti me    tu cog - no - vi - sti

*[Repeat Antiphon]*

ses - si - o - nem me - am    et re - sur - re - cti - o - nem me - am.

**Gloria Patri**

Glo - ri - a Pa - tri et Fi - li - o et Spi - ri - tu - i San - cto si - cut e - rat

*[Repeat Antiphon]*

in prin - ci - pi - o et nunc et sem - per et in se - cu - la se - cu - lo - rum. A - men.

**Antiphon**
*I have risen and even now am with thee, alleluia.*
*Thou hast laid thy hand upon me, alleluia.*
*Thy knowledge is become marvellous, alleluia, alleluia.*

**Psalm Verse**
*Lord, thou hast judged me and known me:*
*Thou hast known my sitting down and my rising up.*

**Gloria Patri**
*Glory be to the Father, and to the Son, and to the Holy Spirit*
*As it was in the beginning, is now, and ever shall be, world without end. Amen.*

## 1b.  Quem queritis in sepulchro

Introit trope 1

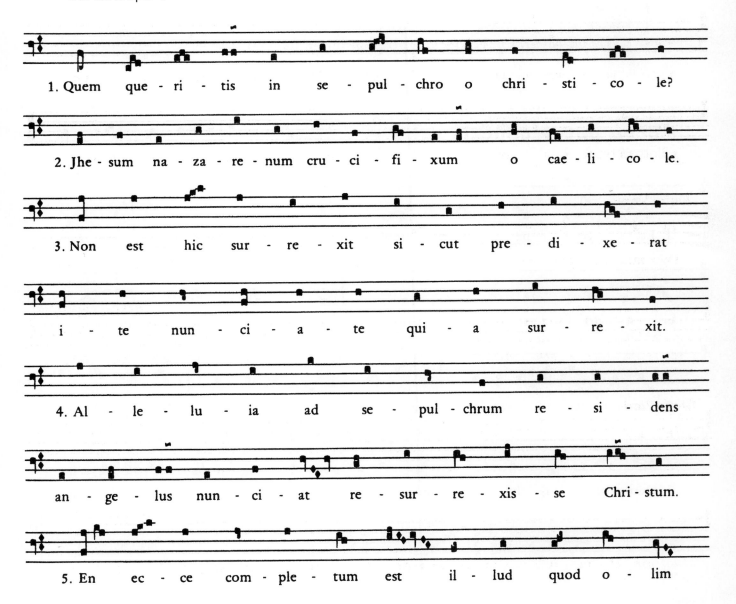

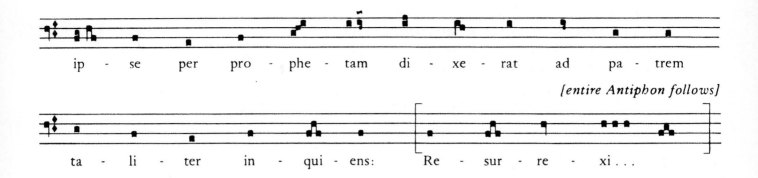

ip - se   per   pro - phe - tam   di - xe - rat   ad   pa - trem

*[entire Antiphon follows]*

ta - li - ter   in - qui - ens:   Re - sur - re - xi . . .

1.[1] *Whom seek you in the tomb, O followers of Christ?*

2.   *The crucified Jesus of Nazareth, O celestial ones.*

3.   *He is not here. He has risen as he had foretold. Go, announce that he has risen.*

4.   *Alleluia. The angel remaining at the tomb announces that Christ has risen.*

5.   *Behold, that is fulfilled which he himself formerly said through the prophet, speaking thus to the Father:* **I have risen**. . . . (rest of Introit follows)

[1]In some sources, the first three lines are given to the angels, the women, and the angels respectively.

## Ecce pater cunctis
Introit trope 2

1. Ec - ce   pa - ter   cun - ctis   ut   ius - se - rat

or - do   per - ac - tis.   Re - sur - re - xi   . . .

2. Vic - tor   ut   ad   cae - los   cal - ca - ta   mor - te   re - di - rem.   Po - su - i - sti . . .

3. Quo   ge - nus   hu - ma - num   pul - sis   er - ro - ri - bus   al - tum

scan - de - - - ret   ad   ce - lum.   Mi - ra - bi - lis . . .

1. *Behold, Father, all has been accomplished as commanded:*
   **I have risen and even now am with thee, alleluia.**

2. *A victor, so that I might return to heaven from crushing death*
   **Thou hast laid thy hand upon me, alleluia.**

3. *So that by this deed humankind might rise from its errant course to high heaven.*
   **Thy knowledge is become marvellous, alleluia, alleluia.**

1c. **Kyrie Cunctipotens genitor**   [ 1 ]  Track 2

*Melismatic version*
*Lord have mercy.*

*Christ have mercy.*
*Lord have mercy.*

Latin version

3. Fons et o - ri - go bo - ne pi - e lux - que per - hen - nis e - ley - son

4. Chri - ste de - i splen - dor vir - tus pa - tris - que so - phi - a e - ley - son

5. Plas - ma - tis hu - ma - nis fa - ctor lap - sis re - pa - ra - tor e - ley - son

6. Ne tu - a dampn - na - tur Jhe - su fa - ctu - ra be - ni - gne e - ley - son

7. Am - bo - rum sa - crum spi - ra - men ne - xus a - mor - que e - ley - son

8. Pro - ce - dens fo - mes vi - te fons pu - ri - fi - cans vis e - ley - son

9. In - dul - tor cul - pe ve - ni - e lar - gi - tor o - pti - me

of - fen - sas de - le sa - cro nos mu - ne - re re - ple e - ley - son

10. Spi - ri - te al - me e - ley - son.

1. *All-powerful Father, God, Creator of all things, have mercy.*

2. *May thy compassion save us, good ruler, have mercy.*

3. *Fountainhead and origin of goodness, Holy one, light everlasting, have mercy.*

4. *Christ, the splendor of God, strength and wisdom of the Father, have mercy.*

5. *Creator of humankind, healer of those who fall, have mercy.*

6. *Lest thy creation be damned, kind Jesus, have mercy.*

7. *The holy breath, the fusion and the love of both [Father and Son], have mercy.*

8. *Advancing flame, source of life, purifying power, have mercy.*

9. *Forgiver of sin, bestower of pardon, erase our offenses, replenish us, give us holy grace, have mercy.*

10. *Most gracious Spirit, have mercy.*

## 1d. Gloria  `1 Track 3`

Qui se - des ad dex - te - ram pa - tris mi - se - re - re no - bis.

Quo - ni - am tu so - lus san - ctus, tu so - lus Do - mi - nus,

tu so - lus al - tis - si - mus Je - su Chri - ste,

cum San - cto Spi - ri - tu in glo - ri - a De - i pa - tris. A - men.

*Glory be to God on high, and on earth, peace to men of good will.*
*We praise thee, we bless thee, we worship thee, we glorify thee*
*We thank thee for thy great glory, Lord God, King of heaven,*
*Lord, the all-powerful Father,*
*Lord, the only-begotten Son, Jesus Christ,*
*Lord God, Lamb of God, Son of the Father,*
*Thou who bearest the sins of the world, have mercy on us,*
*Thou who bearest the sins of the world, accept our prayer for forgiveness,*
*Thou who sittest at the right hand of the Father, have mercy on us.*
*For thou only art holy, thou only art Lord,*
*thou only, Jesus Christ, with the Holy Spirit,*
*art most high in the glory of God the Father. Amen.*

## 1e. **Haec dies**

 Track 4

Gradual

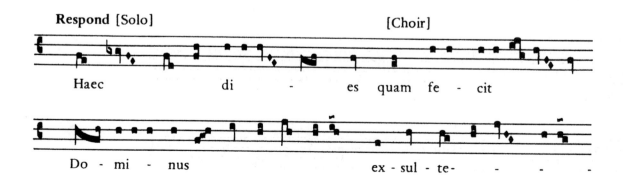

**Respond [Solo]**                                    [Choir]

Haec di - es quam fe - cit

Do - mi - nus ex - sul - te -

-mus     et le - te - mur

in e - a

**Verse [Solo]**

Con - fi - te - mi - ni Do - mi - no

quo - - - - - ni - am bo - - - nus

quo - ni - am in sae - - - cu - lum

**[Choir]**

mi - se - ri - cor - di - a e - ius

*responsorial = solo / choir*

**Respond**
*This [is] the day which the Lord made. Let us exult and rejoice in it.*

**Verse**
*Trust in the Lord, because he is good, because his mercy endures forever.*

## 1f.  **Alleluia Pascha nostrum**

1  Track 5

*Jubilus*

**Alleluia [Solo]**        * **[Choir]**

Al - le - lu - ia    Al - le - lu - ia

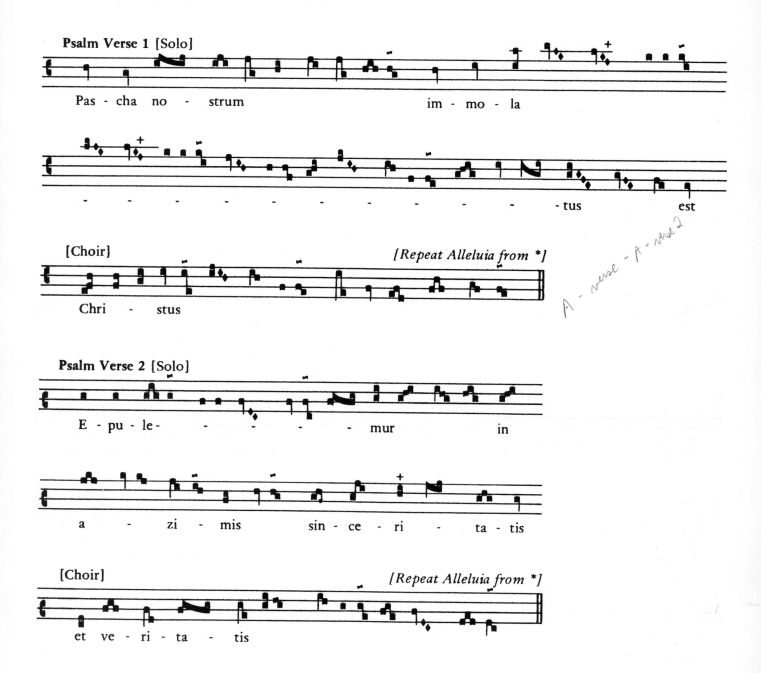

Psalm Verse 1 [Solo]

Pas - cha no - strum  im - mo - la

- - - - - - - - -tus  est

[Choir]  [Repeat Alleluia from *]

Chri - stus

Psalm Verse 2 [Solo]

E - pu - le - - - mur  in

a - zi - mis  sin - ce - ri - ta - tis

[Choir]  [Repeat Alleluia from *]

et ve - ri - ta - tis

*Alleluia.*

**Verse 1:**
*Christ our Passover [offering] is sacrificed.*

**Verse 2:**
*Let us observe the feast with the unleavened bread of sincerity and truth.*

## 1g. Fulgens praeclara

Prose (Sequence)

Al - le - lu - ia

1a. Ful - gens prae - cla - ra ru - ti - lat per or - bem ho - di - e di - es in quo
1b. De ho - ste su - per - bo quem Je - sus tri - um - pha - vit

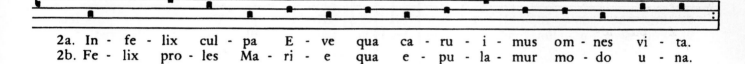

Chri - sti lu - ci - da nar - ran - tur o - van - ter pre - li - a.
pul - chre ca - stra il - li - us per - i - mens te - ter - ri - ma.

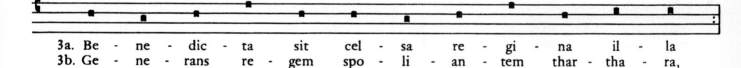

2a. In - fe - lix cul - pa E - ve qua ca - ru - i - mus om - nes vi - ta.
2b. Fe - lix pro - les Ma - ri - e qua e - pu - la - mur mo - do u - na.

3a. Be - ne - dic - ta sit cel - sa re - gi - na il - la
3b. Ge - ne - rans re - gem spo - li - an - tem thar - tha - ra,

4a. Pol - len - tem iam in e - the - ra.
4b. Pa - tris se - dens ad dex - te - ram

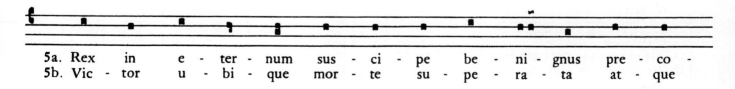

5a. Rex in e - ter - num sus - ci - pe be - ni - gnus pre - co -
5b. Vic - tor u - bi - que mor - te su - pe - ra - ta at - que

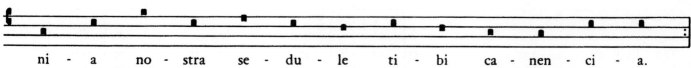

ni - a no - stra se - du - le ti - bi ca - nen - ci - a.
tri - um - pha - ta po - lo - rum pos - si - dens gau - di - a.

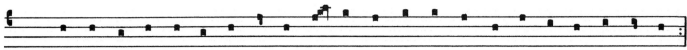

6a. O Mag-na O cel-sa O Pul-chra cle-men-ci - a Chri-sti lu-ci-flu-a O al - ma.
6b. Laus ti - bi ho-nor-que ac vir-tus qui no-stram an - ti-quam le - vi - a - sti sar - ci-nam.

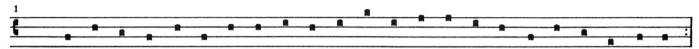

7a. Ro - se - o cru - o - re ag-ni be - ni-gnis-si - mi em-pta flo - ri - da mi-cent hec au - la.
7b. Po - ten - ti vir - tu - te no-stra qui la - vit fa - ci - no - ra tri - bu - it do - na ful - gi - da.

8a. Stu - pens val - de in me - met iam mi - ror ho - di - er - na.
8b. Tan - ta in - di - gnis pan - de - re no - bis sa - cra - men - ta.

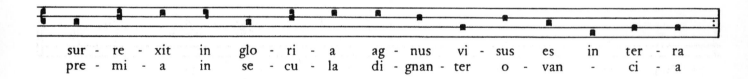

9a. Stir - pe da - vi - ti - ca or - tus de tri - bu iu - da le - o po - tens
9b. Fun - dens o - lim ar - va reg - na pe - tens su - pe - ra iu - stis red - dens

sur - re - xit in glo - ri - a ag - nus vi - sus es in ter - ra
pre - mi - a in se - cu - la di - gnan - ter o - van - ci - a

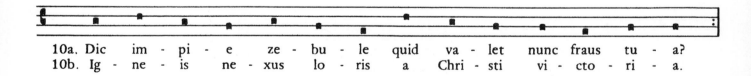

10a. Dic im - pi - e ze - bu - le quid va - let nunc fraus tu - a?
10b. Ig - ne - is ne - xus lo - ris a Chri - sti vi - cto - ri - a.

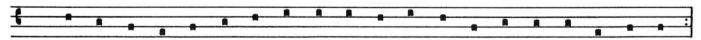

11a. Tri - bus lin - gue am - mi - ra - mi - ni quis au - di - vit ta - li - a my - ste - ri - a
11b. Ut mors mor-tem sic su - pe - ra - ret re - i per - ci - pe - rent ta - lem gra - ti - am.

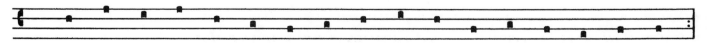

12a. Iu - de - a in - cre - du - la cur ma - nes ad - huc in - ve - re - cun - da?
12b. Per - spi - ce Chri - sti - co - las qua - li - ter le - ti ca - nunt in - cli - ta.

[1]Note change in clef.

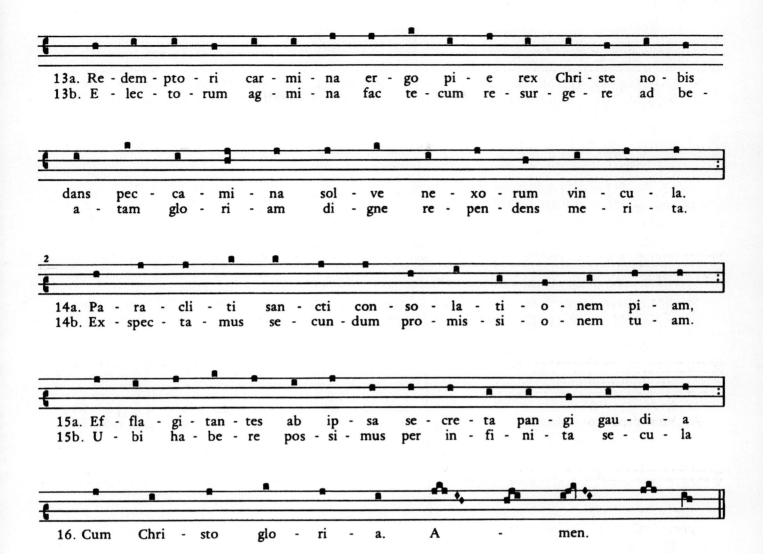

13a. Re - dem - pto - ri   car - mi - na   er - go   pi - e   rex   Chri - ste   no - bis
13b. E - lec - to - rum   ag - mi - na   fac   te - cum   re - sur - ge - re   ad   be -

dans   pec - ca - mi - na   sol - ve   ne - xo - rum   vin - cu - la.
a - tam   glo - ri - am   di - gne   re - pen - dens   me - ri - ta.

14a. Pa - ra - cli - ti   san - cti   con - so - la - ti - o - nem   pi - am,
14b. Ex - spec - ta - mus   se - cun - dum   pro - mis - si - o - nem   tu - am.

15a. Ef - fla - gi - tan - tes   ab   ip - sa   se - cre - ta   pan - gi   gau - di - a
15b. U - bi   ha - be - re   pos - si - mus   per   in - fi - ni - ta   se - cu - la

16. Cum   Chri - sto   glo - ri - a.   A - men.

[2]Note change in clef.

1a. *Lightning bright, this day shines throughout the world, the day in which the glorious battle of Christ is joyfully proclaimed.*

1b. *for Jesus has triumphed beautifully over the proud foe, annihilating his odious encampment.*

2a. *Unhappy sin of Eve which deprived us all of life,*

2b. *Happy son of Mary, by whom we feast together.*

3a. *Blessed be that exalted Queen*

3b. *who gave birth to the King who plundered Hell,*

4a. *the King already powerful in heaven*

4b. *who sits at the right hand of the Father.*

5a. *Eternal King, graciously accept our praise, sung unceasingly to thee,*

5b. *Victor everywhere over conquering, triumphant Death, proprietor of heavenly joy.*

6a. *O great, O lofty, O beautiful mercy of Christ, illuminating and sweet,*

*6b. Praise, honor and power to thee who lifted our ancient burden.*

*7a. The blooming palaces of Heaven glow, purchased by the rosy wounds of the most blessed Lamb.*

*7b. By his mighty virtue, he cleansed our sins and distributed radiant gifts.*

*8a. Stunned within myself, already I marvel at this epoch*

*8b. in which such holy things are extended to us, the unworthy.*

*9a. From the root of David, descended from the tribe of Judah, a powerful Lion, he has risen in glory—he who seemed a lamb on earth,*

*9b. and of old founded the earth, now seeking the realm above, rendering rewards to the just, in merited joy eternal.*

*10a. Say, cursed Prince [of Hell], what is thy deceit worth*

*10b. now that you are bound in fiery bonds by the victory of Christ?*

*11a. Tribes, tongues—stand amazed. Whoever has heard of such mysteries*

*11b. that death should so conquer Death, that creation might receive such grace.*

*12a. Incredulous Judea, why do you remain still unconvinced?*

*12b. Look upon the followers of Christ, how joyfully they sing*

*13a. songs directed toward the Savior. Therefore holy King, Christ, release us from sin's binding chains.*

*13b. Let the host of the elect arise with thee to blessed glory, in reward for deserved merit.*

*14a. We look for the blessed consolation of the Holy Spirit*

*14b. according to thy promise,*

*15a. Entreating to be filled with special joy,*

*15b. which we may possess forever and ever*

*16. with Christ in glory. Amen.*

## 1h. Credo

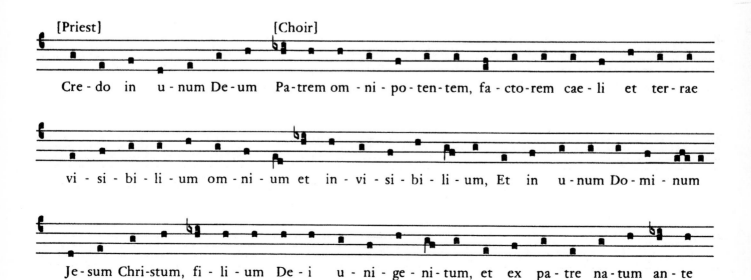

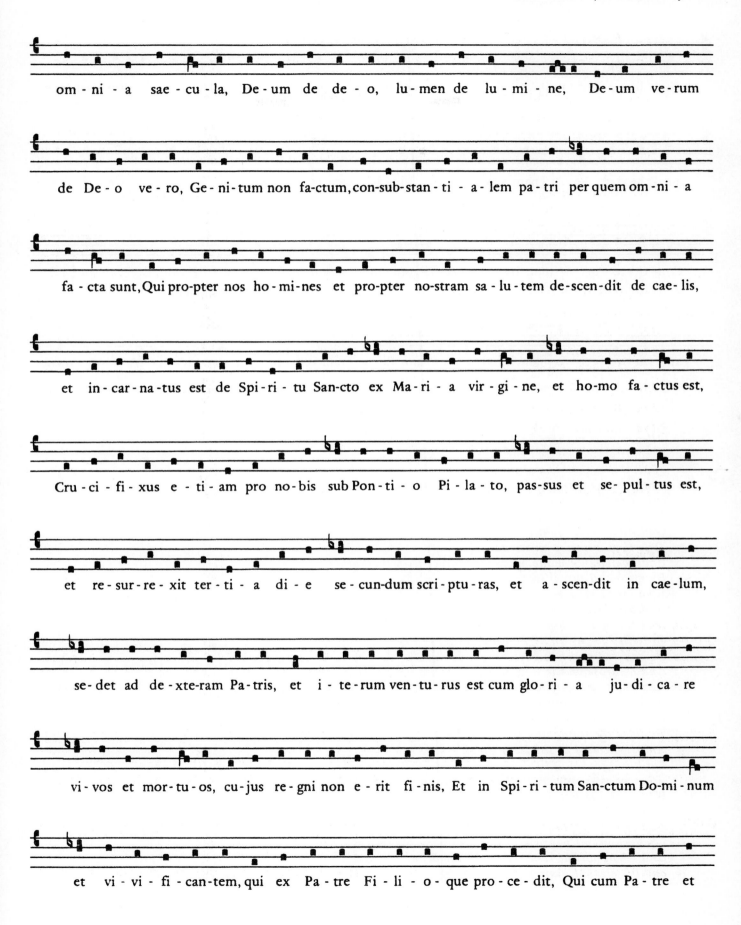

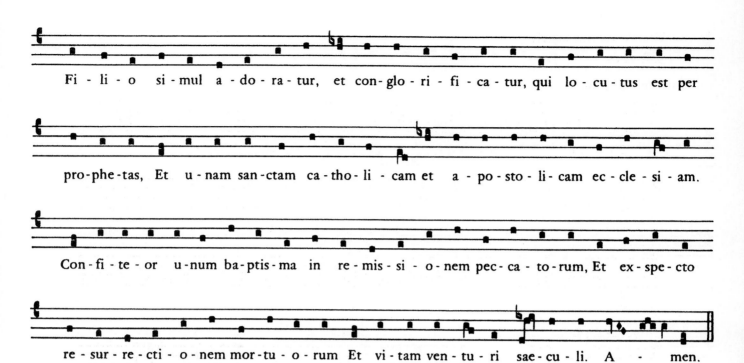

Fi - li - o  si - mul  a - do - ra - tur,  et  con - glo - ri - fi - ca - tur, qui  lo - cu - tus  est  per

pro - phe - tas,  Et  u - nam  san - ctam  ca - tho - li - cam  et  a - po - sto - li - cam  ec - cle - si - am.

Con - fi - te - or  u - num  ba - ptis - ma  in  re - mis - si - o - nem pec - ca - to - rum,  Et  ex - spe - cto

re - sur - re - cti - o - nem mor - tu - o - rum  Et  vi - tam ven - tu - ri  sae - cu - li.  A  -  men.

*I believe in one God*
*All-powerful Father*
*Creator of heaven and earth,*
*of all things visible and invisible,*
*and [I believe] in one Lord Jesus Christ,*
*only-begotten Son of God,*
*Born of the Father before all time,*
*God from God, Light from Light,*
*True God from the true God,*
*Engendered, not made, of one substance with the Father*
*By whom all things were made,*
*Who for us men and for our salvation descended from heaven,*
*And was incarnate of the Holy Spirit through the Virgin Mary*
*And was made man.*
*Crucified for us under Pontius Pilate,*
*He suffered and was buried,*
*And he arose on the third day, according to the Scriptures,*
*And he ascended to heaven, and sits at the right hand of the Father.*
*And he, whose kingdom will have no end,*
*Shall come again in glory,*
*To judge the living and the dead.*
*And [I believe] in the Holy Spirit*
*Lord and source of life,*
*Who proceeds from Father and Son,*
*Who with the Father and Son together is worshipped and glorified,*
*Who spoke through the prophets,*
*And [I believe] in one holy, universal, and apostolic church,*
*I believe in one baptism for the remission of sins,*
*And I look for the resurrection of the dead,*
*and life eternal. Amen.*

1i. **Terra tremuit**

Offertory

*[Repeat Alleluia from end of Verse 1 at \*]*

**Verse 3 [Solo]**

I - bi   con - fre - git

cor - - - nu   ar - cum

scu - tum   et   gla - di - um

et   bel - - - - lum   il - lu - mi - nas   tu

mi - ra - bi - - - - li - ter

*[Repeat Alleluia from end of Verse 1 at \*]*

a   mon - ti - bus   ae - ter - nis

**Antiphon**
*The earth trembled and was still*
*When God arose in judgement, alleluia.*

**Verse 1**
*God is known in Judea,*
*In Israel his name is great, alleluia.*

**Verse 2**
*And his camp was made in peace,*
*And his dwelling place in Sion, alleluia.*

**Verse 3**
*There he destroyed the horn, bow, shield, and sword and war,*
*Thou marvellously radiant from the eternal mountains, alleluia.*

## 1j.  Sanctus

San - ctus  San - ctus  San - ctus  Do - mi - nus

De - us  Sab - ba - oth  Ple - ni  sunt cae - li  et  ter - ra  glo - ri - a

tu - a  Ho - san - na  in  ex - cel - - - - sis

Be - ne - di - ctus  qui  ve - nit  in  no - mi - ne  Do - mi - ni

Ho - san - na  in  ex - cel - - - - - sis.

*Holy, holy, holy, Lord God of hosts.*
*Heaven and earth are full of thy glory.*
*Hosanna on high!*
*Blessed is he who comes in the name of the Lord.*
*Hosanna on high!*

## 1k.  Agnus Dei   [ 1  Track 6 ]

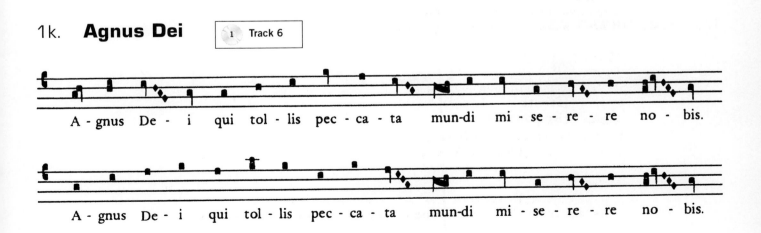

A - gnus  De - i  qui  tol - lis  pec - ca - ta  mun-di  mi - se - re - re  no - bis.

A - gnus  De - i  qui  tol - lis  pec - ca - ta  mun-di  mi - se - re - re  no - bis.

A - gnus De - i  qui tol - lis pec - ca - ta  mun-di  do - na  no - bis  pa - cem.

*Lamb of God, who bearest the sins of the world, have mercy on us.*
*Lamb of God, who bearest the sins of the world, have mercy on us.*
*Lamb of God, who bearest the sins of the world, grant us peace.*

## 1l.   **Pascha nostrum**
Communion

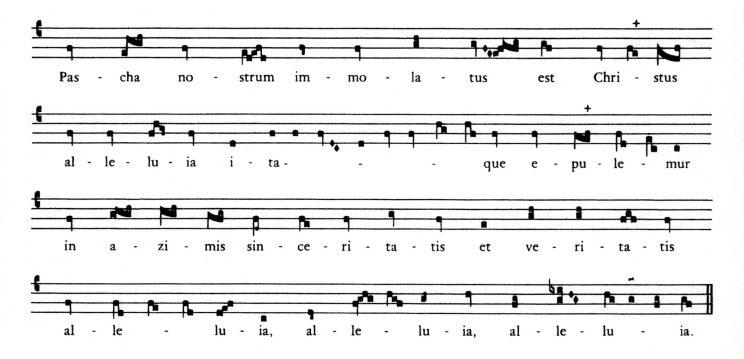

Pas - cha  no - strum im - mo - la - tus  est  Chri - stus

al - le - lu - ia  i - ta - que  e - pu - le - mur

in  a - zi - mis  sin - ce - ri - ta - tis  et  ve - ri - ta - tis

al - le - lu - ia,  al - le - lu - ia,  al - le - lu - ia.

*Christ our Passover [offering] is sacrificed, alleluia.*
*Therefore let us observe the feast with the unleavened bread of sincerity and truth.*
*Alleluia, alleluia, alleluia.*

## 1m.   **Ite, missa est**

[Priest]    I - te,        mis - sa  est.
[Response] De - o        gra - ti - as.

**Priest:**
*Go, it is finished.*

**Response:**
*Thanks be to God.*

The foundation of the art music tradition of western Europe is the monophonic chant of the occidental Christian Church. Sacred chant was the common musical experience of those who created and performed music from late antiquity through the sixteenth century and was the base from which a rich polyphonic tradition developed. Several chant dialects existed in the early Middle Ages, but the historically dominant one is Gregorian chant, so called because of a legend that Pope Gregory I (c. 540-604) was principally responsible for it. Gregorian chant stems from a Roman chant tradition that was transmitted at the instigation of Charlemagne to the Franks around 800. The melodies learned from Roman singers were codified into a system of modes and eventually were notated by the Franks. The earliest substantial written sources of Gregorian chant are Frankish and date from the late ninth and early tenth centuries, decades after oral receipt of the music.

The Mass, the central rite of the Christian church, was celebrated in chant. The principal musical elements of the Roman Mass liturgy are commonly separated into two categories: Proper and Ordinary. The Proper chants, so categorized because their texts are specific to a particular feast day, are the Introit, Gradual, Alleluia, Offertory, and Communion. These elements were fixed liturgically and musically quite early, long before the Ordinary was standardized. The Ordinary items are, by definition, those whose texts remain constant throughout the Church year. Modern convention enumerates them as Kyrie, Gloria, Credo, Sanctus, and Agnus Dei, but in medieval times the Credo was not included in collections or cycles of Ordinary. Moreover, for centuries the Kyrie, Gloria, Sanctus and Agnus Dei were regularly elaborated with additional Latin text. It was not until the thirteenth century that complete Ordinary cycles became common, and not until the Council of Trent (1542-1563) that all "extra words" were officially expunged from the Ordinary. Many of the Ordinary melodies were composed later than the Proper, and they differ demonstrably in musical style from earlier chants. The term *Frankish chant* is often used to distinguish the newer-style melodies from the older Gregorian chant.

The chants of the Mass are also classified according to manner of text setting and mode of performance. Chants are characterized as *syllabic* when most text syllables bear only one note, as *neumatic* when most syllables are sung to several notes, and as *melismatic* when long vocalizations (called *melismas*) extend individual syllables. Each piece is normally intoned by a single singer (*cantor* or priest), who sets the pitch for the choir. The most melismatic and virtuosic chants (Gradual and Alleluia, Nos. 1e, 1f) are performed responsorially. A soloist sings most of the melody, and the choir responds to him at the ends of sections. The Ordinary and the Proper chants with antiphons (Introit, Offertory, and Communion, Nos. 1a, 1i, 1l) are chiefly executed by the choir.

Function and position within the liturgy account for characteristic differences among the principal sung Mass items, which are indicated in the following brief descriptions.

**1a.** The *Introit* takes its name from its entrance or processional function, for during the Introit the clergy and choir assemble. The Introit consists of an antiphon and a psalm tone. The antiphon is an individual melody, while the psalm tone is a formula standard for all Introits in a particular mode. In the sixth century, the antiphon was followed by an entire psalm, but by the tenth century the psalm had been scaled down to a single verse and the *Gloria Patri* or Doxology. The antiphon frames the psalm verse and Doxology, both of which are chanted to the psalm tone, as follows: antiphon—psalm verse—antiphon—*Gloria Patri*—antiphon. Introit antiphons are neumatic in style, while the verses are declaimed syllabically. The Easter Introit *Resurrexi* is classified in mode 4 (plagal deuterus) because it ends on E (called the *final*) and ranges no higher than the fourth above E. The psalm tone chosen is that for mode 4, which has a as its reciting tone. (See No. 3 for principles of mode and modal classification.)

**1b.** Gregorian Introits were elaborated in the tenth and eleventh centuries by appended phrases that are called *tropes* in early manuscripts. In the southwestern Frankish kingdom *Quem queritis in sepulchro* served as a prefatory trope to the Easter Introit *Resurrexi*. (In other regions it occurred in the pre-Mass services or at the end of Matins.) This three-line dialogue between the angels and the women at Christ's tomb (see the Gospel of Luke, Chapter 24) is famous as the cradle of liturgical drama.

*Ecce pater cunctis* is a more conventional type of trope. It consists of three phrases, each of which prefaces a section of the Introit. Care is taken to create smooth textual and musical conjunctions between Introit and interpolated trope phrases. A full performance of the Easter Introit with tropes would be quite long and would consist of: *Quem queritis*—antiphon—psalm verse—antiphon with trope *Ecce pater cunctis*—*Gloria Patri*—antiphon (probably with another trope). The trope lines would have been sung by soloists, antiphon and verses by the choir. Tropes resemble introits in their neumatic text setting, but differ in characteristic melodic motion. They tend to follow scale patterns and do not so often reiterate individual pitches. They were composed later than the antiphon melodies and constitute part of the Frankish chant repertory.

**1c.** The *Kyrie,* the one Mass element in Greek, is a ninefold prayer for mercy. Medieval Kyries existed in two equally valid configurations: one melismatic with Greek text only; the other syllabic with Latin text elaborating the attributes of the Godhead. Both versions of the Kyrie *Cunctipotens genitor* are presented here. The melody exhibits the characteristic traits of late Frankish chant—lucid, repetitive phrase structure and directed, tonally focused melodic motion. Its phrases define an axis of a fifth (D-a) plus a third (a-c). The melody belongs to mode 1 even though it ends not on the normal final of that mode, D, but on the related tone a. In the twelfth century such related tones became codified as *cofinals.*

**1d.** The *Gloria* is a long hymn of praise to God. Its point of departure is the celestial hymn from the Nativity story in Saint Luke's Gospel (Luke 2:14). It is omitted from the Mass in the penitential seasons of Advent and Lent. This Gloria melody is gently neumatic and features a recurring melodic shape, which is freely adapted to different text units (compare *bone voluntatis, qui tollis peccata*, and *quoniam tu solus*). This basic shape centers on the final and establishes the mode 4 quality of the piece.

**1e.** The *Gradual* is a responsorial chant sung between the reading of the Epistle and the Gospel, at a moment of meditation in the service. Gradual melodies are melismatic in style; the text is almost lost in a sweeping surge of melody. *Haec dies* belongs to a family of graduals that use a traditional mode 2 melody type (for another example, see the gradual *Tecum principium* of the first Christmas Mass in the *Liber Usualis*). This melody hovers continually about the final, a, and the reciting note of the psalm tone, c. Some melismas recur (compare *exsultemus* of the Respond and *saeculum* of the Verse), but the course of the Gregorian melody is far less predictable than, for example, that of the melismatic Frankish Kyrie (see No. 1c). All graduals possess a large, tripartite, sectional structure of respond—psalm verse—respond. Unlike the Introit, the psalm verse is not sung to a standard formula.

**1f.** The *Alleluia* is sung right after the Gradual, before the Gospel reading. Alleluias resemble Graduals in their melismatic character and responsorial manner of performance. They project a tone of ecstatic celebration through extended vocalizations and repetition of the word *alleluia*. Alleluias are normally tripartite (alleluia—verse—alleluia), but because of the special jubilation of the day the Easter alleluia had a second verse (alleluia—verse 1—alleluia—verse 2—alleluia).[1] The long melisma following the word *alleluia* is called the *jubilus*. The echo of the alleluia and *jubilus* at the end of verse 1 (on the word *Christus*) is a common trait, as are intermittent repetitions of short figures. The mode 7 character of this chant is projected from the beginning in the rise from G to d and is confirmed subsequently by emphasis on the upper part of the octave. The Alleluia is dropped during Lent, a season of penitence, and a tract takes its place. For a slightly different version of this chant, see No. 10.

**1g.** As early as the ninth century, a new piece was sung after the Alleluia in both the western and eastern Frankish realms. In its melismatic version, this new piece was known as a *sequence*, in its texted version as a *prose*. The Easter prose usually sung in west Frankish churches was *Fulgens praeclara*. Proses are Frankish, not Gregorian, in origin and possess the clear formal organization typical of Frankish composition. Series of paired lines in prose texts invite repeated musical phrases within each group or couplet. The result is a musical plan of *x a a b b c c . . .*, with *x* an opening line without a partner. Variations in length between successive couplets produce interesting asymmetries within this regular plan. In *Fulgens praeclara*, for example, the first four couplets become successively shorter, while the fifth couplet starts a group of long, sweeping phrases. Because proses are always syllabic in text setting, the differences in phrase lengths are very apparent. In the twelfth century, the texts shift from prose to poetry and become much more even in pacing (see No. 7b).

Most of the main phrases of *Fulgens praeclara* end with a stock three-note cadence figure, but the placement of this figure changes over the course of the piece from a relatively low position (G, a, b as cadence tones) to an unexpectedly high position at the end (e). Such a melody does not fit easily into one of the standard eight modal categories.

Proses rightly belong to the Proper, for their texts relate to specific feasts: *Fulgens praeclara* celebrates the triumphant victory of the Resurrection. However, they are not included in the traditional list of the Proper because they were not part of the earliest Church liturgy and were never codified within the Western Church. Most proses were banned from the liturgy in the sixteenth century by decree of the Council of Trent.

There is considerable debate on how proses were performed. Couplets may have been sung antiphonally by two choral groups, or soloists may have sung the text (prose) while a choral group simultaneously vocalized the melody (sequence).

**1h.** The *Credo* is a concise affirmation of Christian belief as formulated by authoritative Church councils. The Credo was mandated in the Carolingian Mass in 798, but was not decreed for the Roman liturgy until 1014. Whereas new melodies were continually composed for the rest of the Ordinary, the Credo text was associated with one principal melody, the so-called authentic tone. This melody consists of a few recitation formulas that are freely adapted to successive text segments. One primary formula starts on a and cadences on G. Another rises from E or D and recites on G. A related figure describes a wavelike curve up to G, then down and back up to G or a. This repetitive melody of restricted range seems particularly suited to congregational singing.

**1i.** The *Offertory* is sung during the presentation of offerings from the congregation. The choir sings the antiphon, which is neumatic in style, but soloists sing the elaborate melismatic verses. During the course of the twelfth century, the verses were abandoned and only the antiphon remained. Usually the end of the antiphon recurs after each verse, but in the source from which this reading is taken, the scribe refers back to the *alleluia* ending verse 1. The text of the Easter offertory is drawn from Psalm 76 (75 in the Vulgate).

**1j.** The *Sanctus* text derives from Isaiah's vision of the seraphim worshipping Jehovah (Isaiah 6:3). It is sung as a choral acclamation, in some cases with congregation participating. Clear phrase or motivic repetition characterizes Frankish Sanctus melodies. In this one, the first and third *Sanctus* exclamations are

---

[1]The two verses derive from Saint Paul's First Epistle to the Corinthians. Chapter 5, verses 7 and 8.

musically identical, *Pleni sunt caeli* and *Benedictus qui venit* begin in parallel, and the two *Hosannas* end identically.

**1k.** Like the *Gloria* and the *Sanctus,* the *Agnus Dei* text is biblically inspired (John 1:29). Its plea for mercy balances that of the Kyrie at the beginning of the Mass. Many Agnus Dei melodies were created during the tenth and eleventh centuries. This one responds to the tripartite text with an *a a′ a* musical structure. The Parisian sources present it as a mode 8 chant ending on G, while the modern *Gradual* prints it in mode 6, ending on F.

**1l.** The *Communion* is an antiphonal chant sung during the distribution of the consecrated bread and wine in the Mass. Its structure originally paralleled that of the Introit: antiphon—psalm verses sung to a standard formula—antiphon. But the psalm was gradually dropped, and by the twelfth century only the antiphon remained. The neumatic mode 6 melody of the Communion *Pascha nostrum* is firmly anchored on the final, F. Its balanced contour emphasizes the thirds above and below this center, a and D.

**1m.** *Ite, missa est* is the standard sentence with which the priest dismisses the communicants. It is from this formula that the "Mass" derives its common name. The melody for this statement is a single mode 2 phrase. The congregation answers "Thanks be to God" on the same phrase.

*Note:* The Easter Mass version presented here is a composite. Propers are from the eleventh-century manuscript Montpellier, Bibliothèque de l'École de Médecine, H 159. The Ordinary is from twelfth- and thirteenth-century Parisian manuscripts that are among the first to specify Mass cycles for particular feasts. The tropes and the prose are from tenth-century Aquitanian sources. For a complete Easter Mass (including chants for all prayers, etc.) as performed in Salisbury cathedral in the thirteenth century, see *Medieval Music,* edited by W. T. Marrocco and N. Sandon (London: Oxford University Press, 1977), pp. 28-47. For the Easter Mass as performed at Nevers cathedral in the twelfth century, see *Music at Nevers Cathedral,* vol. 2, by N. van Deusen, (*Musicological Studies,* vol. XXX/2 [1980], pp. 233-258).

## 2.  First Vespers on the Feast of the Nativity of the Lord (excerpts)
### 2a.  Deus in adjutorium
Opening versicle

**Versicle**

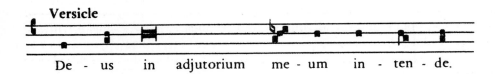

De - us    in   adjutorium   me - um    in - ten - de.

**Response**

Do - mi - ne    ad   adjuvandum   me   fe - sti - na.

**Gloria Patri**

Glo - ri - a    Patri  et  Filio,  et  Spi - ri - tu - i  San - cto,  Si - cut  erat  in  principio,

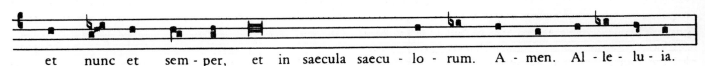

et    nunc  et   sem - per,   et  in  saecula  saecu - lo - rum.   A - men.   Al - le - lu - ia.

**Versicle**
*O God, reach out to help me.*

**Response**
*O Lord, hasten to my aid.*

**Gloria Patri**
*Glory be to the Father and to the Son and to the Holy Spirit, as it was in the beginning, is now, and shall be forever. Amen. Alleluia.*

## 2b.  **Rex pacificus**
Antiphon and Psalm 112

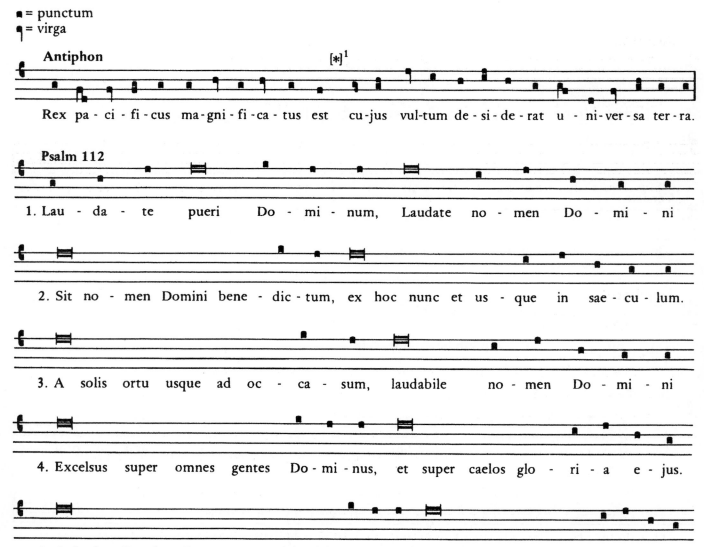

**Antiphon**

Rex pa - ci - fi - cus ma - gni - fi - ca - tus est  cu - jus vul - tum de - si - de - rat u - ni - ver - sa ter - ra.

**Psalm 112**

1. Lau - da - te  pueri  Do - mi - num,  Laudate no - men  Do - mi - ni

2. Sit no - men Domini bene - dic - tum, ex hoc nunc et us - que  in  sae - cu - lum.

3. A  solis  ortu  usque  ad  oc - ca - sum,  laudabile  no - men  Do - mi - ni

4. Excelsus  super  omnes  gentes  Do - mi - nus,  et  super  caelos glo - ri - a  e - jus.

5. Quis sicut Dominus Deus noster, qui in altis ha - bi - tat,  et humilia respicit in caelo et in ter - ra?

[1]The antiphon is intoned by a soloist. The asterisk here and in No. 2c indicates where the choir enters. On repetitions, the choir sings the entire antiphon.

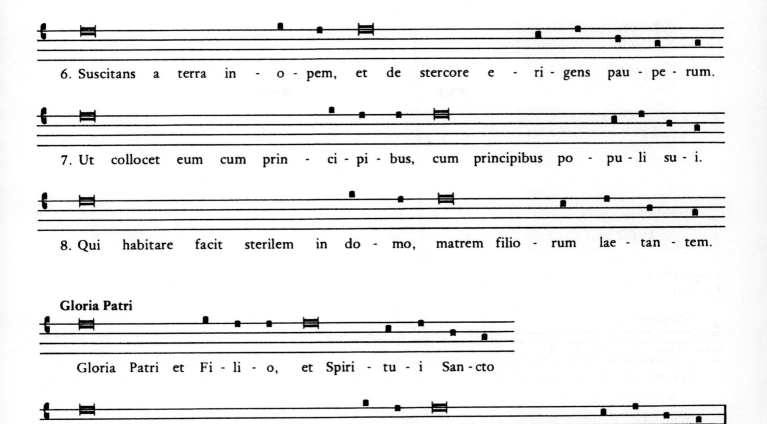

6. Suscitans a terra in - o - pem, et de stercore e - ri - gens pau - pe - rum.

7. Ut collocet eum cum prin - ci - pi - bus, cum principibus po - pu - li su - i.

8. Qui habitare facit sterilem in do - mo, matrem filio - rum lae - tan - tem.

**Gloria Patri**

Gloria Patri et Fi - li - o, et Spiri - tu - i San - cto

Sicut erat in principio et nunc et sem - per, et in saecula saecu - lo - rum. A - men.

**Antiphon**

*The King of Peace is magnificent in glory,*
*the whole world desires his countenance.*

**Psalm 112**

1. *Praise the Lord, you children of the Lord, praise the name of the Lord.*

2. *Blessed be the name of the Lord now and evermore.*

3. *From sunrise to sunset, praise the name of the Lord.*

4. *Exalted above all nations is the Lord, and his glory extends beyond the heavens.*

5. *Who is like the Lord our God, who dwells on high but deigns to regard the lowly in heaven and on earth?*

6. *He raises the weak man from the ground, and lifts the poor man from the dunghill,*

7. *So that he may place him among the princes, the princes of his own people.*

8. *He it is who makes the barren woman in the house to be the happy mother of children.*

**Gloria Patri**

*Glory be to the Father and to the Son and to the Holy Spirit, as it was in the beginning, is now, and shall be forever. Amen.*

## 2c.  **Magnificatus est**

Antiphon and Psalm 124

■ = punctum
◀ = virga

Mag - ni - fi - ca - tus est Rex pa - ci - fi - cus    su - per om - nes re - ges u - ni - ver - sae ter - rae.

**Psalm 124**

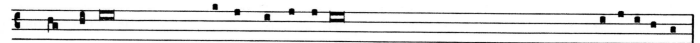

1. Qui con-fidunt in Domino si-cut mons Si-on non commovebitur in aeternum qui habitat in Je-ru-sa-lem.

2. Montes in circuitu ejus et Dominus in circuitu *populi sui*,[1] ex hoc nunc et usque *in saeculum.*

3. Quia non relinquet Dominus virgam peccatorum super *sortem justorum*, ut non extendant justi ad iniquitatem *manus suas.*

4. Benefac *Domine bonis* et *rectis cordes,*

5. Declinantes autem in obligationes adducet Dominus cum operantibus *iniquitatem* pax su*per Israel.*

### Gloria Patri

Gloria Pa*tri et Filio* et Spiri*tui Sancto*
Sicut erat in principio et *nunc et semper*, et in saecula saecu*lorum. Amen.*

### Antiphon

*More glorious is the King of Peace*
*than all the kings of the whole world.*

### Psalm 124

*1. He who trusts in the Lord is like Mount Sion, through eternity he shall not be moved; he who dwells in Jerusalem,*

*2. As the mountains encompass him, so the Lord encompasses his people, henceforth and forever more.*

*3. For the Lord does not let the scourge for sinners rest upon the fate of the righteous, lest the righteous extend their hands to evil deeds.*

*4. Do good, O Lord, to the virtuous and to the upright in heart,*

*5. But may the Lord work justice upon those who stray from right ways, and upon those who do evil. Peace upon Israel.*

### Gloria Patri

*Glory be to the Father and to the Son and to the Holy Spirit, as it was in the beginning, is now, and shall be forever. Amen.*

[1]The italics indicate where the medial and terminal inflections occur in each verse.

## 2d. Veni redemptor gentium

Hymn

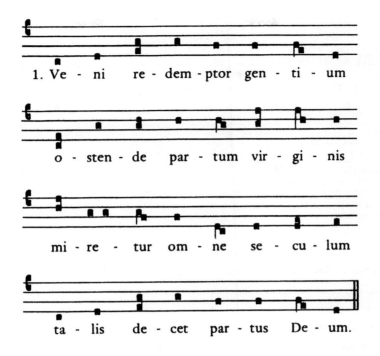

1. Ve - ni re - dem - ptor gen - ti - um

o - sten - de par - tum vir - gi - nis

mi - re - tur om - ne se - cu - lum

ta - lis de - cet par - tus De - um.

1. Veni redemptor gentium
   ostende partum virginis
   miretur omne seculum
   talis decet partus Deum.

2. Non ex virili semine
   sed mystico spiramine
   verbum Dei factum caro
   fructusque ventris floruit.

3. Alvus tumescit virginis
   claustra pudoris permanent
   vexilla virtutum micant
   versatur in templo Deus.

4. Procedens de thalamo suo
   pudoris aula regia
   geminae gigas substantiae
   alacris ut currat viam.

5. Egressus ejus a patre
   regressus ejus ad patrem
   excursus usque ad inferos
   recursus ad sedem Dei.

6. Aequalis aeterno patri
   carnis trophaeo accingere
   infirma nostri corporis
   virtute firmans perpeti.

1. *Come, savior of the gentiles,*
   *make known the virgin birth,*
   *an eternal marvel.*
   *Such a birth is fit for God.*

2. *Not from seed of man*
   *but from wondrous breath of life*
   *the word of God was made flesh*
   *and the fruit of the womb blossomed.*

3. *The virgin's belly swells*
   *but the bastions of chastity remain.*
   *Banners of virtue shine,*
   *God is in his temple.*

4. *Proceeding from his marriage bed*
   *a royal palace of chastity*
   *begotten of two substances*
   *that he might run the course quickly.*

5. *His going-out is from the Father*
   *his return is to the Father,*
   *ranging as far as Hell,*
   *he hastens back to the seat of God.*

6. *Equal with the eternal Father,*
   *armed with victory over the flesh,*
   *securing with constant virtue*
   *the infirmities of our body.*

7. Praesepe jam fulget tuum
   lumenque nox spirat novum
   quod nulla nox interpolet
   fide quo jugi luceat.

7. *Your manger already shines*
   *and the night is alive with new light*
   *that no night can diminish.*
   *May it perpetually radiate with faith.*

## 2e.   **Benedicamus Domino**
Closing versicle

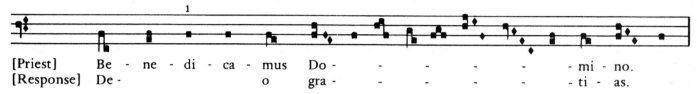

<sup>1</sup>The two puncta on D are omitted in the response.

**Priest**
*Let us bless the Lord.*

**Response**
*Thanks be to God.*

In addition to the Mass, medieval Christian worship included a series of eight Divine Offices sung at specified times each day and night. Chanting of the psalms was the core of Office ritual. In Benedictine monastic use (established around A.D. 535), the entire psalter of 150 psalms was to be sung over the course of each week of the year. Every psalm was framed with an antiphon that, in the earliest usage, recurred after each verse.

The Office liturgy was less settled than that of the Mass, and the texts and melodies sung on specific feasts varied somewhat from place to place and century to century. These excerpts from First Christmas Vespers (the Office sung at dusk on Christmas Eve) represent late eleventh-century practice at a Benedictine monastery near the north Italian town of Lucca. The main elements in this vespers service are outlined below. Asterisks indicate the musical items included in this volume.

*2a. Versicle: *Deus in adjutorium*
*2b. Antiphon *Rex pacificus* and Psalm 112, *Laudate pueri*
*2c. Antiphon *Magnificatus est* and Psalm 124 *Qui confidunt*
    Antiphon *Completi sunt dies* and Psalm 125 *In convertendo*
    Antiphon *Ecce completa sunt* and Psalm 131 *Memento Domine*
    Reading
    Responsory: *Verbum caro factum est,* verse 1 *In principio;*
       verse 2 *Gloria honor deo*

*2d. Hymn: *Veni redemptor gentium*
    Prayers
    Antiphon *Cum esset desponsata* and Canticle *Magnificat anima mea*
    Prayers
*2e. Versicle: *Benedicamus Domino*

**2a, e.** The versicles *Deus in adjutorium* and *Benedicamus domino* with their responses are the standard opening and closing statements of nearly every Office. The opening versicle is recited on a relatively plain tone in the manner of a psalm. On high feast days, the *Benedicamus domino* is sung to a rather elaborate melody, a terminal melisma from the Marian responsory *Styrps Jesse*. In the twelfth and thirteenth centuries, the versicle was often replaced (or, in a sense, elaborated) by a versus or conductus whose closing lines incorporated the liturgical text (see Nos. 6 and 12b). The plain versicle was also often set polyphonically.

**2b, c.** The antiphons frame the Old Testament psalms with New Testament texts appropriate to the feast of Christmas. The antiphons are sung to distinctive melodies of plain, unornate character, while the psalm verses are recited syllabically on the standard *psalm tone* designated to go with all antiphons in a particular modal category. Because *Rex pacificus* is in mode 8 and *Magnificatus est* in mode 7, their psalms are chanted to the mode 8 and mode 7 tones respectively. These psalm tone formulas center on a principal reciting tone (d for mode 7, c for mode 8), which is inflected at beginning, middle, and end. By the eleventh century only the first verse had the initial inflection. Subsequent verses began directly on the reciting tone. The other inflections are placed so as to project the sense and poetic form of individual textual segments. The medial inflection (*mediatio*) marks the caesura within each psalm verse, while the terminal inflection (*differentia*) defines its end. Because the antiphon recurs at the end of the psalm, the termination of the tone varies according to the initial pitch of the antiphon. The Christian Doxology (Gloria Patri) is regularly appended to the end of each psalm.

**2d.** *Hymns* are songs of praise with strophic poetic texts. The practice of hymn singing is traditionally associated with St. Ambrose of Milan (fourth century), to whom several hymn texts are attributed. Because little liturgical control was exercised over them, hymns for particular services and melodies for specific texts varied considerably from one locale or one occasion to another. *Veni redemptor gentium* is among the oldest hymns sung at Christmas vespers. Its early vintage is signaled by the absence of a regular rhyme scheme (compare No. 7c).

Musically, hymns consist of a single melodic strophe to which successive stanzas of the poem are sung. Each musical phrase normally corresponds to a poetic line. This mode 1 melody is rounded off by a repetition of the opening phrase for the fourth line of the stanza. The two middle phrases both end away from the modal final and sketch an arch rising to and falling away from the melodic high point. Such orderly, balanced phrase relationships are common in hymns and enhance the patterned regularities of their poetic texts. A fifteenth-century polyphonic setting of this melody with different (later) text is presented as No. 26.

# 3. Modal Formulas

**3a.** 9th-Century Series from **Commemoratio brevis de tonis et psalmis modulandis**

**3b.** 12th-Century Series from **De Musica** by John (of Afflighem)

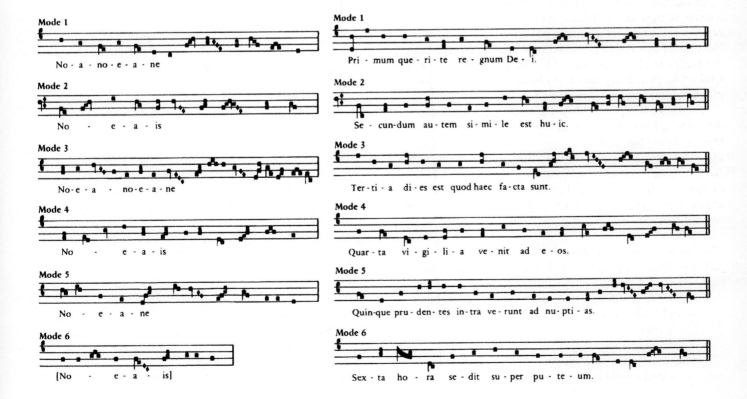

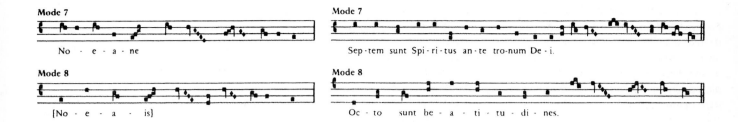

Most modern textbooks explain mode from a Renaissance perspective, thereby engendering much needless confusion about medieval chant. Because of this, it seems worthwhile to give a capsule account of principles that were fundamental to the earliest theorizing about mode.

Frankish musicians adopted the concept of mode as a way of classifying and controlling a vast repertory of monophonic melodies that were already in existence. The melodies they knew in the ninth and tenth centuries were not composed in conformity with "mode"; the modal classification was imposed *ex post facto* on the melodies.[1] Modal theory did not spring into being as a fixed system but evolved gradually and changed over several centuries. Certain core concepts of the earliest modal theory did persist through later stages and can be considered the nucleus of the modal classification system. These core concepts may be outlined as follows:

**1.** There are four modal *finals*, that is, possible locations within the total pitch system on which a melody may end. These four finals are distinguished from each other by the pattern of whole and half steps around them. They are numbered in Greek in ascending order:

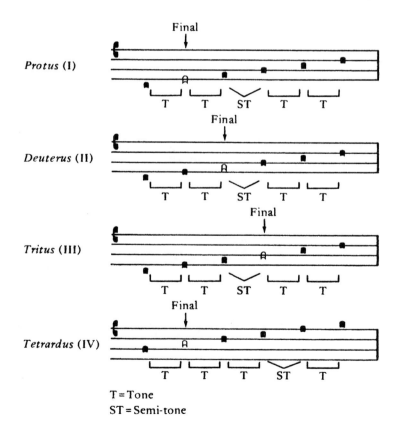

T = Tone
ST = Semi-tone

[1] It is partly because of this that certain melodies, such as No. 1g, do not fit very well within a standard modal category.

**2.** The four modal finals are normally located on the pitches D, E, F, and G, but *protus* melodies may also end on a, *deuterus* melodies on b natural, and *tritus* melodies on c. *Tetrardus* melodies have no alternative location, as no other pitch within the diatonic octave is surrounded by the same pattern of whole and half steps as G. (These relationships will be readily apparent if, in the example above, you shift the C-clef down to the second line from the bottom of the staff. Only in *tetrardus* will the whole and half step pattern around the final change.)

**3.** Each of the four basic modal categories has two subdivisions, authentic and plagal. Authentic melodies range above the final, usually to the upper fifth and beyond to the seventh or octave. Plagal melodies move within the fourth below and the fourth above the final. Put most simply, the final stands at the bottom of the range of the archetypal authentic melody, and midway in the range of the archetypal plagal melody.

The authentic/plagal subdivision resulted in an eightfold system of modal classification. This eightfold system had two equivalent sets of labels, one based on the Greek numbering and emphasizing the four finals; the other Latin and emphasizing the eight combinations of range and final. This latter nomenclature is the one used in modern chant books.

|  | *Greek labels* | *Latin labels* |
|---|---|---|
| D mode: | protus authentic | mode 1 |
|  | protus plagal | mode 2 |
| E mode: | deuterus authentic | mode 3 |
|  | deuterus plagal | mode 4 |
| F mode: | tritus authentic | mode 5 |
|  | tritus plagal | mode 6 |
| G mode: | tetrardus authentic | mode 7 |
|  | tetrardus plagal | mode 8 |

For pedagogical purposes, medieval musicians illustrated the eight modes in series of short melodies or *neumae*. These incorporated the essence of the modal character, principally by dwelling in the appropriate space around the final. The eight modal formulae still are helpful aids to absorbing the special quality of each mode. Two series of such formulae are presented here, one from the late ninth century, the other from the twelfth. The later melodies are somewhat longer and more elaborate and tend to cover wider ranges, thus maximizing the difference between authentic and plagal. The earliest modal formulae were sung to "nonsense syllables" of Greek origin. Later ones were sung to pious texts written especially for the purpose, each of which begins with the number appropriate to the modal melody.

## 4a. Rex caeli Domine
Organum at the fourth
from **Musica Enchiriadis**[1]

1    Track 7

[1] The order of text in lines 1a and 1b has been changed to conform with the monophonic version.

## Rex caeli Domine
Sacred song
Principal melody of No. 4a

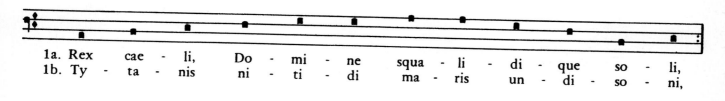

*King of heaven, Lord of the rough earth,*
*of the brilliant Titan (sun) and the resounding sea,*
*Thy humble servants, in worshipping with pious songs,*
*entreat thee to order their deliverance from diverse evils.*

## 4b.  Sit gloria Domini

Organum at the fifth with octave doubling
from **Musica Enchiriadis**[1]

Organal voice doubled
Principal voice
Organal voice
Principal voice doubled

Sit glo-ri-a Do-mi-ni in sae-cu-la;

le-ta-bi-tur Do-mi-nus in o-pe-ri-bus su-is.

[1]The notational signs in the manuscript belong beside the principal voice, not beside the doubled organal voice. This accounts for the difference between my transcription and other published transcriptions.

## Sit gloria Domini

Psalm 103, verse 31, sung to the psalm tone of mode 3
Principal melody of No. 4b

Sit glo-ri-a  Do-mi-ni  in sae-cu-la;  le-ta-bi-tur Do-mi-nus in  o-pe-ri-bus su-is.

*The Lord's glory is forever;*
*the Lord will rejoice in his works.*

## 4c.  GUIDO OF AREZZO (c. 991-after 1033)

**Ipsi soli**

Organum
from **Micrologus**

Principal voice (●)
Organal voice (○)

Ip - si___ so - li_____ ser - vo fi - dem___

Ip - si___ me to - ta de - vo - ti - o - ne com - mit - to.

## Ipsi soli
Antiphon
Principal melody of No. 4c

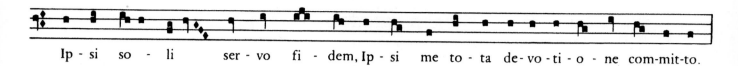

Ip - si   so - li      ser - vo   fi - dem, Ip - si   me to - ta de - vo - ti - o - ne com-mit-to.

*In him alone is my trust;*
*To him I wholly consecrate myself.*

## 4d. Kyrie Cunctipotens genitor
from **Ad organum faciendum**
See No. 1c for the principal melody of No. 4d.

Cun - cti - po - tens , ge - ni - tor de - us  om - ni - cre - a - tor  e - lei - son

Chri - ste  de - i  splen - dor  vir - tus  pa - tris - que  so - phi - a  e - lei - son

Am - bo - rum  sa - crum  spi - ra - men  ne - xus  a - mor - que  e - lei - son.

For translation of No. 4d, see No. 1c.

## 4e. Alleluia in 5th performance mode
Organum with elaborated organal voice
from **Ad organum faciendum**

Organal voice (o)
Principal voice (●)

Al - le -   lu -              ia

## Alleluia Justus ut palma
Principal melody of No. 4e

Al - le  -  lu  -  ia

In the later ninth century, at the time when chant notations began to proliferate, references to singing simultaneously at more than one pitch level appear. This manner of singing, which was called *organum*, is the ancestor of Western polyphony. Organum was conceived as a special performance practice in which a chant could be magnified through parallel singing at the fourth or the fifth below. Even more resonant sound could be achieved by doubling the principal voice (the original chant) or the organal voice (the one in parallel) at an octave above or below. Such doublings occurred automatically when men and boys sang organum together. To sound well, organum had to be performed at a deliberate tempo and with care for correct intervals.

Because the earliest organum was improvised, it was hardly ever notated. A few short examples accompanying theorists' explanations of how to produce organum are the main surviving traces of an apparently widespread practice. The two earliest (c. 850) treatises to explain organum, the *Musica Enchiriadis* and the *Scolica Enchiriadis,* explain two types of organum, one at the fourth, the other at the fifth, below the chant. Organum at the fifth was strictly parallel (No. 4b), but organum at the fourth mixed parallel fourths with oblique and converging motion between the voices (No. 4a). As the theorists explained this type of organum, the organal voice often had to hold stationary in order to avoid a tritone and to facilitate unison convergence at the ends of phrases. Octave doubling was permitted in both types of organum.

Over a half-century after the *Enchiriadis* treatises, the Italian monk Guido of Arezzo also explained organum at the fourth as practiced in his locale (c. 1030). Although Guido's rules differ from the earlier ones, the musical results are similar. His examples include all four phrases of an office antiphon *Ipsi soli* (Ex. 4c). Because the organal voice is often frozen on one pitch, organum at the fourth includes a variety of intervals–unisons, major seconds, and thirds–besides fourths. The fourths were considered primary. The others were not called dissonant, but happened incidentally as the two parts converged on unison cadences or diverged at the beginnings of phrases.

Late eleventh-century theorists teach a radically different kind of organum based on a mix of fourths, fifths, and octaves. The treatise *Ad organum faciendum* (*"How to make organum"*) (c. 1100), which originated in northern France, shows an entire Kyrie performed according to new principles (No. 4d). The two voices proceed now in contrary, now in parallel, directions and always begin or end phrases on unison or octave. The organal voice has moved from below to a position above the chant. In most of the examples, the voices move entirely note against note, but in one the organum has a flourish of additional notes (No. 4e). The discrepancy in number of notes obviously raises problems of rhythmic synchronization between the two lines. Such problems became increasingly prominent as organal voices became more elaborate (see No. 9a, b).

**5.**   <u>WULFSTAN OF WINCHESTER (?)</u> (fl.990)
## Alleluia Te martyrum    | 1  Track 9 |
Organum

Organal voice

Al - le - - - lu - - - ia

Principal voice

¹**x** = another possible interpretation.

² **-** and **t** indicate a longer rhythmic duration.

³ ⤴ indicates a liquescent (see page xv).

*Alleluia. The shining white army of martyrs praises thee, Lord. Alleluia.*

The earliest substantial repertory of organum still extant stems from the cathedral of Winchester, in the south of England. It dates from around A.D. 1000 and has been tentatively attributed to the monk Wulfstan of Winchester. The Winchester repertory contains organal voices for Office responsories and for such Mass items as Kyries, Gloria tropes, tracts, sequences and Alleluias. The organa are difficult to reconstruct, not only because the organal voices are notated alone without their companion principal voices, but also because the original neumes indicate contour but not specific pitches or intervals. Plausible reconstructions of the music depend upon procedural rules formulated in early organum treatises. The precepts for organum at the fourth are most pertinent to the Winchester organa, but they do not account fully for the movement of the organal voice as written.

The *Alleluia Te martyrum* (No. 5) for the Feast of the Holy Innocents (December 28) shows the voices moving note against note except for ends of phrases, where the organal voice often has an extra tone before the unison merger. The two voices differ greatly in melodic movement. The chant has a pronounced melodic contour, while the organal line often holds stationary on a boundary tone as stipulated in the theory. Parallel motion occurs but by no means dominates. Although as a rule the theorists position the organal voice below the principal, here it stands above when the chant rises to an upper cadence tone (as in phrase 1). Many intervals besides fourths sound between the openings of phrases and their unison cadences. The intervallic flux and the varied degrees of blending create an attractively modulated sound, which was praised by some theorists as a particularly fit ornament to sacred music.

## 6. Castitatis lilium effloruit

Versus

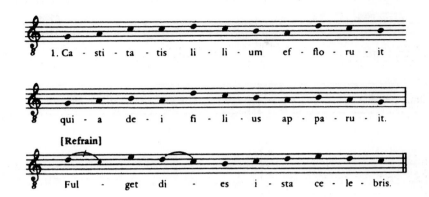

1. Ca - sti - ta - tis li - li - um ef - flo - ru - it

qui - a de - i fi - li - us ap - pa - ru - it.

[Refrain]

Ful - get di - es i - sta ce - le - bris.

1. Castitatis lilium effloruit
   quia Dei filius apparuit.
   Fulget dies ista celebris.

2. Rege nato exultat in laudibus
   multitudo celestis exercitus.
   Fulget dies ista celebris.

4. Ad videndum monent ire protin
   stella magos et pastores angelus.
   Fulget dies ista celebris.

5. Salvatorem pastores annuntiant
   Deum natum magi donis predicant.
   Fulget dies ista celebris.

6. Virgo mater servat hec in animo
   et per cuncta benedicit Domino.
   Fulget dies ista celebris.

1. *The lily of purity has blossomed*
   *for the son of God has appeared.*
   *May this festal day shine forth!*

2. *At the birth of the King*
   *let the multitude of the heavenly host rejoice with praises.*
   *May this festal day shine forth!*

4. *The star tells the wise men, and the angel tells the shepherds*
   *to go immediately to see [him].*
   *May this festal day shine forth!*

5. *The shepherds announce the Savior,*
   *the wise men fortell the birth of God with gifts.*
   *May this festal day shine forth!*

6. *The virgin mother keeps these things in her heart*
   *and blesses the Lord before all.*
   *May this festal day shine forth!*

(five stanzas of twelve)

From the tenth century on, principles of regular syllable count, rhyme, end accent, and strophic parallelism increasingly assert themselves in European poetry. Sacred poems written according to such principles were often set to music in the eleventh and twelfth centuries. Such compositions were called *versus* in southern Europe, *conductus* in Paris and regions north. The versus had no specified place in the liturgy. They were variously sung in the course of processions, attached to the *Benedicamus Domino* (the standard versicle closing each Office, see No. 2e), or inserted into services on special feast days sometimes before a reading. The majority of them are appropriate to the Christmas season.

The regular poetic forms of the versus had decisive impact on the musical settings. Composers responded to even text lines with balanced phrases, to terminal rhymes with clear cadential punctuations, to parallel strophes and recurrent refrains with clear-cut repetitions. In *Castitatis lilium,* a widely circulated versus from about 1100, the coordination of poem and music produces a highly ordered musical structure. The two rhyming verse lines are paired through parallel phrases, both focused tonally on G. The separate refrain phrase is placed in a contrasting higher register and centers on c. All three phrases end with the same easily recognizable cadential formula, a three-note descending figure. In the first phrase, this figure falls to B, an unstable, "open"-sounding pitch, while in the second it closes on the most stable melodic pitch, G. The progression from tension to resolution produced by these differentiated cadence tones fuses the two phrases into a single structural unit. Ordered tonal structure of this sort is a hallmark of late medieval monophony. The principles of tonal tension and resolution realized in this repertory are basic to much later Western music.

## 7a. Ave regina caelorum

Votive antiphon

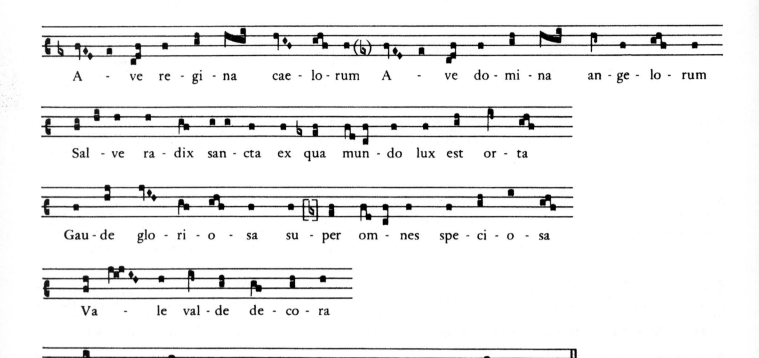

A - ve re - gi - na cae - lo - rum A - ve do - mi - na an - ge - lo - rum

Sal - ve ra - dix san - cta ex qua mun - do lux est or - ta

Gau - de glo - ri - o - sa su - per om - nes spe - ci - o - sa

Va - le val - de de - co - ra

et pro no - bis sem - per Chri - stum ex - o - ra.

*Hail, Queen of Heaven.*
*Hail, Mistress over the angels.*
*Hail, Holy Source*
*from which light entered the world.*
*Rejoice, Glorious One,*
*beautiful beyond measure.*
*Prosper greatly, most comely one,*
*and pray for us always to Christ.*

## 7b. Veni sancte spiritus

Prose

Track 10

1a. VENI SANCTE SPIRITUS, et e - mit - te cae - li - tus lu - cis tu - ae ra - di - um.

1b. Ve - ni pa - ter pau - pe - rum, ve - ni da - tor mu - ne - rum, ve - ni lu - men cor - di - um.

1a. *Come Holy Spirit and send forth the ray of thy light divine.*

1b. *Come Father of the poor, come Giver of bounty, come Light of the heart.*

2a. *Best comforter, sweet friend of the soul, gentle refuge,*

2b. *Rest in labor, relief in anxiety, solace in distress.*

3a. *O most blessed Light, fill the inmost hearts of thy faithful.*

3b. *Without thy divine power, nothing is bright, nothing is innocent.*

4a. *Cleanse what is soiled, moisten what is arid, heal what is injured.*

4b. *Bend what is rigid, warm what is frigid, govern that which errs.*

5a. *Give to thy faithful, who trust in thee, the sevenfold sacred gifts,*

5b. *Give them the reward of virtue, salvation at death, and perpetual joy. Amen.*

## 7c. Pange lingua gloriosi corporis
Hymn

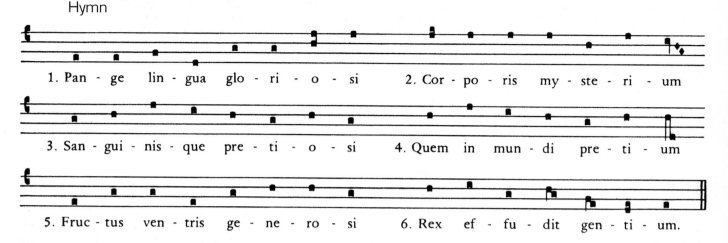

1. Pan - ge   lin - gua   glo - ri - o - si    2. Cor - po - ris   my - ste - ri - um

3. San - gui - nis - que   pre - ti - o - si    4. Quem in   mun - di   pre - ti - um

5. Fruc - tus   ven - tris   ge - ne - ro - si    6. Rex   ef - fu - dit   gen - ti - um.

1. Pange lingua gloriosi
   Corporis mysterium
   Sanguinisque pretiosi
   Quem in mundi pretium
   Fructus ventris generosi
   Rex effudit gentium.

2. Nobis natus nobis datus
   Ex intacta virgine
   Et in mundo conversatus
   Sparso verbi semine
   Sui moras incolatus
   Miro clausit ordine.

4. Verbum caro panem verum
   Verbo carnem efficit
   Fitque sanguis Christi merum
   Et si sensus deficit
   Ad firmandum cor sincerum
   Sola fides sufficit.

6. Genitori genitoque
   Laus et jubilatio
   Salus honor virtus quoque
   Sit et benedictio
   Procedenti ab utroque
   Compar sit laudatio.

(four stanzas of six)

1. Sing, [my] tongue,
   the mystery of the glorious body
   and the precious blood
   which the king of the gentiles,
   fruit of a noble womb,
   shed as ransom for the world.

2. Born to us, given to us
   from an untouched virgin
   and sent back into the world
   with the scattered seed of the Word,
   Dwelling here, he concluded his stay
   with wonderful control.

4. The Word made Flesh produces true bread,
   the flesh from the Word,
   and the blood of Christ makes pure wine.
   And if understanding fails,
   faith alone suffices
   to support a sincere heart.

6. To the Father and the Son
   be praise and jubilation
   salvation, honor, power
   and blessing also
   proceeding from both
   may both have equal praise.

## 7d. Aeterna Christi munera
Hymn
Model for melody of No. 7c

Ae - ter - na   Chri - sti   mu - ne - ra,   et   mar - ty - rum   vi - cto - ri - as,

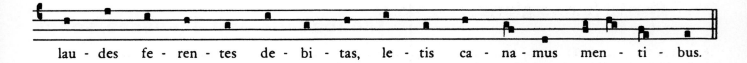

lau - des   fe - ren - tes   de - bi - tas,   le - tis   ca - na - mus   men - ti - bus.

*The eternal gifts of Christ*
*and the victories of martyrs,*
*bearing well-deserved praises*
*we sing of these things with joyful spirits.*

(stanza one of seven)

Composition of liturgical chant did not cease with the consolidation of Gregorian and Frankish repertories in the tenth century but continued on into the later Middle Ages. Like the *versus*, late medieval antiphons and sequences were responsive to contemporary poetic style.

**7a.** *Ave regina caelorum*, a twelfth-century composition, is one of the four celebrated Marian antiphons incorporated into the office of Compline in the thirteenth century. It is a votive antiphon, a song of praise and prayer to the Virgin Mary that stands independent of any psalm (for traditional Office psalmody see No. 2b). The melody reflects the symmetries of the rhymed poetic text and shares the orderly character of earlier Frankish chant. It is carefully shaped through phrase repetition and variation and unambiguously defines the final, c, as its tonal center. Not only are melodic units balanced above and below c, but c is a constant reference point for phrase beginnings and endings. A three-note cadence figure, d-e-c(-c), closes all main phrases except the penultimate one, which remains suspended on the third above the final. The oldest notated version of *Ave regina caelorum* is on G, but the notation early standardized on c (with b-flat), probably because it fit better on the four-line staff. In the fifteenth and sixteenth centuries, the plainsong *Ave regina caelorum* became the foundation for a number of polyphonic motets (see Nos. 24b, 28, 41). For a variant version of this tune, used in the English (Sarum) rite, see No. 24c.

**7b.** Under the impact of symmetrical, rhymed poetry, the sequence lost its irregular prose qualities and became extraordinarily uniform in structure. The Pentecost sequence *Veni sancte spiritus*, whose text is attributed to Pope Innocent III (1160-1216), dates from the late twelfth century. It possesses the repetitive shape of the early sequence (*aa bb cc* . . .) but lacks its intriguing irregularities (see No. 1g). Because every text unit is a rhymed verse of three times seven syllables, the main phrases are entirely even in length. Moreover, their three internal subdivisions are consistently defined by rhyme and by register and melodic contour. The first large phrase, for example, is partitioned into three segments of parallel contour, the first and last of which are anchored on the final, the middle one set apart on the upper fifth.

The entire melody is governed by fifth and octave relationships and adheres to a D-a-d framework. Just as each main text unit ends with the same rhyme, so every main phrase unit, except the fourth, closes on the final, D. Similar cadence figures reinforce the invariant final rhyme. The systematic organization and predictable course of this music stand in sharp contrast to the fantasy of contemporary polyphony (see Nos. 10, 11).

**7c.** Late medieval hymns are similar in form to their predecessors except for the presence of rhyme as a regular poetic feature (see No. 2d). One of the most famous hymns of the thirteenth century is *Pange lingua gloriosi corporis*, written for the newly instituted feast of Corpus Christi (1264). The hymn is in six-line stanzas of alternate eight- and seven-syllable lines,[1] with an *ababab* rhyme scheme. The verse observes a consistent trochaic meter (a / ᴗ accentual scheme).

The third-mode melody principally associated with this text is not freshly composed but has been adapted from an earlier tune originally invented for a four-line hymn stanza in iambic dimeter (ᴗ / ᴗ / ᴗ /). The earlier melody is shown here (No. 7d) with the first strophe of *Aeterna Christi munera*, a fifth-century hymn in praise of martyrs. The basic structure of the model is preserved in the *Pange lingua* adaptation, but certain pitches and melodic gestures receive a new degree of emphasis. This *Pange lingua* melody later served as a point of departure for an extraordinary polyphonic Mass by Josquin Desprez (see No. 34).

[1]The stanza is actually modelled on a celebrated sixth-century hymn, *Pange lingua gloriosi proelium*, by Venantius Fortunatus. A fourteenth-century attribution of the Corpus Christi office to Saint Thomas Aquinas is no longer accepted.

## Troubadour and Trouvère songs

**8a.** <u>BERNART DE VENTADORN</u> (?c. 1130/40-c. 1190/1200)

**Can vei la lauzeta mover**

Track 11

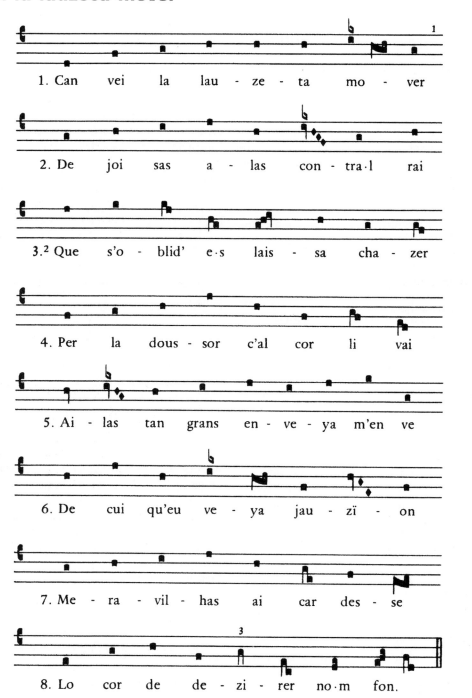

1. Can vei la lau - ze - ta mo - ver

2. De joi sas a - las con - tra·l rai

3.[2] Que s'o - blid' e·s lais - sa cha - zer

4. Per la dous - sor c'al cor li vai

5. Ai - las tan grans en - ve - ya m'en ve

6. De cui qu'eu ve - ya jau - zï - on

7. Me - ra - vil - has ai car des - se

8. Lo cor de de - zi - rer no·m fon.

[1]Some manuscripts have B♭s as indicated above the staff.

[2]Lines 3 and 4 are reversed in the manuscript from which this melody is drawn.

[3]This figure is called a *plica* and is sung as G-liquescent F.

1. Can vei la lauzeta mover
   De joi sas alas contra.l rai
   Que s'oblid' e.s laissa chazer
   Per la doussor c'al cor li vai,
   Ai, tan grans enveya m'en ve
   De cui qu'eu veya jauzïon,
   Meravilhas ai car desse
   Lo cor de dezirer no.m fon.

2. Ai, las, tan cuidava saber
   D'amor e tan petit en sai!
   Car eu d'amar no.m posc tener
   Celeis don ja pro non aurai.
   Tout m'a mo cor e tout m'a me,
   E se mezeis e tot lo mon,
   E can se.m tolc, no.m laisset re
   Mas dezirer e cor volon.

3. Anc non agui de me poder
   Ni no fui meus de l'or' en sai
   Que-m laisset en sos olhs vezer
   En un miralh que moult me plai.
   Miralhs, pus me mirei en te,
   M'an mort li sospir de preon
   C'aissi-m perdei com perdet se
   Lo bels Narcisus en la fon.

4. De las domnas me dezesper.
   Ja mais en lor no-m fiarai,
   C'aissi com las solh chaptener,
   Enaissi las deschaptenrai.
   Pois vei c'una pro no m'en te
   Va leis que-m destrui e-m cofon,
   Totas las dopt' e las mescre,
   Car be sai c'atretals se son.

5. D'aisso.s fa be femna parer
   Ma domna, per qu'e.lh o retrai,
   Car no vol so c'om deu voler
   E so c'om li deveda, fai.
   Chazutz sui en mala merce,
   Et ai be faih co.l fols en pon;
   E no sai per que m'esdeve
   Mas car trop puyei contra mon.

6. Merces es perduda per ver,
   Et eu non o saubi anc mai,
   Car cilh qui plus en degr'aver
   No.n a ges, et on la querrai?
   A, can mal sembla, qui la ve,
   Qued aquest chaitiu deziron
   Que ja ses leis non aura be
   Laisse morir, que no l'äon!

1. *When I see the lark beat his wings*
   *for joy against the sun's ray,*
   *until he forgets to fly and plummets down,*
   *for the sheer delight which goes to his heart,*
   *alas, great envy comes to me*
   *of those whom I see filled with happiness,*
   *and I marvel that my heart*
   *does not instantly melt from desire.*

2. *Alas, I thought I knew so much about love,*
   *and really I know so little,*
   *for I cannot keep myself from loving her*
   *from whom I shall have no favor.*
   *She has stolen from me my heart, myself,*
   *herself, and all the world.*
   *When she took herself from me, she left me nothing*
   *but desire and a longing heart.*

3. *Never have I been in control of myself*
   *or even belonged to myself from the hour*
   *that she let me gaze into her eyes—*
   *that mirror that pleases me so greatly.*
   *Mirror, since I saw myself reflected in you,*
   *deep sighs have been killing me.*
   *I have lost myself, just as*
   *handsome Narcissus lost himself in the fountain.*

4. *I despair of women,*
   *no more will I trust them,*
   *and just as I used to defend them,*
   *now I shall denounce them.*
   *Since I see that none aids me*
   *against her who destroys and confounds me,*
   *I fear and distrust them all*
   *for I know well they are all alike.*

5. *In this my lady certainly shows herself*
   *to be a woman, and for it I reproach her,*
   *for she wants not that which one ought to want,*
   *and what is forbidden, she does.*
   *I have fallen out of favor*
   *and have behaved like the fool on the bridge;*
   *and I don't know why it happened*
   *except because I tried to climb too high.*

6. *Mercy is lost, in truth,*
   *though I never received it,*
   *for she who should possess it most*
   *has none, so where shall I seek it?*
   *Ah, one who sees her would scarcely guess*
   *that she just leaves this passionate wretch*
   *(who will have no good without her)*
   *to die, and gives no aid.*

7. Pus ab midons no. m pot valer
Precs ni merces ni.l dreihz qu'eu ai,
Ni a leis no ven a plazer
Qu'eu l'am, ja mais no.lh o dirai.
Aissi.m part de leis e.m recre;
Mort m'a e per mort li respon,
E vau m'en, pus ilh no.m rete,
Chaitius, en issilh, no sai on.

8. Tristans, ges non auretz de me,
Qu'eu m'en vau, chaitius, no sai on.
De chantar me gic e.m recre,
E de joi e d'amor m'escon.

7. *Since with my lady neither prayers nor mercy*
*nor my rights avail me,*
*and since she is not pleased*
*that I love her, I will never speak of it to her again.*
*Thus I part from her, and leave;*
*she has killed me, and by death I respond,*
*since she does not retain me, I depart,*
*wretched, into exile, I don't know where.*

8. *Tristan, you will have nothing from me,*
*for I depart, wretched, I don't know where.*
*I quit and leave off singing*
*and withdraw from joy and love.*

## 8b. PEIRE VIDAL (fl. 1175-1210)
### Baros de mon dan covit

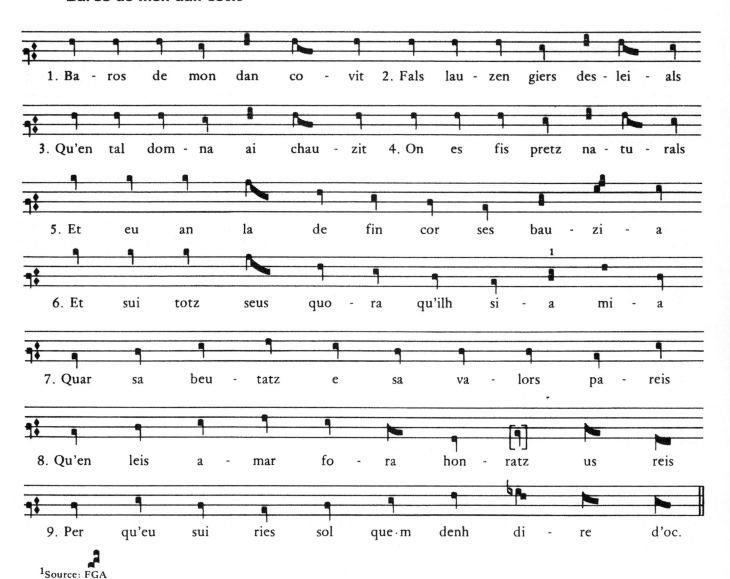

1. Ba - ros de mon dan co - vit 2. Fals lau - zen giers des - lei - als

3. Qu'en tal dom - na ai chau - zit 4. On es fis pretz na - tu - rals

5. Et eu an la de fin cor ses bau - zi - a

6. Et sui totz seus quo - ra qu'ilh si - a mi - a

7. Quar sa beu - tatz e sa va - lors pa - reis

8. Qu'en leis a - mar fo - ra hon - ratz us reis

9. Per qu'eu sui ries sol que·m denh di - re d'oc.

[1] Source: FGA

1. Baros, de mon dan covit[1]
   Fals lauzengiers deslïals,
   Qu'en tal domna ai chauzit
   Ont es fis pretz naturals.
   Et ieu am la de cor e ses bauzïa,
   E sui totz sieus, quora qu'ilh sïa mïa.
   Qu'a sa beutat e sa valor pareis
   Qu'en lieis amar honratz fora us reis;
   Per que.m tieng ric, sol que.m deinh dire d'oc.

1. Barons, I defy false, faithless slanderers to harm me, for my choice has fallen on such a one in whom there is noble and natural merit; and I love her truly and without deceit, and am wholly hers no matter when she be mine. Since by her beauty and worth it is clear that, in loving her, a king would be honoured, I therefore deem myself rich, if only she deigned to say "yes" to me.

2. Anc res tan no m'abellit
   Cum sos adreitz cors lïals,
   On son tug bon aip complit
   E totz bes, senes totz mals.
   E pus tot a quan tainh a drudarïa,
   Ben sui astrucs, sol que mos cors lai sïa;
   E si merces, per que totz bos aips creis,
   Mi val ab lieis, be.us puesc dir ses totz neis,
   Qu'anc ab amor tant ajudar no.m poc.

2. Never did anything so delight me as her true and loyal person, in whom are all qualities complete and good, without any defects. And since she has all that pertains to loving, I am most fortunate, if only I were there with her; and if pity, through which every quality increases, is of help to me with her, then I can indeed say to you, without any reserve, that it could never have helped me so much in love before.

3. Chant e solatz vei fallit,
   Cortz e dons e bos ostals;
   e domnei no vei grazit—
   Si.lh domn'e.l drutz non es fals.
   Aquel n'a mai que plus soven galïa,
   No.n dirai plus mas cum si vuelha sïa.
   Mas peza me quar ades non esteis
   Lo premiers fals que comenset anceis;
   E fora dreitz, qu'avol eixample moc.

3. Song and solace I see neglected, court-gatherings and gifts and fine hospitality; and love-service I see not favoured, unless the lady and lover are false. He gains most from it who most often betrays; I'll say no more of it but be it as it will. Yet it grieves me that he didn't perish at once, the first knave who started it all; and it would have been right, for he set a wicked example.

4. Mon cor sent alegrezit
   Quar me cobrara'N Barrals.
   Ben aja selh que.m noirit,
   E Dieus, quar ieu sui aitals!
   Que mil salut mi venon cascun dïa
   De Cataluenha e de Lombardïa,
   Quar a totz jorns pueja mos pretz e creis
   Que per un pauc no mor d'enveja.l reis,
   Quar ab donas fas mon trep e mon joc.

4. I feel my heart full of happiness, for Lord Barral will again have me with him. Fortune favour him who raised me, and God, that I am such as I am! For a thousand love letters come to me each day from Catalonia and Lombardy, and every day my merit grows and increases, so that the king is almost dying of envy, and with the ladies I dance and play as I will.

(four stanzas of seven)

[1]The lack of an identifiable authentic version of the song is exemplified in discrepancies between the text in the critical edition and that in the music manuscript.

## 8c. GAUCELM FAIDIT (?c.1150-c.1220)
**Fortz chausa es** [1199]

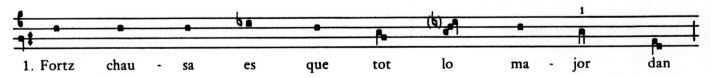

1. Fortz chau - sa es que tot lo ma - jor dan

[1]The plica indicates a liquescent note between the main pitch and the following neume.

2. E·l    ma - jor    dol    las    qu'ieu    anc    mais    a - gues

3. E    so    don    dei    totz - temps    plai - gner    plo - ran

4. M'a - ven    a    dir    en    chan - tan    e    re - trai - re

5. Car    cel    qu'e - ra    de    va - lor    caps    e    pai - re

6. Lo    rics    va - lens    Ri - chartz    reys    dels    En - gles

7. Es    mortz.    Ai    Dieus    cals    perd'    e    cals    dans    es

8. Cant    es - trains    motz    e    cant    greus    ad    au - zir

9. Ben    a    dur    cor    totz    hom    q'o    pot    sof - frir.

[2]Source: A-F.

1. Fortz chausa es que tot lo major dan
   e-l major dol, las! q'ieu anc mais agues,
   e so don dei totztemps plaigner ploran,
   m'aven a dir en chantan e retraire—
   Car cel q'era de valor caps e paire
   lo rics valens Richartz, reis dels Engles,
   es mortz— Ai Dieus! cals perd'e cals dans es!
   cant estrains motz, e cant greus ad auzir!
   Ben a dur cor totz hom q'o pot sofrir.

1. *It is a very cruel event, the greatest misfortune*
   *and the greatest sorrow, alas, that I have ever had*
   *one which I must always lament, weeping,*
   *that I must tell and recount in song*
   *for he who was the head and father of valor,*
   *the strong, powerful Richard, king of the English,*
   *is dead—Alas God! what a loss, what a blow!*
   *such a harsh statement, so painful to hear,*
   *hard of heart is any man who can endure it.*

2. Mortz es lo reis, e son passat mil an
   c'anc tant pros hom non fo, ni no-l vi res,
   ni mais non er nulls hom del sieu semblan
   tant larcs, tant rics, tant arditz, tals donaire,
   q'Alixandres, lo reis qui venquent Daire,
   non cre que tant dones ni tant meses,
   ni anc Karles ni Artus plus valgues,
   c'a tot lo mon si fetz, qui-n vol ver dir,
   als us doptar et als autres grazir.

3. Meravill me del fals segle truan,
   co-i pot estar savis hom ni cortes,
   puois re no-i val beill dich ni faich prezan,
   e doncs per que s'esfors om, pauc, ni gaire?
   q'eras nos a mostrat Mortz que pot faire,
   q'a un sol colp a-l meillor del mon pres,
   tota l'onor, totz los gaugs, totz los bes;
   e pos vezem que res no-i pot gandir,
   ben deuri' hom meins doptar a morir!

7. Ai! Seigner Dieus! vos q'etz vers perdonaire,
   vers Dieus, vers hom, vera vida, merces!
   Perdonatz li, que ops e cocha l'es,
   e no gardetz, Seigner, al sieu faillir,
   e membre vos cum vos anet servir!

(four stanzas of seven)

2. *The King is dead, and not for a thousand years*
   *has there been, or has anyone seen, so splendid a man,*
   *nor was there ever a man equal to him,*
   *so open, so powerful, so courageous, so generous*
   *so I believe not even Alexander, the king who vanquished*
     *Darius,*
   *gave or distributed as much as he,*
   *nor were Charlemagne nor King Arthur more valiant*
   *for to speak the truth, he knew*
   *how to dominate some in this world, and to be kind*
     *to others.*

3. *I marvel that in this false, deceitful age*
   *there can be any wise and courtly man,*
   *for neither fair words nor fine deeds ensure these qualities,*
   *and then, why should a man exert himself little or much,*
   *when Death has shown us what he can do*
   *at one blow claiming the world's best—*
   *all honor, all joys, all good—*
   *and since we see that it is inescapable,*
   *man ought not to fear dying so much.*

7. *Alas, Lord God! you who are the true forgiver of sins,*
   *true God, true man, true life—have mercy!*
   *Pardon him [Richard], for he has need of your grace,*
   *Lord, do not remember his sins,*
   *but remember how he was going to serve you.*

## 8d. Chevalier mult estes guariz
Crusaders' song (1147)

1. Che - va - lier mult es - tes gua - riz 2. Quant Deu a vus fait sa cla - mur

3. Des Turs e des A - mo - ra - viz 4. Ki li unt fait tels des - ho - nors

5. Cher a tort unt ses fieuz sai - siz 6. Bien en de - vums a - veir do - lur

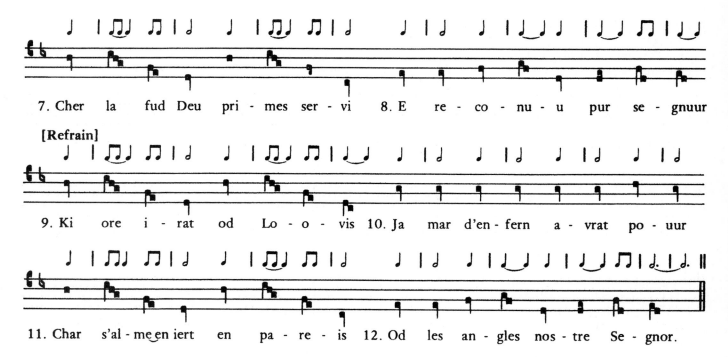

7. Cher  la  fud  Deu  pri - mes  ser - vi  8. E  re - co - nu - u  pur  se - gnuur

[Refrain]

9. Ki  ore  i - rat  od  Lo - o - vis  10. Ja  mar  d'en - fern  a - vrat  po - uur

11. Char  s'al - me en iert  en  pa - re - is  12. Od  les  an - gles  nos - tre  Se - gnor.

1. Chevalier mult estes guariz
   Quant Deu a vus fait sa clamur
   Des Turs e des Amoraviz
   Ki li unt fait tels deshonors
   Cher a tort unt ses fieuz saisiz
   Bien en devums aveir dolur
   Cher la fud Deu primes servi
   E reconuu per segnuur.

   Ki ore irat od Loovis
   Ja mar d'enfern avrat pouur
   Char s'alme en iert en pareis
   Od les angles nostre Segnor.

2. Pris est Rohais ben le savez
   Dunt crestiens sunt esmaiez
   Les musteirs ars e desertez
   Deus n'i est mais sacrifiez.
   Chevaliers cher vus purpensez
   Vus ki d'armes estes preisez
   A celui voz cors presentez
   Ki pur vus fut en cruiz drecez.

   Ki ore irat od Loovis ....

7. Alum conquere Moises
   Ki gist el munt Sinai
   A Saragins nel laisum mais
   Ne la verge dunt il partid
   La roge mer tut ad un fais
   Quant le grant pople le seguit
   E pharon revint apres
   El e li suon furent perit.

   Ki ore irat od Loovis ....

(three stanzas of seven)

*1. Knights, you are well protected*
*since God has pleaded his case to you.*
*The Turks and Almoravids [an Atlas mountain tribe]*
*have done him such injustice*
*for they have wrongly seized his fiefs.*
*We should certainly feel distressed at this*
*for there God was first served*
*and recognized as Lord.*

*[Refrain] He who goes with Louis [King Louis VII]*
*need never fear Hell*
*His soul will certainly go to Paradise*
*where our Lord's angels are.*

*2. Rohais has been taken, as you well know—*
*hence Christians are dismayed—*
*the monasteries burned and deserted*
*God is no more sacrificed there.*
*Knights, reflect on this,*
*you who are renowned in arms,*
*present your hearts to him*
*who for you was raised on the Cross.*

*He who goes with Louis ....*

*7. Rouse yourselves to win Moses*
*who dwelt on Mount Sinai.*
*Leave him not to the Saracens*
*nor the rod with which he parted*
*the Red Sea at one blow*
*when the great host followed him*
*and Pharaoh followed after*
*and perished with his men.*

*He who goes with Louis ....*

## 8e.  GACE BRULÉ (c. 1160-after 1213)
### Biaus m'est estez

1. Biaus m'est es - tez quant re - ten - tist la brueil - le

2. Que li oi - sel chan - tent par le bos - cha - ge

3. Et l'er - be vert de rou - se - e se mueil - le

4. Qui re - splen - dir la fait lés le ri - va - ge.

5. De bone a - mor vueill que mes cuers se dueil - le

6. Car nus fors moi n'a vers li ferm co - ra - ge

7. Et non - por - quant trop est de haut pa - ra - ge

8. Ce - le cui j'aim n'est pas drois que me vueil - le.

1. Biaus m'est estez que retentist la brueille
   Que li oisel chantent par le boschage,
   Et l'erbe vert de la rousee mueille
   Qui resplendir la fait lés le rivage.
   De bone Amor vueill que mes cuers se dueille,
   Car nus fors moi n'a vers li ferm corage;
   Et nonporquant trop est de haut parage
   Cele cui j'aim n'est pas drois que me vueille.

2. Fins amans sui, comment qu'Amours m'acueille,
   Car je n'aim pas con hom de mon eage,
   Qu'il n'est amis qui aint ne amer sueille,
   Qui plus de moi ne truist amour sauvage.
   He las, chaitis! ma dame a cui s'orgueille?
   Vers son ami, cui dolour n'assouage.
   Merci, Amors, s'ele esguarde parage,
   Donc sui je mors, més pensés que me vueille.

3. De bien amer Amours grant sens me baille,
   Si m'a traï s'a ma dame n'agree;
   La volenté pri Dieu que ne me faille,
   Car mout m'est bel quant u cuer m'est entree;
   Tout mi pensé sunt a li, u que j'aille,
   Ne rienz fors li ne me puet estre mee.
   De la dolour dont souspir a celee;
   A mort me rent, ainz que longues m'asaille.

4. Mes bien amers ne cuit que rienz me vaille,
   Quar pitiez est et mercis oublïee
   Envers cele qui si grief me travaille
   Que gieus et ris et joie m'est veee.
   He las, chaitis! si dure dessevraille!
   De joie part et la doleur m'agree,
   Dont je souspir coiement, a celee;
   Si me rest bien, comment qu'Amours m'assaille.

5. De mon fin cuer me vient a grant mervoille,
   Qui de moi est, et si me vuet ocire
   K'a essïent en si haut lieu tessoille;
   Donc ma dolour ne savroie pas dire;
   Ensinc sui morz, s'Amours ne me consoille;
   Car onques n'oi par li fors poinne et ire,
   Mais mes sire est, si ne l'os escondire:
   Amer m'estuet, puis qu'il s'i aparoille.

1. I love the summer, when the forest resounds
   because the birds sing in the trees,
   and the green grass dampens with dew
   and thus shines along the shore.
   It causes my heart to suffer from good Love
   because no one except myself approaches it with bold heart;
   however, she whom I love is of too high a position;
   it is not right that she want me.

2. I am an honest lover, however Love may receive me,
   because I do not love like a man of my age,
   for there is no lover who has ever loved
   who has found love wilder than I.
   Alas, wretch! towards whom does my lady pride herself?
   Towards her lover, whose travail she does not assuage.
   Mercy, Love, if she looks at [social] position,
   then I am dead, never think that she wants me.

3. Love generously grants me to love well,
   but has betrayed me if it please not my lady;
   I pray God's will that he not fail me,
   because I very much like how much she has
        entered my heart.
   All my thoughts are of her, wherever I may go,
   nor can anything but her be my salvation
   from the pain from which I secretly sigh;
   I give myself up to death, before it besieges me too long.

4. But I do not believe that loving well helps me at all,
   because pity and mercy are forgotten
   as far as she who so heavily burdens me is
        concerned,
   because games, and laughter and joy are denied me.
   Alas, wretch! such a hard privation!
   I leave joy and pain embraces me
   from which I silently, secretly sigh;
   so I resist well, although Love besieges me.

5. It comes as a great surprise to me that my honest heart
   which is mine, wishes to kill me,
   which speaks knowledgeably in such a high place
   that I would not know how to speak my pain;
   thus I am dead, unless Love counsels me
   for I hear only from him of pain and wrath,
   but he [Love] is my lord, so I dare not hide it;
   I must love, since he so decides it.

6. A mie nuit une dolors m'esvoille,
   Que l'endemain me tolt joer et rire;
   Qu'a droit consoil m'a dit dedans l'oroille:
   Que j'ain celi pour cui muir a martire.
   Si fais je voir, més el n'est pas feoille
   Vers son ami qui de s'amour consire.
   De li amer ne me doi escondire,
   Non puis noier, mes cuers s'i aparoille.

7. Guy de Ponciaus, GASCOZ, ne set que dire:
   Li dex d'amours malement nos consoille.

6. *At midnight a pain awakens me*
   *that takes laughing and playing from me on the*
      *morrow;*
   *because it correctly said to me, into my ear:*
   *that I love her for whom I die in agony.*
   *So I reveal it, for the man who obtains love*
   *can never be crazy toward his beloved.*
   *I should not hide from myself that I love her,*
   *I cannot deny it, my heart decides it.*

7. *Guy of Ponciaux, a Gascon, knows not what to say:*
   *the god of Love counsels us badly.*

—Translation by Leslie Morgan

## 8f. GUILLAUME D'AMIENS (fl. late 13th century)
## Prendes i garde

Rondeau

1. Pren - des i gar - de__ s'on nous__ re - gar - de
2. S'on nous re - gar - de__ di - tes le moi.
3. C'est tout la jus en__ cel - [le] bos - chai - ge.
4. Pren - des i gar - de__ s'on nous__ re - gar - de.
5. La pas - tou - re - le__ u gar - doit va - ches
6. "Plai - sant bru - ne - te__ a vous m'oc - troi."
7. Pren - des i gar - de__ s'on nous__ re - gar - de
8. S'on nous re - gar - de__ di - tes le moi.

Prendes i garde, s'on nous regarde[1]
S'on nous regarde, dites le moi.
C'est tout la jus en cel boschaige.
Prendes i garde, s'on nous regarde.
La pastourele u gardoit vaches
"Plaisant brunete, a vous m'octroi."
Prendes i garde s'on nous regarde
S'on nous regarde, dites le moi.

*Take care, lest anyone see us,*
*if someone sees us, tell me.*
*It's just there in that wooded grove.*
*Take care lest anyone see us.*
*The peasant lass was looking after the cows,*
*"Charming brunette, I offer myself to you."*
*Take care lest anyone see us,*
*If someone sees us, tell me.*

[1]Some versions of this text have the personal pronoun *me,* others *nous.* I have chosen the latter reading because it better conveys the situation.

A brilliant flowering of secular song in vernacular tongues took place in the twelfth and thirteenth centuries. Two central poet-musician groups involved were the troubadours in southwest Europe, whose dialect was the *langue d'oc,* and the trouvères of the northwest, who spoke the *langue d'oïl.* Central to their poetry was the celebration of love as an elevating, joyful and refined experience—a tradition summarized under the modern term *courtly love.* Although love was the central topic, their songs also included political and moral themes, laments, satires, literary and social debates, and even popularized religious subjects such as miracles.

The poems are strophic verse organized by rhyme and number of syllables in lines. The regularities of poetic structure are emphasized through regularities in musical patterns. Successive strophes are normally sung to the same melody, and successive rhymed couplets often receive identical musical phrases. Troubadour and trouvère poetry was conceived as song, but the music was not always copied with the poems. In fact, most of the troubadour melodies are lost. Those melodies (troubadour or trouvère) that do survive exhibit great variety in formal shape, melodic movement, and tonal focus. They tend to be quite different in sound from older or contemporary liturgical chant.

Two major performance issues are associated with twelfth- and thirteenth-century secular song. One is rhythmic, for with the exception of a few late sources the songs survive in a chant notation that is rhythmically neutral. Some scholars argue the music should be sung in free rhythm based on appropriate text declamation. Others consider that the rhythmic modes developed for polyphony in the late twelfth century (see comment on No. 10) should be applied. The latter view was particularly prevalent in the early twentieth century and has guided many of the published transcriptions, but the weight of recent scholarship is toward nonmetric interpretation. The other major performance problem for this repertory concerns accompaniment. Pictorial representations suggest that instruments may have accompanied song performances, but there is no conclusive evidence, positive or negative, on this point. Only single melodies are recorded in the manuscripts, but modern concert and recorded performances regularly include instrumental accompaniments. These differ widely in nature, but often find inspiration in living ethnic traditions, such as those of North Africa. The listener should be aware of the large degree of individual interpretation inevitable in any performance of this music.

The songs included here have been chosen to illustrate a broad cross-section of text subjects and musical shapes. They are all (save for No. 8f) presented in nonmetrical notation. The comments refer to some metrical transcriptions for comparison. When melodies are preserved in several manuscripts they often differ from each other, hence recorded versions may well deviate somewhat from the reading edited here.

**8a.** The troubadour Bernart de Ventadorn (? c. 1130/40c. 1190/1200) rose to prominence at the court of Queen Eleanor of Aquitaine. His *canso Can vei la lauzeta mover* circulated widely, and at least five other poets fashioned texts to its melody. The poem vividly expresses the passion, and the anguish, of courtly love in stanzas of eight eight-syllable lines rhymed *ababcdcd.* Each line is set as a single phrase in which neumatic groups and single tones are judiciously mixed. Unlike most of Bernart de Ventadorn's songs, no phrase repetition occurs within the stanza. The melody is through-composed. Successive phrases show careful attention to registral tension and to the quality of cadential pitches. The D-a fifth outlined in the opening ascent sets the tonal focus, and the melody ends on the D.

**8b.** Peire Vidal (fl. 1175-1210) probably knew Bernart de Ventadorn at the court of Raimon V, Count of Toulouse, and was a supporter of Richard the Lionhearted, Eleanor of Aquitaine's eldest son. His *Baros de mon dan covit* combines general courtly love sentiments with apparent references to a specific situation and mock boastings about his own prowess as warrior and lover. The poetic stanzas combine eight- and ten-syllable lines, which result in differing lengths of musical phrases. Melodic repetitions group the text lines in pairs as follows:

| Text: | 8a | 8b | 8a | 8b | 10c | 10c | 10d | 10d | 10e |
|-------|----|----|----|----|-----|-----|-----|-----|-----|
| Music: | a | a' | a | a' | b | b' | c | c' | d |

The *a* phrase is an elaborate recitation around the pitch a. Subsequent phrases possess more varied melodic contours. The differentiation of cadential tones for repeated phrases (a technique noted in the sacred *versus,* see No. 6) is an important structural technique continued in fourteenth-century polyphonic song (see No. 18).

**8c.** *Fortz chausa es* by Gaucelm Faidit (? c. 1150–c. 1220) is a lament or *planh* on the death of Richard the Lionhearted, King of England (d. 26 March 1199). The effect of a spontaneous outpouring of grief is achieved in the melody through unexpected shifts in vocal register, irregularly placed melismas, striking intervals (e.g. in line 7 a major sixth, in lines 7-8 a tritone), and the avoidance of phrase repetitions. The fluctuation in tonal focus also contributes to the mood of distress.

For metrical interpretations of these three songs, see F. Gennrich, *Der Musikalische Nachlass der Troubadours,* Summa Musicae Medii Aevi III (1958), pp. 43, 67, and 108.

**8d.** *Chevalier mult estes guariz* is a crusaders' song from the 1147 campaign led by King Louis VII of France, first husband of Eleanor of Aquitaine. The text is an exhortation to the knights, assuring them salvation for their participation in the holy cause. Each eight-line verse is followed by a morale-raising four-line refrain. The verses were probably sung by one or more soloists, the refrain by the entire company. The simple melodic shapes and multiple repetitions seem calculated to ensure comprehension and memorability. The first three verse couplets are sung to essentially the same melody. The contrasting melody for the last couplet prepares the refrain music and is repeated exactly for the last refrain couplet.

The square notation of the edition reproduces that of the source. For a metrical interpretation, see *Troubadours, Trouvères and Minne-Meistersinger,* ed. F. Gennrich, Anthology of Music vol. 2 (1960), p. 42.

**8e.** With the trouvères of northern France, both poetic sentiments and musical shapes incline to conventional paths. The music of *Biaus m'est estez,* a love song by Gace Brulé (c. 1160-after 1213), is cast in the *a a b* form especially favored by the trouvères. This pattern persists as the conventional form of the fourteenth-century French ballade (see No. 18a). In Brulé's melody, the two phrases of the *a* section alternate open and closed endings and complement each other in contour. The general tendency of the first is upward from D to a; of the second, downward from a to D. The *b* section balances the two *a*s in length and itself divides into two equal parts. Its first phrase pair achieves the melodic high point of the stanza and closes with the second element of the *a* section. Its second phrase pair gravitates

toward the lower part of the range and holds to the established alternation of open and closed endings. The setting is very regular and controlled in construction.

**8f.** The courtly troubadour and trouvère repertories furnish hardly any examples of the refrain forms—ballade, rondeau and virelai—that became standard in the fourteenth century (see No. 18). However, the French rondeau, a dance song, flourished in more lowly cultural spheres during the thirteenth century.[1] Monophonic rondeaus appear often as interpolations in thirteenth-century French *romans,* and rondeau refrains were commonly quoted in thirteenth-century motets.

*Prendes i garde,* a song by the trouvère Guillaume d'Amiens that occurs as an interpolation in the *roman Renart le Nouvel,* has a robust frankness of tone quite alien to troubadour and trouvère lyrics, though common enough in French motet texts (see No. 13f). The refrain consists of just two lines sung to parallel phrases, the first of which has an open, the second a closed, ending. This refrain interacts with two verses to produce the following poetic scheme:

| Text: | refrain- | short verse- | half of refrain- | long verse- | refrain |
|---|---|---|---|---|---|
| | 2 lines | 1 line | 1 line | 2 lines | 2 lines |
| Music: | AB | a | A | ab | AB |

The verse lines are fashioned to be sung to the refrain melody—an extraordinary economy of musical means. When accompanying a dance, the verses were probably sung by soloists, the refrains by the whole group.

In the fourteenth century, the simple, syllabic thirteenth-century rondeau was transformed textually through assimilation into the courtly tradition and musically through melismatic elaboration and polyphonic texture (No. 18b). It was further transformed in the fifteenth century through expansion of the refrain to a four- or five-line unit and a corresponding enlargement of the verses (see Nos. 30, 31).

For a motet that incorporates a version of this rondeau refrain see No. 325 in *The Montpellier Codex,* ed. H. Tischler, Recent Researches in the Music of the Middle Ages and Early Renaissance, vols. VI and VII (1978), pp. 199-200.

[1]A repertory of more refined Latin rondeaus survives in one of the principal manuscripts of Notre-Dame polyphony (see comment on No. 10). An *a a b* musical scheme was used by troubadours and trouvères, but rarely in association with a refrain, which is a necessary constituent of the ballade (see No. 18a).

## 9a. Viderunt Emmanuel

Aquitanian versus

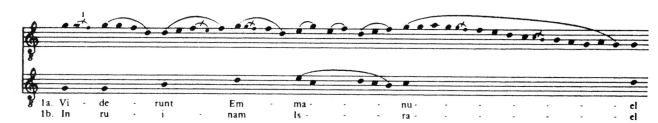

1a. Vi - de - runt Em - ma - nu - el
1b. In ru - i - nam Is - ra - el

pa - tris u - ni - ge - ni - tum
et sa - lu - tem po - si - tum

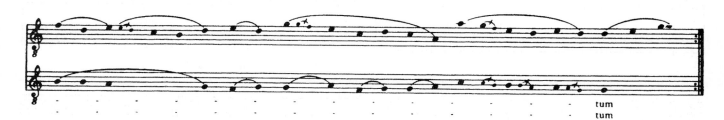

tum
tum

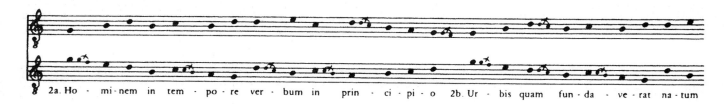

2a. Ho - mi - nem in tem - po - re ver - bum in prin - ci - pi - o  2b. Ur - bis quam fun - da - ve - rat na - tum

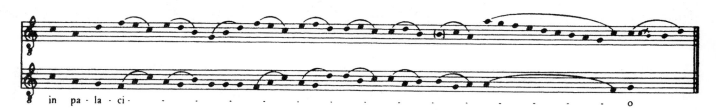

in pa - la - ci - o

¹ ⨍ indicates a liquescent (see page xv).

Viderunt Emmanuel
patris unigenitum
In ruinam Israel
et salutem positum.
Hominem in tempore
verbum in principio,
Urbis quam fundaverat
natum in palacio.

*They have seen the Savior,*
*the only-begotten Son of the Father,*
*appointed for salvation,*
*in the collapse of Israel.*
*A man in this temporal world,*
*the Word from the beginning,*
*born in a palace*
*of the city which he had founded.*

## 9b. Kyrie Cunctipotens genitor

from **Codex Calixtinus**

See No. 1c.

ne - xus     a - mor - que   e - · - · - · - · - · - · - · - lei - son.

For translation of No. 9b, see No. 1c, lines 1, 4 and 7.

Twelfth-century polyphony differs markedly in character and technique from the organa of about 1000 sung at Winchester (No. 5). The organal voice usually starts above the principal one and continues in contrary motion to it. The voices often cross and are as likely to end a phrase on the octave or fifth as on a unison. The organal part is frequently more active than its partner, responding to a single pitch in the main voice with a group of notes (for a pedagogical example, see No. 4e). No longer a subordinate accompaniment, the organal voice stands out as an independent line, differing from the other both in melodic and in rhythmic motion. The kinds of works set polyphonically have changed, too. Most polyphonic pieces to survive from the early twelfth century are not based on liturgical chant but are sacred *versus* in which both voices are recently composed (and may, indeed, have been created together). They share many characteristics of the monophonic *versus* (see No. 6), but the music is in two parts.

9a. The principal early twelfth-century repertory known to us stems from Aquitaine in the southwest of present-day France. Most texts label this repertory "Saint-Martial" polyphony, after a famous monastery of the region, but the term "Aquitanian polyphony" better expresses the regional diffusion of the style. Viderunt Emmanuel is a two-part versus from the Aquitanian repertory.[1] Among its striking aspects are the close coordination of music with poetry and the careful attention to line and texture. The compact poem has four lines of fourteen (seven plus seven) syllables each, which rhyme in pairs. Parallel melodies for each pair of text lines produce a musical shape of *a a b b'*. Extended melismas close the first and last sections (*a* and *b'*) and emphasize the ends of main poetic lines. Textural changes also articulate poetic units. The first seven-syllable segment of line 1 has a florid setting, while the second segment has a plainer contrapuntal texture. Stock figures that expand and contract from one perfect consonance to another are common in the note-against-note passages and stand out especially in the final melisma (palacio). The regular three-note groupings in this last melisma suggest some sort of regular rhythmic patterning as well. The notation itself is

[1] It is not a Gradual trope for the third Christmas Mass as sometimes represented.

indeterminate about rhythmic detail and about coordination between parts whenever direct note-against-note motion is abandoned. Voice alignments suggested in this edition are based on consonance and on typical voice-leading patterns. The transcription preserves some of the inherent rhythmic indeterminacy of the twelfth-century notation and invites performers to experiment with various modes of realization, from free to metric interpretations. Most metric interpretations of this music are based on the rhythmic modes of late twelfth-century Parisian discant (see comment to No. 10).

**9b.** A small but significant collection of northern French polyphony from mid-century (c. 1160?) is preserved in the *Codex Calixtinus,* a pilgrimage guide to the shrine of Saint James of Compostela. The *Calixtinus* repertory includes *conductus* (the northern equivalent of *versus*) and a few liturgical pieces. The conductus resemble the Aquitanian *versus* in musical idiom. Some of the liturgical settings, however, possess florid organal voices that foreshadow the elaborately melismatic organa of Leonin (see No. 10).

A two-voice *Cunctipotens genitor,* attributed to a Prefect Gauthier, illustrates the extreme of this florid style. The upper voice consistently decorates the primary consonances (unison, fourth, fifth, and octave) that link it to the chant. Much of the decoration is formulaic: stepwise scale motion, turns around a central note, conjunct thirds rising from unison to fifth. The underlying principles of voice leading here are very much like those illustrated in the *Cunctipotens genitor* from *Ad organum faciendum* (No. 4d), but the decoration smooths out the organal line and endows it with melodic grace. Plainsong settings of this sort initiate a new tradition of treating the preexisting chant as a subordinate supporting voice in polyphony.

As in the Aquitanian sources, the *Calixtinus* notation is rhythmically indeterminate. The lines that the original scribe draws through the score (preserved in the transcription) define main phrases or subphrases, but details of voice coordination were worked out by the performers. The figures in the organal voice may have been rendered as fairly quick ornaments between stable, consonant intervals, but they have also been interpreted in modal rhythm.

**Plate 2.** Florence, Biblioteca medicea-laurenziana Pluteo 29.1, f. 109r. Original notation of Alleluia Pascha nostrum (No. 10b), opening.

## 10a. LEONIN (c. 1135-c. 1201)
### **Alleluia Pascha nostrum**
Organum duplum
See No. 1f.

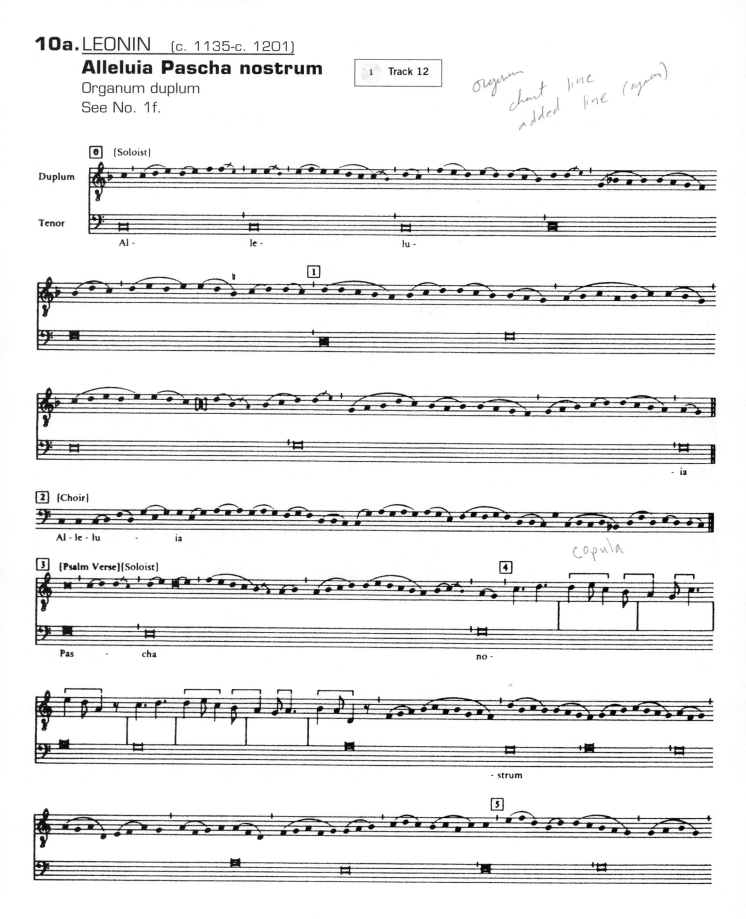

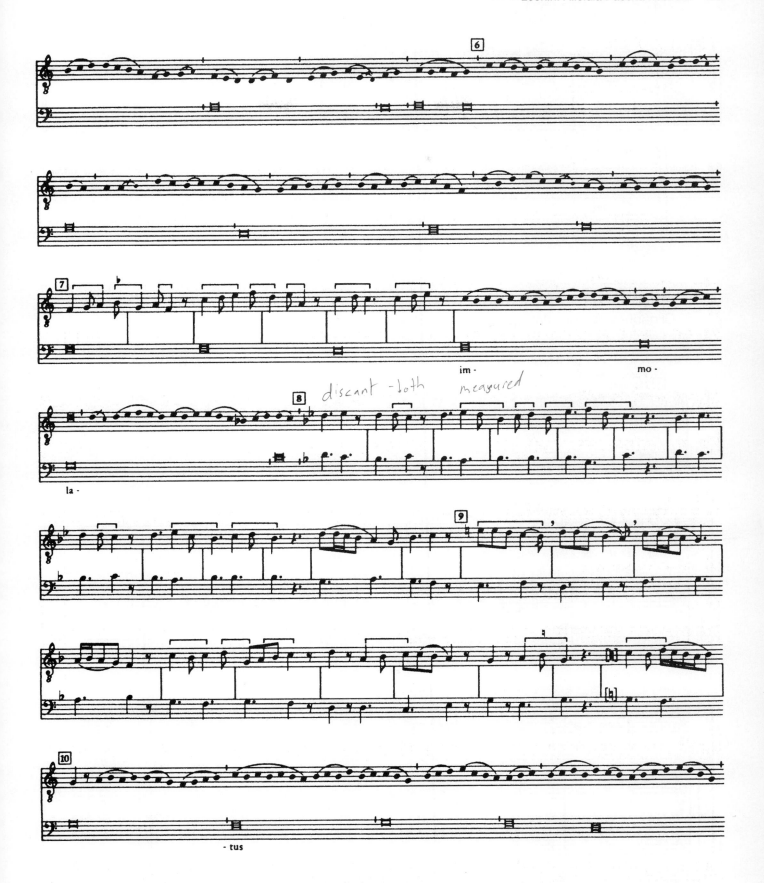

est.

[Choir]                                                                                      [Repeat Alleluia]

Chri    -    stus

For translation of No. 10a, see No. 1f.

## 10b. **Alleluia Pascha nostrum**
### Organum duplum (later revision of verse)

*Leoninus → Perotinus*

*clausalae - substitute pieces*

Alleluia as in No. 10a, [0] through [2]

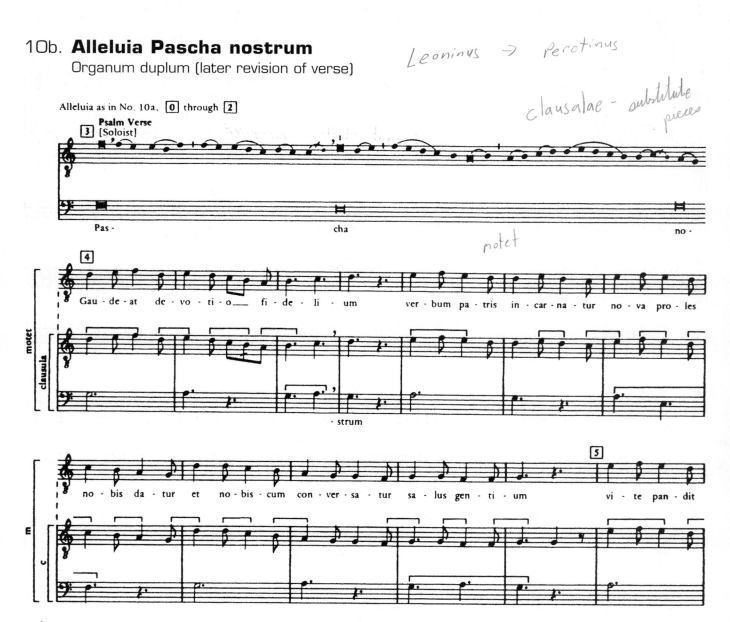

*notet*

Pas -                                      cha                                                            no -

Gau - de - at  de - vo - ti - o__ fi - de - li - um    ver - bum pa - tris in - car - na - tur  no - va pro - les

- strum

no - bis da - tur  et  no - bis - cum con - ver - sa - tur  sa - lus gen - ti - um      vi - te pan - dit

[1]The symbol ʼ indicates variously a change in tenor syllable, a phrase break, or a pause for breath.

A - ve Ma - ri - a fons le - ti - ci - e vir - go pu - ra pi - a ____ vas mun - di - ci -

- e ____ te vo - ce va - ri - a lau - det so - bri - e gens ____ le - ta so - bri - a gau - dens va - ri -

- e pro - mat ec - cle - si - a lau - des ho - di - e so - net in Ma - ri - a vox ec - cle - si - e

hec ____ sol - vit scri - ni - a I - sa - i - e re - se - rens ____ hos - ti - a ____ clau - sa pa - tri -

²In motet version, B♭ throughout tenor.

³Motet source: F-G-A-G-F.

**Motet No. 1**

*Rejoice, devoted souls of the faithful,*
*the word of the Father is made flesh,*
*a new child is given to us,*
*and for us the salvation of mankind is accomplished.*
*He extends the gift of life,*
*while he dutifully endures*
*the punishment of death.*
*The prince of the world is driven away,*
*because he understands*
*that he who has perished*
*is released through death.*
*By his own right, he is thus deprived,*
*for he has desired*
*to substitute himself for another*
*although he had done no wrong.*

**Motet No. 2**

*Hail Mary*
*fount of joy,*
*pure, holy virgin,*
*vessel of chastity.*
*With varied voices*
*a joyful, temperate people*
*praises thee soberly.*
*Rejoicing in manifold ways,*
*let the Church*
*express its praise today.*
*Let the voice of the Church*
*sound for Mary.*
*She provides the clue*
*to Isaiah,*
*revealing the final victim*
*to the nation,*
*giving supreme jurisdiction*
*to the King of glory*
*through whose grace alone,*
*full of mercy,*
*a sacrifice was made*
*the last of all sacrifices.*

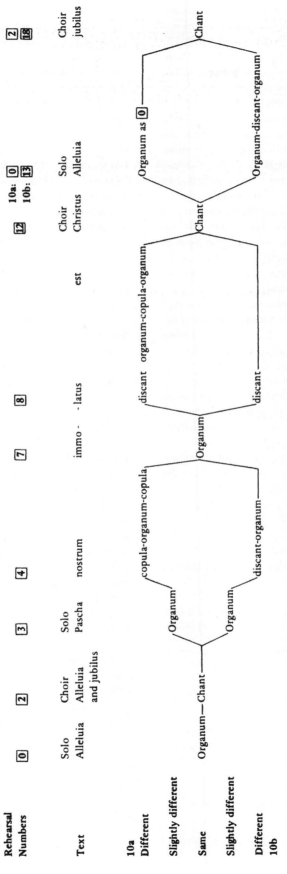

**Figure 1.** Comparison between early and revised versions of *Alleluia Pascha nostrum.*

Late in the twelfth century, in the great cathedral and university town of Paris, there sprang up a polyphonic tradition that was to exert commanding influence for more than a century. The music of this time and place is usually called Notre Dame polyphony, after the new Gothic cathedral rising in Paris, and its early stages are put at around 1170, contemporary with the building of the cathedral. Important contributions of the Notre Dame composers were a highly ornate melismatic organum style, polyphony in three and four independent parts, and (most important for the future) a system for coordinating parts rhythmically and a notation for communicating rhythm. Although many musicians must have contributed to these developments, an anonymous English theorist of the late thirteenth century ("Anonymous IV"[1]) singles out two as especially prominent and creative. One is Magister Leonin (c. 1135-c. 1201),[2] the best creator of organum, who made a *Magnus liber organi* ("Big Book of Organum"). The other is Magister Perotin, active around the turn of the century, who was the best creator of discant and composed splendid three- and four-part organa.

Leonin's *Magnus liber organi* is an impressive cycle of two-part graduals, alleluias, and Office responsories for major feasts of the Church year. Among them is the Easter *Alleluia Pascha nostrum* (No. 10a). Leonin includes only responsorial chants within the *Magnus liber* and sets only the soloist's portions polyphonically. As performed, the pieces are composites of two-part polyphony sung by soloists and chant sung monophonically by the choir (see rehearsal numbers 2 and 12; refer to No. 1f for the given chant).[3] The polyphonic sections are also composites and include three kinds of contrasting texture:

1. Melismatic organum style: Unmeasured chant notes are sustained in the principal voice, called the *tenor;* above them the organal voice, or *duplum,* sings long, ornate melismatic phrases. Both parts are in free, unmeasured rhythm[4] (see beginning to [2], [3], etc.).

2. Discant style: Both tenor and duplum are in measured rhythms and move at similar rates of speed (see rehearsal numbers [8] to [10]). The chant proceeds much more quickly than in organum style.

3. *Copula:* A special kind of passage in paired phrases, characterized by the thirteenth-century theorist John of Garland as antecedent and consequent in relationship. The tenor is in unmeasured, sustained notes, while the duplum has measured rhythms (see [4], [7], and [11]).

The measured rhythms in Notre Dame polyphony are controlled by conventional *rhythmic modes,* which are modular rhythmic patterns consisting of measured long and short values, *longa* and *brevis.* In the discant section at [8], the tenor takes the fifth rhythmic mode, a series of Longs. The duplum works in the first rhythmic mode, which alternates a Long and a Short value one-half the duration of the preceding Long. Distinctive patterns of ligatures (indicated by horizontal brackets in the edition) and single notes provide the code for the intended mode. Leonin's discant sections are usually placed on prominent melismas in the chant. The one in this setting coincides with a massive forty-seven-note melisma on the third syllable of *immolatus.* Such a section is called a *discant clausula.*

Elsewhere organum style prevails, punctuated only occasionally by copula. Primary consonances (unison, fourth, fifth, octave) control the counterpoint throughout, no matter how florid or discantal the texture.

Later generations of Parisian singers continued to perform from Leonin's *Magnus liber organi* but did not consider his settings to be fixed, immutable compositions. The preexisting chant foundation remained stable, but segments of Leonin's polyphony were often replaced by new settings of a particular portion of chant. Two kinds of "modernizing" changes were especially common:

1. recomposition of organum-style sections in discant texture;
2. replacement of early discant clausulas by new discant clausulas of more regular construction.

A revised verse of the *Alleluia Pascha nostrum* found in one of the central Notre Dame sources shows the recomposition process (No. 10b). The main changes (here cued to the editorial rehearsal numbers) are:

1. At [4], a discant clausula on *nostrum* replaces the earlier copula-organum setting.
2. At [8], a new discant clausula replaces the original clausula on *immolatus.*
3. At [13], a new Alleluia setting, with a long central discant section, is provided for the repeat of the Alleluia.

The net effect of these insertions or substitutions, summarized in Figure 1, is to increase the proportion of discant in the piece. The new discant clausulas differ from earlier ones in their more orderly rhythmic nature. Regular tenor rhythms of uniform length sometimes encourage even phrasing in the duplum, sometimes interact with contrasting duplum phrasing (see between [4] and [5]). Repetition of the tenor melody (within the first clausula at [6], within the third at [15], [16], [17]) expands the new discant clausulas in length and fosters independent structural organization within them. The first clausula of No. 10b divides into two sections that begin similarly, almost like parallel strophes

---

[1]This theorist is so named because his treatise is printed as the fourth anonymous work in Ch. E. H. de Coussemaker's *Scriptorum de musica medii aevi nova series,* vol. 1 (Paris: 1864). The standard modern edition and commentary is F. Reckow's *Der Musiktraktat des Anonymous 4,* Beihefte zum Archiv für Musikwissenschaft, vols. IV and V (Wiesbaden: Franz Steiner Verlag, 1967).

[2]Dates from C. Wright, "Leoninus, Poet and Musician," *Journal of the American Musicological Society* 39 (1986), p. 31-32.

[3]Note that Leonin's setting moves the eighth-mode chant from its normal position on G down a fifth to C. The version of the chant as sung at Paris in the late twelfth century differs in details from the early version, No. 1f.

[4]The rhythm of the duplum has been subject to controversy. It has been rendered modally, but recent scholarship indicates that it was not conceived in fixed rhythmic patterns.

(compare ④ with ⑥). The repeated tenor melody of the Alleluia discant creates a repetitive harmonic background, even though each statement occurs at a different point in the rhythmic pattern (⑭ and after).

Early in the thirteenth century, the dupla of the newer discant clausulas were given Latin texts, a procedure that transformed the discant clausula into a *motet* (from the French *mot*, which means

"word"). The texts provided an appropriate devotional message and also sharpened the articulation of the upper voices, clarifying both phrasing and rhythmic detail. In No. 10b, the motet versions are shown in parallel with the original discant clausulas at ④ and at ⑧. Although at first imbedded within the organa of the *Magnus liber,* the motet took on an independent life of its own during the first half of the thirteenth century (see No. 13).

## 11. PEROTIN (?) (fl. 1200)
### Alleluia Pascha nostrum
Organum triplum
See No. 1f.

[Soloists]

[1]The symbol ⸴ indicates variously a change in tenor syllable, a phrase break, or a pause for breath.

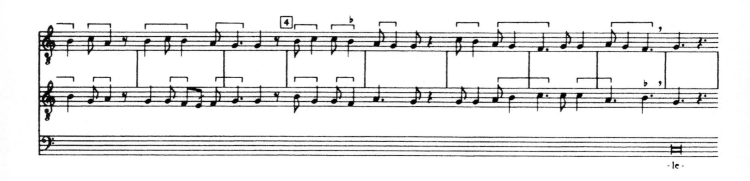

- le -

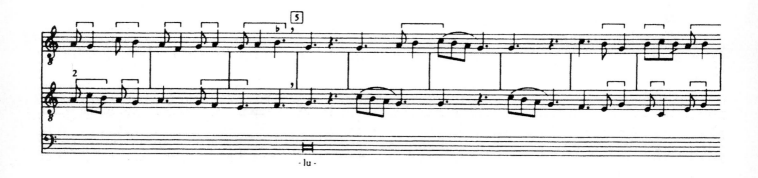

- lu -

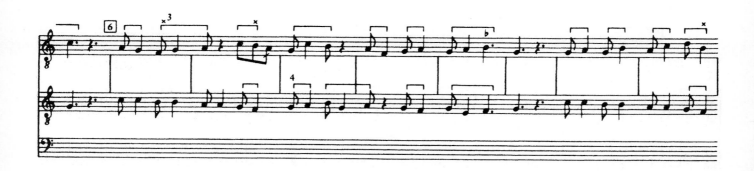

[2]B in ms.

[3]The tritones marked x might be left as they are or eliminated at the discretion of the performers.

[4]Ligatures as W2.

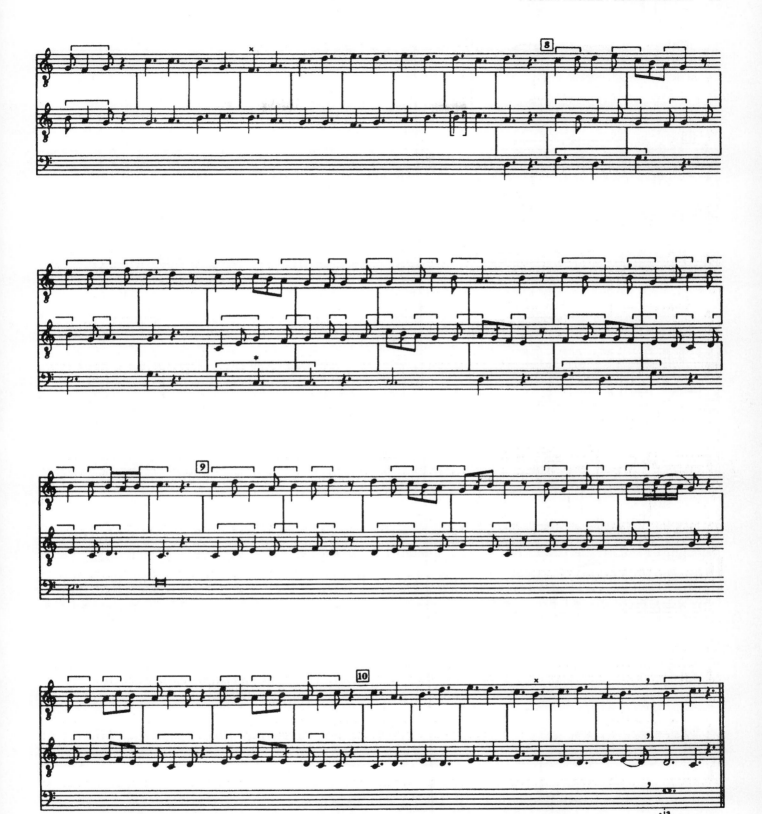

[Choir]

Al - le - lu - · · ia

Pas -

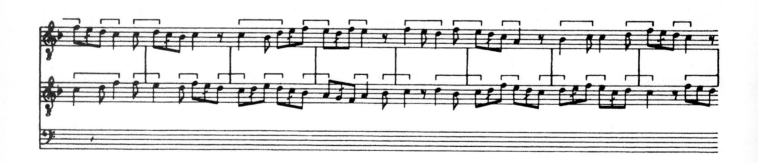

- cha          no -

- strum

im -

- mo -                    - la

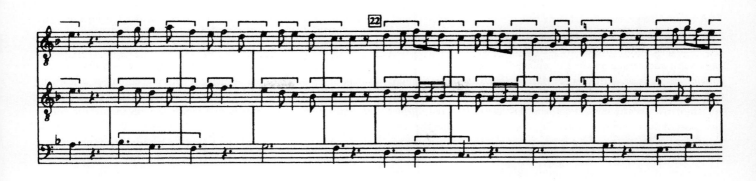

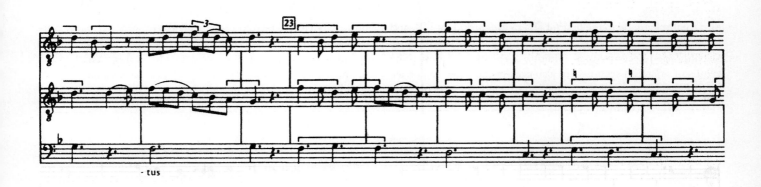

- tus

est.

Chri-          stus

[Repeat Alleluia]

For translation of No. 11, see No. 1f.

A second stage of Notre Dame polyphony is associated with Magister Perotin (fl. 1200), the master of discant to whom three- and four-part compositions are attributed. Some of Perotin's *organa tripla* and *organa quadrupla* replaced two-part organa of the *Magnus liber organi*. A three-part *Alleluia Pascha nostrum* thought to be by Perotin is based on the same chant as Leonin's (No. 10a) and similarly takes in only the soloists' passages: the initial *Alleluia* and most of the verse. In sound, it differs noticeably from the two-voice setting, for the two upper voices (*triplum* and *duplum*) produce fuller sonorities and provide more contrapuntal interplay over the tenor than a single duplum. Rhythmic modes are more pervasive and now synchronize triplum and duplum in sustained-note organum texture as well as in discant. The rhythmic modes are also more varied than in earlier Notre-Dame music. Within just the opening *Alleluia* of No. 11 the upper voices shift from the third rhythmic mode to the first (at [2]) to the second (at [4]), and so on. A distinctive passage (after [7]) in undifferentiated Longs, the fifth mode, contributes additional rhythmic variety. The lengths of organum sections are also greatly expanded. Whereas, for example, Leonin makes just one short melodic gesture over the

first tenor note of the *Alleluia*, Perotin provides ten phrases! His opening section is about five times the length of Leonin's.

Perotin's setting includes three discant clausulas—one in the *Alleluia* and two in the verse. Those in the verse—on *nostrum* and *(immo)latus*—correspond exactly to the placement of discant in the revised two-part version (No. 10b). The duplum of Perotin's second clausula ( [20] ) is in fact identical with that of the corresponding clausula in No. 10b (at [8]). Possibly Perotin appropriated the two-part clausula and wrote a triplum to it, or perhaps the two-part version was a reduction of the three-voice clausula.

Attractive features of Perotin's organum are the variety in rhythmic movement, the interplay between the two upper parts, which now overlap, now coincide in phrasing, and the fluctuations of consonance and dissonance over sustained tenor tones. The leisurely, unpredictable unfolding of the organum passages contrasts vividly with the discant clausulas' ordered pace, controlled by uniform rhythmic patterns in the tenor. Within the clausulas, tenor and duplum tend to phrase together, but the triplum often bridges their phrases and so creates longer spans of motion over their short repeated units.

## 12.    Conductus
### 12a. **Deus in adjutorium**
Conductus sine cauda

[1]An accidental in parentheses carries through from a previous sharp or flat in the line.

um, 3. ad do - lo - ris re - me - di - um 4. fe - sti - na in au - xi - li - um,
re 7. ti - bi, Chri - ste, rex glo - ri - e: 8. Glo - ri - a ti - bi, Do - mi - ne!
um, 3. qui es De - us in se - cu - la 4. se - cu - lo - rum, in glo - ri - a!
ya: 7. a - men, a - men, al - le - lu - ya: 8. a - men, a - men, al - le - lu - ya!

1. O God, reach out
   to aid those in distress.
   To cure their anguish,
   hasten with help.

2. So that our chorus might sing psalms
   and utter praises
   to thee, Christ, King of Glory,
   Glory be to thee, Lord.

3. O Christ, deign to take pity
   on all those who believe in thee,
   thou who art God in glory
   forever and ever.

4. Amen, amen, alleluia. (4 times)

## 12b. **O tocius Asie**
Conductus cum cauda

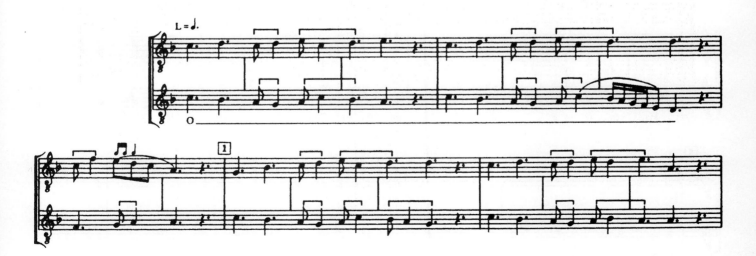

de cu - ius vi - cto - ri - a    pro - tec -

to - rem    vir - gi - num    Be - ne - di - ca - mus Do -

- mi - num

O tocius Asie gloria
Regis Alexandrie filia
Graecie gimnasia
Coram te Maxentia
Dia confudit philosophia
De cuius victoria
Protectorem virginum
Benedicamus Dominum.

*O glory of all Asia*
*daughter of the King of Alexandria*
*in thy presence, Maxentia,*
*the goddess Philosophy*
*has secured the schools in Greece,*
*and because of her victory,*
*we bless the Lord,*
*protector of women.*

Besides the chant settings of the *Magnus liber organi,* the Notre Dame sources also preserve a quantity of nonliturgical conductus, most of them in two- or three-voiced polyphony. Like their near relatives, the *versus* (Nos. 6 and 9a), the Notre Dame conductus are settings of rhymed, strophic Latin poems. Those on sacred subjects commonly were introduced in the Offices to accompany processional actions. Like the motet, polyphonic conductus belong to the realm of discant: The voices are governed by consonance and proceed in rhythmic modes. But in contrast to the motet, conductus are newly composed in all voices and have but one text sung simultaneously by all participants.

Thirteenth-century theorists distinguish two kinds of conductus: a plain type designated as *sine cauda* and a more elaborate type *cum cauda.* The caudas (literally, "tails") are melismatic vocalizations on a single syllable. *Deus in adjutorium* (No. 12a) is a relatively plain three-voiced conductus *sine cauda.* The text setting very directly matches each syllable with an element of the rhythmic mode. (Note that the mode could be interpreted as

mode 2 or as mode 1 with an "upbeat.") Each text line receives a separate musical phrase, and each four-line strophe is sung to the same music. The music strongly reinforces the regular, repetitive qualities of the poetic structure. Because the text, rather unusually, elaborates the versicle sung at the beginning of each Office— *Deus in adjutorium meum intende* ("O God reach out to help me," see No. 2a)—this conductus must have begun major Offices on important feast days.

Poetic structure is less obvious and far less a controlling force in the conductus *cum cauda O tocius Asie* (No. 12b). The single strophe of ten irregular lines is engulfed by three long melismas— one at the beginning, one after line 5, and one at the end. The voices in the caudas converge and diverge from perfect consonances in a manner reminiscent of melismas in Aquitanian versus (see No. 9a). This conductus has been associated with the Crusade of 1248, but its music represents a style current some fifty years earlier. Judging from the last text line, it was intended to close one of the Offices that regularly end with the versicle *Benedicamus Domino* ("Bless the Lord").

# 13th-Century Motets (to c. 1250)

## 13a. Discant clausula on Regnat
### from Alleluia Hodie Maria virgo

## 13b. Ad solitum vomitum/Regnat
Two-voice motet

## 13c. Ad solitum vomitum/Regnat
Three-voice conductus motet

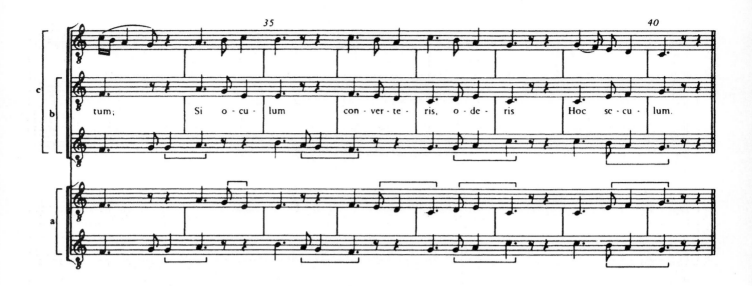

**Motetus of Nos. 13b, c; Triplum of No. 13c**
*Lest you return to your usual vomit,*
*tremble for your deserved ruin.*
*Bewail the past*
*and foster some good purpose.*
*Go not to the brothels*
*lest through them you perish.*
*Prepare for a sudden end,*
*and beware a forbidden return*
*to a troubled death.*
*If you will but look about you,*
*you will hate this age.*

**Tenor**
*She reigns* (from *Alleluia Hodie Maria virgo*, No. 13e).

# 13d. Depositum creditum/Ad solitum vomitum/Regnat
Latin double motet

For translation of tenor and motetus, see No. 13b.

**Triplum**
*When you should guard established beliefs,*
*undertake no unlawful obligations.*
*You should declare this to yourself*
*if you desire merit.*
*You should flee corrupting delights,*
*fear them,*
*beware ill-omened riches,*
*hold to lawful allegiance,*
*not hastily granted.*
*Through lamenting [your faults]*
*make firm forever your easily provoked emotions,*
*and to heavenly God alone*
*dedicate yourself.*

# 13e. Alleluia Hodie Maria virgo
(Feast of the Assumption of the Virgin)
Source chant for **Regnat** clausula

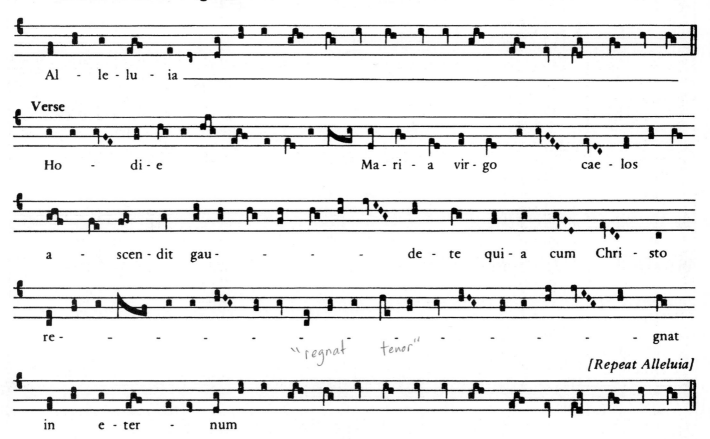

*Alleluia. Today the Virgin Mary ascends to heaven.*
*Rejoice, because she reigns with Christ eternally.*

## 13f. L'autre jour/Au tens pascour/In seculum

French double motet

See No. 1e.

Track 13

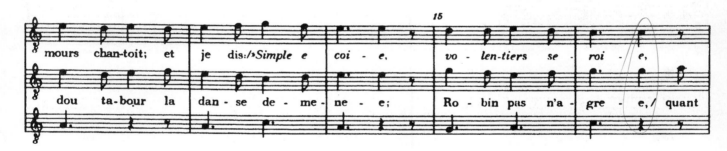

**Triplum**

*The other morning by a valley at daybreak,*
*I found a shepherdess, and I watched her.*
*She was alone, singing of love, and I said:*
**"Sweet and gentle one, I would gladly be your lover,**
**If it pleases you."**
*She replied most sensibly,*
*"Leave me alone sir, return to your region.*
*I love Robin truly and I have given him my love,*
*I love him more than anyone.*
*He has gone to play in the woods beneath the bower.*
*It would be vile of me not to love him,*
*for he loves me faithfully.*
*Never would I seek to leave him for you."*


**Motetus**

*At Eastertide all the shepherd folk from one region*
*gathered together at the bottom of a valley.*
*In the meadow Herbert led the dance with pipe and tabor.*
*Robin was not pleased when he saw it,*
*but out of defiance would do a better* estampie.

*Then he grabbed his drone, seized his hat, tucked up his tunic,*
*and did the jolly* estampie *for the love of his sweetheart.*
*Rogier, Guiot, and Gautier are very envious indeed.*
*Not one of them laughs, but they say defiantly*
*that before nightfall his pipe will be broken.*

### Tenor
*Forever* (from the Easter Gradual *Haec dies,* see No. 1e).

Motets originated in the early thirteenth century through the practice of supplying text to the duplum of discant clausulas within Notre Dame organa (see No. 10b). In the course of the century, motets were separated from their original context and performed as independent pieces. The motet in fact became the leading genre of the 1200s and was the focus of the most progressive trends in composition. Chief among these were a flexible rhythmic language liberated from modal units, a new notation capable of specifying individual durations not bound by conventional patterns, and a complex polyphony of three genuinely independent lines. In addition, the motet established a foundation for polyphonic secular art song, which rose to prominence in the fourteenth century. The development of the motet can be divided conveniently into two phases, an early one illustrated in Nos. 13a-d, f and a later one illustrated in Nos. 15a-d.

The complex of works Nos. 13a-d summarizes the earliest developments through several versions of one piece. No. 13b began life as a discant clausula within the *Alleluia Hodie Maria virgo* (Nos. 13a, e) and became a two-part motet through addition of text to the duplum voice. The twofold statement of the tenor melody (repeat at m. 21), the regularity in phrasing, and the carefully calculated overlaps between tenor and duplum phrases, are typical of the mature discant clausula. Over the first tenor statement, the motetus observes three-measure phrases; over the second statement it shifts to two- and four-measure phrases arranged to overlap the short, regular tenor units.

A motet for three voices (No. 13c) is created by superimposing a third voice (*triplum*) upon the tenor-motetus pair. This third voice adopts the motetus text along with its phrasing. It crosses the other two parts freely, often cutting below the tenor. The shared text in triplum and motetus has led modern writers to call such works *conductus motets.*

No. 13d is a more radical transformation of the original two-voice motet. It is a Latin double motet, produced through the addition of another triplum with a different text from the motetus. This triplum blends with the mode 3 rhythm of the other two voices, but is independent in phrasing, often bridging the shorter units of the others. Its text borrows the rhymes of the motetus poem, and launches similar urgent exhortations to moral reform. The double motet—a three-voice composition with separate texts in triplum and motetus and plainsong tenor—became the standard motet type of the thirteenth century.

No. 13f is a double French motet of the sort that was in vogue by mid-century. The tenor *In seculum,* one of the most popular choices among thirteenth-century motet composers, comes from the Easter Gradual *Haec dies* (see No. 1e). Despite this foundation of sacred chant, the upper voices are completely secular in subject, although the motetus preserves a seasonal connection in its opening reference to Eastertide. The secularization of the motet, indicative of a drift toward courtly and university spheres, is a highly significant trend interconnected with emergence of the genre as the most technically demanding and artistically challenging music of the day.

*L'autre jour/Au tens pascour/In seculum* is cast in modal rhythms, the tenor in a standard three-note mode 5 pattern, the other two in mode 1. Motetus and triplum are homogeneous in character and share the same ranges and rhythmic movement. Both possess obviously tuneful qualities and cohere as melodies quite independently of the tenor foundation. In this respect, they hark back to trouvère song. Their focus on the c-e-g fifth does respond to the tenor's emphasis on c.

The composer's concern for formal clarity is apparent at the midpoint of the piece. There, just as the tenor melody repeats (m. 22), the two upper voices refer melodically to the opening (mm. 1-2) but with the voice parts exchanged. In the next century, consistent periodic repetitions were to become a central element in motet composition, fostering pronounced expansion in length and new levels of complexity (see Nos. 16, 17).

## 14. "A CERTAIN SPANIARD"
### In seculum breve
Instrumental hocket
See No. 1e.

Track 14

Although little ensemble instrumental music survives from the thirteenth century, some motet collections preserve a few un-texted, presumably instrumental, pieces devoted to a special technique called *hocket.* Hocket is a rhythmic device for two performers featuring interruptive rests in one voice that are filled in by the other. An evenly paced tenor typically supports the two hocketing parts and provides a foil to their spirited interchanges. The tenor melisma *In seculum* (see Nos. 1e and 13f) was a favorite vehicle for hockets. *In seculum breve* takes its name from the tenor incipit and from the prevailing short note value, the breve (transcribed here as an eighth note). The tenor melody is stated twice through in mode 2 units, while the two upper voices deftly cooperate in a continuous lively countermelody. Their lines are erratic in movement, broken by eccentric pauses or truncations that are, so to speak, "plugged up" by the companion voice. This piece exists in another, less virtuosic version, *In seculum longum,* which moves at the slower pace of the long (dotted quarter note in transcription).[1] The *longum* version would appear to be the

"French hocket" *In seculum* attributed by the theorist "Anonymous IV" to "a certain Spaniard."[2] According to Anonymous IV, the change from mode 5 (*longum*) to mode 2 (*breve*) was due to Parisian performers. Yet another arrangement adds a texted *quadruplum* to the hocket.[3]

The technique of hocket was not invented in these mid-thirteenth-century pieces but may be traced back to Notre Dame organa and conductus caudas. It was recognized as an independent subspecies of discant by theorists of the time. In the fourteenth century, hocket becomes absorbed into the motet, where it serves both ornamental and structural functions (see No. 17).

———

G. A. Anderson, Corpus Mensurabilis Musicae 75 (1977), p. 137-138.

[2]*Der Musiktraktat des Anonymous 4*, vol. 1, ed. F. Reckow, Beihefte zum Archiv für Musikwissenschaft, vol. IV (1967), p. 61.

[3]*The Montpellier Codex*, Part I, ed. H. Tischler, Recent Researches in the Music of the Middle Ages and Early Renaissance, vol. II (1978), p. 1, No. 2.

[1]Published in *Compositions of the Bamberg Manuscript,* edited by

# 13th-Century Motets (after c. 1250)

## 15a. El mois de mai/De se debent bigami/Kyrie   1  Track 15
Bilingual motet

**Triplum**

*In the month of May when the thrush sings,*
*when the gladiolus, and the rose, and the lily bloom,*
***then those in love should be joyful.***
*I will rejoice, for I am the faithful lover*
*of the most beautiful one in all these lands.*
***I have set my whole heart on loving her,***
***I will never cease*** *for as long as I live.*
*The great beauty of her shining face,*
*her pretty body made so wonderfully,*
*make me always think of her.*

**Motetus**
*Bigamists should complain against themselves, not against the pope,*
*for they despoil themselves of the privilege of clergy,*
*but now from their own deed they can learn*
*and with Ovid confess this to be the truth:*
**"Virtue is no less to guard possessions than to seek them."**

**Tenor**
*Kyrie.*

# 15b. On parole de batre/A Paris/Frese nouvele

French double motet on secular tenor

[1] Track 16

[1] Throughout the piece groups of two eighth notes (♪♪) should be performed unevenly as ♪♪.

**Triplum**

*The talk is of threshing and winnowing,*
*of digging and ploughing.*
*Such pastimes are not at all to my liking.*
*For there is nothing*
*like having one's fill*
*of good clear wine and capons,*
*and being with good friends,*
*hale and hearty,*
*singing,*
*joking*
*and in love,*
*and having all one needs*
*to give pleasure to beautiful women*
*to one's heart's content.*
*All of this is to be had in Paris.*

**Duplum**

*Morning and night in Paris*
*there is good bread to be found, good clear wine,*
*good meat and fish,*
*all manner of friends*
*of lively minds and high spirits,*
*fine jewels and noble ladies*
*and, in the meantime,*
*prices to suit a poor man's purse.*

**Tenor**

*Fresh strawberries! Nice blackberries!*
*Blackberries, nice blackberries!*
                —Translated by Michael J. Freeman

## 15c. Alle psallite cum luya/Alle psallite cum luya/Alleluya

1    Track 17

Latin voice-exchange motet (English)

**Triplum** and **Motetus**
*"Alle," sing with "luya."*
*"Alle," sing loudly with "luya."*
*"Alle," with heart totally committed to God sing with "luya."*

**Tenor**
*Alleluia.*

## 15d. PETRUS DE CRUCE (fl. 1290)
### Aucun ont trouvé/Lonc tans/Annuntiantes

French double motet

 1 Track 18

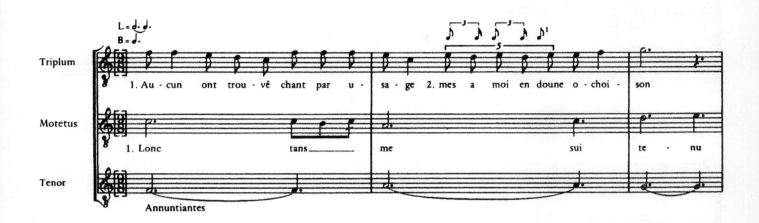

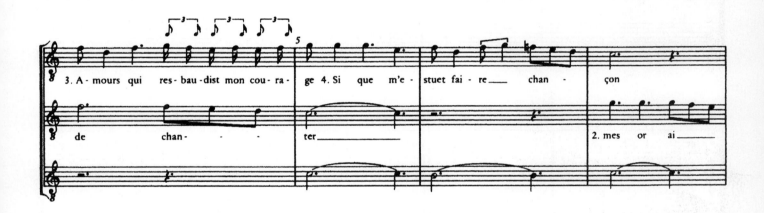

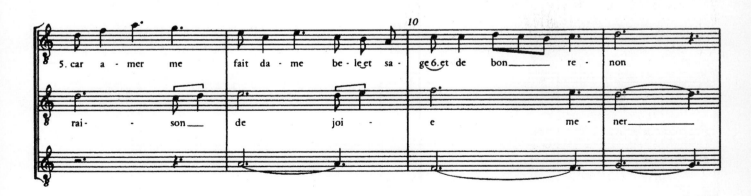

[1]Rhythms above the staff indicate alternate ways of performing groups of four or more semibreves according to early fourteenth-century theorists.

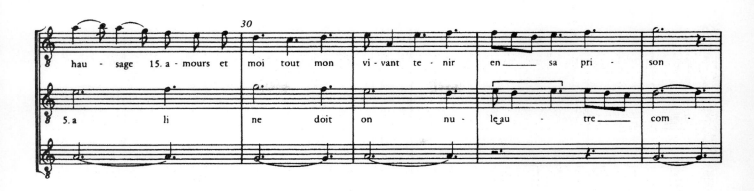

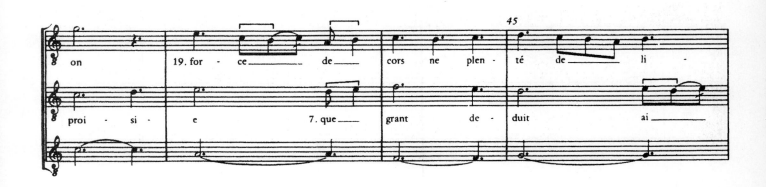

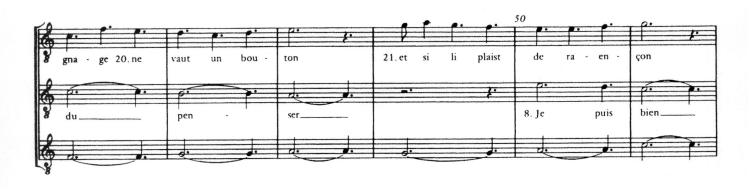

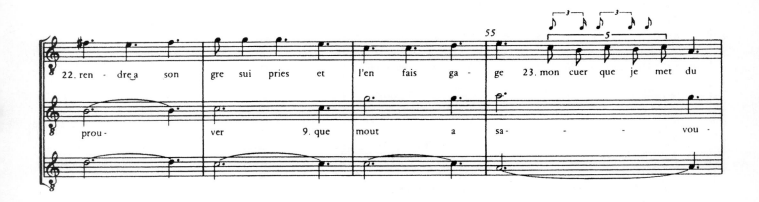

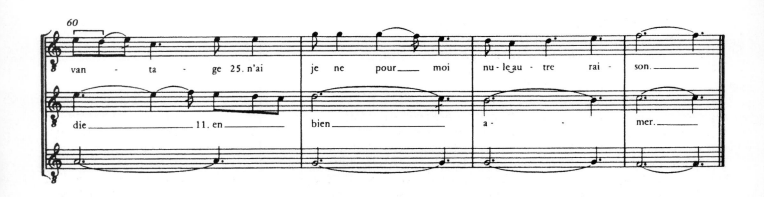

**Triplum**

*There are men who live by writing songs,*
*but I am inspired*
*by a love that so fills my heart with joy*
*that I can't stop myself writing a song.*
*For a fair and lovely lady, of high repute,*
*has made me love her*
*and I, who have pledged myself to serve her*
*all my days, loyally*
*and with no thought of betrayal,*
*shall sing, for from her do I hold such a sweet bequest*
*that it alone can give me joy.*
*It is this thought which soothes my sweet sorrow*
*and gives me hope of a cure for it.*
*At the same time,*
*Love may well complain of my arrogance*
*and hold me prisoner all my days;*
*I wouldn't think the worse of her for that.*
*She knows how to lay siege so cleverly*
*that there is no defence against her;*
*neither might nor rank*
*is of the slightest use.*
*And if it pleases her to give back my ransom at her will,*
*I shall be her captive and give my heart as surety*
*by putting it completely at her disposal.*
*And I beg for mercy, since I have no alternative,*
*no other words to say for myself.*

**Duplum**

*Long have I refrained from singing,*
*but now I have reason to show my joy*
*since true love has led me to desire*
*the most accomplished lady*
*to be found in the whole world.*
*No other can be compared to her,*
*and when I so love such a precious lady*
*that I have great pleasure merely in thinking about her,*
*well do I know*
*that a life of true love*
*is very pleasant,*
*whatever people say.*

**Tenor**

*ANNUN(TIANTES) from the Gradual*
**Omnes de Saba** *for Epiphany.*
　　　　　—Translated by Michael J. Freeman

The last decades of the thirteenth century are an epoch of transition and change in motet composition. No single motet type dominates. Tenors, formal procedures, rhythmic textures become remarkably diverse. Versatile new notational techniques enable, and even encourage, far-reaching experimentation with rhythms. Nos. 15a-d indicate the variety of compositions coexisting in one collection of late-thirteenth- to early-fourteenth-century motets, sections 7 and 8 of the great Montpellier motet codex.

Two prominent trends of the late thirteenth century evident in Nos. 15a and 15b are tenor parts from sources other than the *Magnus liber organi* clausulas and heterogeneous textures produced through increased differentiation among voices. In both these motets the *tripla* are strongly profiled and much more rhythmically active than the other two parts. The greater activity involves shorter note values (*semibreves*, here transcribed as sixteenth notes [No. 15a] and eighth notes [No. 15b]) and continuous motion that obliterates the periodic patterns of rhythmic modes. The texture divides into two layers: a prominent, energetic triplum with much text and many notes; a slower motetus and tenor that are relatively homogeneous in motion. Phrasing in triplum and motetus is irregular and unpredictable. The melodies are released from the regular modules of rhythmic mode.

A tendency toward complete secularization manifests itself in some motets when secular songs become tenors. The tenor of No. 15b is a street vendor's cry—presumably from Paris, since triplum and motetus speak of the joys of good living in that city. Adoption of secular tenors has important structural consequences. The memorable short phrases and audible repetitions of *Frese nouvele* produce clear periodic structure and firm tonal focus. The tenor of No. 15a makes a similar repetitive foundation. It comes from an unusual plainsong source, the first phrase of the Kyrie *Cum jubilo* (Kyrie IX in modern Vatican editions). The triplum of this motet quotes popular refrains (see italics in text).[1] Such quotation occurs frequently in mid- to late-13th-century motets and is another symptom of the secular leanings of the genre. The term *motet enté* is commonly used to signal the grafting on of preexistent refrains.

Motets of this sort are often called *Franconian* motets, after the theorist Franco of Cologne, who codified a new notational system in which individual durations could be explicitly notated independent of any mode.

---

[1]The Montpellier Codex preserves another version of this motet with a different, less active triplum; No. 286 in *The Montpellier Codex*, ed. Hans Tischler, Recent Researches in the Music of the Middle Ages and Early Renaissance, vols. VI and VII, p. 126.

English composers favored a distinctive type of motet, sacred in nature and strongly periodic in organization. *Alle psallite cum luya* (No. 15c) is a model of the favorite English technique of *voice exchange,* in which triplum and motetus swap melodies in successive phrases. This procedure generates proselike series of repeated phrases that differ only in distribution of lines among performers. The tenor of *Alle psallite* displays an unusual reiterative melodic structure. Its phrases expand successively from three to four to five measures, each following the general contour of the first segment and ending on D. Pieces such as this may have had a bearing on the periodic modes of organization adopted by French composers in the fourteenth century.

A composer-singer named Petrus de Cruce is known for a most individual manner of composition featuring extreme subdivision of the standard "short" value, the breve. As in No. 15d, subdivisions of five, six, or seven semibreves prevail in the triplum, which greatly surpasses the other voices in melodic and rhythmic activity. Relative to the triplum, motetus and tenor are considerably slowed in motion, an exaggeration of a tendency apparent in Nos. 15a and b. The proliferation of short time values in the triplum forces a wholesale expansion of time scale, so that the traditional mode 1 and mode 5 rhythms in motetus and tenor respectively are sung two to three times more slowly than before. Because the triplum line stands out so separately, the effect is much like a song with accompaniment.

In form, No. 15d divides into two sections distinguished by tenor organization. In the first section, the tenor presents its F-mode melody in traditional three-note mode 5 modules. In the second section, the tenor repeats its melody as a continuous, unpatterned series of longs. This varied repetition presages diminution procedures common in the fourteenth century (see No. 17).

## 16. PHILIPPE DE VITRY (1291-1361)
### Tribum que/Quoniam secta/Merito hec patimur

Isorhythmic motet

Track 19

[1] A colored facsimile of the original notation may be found in *Schriftbild der Mehrstimmigen Music*, ed. H. Besseler and P. Gülke, Musikgeschichte in Bildern, Vol. III, Lfg. 5, pp. 56-57.

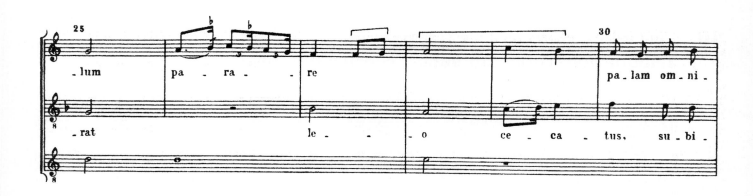

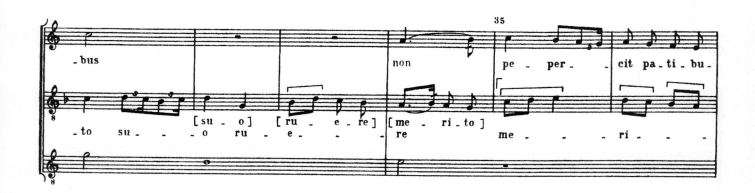

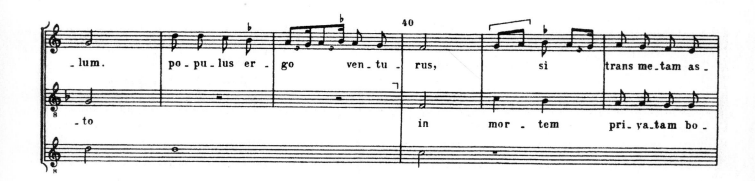

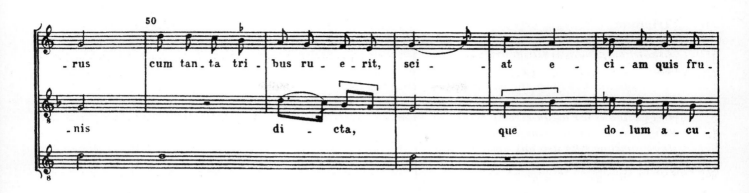

**Triplum**[1]

*Furious Fortune did not fear*
*to turn quickly against the tribe*
*that did not recoil from a shameless rise [to power]*
*when she did not spare the governing leader of the tribe*
*from the pillory,*
*to be established as an eternal public example.*
*Therefore let future generations know*
*that someone who ascends through fear*
*may perhaps fall, as such a tribe has fallen.*
*As for him whose prosperity has sunk to the depths:*
*Winter coming after warm west winds hurts all the more;*
*after rejoicing, lamentation is the more painful,*
*whence there is nothing better*
*than to have had no success.*

**Motetus**

*Since with the plots of thieves and*
*the den of shady dealers*
*the fox, which gnawed at the cocks*
*in the time when the blind lion reigned,*
*has suddenly been hurled down*
*to his reward in death*
*and deprived of property,*
*the cock sings the sayings of Ovid*
*which hammer home the point:*
*All human things hang on a fine thread,*
*and when it breaks suddenly,*
*they collapse.*

**Tenor**

*We suffered this deservedly,* from the Responsory **Merito hec patimur,** sung at Matins on the
third Sunday of Lent.

[1]The texts refer to cataclysmic political events that occurred at the French court in the spring of 1315.

Around 1320, the experimental diversity of late-thirteenth-century French polyphony begins to give way to a new stylistic consensus. This consensus involves clarification of genres (polyphonic secular song splits off from the motet), standardization of compositional procedures, and expansion of the notational system to include a larger spectrum of durational levels and to incorporate duple as well as triple relationships at every level. The earliest treatises explaining the new performance and notational techniques characterize them as the *ars nova* (new practice or art) in contrast to the *ars vetus* (old practice or art) codified in the late thirteenth century by Franco of Cologne. Modern scholars consequently adopted the term *ars nova* to designate French music of the first three quarters of the fourteenth century, *ars antiqua* (old art, with connotations of old-fashioned) to denote thirteenth-century French music.

In the new practice, the spectrum from longest to shortest durations was divided into five levels (maxima-long-breve-semibreve-minim). Each note type could be connected to its adjacent levels by a duple or a triple relationship (for example, a breve might equal either 2 or 3 semibreves). The official acceptance of duple or "imperfect" relationships permitted considerable rhythmic variety and contrast both within compositions and from one composition to another.

Whereas in the old art the ratio between the longest precise durational value (perfect long) and the shortest (semibreve) was 9:1 (a perfect long was divided into 3 breves, each worth 3 semibreves: 3 x 3 = 9), in the new art the ratio of longest (*maxima*) to shortest (*minima*) could be as large as 81:1 (a perfect maxima consisted of 3 longs, each worth at most 27 minims: 3 x 27 = 81). The new art or practice thus allowed an extraordinarily wide range of rhythmic motion within a piece, with some voices moving in very quick notes and some paced in broad longs or maximas.

The Parisian poet, musician, and cleric Philippe de Vitry (1291-1361) was a leading inventor and teacher of the new practices and is credited by one fifteenth-century observer with founding "a new manner of motets."[1] De Vitry's *Tribum que/Quoniam secta/Merito hec patimur* from 1315 represents an early stage in the crystallization of the *ars nova* motet. Texture is among its most striking features. Triplum and motetus move in similar rhythms and in fairly short note values, while the tenor stands apart with its own slow, deliberate pace. Indeed, the old-fashioned mode 2 rhythmic pattern has become so elongated as to be nearly unrecognizable (compare the tenor of No. 14). The difference in motion is so great that modern notation is forced to measure the two layers differently: the tenor in a broad triple meter, motetus and triplum in shorter duple units corresponding to the (novel) duple relationship between long and breve. Such nesting of different rates of motion creates the two-layered texture characteristic of the *ars nova* motet.

The long temporal spans of de Vitry's motets are ordered and articulated by periodic recurrences of certain musical elements, especially the tenor rhythmic pattern, or *talea*. The modern term for such large-scale rhythmic periodicity is *isorhythm* (single-rhythm). The tenor rhythm in *Tribum que* clearly derives from thirteenth-century practice, but later de Vitry motets have longer,

more individual taleas. Among the important periodicities in *Tribum que* are the pitch sequence E-D-D, which from measure 10 on occurs at regular twelve-measure intervals in the tenor, and the triplum and motetus melodies that recur in alternation over these fixed tenor pitches (see Figure 2). In addition, the triplum adheres to a fixed series of phrase lengths from measure 10 on (4 m., 3 m. [+] 5 m.), and the motetus is punctuated every ten or eleven measures by prominent rests just when the tenor sounds its repeated Ds. The net effect is to divide the motet into three strophic periods that are related rhythmically and melodically (see Figure 2). Octave and fifth G sonorities on the first D of each tenor E-D-D reinforce the periodicity. The repetition of the tenor melody or *color* (in fourteenth-century terminology), which begins at measure 43, cuts across the threefold division of the motet.

A new harmonic sense also characterizes the *ars nova* motet. Individual harmonic arrivals stand out as rhythmic punctuations and as resolutions of unstable imperfect consonances into stable perfect consonances (e.g. m. 13, m. 20). Outer-voice motion from major sixth to octave becomes the standard cadence formula for the fourteenth century. Focused harmonic arrivals foster clear tonal organization in de Vitry's motets. *Tribum que* begins and ends on F sonorities that contrast with the recurrent G arrivals produced by the principal melodic and rhythmic periodicities.

---

[1]It is doubtful that de Vitry codified his teaching in a written treatise called *Ars Nova*. The texts usually associated with him are probably second- or even third-hand reports of his teaching.

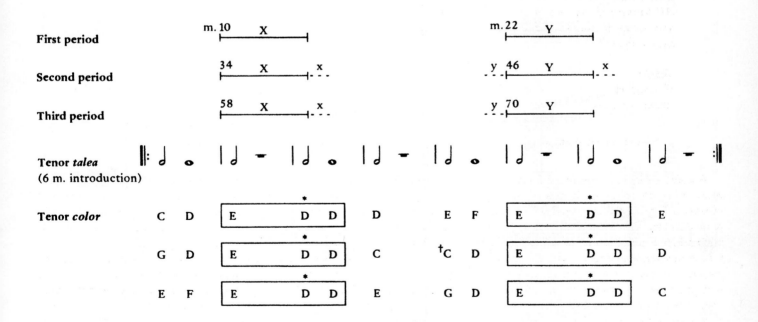

X and Y stand for passages that recur regularly, x and y for elements found only in the last two cycles.

*G-d-g sonority
†Color repeats from here.

**Figure 2.** Design of de Vitry's *Tribum que/Quoniam secta/Merito hec patimur* (No. 16).

## 17. GUILLAUME DE MACHAUT (c. 1300-1377)
### Bone pastor Guillerme/Bone pastor qui pastores/Bone pastor
Isorhythmic motet

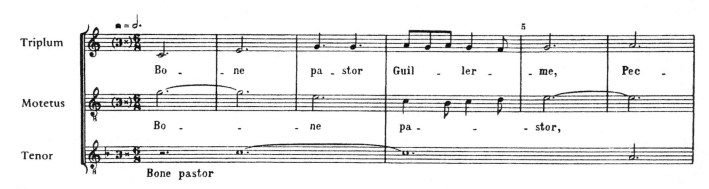

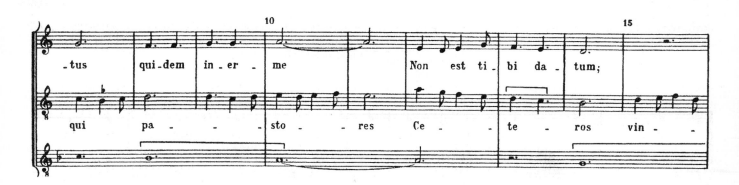

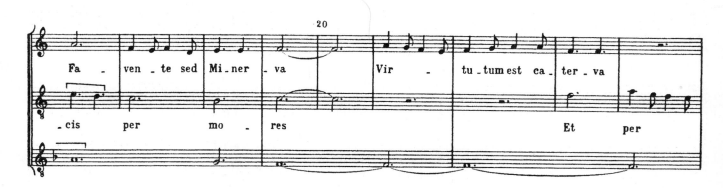

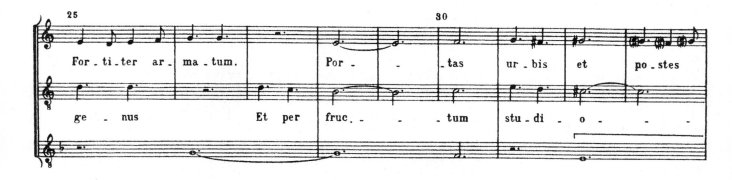

<sup>1</sup>G# in some manuscripts.

**Triplum**

1. *Good shepherd William*
   *A defenseless breast*
   *is not given to thee*
   *But with the help of Minerva*
   *it is strongly armed*
   *with a troop of virtues.*

2. *You fortify the gates and the doors*
   *of the city lest the enemy*
   *destroy the city,*
   *The world, the devil and the flesh*
   *with whose bitter sting*
   *many are bitten.*

3. *The mitre that crowns your head*
   *With its two horns portrays*
   *The two testaments,*
   *Which the mitre bearer*
   *must have like ornaments*
   *of a pure mind.*

4. *And because you are steeped*
   *and wholly involved*
   *with worship*
   *Your neck is worthy*
   *to bear the mitre, so that the symbols*
   *may be equal to the signified.*

5. *Displaying care for the people,*
   *You wish, just as each tries*
   *to help those that stray,*
   *To draw them with the upper part*
   *of your staff*

6. *With the other part,*
   *which is the middle,*
   *to administer to the sick*
   *With the third part*
   *you know how to sting*
   *those who resist.*

7. *You feed your sheep with preaching*
   *and with praiseworthy conversion,*
   *and finally with sensitive*
   *pleading.*

8. *After this destitution*
   *may this King, doer of all things,*
   *who spares the humble,*
   *Grant a stable rule*
   *for those who falter.*

**Motetus**

1. *Good shepherd who excels other shepherds*
   *in conduct and in lineage*
   *and in the fruit of study*
   *bearing human understanding as far*
   *as heaven.*

2. *O William, properly adorned,*
   *a King who powerfully rules All*
   *Has predestined you to grace*
   *his house, as shepherd of Reims.*

3. *He has chosen you, an honorable vessel,*
   *A distinguished vessel,*
   *From whom nothing may be brought forth*
   *except that which is worthy.*

4. *He gave you, a special vessel,*
   *To himself, the King,*
   *He gave you, a universal vessel,*
   *to his flock.*

**Tenor**

*Good shepherd* (source unidentified)

Guillaume de Machaut (c. 1300-1377), known to posterity as the major French poet of the fourteenth century, is the composer whose work dominates the *ars nova* repertory. Over 140 of his compositions survive, the majority of them songs. Machaut's 23 motets and one complete Mass Ordinary incorporate principles of isorhythm similar to those in de Vitry's motets.

Machaut's *Bone pastor Guillerme/Bone pastor qui pastores/ Bone pastor,* from 1324, is the earliest of his datable works. It is a full-fledged isorhythmic motet. The tenor talea, a complex rhythm covering eight notes, is presented four times in its original form, then four times in values reduced by half (m. 97 to the end). This process is called *diminution.* The talea splits the tenor color into two balanced halves, the first of which moves from c down to F (mm. 1-24), the second of which descends to D and returns to F (mm. 25-48). The complete color occurs twice in each section. An intricate hierarchy of duple divisions thus governs the formal organization. Two main sections in the ratio 2:1 are each divided by two color statements, which in turn are each bisected by two talea statements. The talea itself breaks into units of two and four notes. Such a periodic organization builds on elements from the thirteenth-century motet, but is far more elaborate than any devised in the preceding century.

The tenor rhythm is plainly recognizable from the three rests that segment it and from its very long terminal note, which is always an F. In the first section the upper voices reinforce the tenor's periodicity not just with consistent cadences on the final F, but also with an unvarying rhythmic pattern that recurs at the junction between taleas (mm. 19-29, 43-53, 67-77). Both rest patterns and fragments of imitation (mm. 21/24, 45/48, 69/72) help the listener to perceive this partial isorhythm in the upper voices. The upper voices are fully isorhythmic in the diminution section. Their recurrent rhythmic patterns coincide exactly with the tenor talea (compare mm. 97-108, 109-120, 121-142). The distinctive upper-voice hockets and the inevitable terminal F cadences ensure recognition of the talea in this section. The increase in rhythmic energy and excitement so apparent in the diminution section is due not only to the tenor acceleration and the sprightly hockets, but also to mensural conflict between the tenor and upper voices. (Technically, the tenor has three-unit perfect breves, the upper voices two-unit imperfect breves.) Because this conflict resolves only at the F cadences, those cadences stand out as stable pillars even more than in the initial statement section.

The standard double-leading-tone cadence abounds in *Bone pastor* (mm. 18-19, 42-43, etc.). This cadence may be thought of in two ways: as a voice leading formula in which two voices move up a half step while the lowest voice (situated a sixth below the highest) descends a tone, or as a harmonic progression from a pair of unstable imperfect consonances (major sixth and major third) to a pair of stable perfect consonances (octave and fifth). Machaut skillfully controls such chord qualities for artistic effect. Doubly imperfect sonorities held in mid-phrase prolong harmonic tension (e.g., mm. 32-33, 59-61). Thirds at cadential arrivals (mm. 67, 130) and delayed resolutions (m. 91) promote forward impetus across some cadences.

# 18. <u>GUILLAUME DE MACHAUT</u>
## Secular songs

### 18a. **Nes que on porroit**
Ballade

1. Nes que on porroit les estoiles nombrer,
   Quant on les voit luire plus clerement,
   Et les goutes de pluie et de la mer,
   Et l'areinne seur quoy elle s'estent,
   Et compasser le tour dou firmament,
   Ne porroit on penser ne concevoir
   Le grant desir que j'ay de vous veoir.

2. Et si ne puis par devers vous aler
   Pour Fortune qui le vuet et deffent,
   Dont maint souspir me convient estrangler,
   Quant à vous pense et je sui entre gent
   Et quant je sui par moy secretement;
   Adonc me fait tous meschiés recevoir
   Le grant desir que j'ay de vous veoir.

3. Car il me fait compleindre et dementer
   Et regreter vostre viaire gent
   Et vo biauté souvereinne et sans per
   El la tres grant douceur qui en descent.
   Einsi me fait languir piteusement,
   Mon cuer esprent et esteint mon espoir
   Le grant desir que j'ay de vous véoir.

1. *No more than one could count the stars*
   *when they are seen to shine most brightly*
   *or the raindrops or drops of water in the sea*
   *or the sand on which the sea extends,*
   *or compass the extent of the firmament—*
   *no more than this could anyone know or imagine*
   *the great desire I have of seeing you.*

2. *And if I cannot come to your side*
   *since Fortune prevents and forbids it,*
   *then I must suppress many sighs*
   *when I think of you in company.*
   *And when I am secluded and alone,*
   *then I brood upon all my troubles from*
   *the great desire I have of seeing you.*

3. *Absent from you, I lament and grieve*
   *and miss your sweet face*
   *and your supreme goodness, without equal*
   *and the great pleasure it creates.*
   *And so I languish piteously*
   *heart afire and hope extinguished because of*
   *the great desire I have of seeing you.*

## 18b. **Quant j'ay l'espart**
Rondeau

Track 20

| | |
|---|---|
| 1.-3. Quant j'ay l'espart<br>De vo regart,<br>Dame d'onnour, | *1.-3. When I have the light<br>of your glance,<br>noble Lady,* |
| 4.-6. Son doulz espart<br>En moy espart<br>Toute doucour. | *4.-6. its sweet light<br>kindles in me<br>all tenderness,* |
| 7.-9. Car main et tart<br>M'esprent son dart<br>De fine amour, | *7.-9. for early and late<br>its dart of pure love<br>enflames me.* |
| 10.-12. Quant j'ay l'espart<br>De vo regart,<br>Dame d'onnour, | *10.-12. When I have the light<br>of your glance,<br>noble Lady* |
| 13.-15. Et me repart<br>D'un ris qui m'art.<br>Mais celle ardour | *13.-15. and am adorned<br>by a smile, I burn,<br>but by the gentle effect* |
| 16.-18. Par son dous art<br>De moy depart<br>Toute doulour. | *16.-18. of this ardour<br>all anguish<br>leaves me.* |
| 19.-21. Quant j'ay l'espart<br>De vo regart,<br>Dame d'onnour, | *19.-21. When I have the light<br>of your glance,<br>noble Lady,* |
| 22.-24. Son doulz espart<br>En moy espart<br>Toute doucour. | *22.-24. its sweet light<br>kindles in me<br>all tenderness.* |

## 18c. Dame a vous sans retollir

Virelai

1.,5. Dame a vous sans re - tol - lir Dong cuer pen - se - e de - sir Corps et a - mour
4. Vos - tre biau - te fait ta - rir Toute au - tre et a - ni - en - tir Et vo dou - cour

Com - me a tou - te la mil - lour Qu'on puist choi - sir Ne qui vi - vre ne mo - rir Puist a ce jour.
Pas - se tout rose en cou - lour Vous doi te - nir Et vo re - gars puet ga - rir Tou - te do - lour.

2. Si ne me doit a fo - lour Tour - ner se je vous a - our Car sans men - tir
3. Bon - te pas - ses en va - lour Tou - te flour en douce o - dour Qu'on puet sen - tir.

(*Refrain*)

1. Dame a vous sans retollir
   Dong cuer pensee desir
   Corps et amour
   Comme a toute la millour
   Qu'on puist choisir
   Ne qui vivre ne morir
   Puist a ce jour.

**Verse 1**

2. Si ne me doit a folour
   Tourner se je vous aour
   Car sans mentir

3. Bonte passes en valour
   Toute flour en douce odour
   Qu'on puet sentir.

4. Vostre biaute fait tarir
   Toute autre et anientir
   Et vo doucour
   Passe tout rose en coulour
   Vous doi tenir
   Et vo regars puet garir
   Toute dolour.

(*Refrain*)

5. Dame a vous sans retollir . . . .

**Verse 2**

2. Pour ce dame je m'atour
   De tres toute ma vigour
   A vous servir

3. Et met sans nul villain tour
   Mon cuer ma vie et m'onnour
   En vo plaisir.

4. Et si Pite consentir
   Wet que me daigniez oir
   En ma clamour
   Je ne quier de mon labour
   Autre merir
   Qu'il ne me porroit venir
   Joie grignour.

(*Refrain*)

5. Dame a vous sans retollir . . . .

**Verse 3**

2. Dame ou sont tuit mi retour
   Souvent m'estuet en destour
   Pleindre et gemir

3. Et present vous descoulour
   Quant vous ne savez l'ardour
   Qu'ay a souffrir

(Refrain)

1. *Lady, to you I unreservedly give*
   *heart, mind, passion,*
   *body, and love,*
   *as to the best Lady*
   *of any that one might choose,*
   *living or dead,*
   *up to this day.*

**Verse 1**

2. *Think me not foolish*
   *if I declare it to you,*
   *for without falsehood*

3. *Your virtue surpasses in worth*
   *any flower of sweet aroma*
   *one could possibly scent.*

4. *Your beauty diminishes and*
   *eclipses any other*
   *and your sweetness*
   *surpasses all: A colorful rose*
   *I must consider you to be,*
   *and your glance can heal*
   *any sadness.*

(Refrain)

5. *Lady, to you I unreservedly give . . . .*

**Verse 2**

2. *For this, madam, I am prepared*
   *with my full sum of strength*
   *to serve you*

3. *and, with no bad intention,*
   *put my heart, my life, and my honor*
   *at your pleasure.*

4. *And if, moved by Pity,*
   *you deign to hear*
   *my cry,*
   *I seek no other reward*
   *for my pains*
   *than that there might come to me*
   *some increased joy.*

(Refrain)

5. *Lady, to you I unreservedly give . . . .*

**Verse 3**

2. *Lady, to whom I constantly return,*
   *often when I am away from you,*
   *I lament and sigh*

3. *and when before you, I blush—*
   *for you are so little aware of the ardor*
   *from which I suffer*

4. Pour vous qu'aim tant et desir
Que plus ne le puis couvrir.
Et se tenrour
N'en avez en grant tristour
M'estuet fenir
Nompourquant jusqu'au morir
Vostres demour.

(*Refrain*)
5. Dame a vous sans retollir . . . .

4. *for you, whom I so much love and desire*
*that I can no longer conceal it.*
*And if toward me you feel*
*no tenderness, I shall have to expire*
*in great sadness,*
*but, nevertheless, I remain yours*
*until death.*

(Refrain)
5. *Lady, to you I unreservedly give . . . .*

Two traditions—the monophonic trouvère song and the polyphonic thirteenth-century motet—contribute to the genesis of polyphonic art song in fourteenth-century France. The songs of Guillaume de Machaut, settings of his own fine poetry, represent the new genre in its full maturity.

The diverse poetic types of the thirteenth century had, by Machaut's time, coalesced into certain stereotyped fixed forms: *ballade, virelai, rondeau,* and *lai.* The repetition schemes particular to these poetic forms carry across to the music and result in standard patterns of musical repetition. Machaut usually sets ballade and rondeau in two- or three-part polyphony, lai and virelai monophonically. In most of the polyphonic settings, only one voice has text. The other, untexted lines traditionally have been interpreted as instrumental, but recent investigation reveals that they too were very likely sung.[1] A cantus-tenor duet is the structural foundation, supplying the basic consonant progressions that control the melodic lines. When a third voice participates, it is a triplum above the cantus in Machaut's earlier works, a contratenor sharing the tenor range in later compositions (No. 18a). The third voice enriches the sonorities of the basic duet and animates the texture with syncopations and entrances off the beat. Irregular and syncopated rhythms, erratic melismatic excursions, and asymmetrical phrases mark Machaut's melodic style. Melismas particularly disrupt the poetic lines in *Nes que on porroit,* a late ballade from about 1363.

Machaut's ballades are poems in three stanzas, all of which end with the same single-line refrain. A single musical strophe serves for all three stanzas. Within stanzas, the music of the opening poetic couplet is repeated for the second couplet, producing an *aab* shape. The first *a* section normally ends with an open cadence, the second with a closed cadence. The closed cadence typically returns at the end of the *b* section. Not infrequently, as in

*Nes que on porroit,* the entire last phrase of the *a* section is brought back at the end of *b*. The melodic material of the final refrain phrase in fact so permeates *Nes que on porroit* that the piece seems generated from it. Machaut himself characterized this piece in a letter as an "unusual and novel" work.

The rondeau form features a refrain that is stated whole at the beginning and end of the verse, and in part after the first verse section. The two verse sections follow the structure of the refrain and are sung to the same music. The text-music relationship is usually represented as follows, with upper-case letters representing music *with refrain text,* and lower-case letters representing the same music with different text.

| Text: | R | v₁ | ½ R | v₂ | R |
|-------|------|-----|------|------|------|
| Music: | *AB* | *a* | *A* | *ab* | *AB* |

Machaut's *Quant j'ay l'espart* (No. 18b), a song in duple meter, follows the rondeau scheme. Its short text is quite engulfed by the melismatic melody. As usual in the rondeau, the first section (*A*) of the refrain ends with an open, non-final-sounding cadence, while the second (*B*) ends with a closed cadence. The middle of the piece thus presents a series of open cadences. The broadly paced tenor of *Quant j'ay l'espart* is typical of early Machaut works. Tenors of his later songs are more active rhythmically and melodically. Duple relationships at all metric levels in *Quant j'ay* are made possible by the new *ars nova* notational system.

In Machaut's time, virelais were considered to be a special kind of ballade surrounded by a refrain. Their musical design is *AbbaA.* Successive verses are sung to the music of the middle section. The virelai *Dame a vous* (No. 18c) appears in one of Machaut's long narrative poems, *Le Remede de Fortune* as a dance piece sung by the poet. The mainly syllabic text setting, a usual virelai feature, is related to the dance function. The shifting rhythmic groups, which cut across expected "measures," give life and energy to the song.

---

[1]C. Page, "The performance of songs in late medieval France," *Early Music,* vol. 10 (1982), pp. 441-450.

**19.** <u>JACOPO DA BOLOGNA</u>   (fl. 1340-60)    Track 21

## Non al suo amante

Madrigale

Non al suo amante più Diana piacque
Quando per tal ventura tutta nuda
La vide in mezzo de le gelide acque

Ch'a me la pastorella alpestra e cruda
Posta a bagnar un leggiadretto velo
Ch'a l'aura il vago e biondo capel chiuda

Tal che mi fece quando gli arde'l cielo
Tutto tremar d'un amoroso gielo.
　　　　—Francesco Petrarca, 1304-1374

*[The goddess] Diana never pleased her lover more*
*when by chance he saw her quite naked*
*among the chilly waters*

*Than I [was pleased] by a rustic, cruel shepherdess*
*intent on washing the graceful wispy veil*
*that protects her pretty blond hair from the breeze*

*So that although the sky burned hot*
*my whole body trembled with the cold chill of love.*

　Whereas French *ars nova* music develops organically from French and English composition of the thirteenth century, Italian polyphony of the fourteenth century or *trecento* (1300s) emerges from a relative void. The rich repertory of secular song in two or three parts produced from about 1340 to 1400 in northern Italy possibly stems from an indigenous unwritten tradition of florid song. Typically, a soloist might decorate a love poem with an elaborate melody, either singing alone or being joined by a companion who supported the main line from below with primary consonances.

　One of the most celebrated early *trecento* songs is a setting of Petrarch's *Non al suo amante* by Jacopo da Bologna (fl. 1340-60). Jacopo's career is associated with the politically powerful della Scala and Visconti families. He sets the poem as a duet for two voices, both fully texted as is usual in the Italian style. Ornate melismas begin and end each phrase, flanking relatively syllabic text delivery. The voices blend euphoniously in perfect and imperfect consonances, merging in sweet unisons at the end of poetic lines. Quick decorative figures grace the upper melody and define it as the more dominant of the two.

The lower line is more sedate in movement, only asserting itself in short bridges between phrases.

The poem is a *madrigale* in form, and consists of two parallel three-line verses followed by a two-line *ritornello*. The musical setting reflects this structure in its single section for both verses and contrasting material for the *ritornello*. Although this standard *aab madrigale* design resembles the French ballade form (see No. 18a), it is quite different in execution: The *a* sections end with the same cadence (not with alternate open and closed cadences), a change in meter sets the *ritornello* apart from the verses, and the weight of length inclines toward the first section (*a*) rather than toward the second (*b*). The rhythmic movement is generally smoother, more flowing, and more predictable than in Machaut's ballades.

Although conceived for singers, songs of this sort were also appropriated by instrumentalists in Italy. The famous Faenza codex (c. 1400), one of the earliest extant collections of keyboard music, includes a very florid arrangement of *Non al suo amante* (not including the *ritornello*) for keyboard instrument.[1]

[1]Published in *Keyboard Music of the Late Middle Ages in Codex Faenza 117*, ed. D. Plamenac, Corpus Mensurabilis Musicae 57 (1972), pp. 94-96.

## 20. GHERARDELLO DA FIRENZE (c.1320/5-1362/3)    Track 22
### Tosto che l'alba
Caccia

As soon as dawn of the fine day appears
the hunters awake: "Get up, get up. It's time!"
Call the dogs: "Hey, hey, Viola! Hey, Primera, hey!"
High on the mountain with good dogs in hand
and the pack quiet
and everyone in order on the field.
I see one of the best of the pack on the scent.
"On the alert!
Everyone beat the brush on all sides—
the quail calls!"
"Ayo, ayo! the young doe is coming to you!
Carbon has seized her and holds her in his mouth."

**Ritornello**
One upon the mountain shouted down
"On to another! on to another!" and sounded his horn.

One of the most entertaining of *trecento* song types is the *caccia* (chase), appropriately named for the hunting subjects of its texts and for the literal "chases"—canons—of its music. *Tosto che l'alba*, by the Florentine composer and cleric Gherardello da Firenze (c. 1320/5-1362/3), has a typically descriptive text larded with natural shouts and cries from the hunting field. The cries are handled realistically in the music, treated as abrupt exclamations, highlighted by special rhythmic devices such as hocket and syncopation (e.g., m. 9, mm. 35-36). The final horn call is rendered onomatopoetically in the rising fourth motive of the concluding melisma (mm. 53-54, 56-57).

Two voices of a caccia are always texted and in canon. A third voice, the tenor, supports them with a relatively sober, untexted line. The two canonic voices always sing exactly the same music, but at a considerable interval of time. In this case, ten semibreves (♩.) separate the two in the first section, six in the second

(m. 47). While the actual canonic relationship is difficult to perceive, its results are plainly audible. The same shouts recur at predictable intervals of time. Different text lines and phrases overlap constantly, producing a vivacious confusion appropriate to the subject.

Like the madrigale, the caccia normally ends with a short, contrasting ritornello. In *Tosto che l'alba* the meter does not change, but quicker rhythms are introduced and the time between the canonic entries is shortened. The opening sequential melisma, stated in the single upper voice, clearly defines a new phase of action.

A facsimile of the original notation of this piece is printed in *The New Grove Dictionary of Music and Musicians*, volume 3, page 575. The beautiful illumination of the page pictures the hound and the doe mentioned in the text and is thought to include a portrait of Magister Gherardello, the composer.

## 21. FRANCESCO LANDINI (c. 1330-1397)
### Questa fanciull'amor
Ballata

(*Refrain*)
1. Questa fanciull'amor fallami pia,
   Che m'a ferito'l cor nella tuo via.

2. Tu m'a', fanciulla, si d'amor percosso,
   Che solo in te pensando trovo posa.

(*Refrain*)
1. *O Love, turn that girl's devotion toward me,*
   *for she has wounded my heart in your manner.*

2. *Young lady, you have so stricken me with love*
   *that only in thinking of you do I find repose.*

3. El cor di me da me tu a' rimosso
   Cogli occhi belli et la faccia gioiosa.

4. Però al servo tuo de! sia pietosa
   Mercè ti chero alla gran pena mia.

(*Refrain*)
5. Questa fanciull'amor . . . .

   Se non soccorri alle dogliose pene
   Il cor mi verrà meno che tu m'a' tolto

   Che la mia vita non sente ma' bene
   Se non mirando'l tuo veçoso volto,

   Da poi fanciulla che d'amor m'a involto
   Priego ch'alquanto a me beningnia sia.

(*Refrain*)
   Questa fanciull'amor . . . .

*3. You have deprived me of my heart
   with your beautiful eyes and cheerful face*

*4. but do take pity on your servant
   I beg you mercy for my great suffering.*

(Refrain)
5. *O Love* . . . .

   *If you do not relieve my painful suffering
   my heart you took from me will wither*

   *For my life is spoiled
   if I do not worship your lovely face.*

   *From now on, young lady who has ensnared me in love,
   be somewhat kind to me, I pray.*

(Refrain)
   *O love* . . . .

The leading composer of the late *trecento* is Francesco Landini (c. 1330-1397), a blind organist who worked in Florence. He is represented by over 150 works in manuscript collections. His popular *Questa fanciull'amor* was not only arranged for keyboard, but was transformed through provision of new texts (a procedure known as *contrafactum*) into Mass movements, a lauda, and a German *Lied*. Landini favored the *ballata*, a refrain song identical in outline to the French virelai (see No. 18c). Its elements are a *ripresa* (refrain), two *piedi*, which are sung to the same music, and a *volta*, which is sung to the *ripresa* music. The form may be diagrammed as:

Music:   A   b   b   a   A
Text:    R   p₁  p₂  v   R

In *Questa fanciull'* the two sections of music are linked by a common final phrase.

Landini's later *ballate* are mostly for three voices. As in this example, cantus and tenor are fully texted and are the main structural voices. The text setting follows the pattern established in the earlier *trecento* (see No. 19), with melismas at beginnings and ends of poetic lines. The upper-voice melody is less ornamented than in Jacopo da Bologna's music, but coheres about a recurrent descending figure placed both cadentially and within phrases (mm. 7, 12, etc., variant mm. 4, 9). In fact, this figure produces the characteristic decoration of the double-leading-tone cadence named the "Landini cadence" or the "under-third cadence" in modern times (mm. 4-5, 20-21). The telling gesture—the cantus drop to a third below its goal tone just before the melodic and harmonic resolution—becomes more of a cliché in the early fifteenth century.

The untexted contratenor in *Questa fanciull'* may reflect French influence, which is often remarked in Landini's late works. The contratenor freely crosses the tenor within phrases, but moves to the fifth at the octave cadences.

Landini is noted also for his concern for tonal cohesion, a quality evident in *Questa fanciull'*. Both its sections end on the D sonority that opened the piece, and both are bisected by a strong internal cadence on E (mm. 11, 29), which contrasts sharply with the central D. Sonorities on A play a pivotal role between D and E and begin both phrases of the *piedi* as well as the terminal melisma in the first phrase of the *ripresa*.

**22.** BORLET (?)

## Ma trédol rosignol joly

Virelai

**Cantus**

*1.4. My sweet, pretty nightingale
who sings "oci, oci, oci"[1]
I pray you
be tender.
Come to me, lovely lady,
By my faith, goddess, have confidence
if "oci, oci, oci" him [?]
my heart will be cleansed of anger
        toward my mistress.*

*2. Lark, flying so high
singing a clear sweet song:
"Liry, liry, liry, liry,"
you go flying.*

*3. To my lady, being mine,
go to her, saying for me
a sweet song:
"Liry, liry, liry,"
this my heart beats [for her].*

**Contratenor**

*1.4. Lark, crying after the nightingale
"oci, oci, oci,"
I pray you this
to make concord
between my pretty lady and me,
and so I pray her
through the nightingale
to have mercy, mercy on me,
by God, mercy, mercy, mercy, mercy,
I ask it faithfully
my lady, my own.*

*2. My sweet, pretty nightingale,
lark flying around and saying
"Tantiny, tantiny, tantiny, tantiny,"
"Liry, liry, liry, liry, liry,"
come talk to me.*

**Tenor**

*Nightingale of the pretty woods,
inflict early ruin upon the scoundrel
and then death.*

[1]Literally "kill, kill." Perhaps intended simply as a bird call here, perhaps of allegorical import.

The rhythmic complexities of the *ars nova* reach their apex late in the fourteenth century in circles associated with the papal court at Avignon and the secular courts of Gaston Fébus, Count of Foix (a region of southwestern France), and the kings of Aragon. Because some theorists, in explaining how to notate intricate new rhythms, characterize the modern style as "more subtle" than the former, this late phase of fourteenth-century music has been christened *ars subtilior*. The increased subtlety of technique is most apparent in French secular songs, but composers of Italian background, familiar with Italian notational concepts, also contributed to it.

One "mannered" type of composition favored in the later fourteenth century is the naturalistic virelai, cousin to the caccia (see No. 20) in its penchant for descriptive text elements. The elaborate bird calls featured in naturalistic virelais invite special sound effects. In *Ma trédol rosignol* these include insistent bird calls on repeated motives and unexpected rhythmic subdivisions of three for two or two for three (mm. 4, 18-19). The rhythmic

complications of the two upper voices stand out sharply against the even tenor, which is a simple song whose text probably veiled some dark political or amorous situation. Texted secular song tenors can be traced back to motets of the later thirteenth century (see No. 15b). The upper voices present an incomplete virelai over the reiterated tenor. Since neither has a verse for the refrain music, the piece is performed as a partial virelai form: *AbbA*. The texts have nothing of the literary skill of Machaut's poems and are little more than vehicles for the virtuosic bird imitations.[1]

[1]A four-voice version of this virelai exists with text *Hé tres doulz roussignol joly*. It is attributed to one Borlet, a musician who is otherwise unknown, unless the name is an anagram of Trebol (Trebor), to whom six songs are attributed in the Chantilly manuscript. It is unclear which of the two versions came first. A transcription of *Hé tres doulz roussignol* is published in W. Apel, *French Secular Compositions of the Fourteenth Century*, Corpus Mensurabilis Musicae 53, (1970), vol. 1, p. 19.

## 23. JOHANNES CICONIA (c.1370-1412)   Track 24

### Sus un' fontayne

Virelai

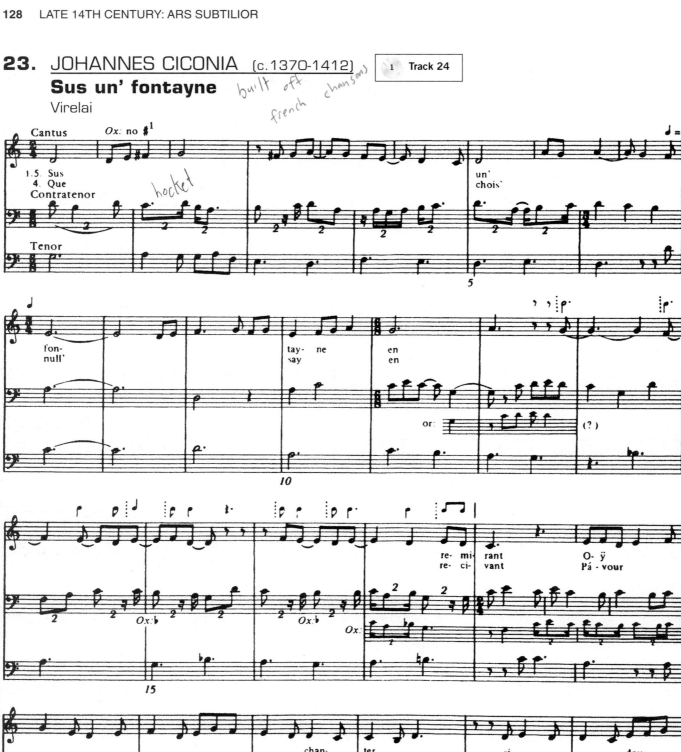

[1]All observations marked *OX* refer to variant readings in a different manuscript.

1. Sus un' fontayne en remirant
   Oÿ chanter si douchement
   Que mon cuer, corps et pensement,
   Remanent pris en atendant

2. D'avoir merchi de ma dolour
   Qui me trepount au cuer forment

3. Seul de vëoir ce noble flour,
   Qui tant cantoit suavement.

4. Que chois' null' say en recivant
   Pavour, tremour et angosment
   Que fere duis certaynement,
   Tant suy de ly vëoir desirant.

5. Sus un' fontayne en remirant
   Oÿ chanter si douchement
   Que mon cuer, corps et pensement,
   Remanent pris en atendant.

1. *By a fountain, gazing about,*
   *I heard such sweet singing*
   *that my heart, body, and mind*
   *were fixed in waiting*

2. *To find pity for that distress*
   *which resounds in my heart,*

3. *Only to see this noble flower*
   *who was singing so sweetly.*

4. *Ignorant of my chances, I experience*
   *fear, trembling, and anguish,*
   *which I certainly ought to bear*
   *so desirous am I of seeing her.*

5. *By a fountain, gazing about,*
   *I heard such sweet singing*
   *that my heart, body, and mind*
   *were fixed in waiting.*

Born and trained in the Flemish city of Liège, Johannes Ciconia (c. 1370-1412)[1] migrated south and eventually settled in northern Italy at Padua (1401-12). An intermediate sojourn in Avignon (probably of extended duration) very likely accounts for the command of intricate rhythms and involved notations evident in some of his works. His virelai *Sus un fontayne,* which dates from around 1390, reveals complete mastery of a rhythmic counterpoint hardly equaled in complexity until the twentieth century.

In both texture and text setting, *Sus un fontayne* recalls Guillaume de Machaut's late ballades (see No. 18a). A single texted voice dominates melodically and is supported by untexted contratenor and tenor. Frequent, unpredictable melismas fragment the poetic lines and extend them asymmetrically. The rhythmic idiom, however, far exceeds Machaut's in complexity. Numerous shifts in mensuration (some only for the span of one note), metric displacements (cantus, mm. 12-17, 75-79), and simultaneous combinations of opposing meters and conflicting subdivisions produce a syncopated, unsettled rhythmic surface. Right from the start, each voice observes different mensural relationships. Duple groupings in one voice constantly cut across triple groupings in another. The rhythmic turmoil ceases only occasionally (and momentarily) at cadences (e.g., mm. 45, 71), or on held sonorities (mm. 7, 34), reference points for performers and listeners alike. Performance of this music obviously demands virtuoso singers and instrumentalists, musicians specially skilled in handling cross-rhythms and fluctuating meters. The rhythmic complexity is not merely abstruse artifice but also is a means of generating tension within phrases and forward momentum within the piece. Moreover, it has significant harmonic effects. In displacing consonances of the underlying discant structure, the contrary groupings create considerable harmonic instability and much passing dissonance.

Another, hidden, subtlety of *Sus un fontayne* is in its references to the work of another Avignon composer, Philippus (Philipoctus) de Caserta(fl. 1370). Ciconia quotes the openings of three ballades by Philippus: *En remirant* (mm. 11-18); *En atendant* (mm. 56-59); and *De ma dolour* (mm. 74-80).[2] In each case both text and music of the borrowed material are woven smoothly into the fabric of Ciconia's virelai—a technical *tour de force*. These quotations may be understood as an act of homage to Philippus or as clever allusions to be appreciated by a privileged inner circle—perhaps both. In any event, they are an added element of skill within the extraordinarily refined, dauntingly complex style of the *ars subtilior* as realized in the 1380s-90s.

[1]In this instance I do not take the dates given in *The New Grove Dictionary of Music and Musicians* (vol. 4, p. 391) but adopt those favored in *The Works of Johannes Ciconia,* edited by M. Bent and A. Hallmark, Polyphonic Music of the Fourteenth Century, vol. 24 (Monaco: Éditions de l'Oiseau-lyre, (1985), pp. IX-X.

[2]The ballades by Philippus are published in W. Apel, *French Secular Compositions of the Fourteenth Century,* Corpus Mensurabilis Musicae 53, (1970), vol. 1, pp. 148, 56, and 145 respectively. Apel accepts a conflicting attribution of *En atendant* to Johannes Galiot and takes an opposite stand on the direction of borrowing (p. XXXIV).

## 24. LEONEL POWER (1370/80-1445)
### 24a. Credo (Opem nobis)

*Mass ordinary*

II (truncated and varied)

For translation of No. 24a, see No. 1h.

## 24b. **Ave regina caelorum**
Motet

For translation of No. 24b, see No. 7a.

## 24c. **Ave regina caelorum**
Melody of Sarum (Salisbury, England) tradition
See No. 7a.

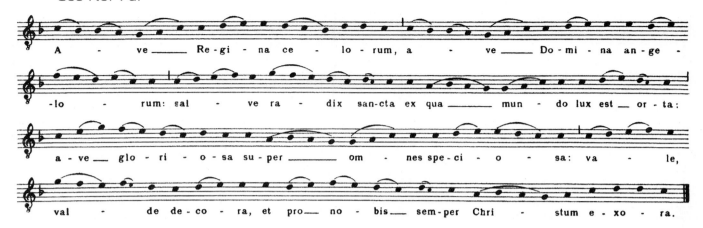

A - ve ___ Re - gi - na ce - lo - rum, a ___ ve ___ Do - mi - na an - ge - 
-lo - rum: sal - ve ra - dix san-cta ex qua ___ mun - do lux est ___ or - ta: 
a - ve glo - ri - o - sa su - per ___ om - nes spe - ci - o - sa: va ___ le, 
val - de de - co - ra, et pro ___ no - bis ___ sem - per Chri - stum e - xo - ra.

From *John Dunstable Complete Works*, ed. M. Bukofzer, 2nd revised edition by M. Bent, I. Bent, and B. Trowell, Musica Britannica 8 (London: Stainer and Bell, 1970), 110.

For translation of No. 24c, see No. 7a.

In the 1420s a new sound ideal so changed the character and course of European music that music historians announce a new epoch, the Renaissance. The immediate source for the new sound quality was to the northwest, in Britain, where English composers had long practiced a distinctive musical dialect. Conditions in the early fifteenth century were particularly favorable for exchange between English and Continental musicians, for the English crown then occupied and controlled vast expanses of territory in what is now France. Moreover, the prime English ally, the Duke of Burgundy, was an enthusiastic patron of music who attracted and maintained many fine musicians at his court.

The leading English composers in this critical period of change were Leonel Power (btw. 1370/80-1445) and his somewhat younger contemporary, John Dunstable (c. 1390-1453). Their works circulated widely on the Continent, and appear in French, Burgundian and Italian manuscripts. Leonel Power is more of a transitional figure than Dunstable, in that his output comprises both works with late fourteenth-century angular rhythms and works in a newer, more settled rhythmic style. Power is the composer most represented in the famous Old Hall manuscript, a collection copied about 1410-15, which is our primary source for the pre-Dunstable phase of English music.[1] The Old Hall manuscript reveals not only distinctive compositional features of English music at the turn of the century, but also a distinctive orientation toward polyphonic settings of the Mass Ordinary. Mass settings are sparse in Continental repertory of the fourteenth and early

fifteenth centuries, but become common by the mid-fifteenth century. Expanding upon a practice already evident in the Old Hall repertory, Power and Dunstable created unified polyphonic Mass cycles. The cyclic Mass subsequently became a principal genre of Renaissance sacred music and was cultivated by generations of composers from the 1440s to the 1590s.

**24a.** A first step toward the complete Ordinary cycle was to pair individual Mass movements, usually Gloria with Credo and Sanctus with Agnus Dei. Leonel Power's Credo *Opem nobis* from the Old Hall manuscript (No. 23) is paired with a Gloria (Old Hall, No. 24), but the musical connection is loose by later criteria. The pairing rests on such features as similarity of clefs and flat signatures, identical voice ranges, isorhythmic structure (but not with the same rhythmic pattern), similarity of texture, and liturgical destination (both are for the feast of St. Thomas of Canterbury, December 29th). The two movements are not based on the same plainsong. That associative device was to become standard by the middle of the fifteenth century.

Stylistically, the Credo *Opem nobis* can be considered a transitional work. It has some old traits, such as isorhythmic construction and modest rhythmic complexity, but also newer ones, such as a single dominant upper voice, occasional quick movement in the lower voices, and a high incidence of thirds and sixths. The preference for imperfect intervals is manifested in parallel motion between voices (mm. 8-9, 15, etc.), in parallel sixth approaches to octave cadences (mm. 22, 41, 129-30), and in triadic outlines in individual voices (mm. 89-90, 133) as well as in rhythmic emphasis of triad members within lines (mm. 46-47, 50-51). The

[1] The manuscript contains but one Dunstable piece, among the additions made to the collection about 1420.

omission of the fifth in many cadences (mm. 14, 42, 68) or the introduction of the fifth after a rest (mm. 23, 33), which avoids a pungent double-leading-tone cadence, gives the cadences a particularly sweet sound. Nearly all the cadences are ornamented with an "under-third" figure, a trademark of early fifteenth-century music. The under-third cadence (also called the Landini cadence, see p. 124 above) preserves the conventional sixth-to-octave progression, but the voice leading is decorated by an intervening melodic third (mm. 13-14 on F, mm. 22-23 on D, with the half step in the bass).

Even the older features of this movement have a somewhat "modern" cast. The isorhythm, which prevails in all three voices, functions more to produce a general consistency of manner than to sectionalize stiffly. The talea, which is stated three times (mm. 1, 55, 109), mainly defines an even series of similar phrases, each punctuated by a brief duet between the lower voices. Because the triplum both monopolizes the single text and has a directed melodic flow, the overall effect is more akin to the chanson than to the fourteenth-century isorhythmic motet. Rhythmic complexity is largely confined to clashes between $\frac{6}{8}$ and $\frac{3}{4}$ groupings, a feature also of Dufay's early works.

Power's handling of the tenor chant also departs from Continental norms of the fourteenth century. The chant—an antiphon sung at Lauds on the feast of St. Thomas of Canterbury—is not quoted exactly but is paraphrased.[2] Power preserves its general contour and tonal focus, but elaborates it with additional notes, which in this case elongate the original considerably. The paraphrase is particularly evident in the brief duets where the tenor breaks away from its slow supporting role and becomes an active voice. In some other early fifteenth-century sacred works based on chant, the plainsong is adopted by the highest voice and elaborated in the principal melodic lines.

**24b.** In addition to polyphonic Mass Ordinaries, English composers specialized in discantal settings of Marian antiphons from the Offices. Leonel Power's *Ave regina caelorum* from the Old Hall manuscript exemplifies the common "English descant style" employed for such utilitarian pieces. The core of the polyphony is the plainsong antiphon. To it an upper and a lower voice are fashioned in such a way as to produce a fundamentally homophonic texture. Although the chant is melodically intact (see No. 24c), it is so transformed under Leonel's rhythms as to lose much of its original identity. The focus of melodic interest is the newly composed upper voice, whose opening triadic outline is an English trademark of the period.

Power projects the text plainly, but does not follow the plainsong in matching verse structure and musical phrases. He ends some phrases within poetic lines (e.g., m. 4 end, m. 6 end), and sometimes slides by beginnings of new lines (e.g., m. 6 beginning, m. 9). The discrepancy between text units and musical phrases is a source of artistic tension in the piece. Most surprisingly, the antiphon's clear tonal focus on C (see above, No. 24c) is utterly masked in this polyphonic setting where the main cadences fall on contrasting F and A sonorities. A change of meter and simplification of rhythm for the last three lines (mm. 15 ff.) articulates the antiphon in two relatively balanced sections. As in the Credo *Opem nobis,* imperfect consonances abound within phrases and frequently occur in parallel (mm. 2-3, m. 10 end, m. 30), while octave-fifth sonorities mark stable phrase endings. Modest liturgical settings such as this were to become popular on the Continent and lead to a new genre of motet (see No. 25).

**24c.** Because the English version of the *Ave regina caelorum* melody differs in detail from the earliest Continental readings (see No. 7a), it is presented here as an adjunct to the Power polyphonic setting.

---

[2]The original chant is printed in *The Old Hall Manuscript,* ed. A. Hughes and M. Bent, vol. 2. Corpus Mensurabilis Musicae 46 (1969), p. 54.

## 25. JOHN DUNSTABLE (c. 1390-1453)  [2 Track 2]
### Beata mater
Motet

From *John Dunstable Complete Works,* ed. M. Bukofzer, 2nd revised edition by M. Bent, I. Bent, and B. Trowell, Musica Britannica 8 (London: Stainer and Bell, 1970), p. 160.

*Blessed mother and unwed virgin,*
*Glorious Queen of the world,*
*Intercede for us to God.*

In a much-quoted passage, the poet Martin le Franc wrote about 1440 that Dufay and Binchois, two prominent composers of the day, "have a new way of making lively concords in *haut* and *bas* music . . . they have adopted the English manner [*contenance angloise*] and follow Dunstable, in consequence of which a wonderful charm renders their music joyful and remarkable."[1] Martin's is but one of several voices claiming the English manner in general, and John Dunstable in particular, as telling influences on Continental composers during the early decades of the fifteenth century. This influence extended to compositional genres as well as to basic elements of musical language. Both the cyclic Mass Ordinary (see Nos. 24a, 27) and the discant motet (sometimes called the song motet or votive motet) were fostered by English composers and subsequently spread to the Continent.

The discant motet grew out of simple "English descant" settings of plainsong antiphons (see No. 24b), but did not necessarily incorporate chant. This new kind of motet with its homogeneous textures, easily grasped rhythms, single texts, and direct devotional message was the antithesis of the complicated, large-scale, polytextual isorhythmic motet inherited from the late fourteenth century. A classic example of the new genre is *Beata mater* by John Dunstable (c. 1390-1453). The upper voice commands attention with its long, elegant phrases unwinding at leisure over two more sedate voices. The text, a Marian antiphon,[2] is clearly audible, whether presented in just one voice or shared by two (duo section). Rhythms flow evenly except for modest flurries of activity just before cadences. The smoothly sculpted surface is undisturbed by polytextual conflict or competition between rival lines. Although independent in rhythmic movement, the lines cohere through a shared harmonic basis that is triadic in nature. Melodic gestures outlining triads[3] (as in mm. 1-2, 7, 28, 66-68) stand out prominently and are probably among the features that attracted Continental composers to Dunstable's musical manner. No chant controls the course of the melody, the sequence of harmonies, or the tonal plan of *Beata mater*. The composer was guided only by the text and his own musical imagination and judgment. The form of the composition is articulated not through recurrent rhythmic patterns but through text units and changes in scoring. Each line of text receives a distinct section of music. The first and last lines are set in full three-voiced texture, while the middle one is a transparent duet. The contrast between duet and three- or four-voice texture becomes a common feature of fifteenth-century sacred music. Besides providing formal articulation and relief from the full ensemble sound, the duets emphasize the contrapuntal interplay of lines in contrast to the more chordal effect of the three- and four-voice writing (see, for example, No. 28).

[1]The original is quoted in G. Reese, *Music in the Renaissance*, (New York: Norton, 1954), pp. 12-13.

[2]In the Sarum rite, this antiphon is sung at Compline on the feast of the Nativity of the Virgin Mary (September 8). Dunstable's setting does not include the plainsong.

[3]This is the modern term. Theoretical recognition of the triad as such was still more than a century distant from Dunstable's time.

# 26. GUILLAUME DUFAY (c.1400-1474)
## Christe, redemptor omnium
## Hymn **In nativitate Dominum**
See No. 2d.

| 2 | Track 3 |

```
1. Chri-ste, red-em-ptor    o-mni-um, Ex        pa-tre, pa-tris   u - ni - ce,
3. Me-men-to    sa-lu-tis au-ctor, Quod          no-stri quon-dam cor-po-ris.
5. Hunc coe-lum, ter-ra, hunc ma-re, Hunc        o-mne quod in  e - is  est.
7. Glo-ri-a    ti-bi  do-mi-ne, Qui              na-tus es de  vir-gi-ne,
```

```
1. So-lus an-te prin-ci-pi-um        Na-tus in ef-fa-bi-li-ter.
3. Ex il-li-ba-ta vir-gi-ne          Na-scen-do, for-mam sum-pse-ris.
5. Au-cto-rem ad-ven-tus tu-i,       Lau-dans ex-sul-tat can-ti-co.
7. Cum pa-tre et san-cto spi-ri-tu   In sem-pi-ter-na sae-cu-la.
```

[Cantus]

Fauxbourdon

Tenor

Christe redemptor

---

2. Tu lu - men tu splen - - dor pa -
4. Sic prae - sens te - - sta - - tur di -
6. Nos quo - que, qui san - cto tu -

2. tris, Tu spes per - en - ni o - - mni - - um
4. es Cur - rens per an - ni cir - - cu - - lum
6. o Re - dem - pti san - gui - ne su - - mus,

2. In - - ten - de quas fun - dunt pre - - ces Tu -
4. Quod so - **lus** a se - de pa - - tris Mun -
6. Ob di - em na - ta - lis tu - - i Hym -

2. i per or - - bem fa - mu - - - li.
4. di sa - lus ad - - ve - ne - - - ris.
6. num no - vum con - - ci - ni - - - mus.

A - men.

[1] The xs over certain notes in the cantus refer to pitches from the plainsong melody.

[2] The middle voice, in small notes, has been realized by the editor according to the principles of fauxbourdon.

[3] Or sing B♮ and preserve a perfect fourth below it.

*For the Nativity of Christ*

1. *Christ, redeemer of all,*
   *from the Father, one with the Father,*
   *alone before the beginning,*
   *of birth inexpressible.*

2. *Thou the light, thou the splendor of the Father*
   *thou the everlasting hope of all,*
   *listen to the prayers*
   *which thy servants pour out throughout the world.*

3. *Remember, author of salvation,*
   *that once in being born*
   *you assumed the form of our body*
   *from an unblemished virgin.*

4. *Thus the present day bears witness*
   *through the course of the whole year*
   *that alone, from the throne of the Father,*
   *thou hadst come for the salvation of the whole world.*

5. *Heaven, earth, and sea*
   *and all that is in them*
   *praising the author of thy arrival*
   *rejoice over this in song.*

6. *We also who are redeemed*
   *by thy sacred blood*
   *because of this day of thy birth*
   *sing a new hymn.*

7. *Glory be to thee, Lord,*
   *who was born of a virgin*
   *with the Father and the Holy Spirit*
   *forever and ever.*

Guillaume Dufay (c. 1400-1474) received his early training as a boy chorister at the cathedral of Cambrai. By 1420 he had migrated from this northern region to Italy, where he served the Malatesta family in Pesaro. In subsequent decades, as his repute as a singer and composer grew, Dufay distributed his activity among Cambrai, northern Italy, and the court of Savoy. From 1458 to his death in 1474 he lived in Cambrai. Dufay was enormously productive as a composer. His output summarizes the main musical genres of the fifteenth century: Mass, motet, and chanson. In his later years, he was sought out by many younger composers, including Johannes Ockeghem. Although Dufay was not alone in absorbing the *contenance angloise,* his was the imagination that crystallized the distinctive musical language of the fifteenth-century Renaissance.

Dufay was among the earliest Continental composers to employ a technique known as *fauxbourdon* for polyphonic settings of certain repetitive liturgical pieces, such as hymns. In Dufay's fauxbourdon settings, two voices, cantus and tenor, are written out, while a third is extemporized by a singer who parallels the cantus a fourth below. Within phrases, cantus and tenor parallel each other in sixths. The result is a series of sixth-third sonorities, imperfect consonances that resolve to perfect octave-fifth consonances at cadences. Fauxbourdon may be viewed as a special way of magnifying a monophonic line, similar in intent to the parallel organum produced in the ninth century. It could be produced "at sight" in a strictly formulaic way, but Dufay's notated fauxbourdon settings display artful embellishment of melody and rhythm.

In *Christe redemptor omnium,* as in other fauxbourdon hymn settings, the plain and the polyphonic versions of the traditional tune alternate. Odd-numbered verses are sung as plainchant, even-numbered ones in fauxbourdon. Dufay paraphrases the chant in the highest voice, gracing it with added tones and shaping it to a triple meter. He especially modifies phrase endings, extending them and applying the under-third formula at the cadence. This sort of fauxbourdon setting is a near relative to the discant or votive motet in its simplicity of texture and vertical orientation (see No. 25). However, the harmonic sound is more uniform and the voices are more dependent rhythmically than in the discant motet. Fauxbourdon early became part of the normal musical syntax of the fifteenth century and was often introduced for a single phrase or a pointed cadential approach in secular as well as in sacred music.

An alternate polyphonic version of *Christe redemptor* by Dufay is not in fauxbourdon, but does paraphrase the chant melody in the superius.[1]

[1]This version may be found in *Guillelmi Dufay Opera Omnia*, vol. 5, ed. H. Besseler, *Corpus Mensurabilis Musicae* 1:5 (1966), pp. 41-42.

# 27.  GUILLAUME DUFAY
## 27a. Agnus Dei
from **Missa Se la face ay pale**    2  Track 4

[1]*Canon:* Tenor crescit in duplo.

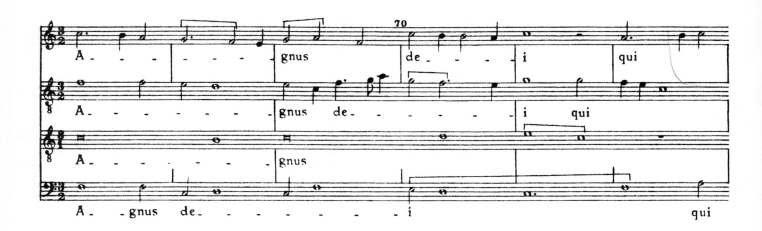

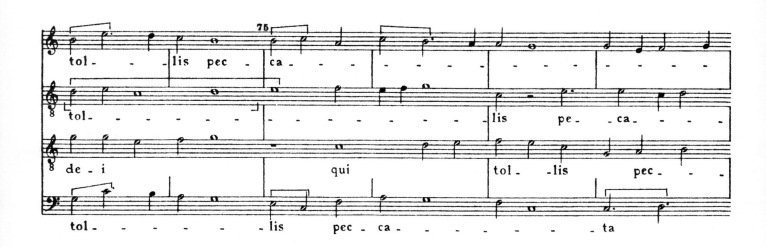

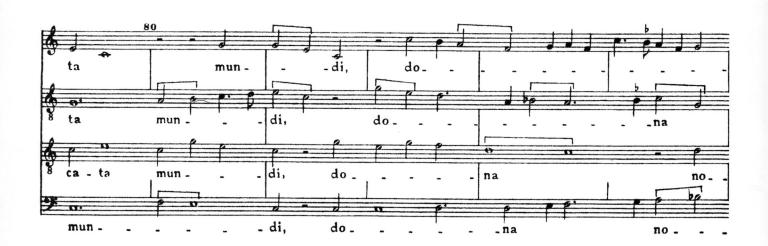

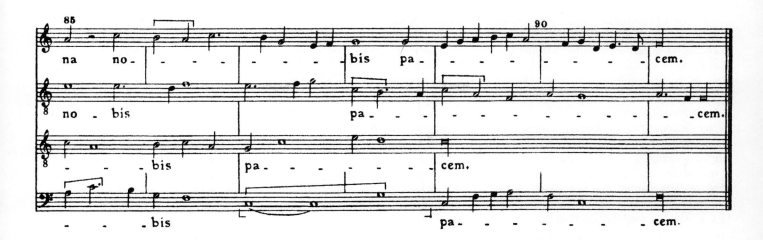

For translation of No. 27a, see No. 1k.

## 27b. **Se la face ay pale**
Tenor of three-voice song

*cyclic masses*
*composers used tunes*
*compositions*
*motto-head motive*

*If my face is pale,*
*the reason is love.*
*That is the principal reason,*
*and it is so bitter for me*
*to love that I would want*
*to throw myself into the sea.*
*Then, seeing this,*
*the fair lady to whom I belong*
*would know that I can have*
*no happiness without her.*

The fifteenth-century cyclic Mass setting germinated from pairings of Ordinary movements (see No. 24a). By the 1440s, Leonel Power and John Dunstable had produced complete, related sets of Gloria-Credo-Sanctus-Agnus Dei. (The Kyrie was late in being admitted because English Kyries were usually "troped" and hence were allied more with the Proper than with the Ordinary.) Power and Dunstable were the first composers to write cantus firmus or "tenor" masses, a specific type of cyclic Mass in which all movements incorporate the same preexistent melody, normally stated in the tenor part. The cantus firmus Mass became the dominant Mass type of the fifteenth century. The impetus behind this new genre still awaits clarification. It was probably connected both with a proliferation of competent singing groups at cathedrals and courts (secular and ecclesiastical) and with the aspirations of composers to practice their craft in substantial musical compositions. The tenor Mass did supplant the isorhythmic motet, which still dignified ceremonial occasions in the 1430s and had been the prime vehicle for display of compositional technique.

Dufay followed the English lead in writing unified Mass cycles. Of his six surviving, unquestionably authentic Mass cycles, four are tenor Masses. The *Missa Se la face ay pale* is thought to be the earliest of these and to date from mid-century.[1] In a departure from English precedent, Dufay took as his cantus firmus the tenor of his own chanson *Se la face ay pale*. Except for wholesale augmentation of durations and suppression of the text, the chanson tenor is quoted exactly in the Mass. Each Mass movement contains at least one full statement of the cantus firmus presented in the tenor.[2] The other voices are unrelated to the borrowed material apart from fleeting moments, as in the second Agnus, measure 60, where the two upper voices briefly refer to the final melisma of the song (just after *puis*). The shared tenor ensures tonal unity and creates a thematic bond among movements. Another primary element of cyclic cohension is a *head*

[1] Scholars now believe that the *Missa Caput* formerly attributed to Dufay is the work of an anonymous English composer.

[2] For a diagram of cantus firmus disposition in the whole Mass, see H. M. Brown, *Music in the Renaissance* (Englewood Cliffs, N.J.: Prentice-Hall, 1976), p. 46.

*motif* or *motto*. This is a contrapuntal fragment quoted at the beginning of each movement (except, in this instance, the Kyrie, where the motto is slightly varied). The first two measures of the Agnus Dei, for example, state the familiar motto, and then continue on in new counterpoint. Even though the Mass movements were heard at widely spaced intervals in the service (see No. 1), the identical opening motif and the recurrent tenor melody guaranteed an audible association among them.

Dufay's characteristically careful handling of texture and line is plain in this Agnus Dei. Cantus firmus disposition and textural contrasts akin to those in Dunstable's *Beata mater* shape each section. The first starts with a high duet and thickens to four parts with the entrance of the cantus firmus. The second Agnus Dei (m. 44) has no cantus firmus. It contrasts two duets of differing range and color before climaxing with an active three-voice texture. The final Agnus Dei (m. 67) continues this build-up by restoring all four voices, the tenor with the remainder of the cantus firmus. The lines are very free rhythmically. Because their rhythms change constantly, no regular meter or pulse develops. The fluid, supple quality of such counterpoint, refined to even greater surface smoothness, becomes a hallmark of sixteenth-century sacred style. Imitations occur sporadically (e.g., mm. 1-2, 27-28), but are less predictable in placement than in Dufay's chansons (see No. 30b). One imitation, in the second Agnus, surprisingly coalesces into a canon at the octave (mm. 51-55).

The lines are linked not through rhythmic coordination but through consonance and underlying harmonic matrices. Within a given phrase or section, the parts tend to outline compatible modules of fourths and fifths. In the initial duet, for example, the cantus centers on the fourth g-c′, while the contra defines the fourth and fifth around c (G-c-g). The beginning of the second Agnus has a different tonal framework centered on F. The cantus outlines the perfect intervals around f (c′-f-c). The contra matches it with an octave grounded on F (F-c-f). Perhaps surprisingly, the tenor does not dictate the tonal realm of the chant. Like the song from which it came, the tenor is solidly anchored on C. The Mass movements, however, all end on F, as do most of their internal sections (see Agnus, mm. 43, 66, 91). It is the presence of the *tenor bassus* that robs the tenor of a controlling tonal function. The emergence of a bass is a noteworthy development in Masses and motets of the later fifteenth century.

# 28. GUILLAUME DUFAY
## Ave regina caelorum [III]

Motet

See No. 7a.

Track 5

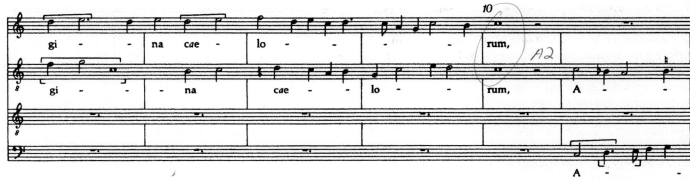

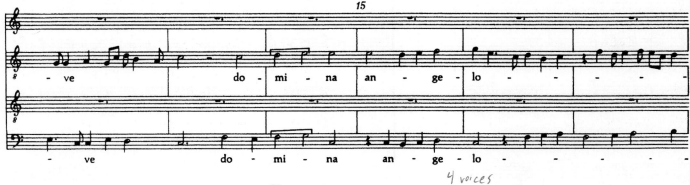

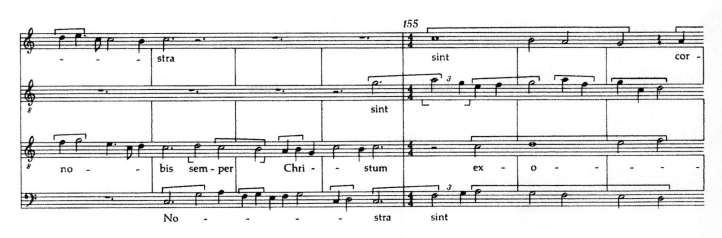

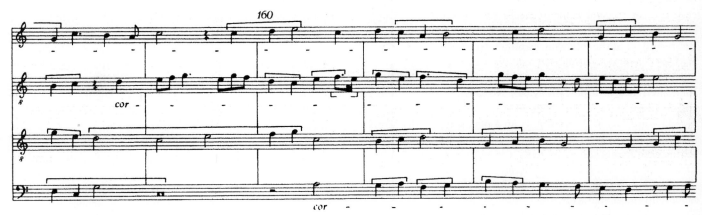

1 Ave regina caelorum
2 Ave domina angelorum
   *Miserere tui labentis Dufay* 86,21
   *Ne peccatorum ruat in ignem fervorum.*
3 Salve radix sancta
4 Ex qua mundo lux est orta
   *Miserere genetrix Domini*
   *Ut pateat porta caeli debili*
5 Gaude gloriosa
6 super omnes speciosa

*Hail Queen of heaven,*
*Hail mistress over the angels.*
**Have mercy on thy dying Dufay**
**Lest, a sinner, he be hurled down into seething**
**hot hellfire.**
*Hail holy source,*
*From which light entered the world.*
**Have mercy, Mother of God,**
**So that the gate of Heaven may be open to the weak.**
*Rejoice, glorious one,*
*Beautiful beyond measure.*

*Miserere supplicanti Dufay*
*Sitque in conspectu tuo mors eius speciosa*
*Vale valde decora*
*Et pro nobis semper Christum exora.*
*In excelsis ne damnemur miserere nobis*
*Et juva ut in mortis hora*
*nostra sint corda decora.*

**Have mercy on thy suppliant Dufay**
**And may his death be beautiful in thy sight.**
*Prosper greatly, most comely one,*
*And pray for us always to Christ.*
**Lest we be damned on high, have mercy on us,**
**And help us so that in the hour of death**
**our hearts may be serene.**

The fifteenth-century spirit of experimentation and innovation is nowhere more apparent than in the realm of the motet. Whereas fourteenth-century continental composers cultivated but one motet type, the isorhythmic, their fifteenth-century successors wrote several kinds of pieces that, in retrospect, can be classified under the heading "motet." Within Dufay's works, we can regard all of the following as motets: traditional, polytextual, isorhythmic motets (composed mainly for ceremonial occasions); fauxbourdon settings of hymns and Magnificats (in which plainsong alternates with polyphony, see No. 26); discant settings of votive prayers (with or without plainsong paraphrase, see No. 25); and sacred compositions on a plainsong cantus firmus, similar in nature to a movement of a cantus firmus Mass. The setting of liturgical and votive texts is a significant change with respect to Machaut's practice in the preceding century. From this time on within the European tradition, the motet maintains a sacred, liturgical character.

Dufay's magnificent setting of the antiphon *Ave regina caelorum* (see No. 7a) from 1464 illustrates not only the transfer of tenor Mass techniques to the motet, but also the extraordinary degree of change wrought in Dufay's style from the 1420s to the 1470s. Dufay's earlier votive motets are modest pieces for three voices,

similar in nature to Dunstable's *Beata mater* (No. 25).[1] By contrast, the late *Ave regina caelorum* is a substantial composition for four voices, conceived in several sections on a large architectural scale. The unusual and very individual text combines the antiphon poem with a newly written prayer to the Virgin from the dying Dufay, whose name appears twice in the text. (In his will of 8 July 1474, Dufay asked that this piece be sung at his deathbed.) The two are interlocked so that pairs of antiphon lines alternate with couplets of Dufay's plea for mercy. In the motet, each of the eight textual segments is treated as a musical section (see Figure 3, below). A concluding ninth segment is an elaborate melismatic expansion of the final plea for composure in the face of death. A change of mensuration midway through the piece creates a large two-part structure, the first part in triple, the second in duple, mensuration. Prominent melismas at the end of each prayer segment (except the third) pair units within the two main divisions. The whole is an imaginative hierarchical structure similar in scope to a large isorhythmic motet, but very different in spirit and conception.

[1]For two earlier settings of *Ave regina caelorum* by Dufay, see *Guillelmi Dufay Opera Omnia*, ed. H. Besseler, *Corpus Mensurabilis Musicae* I, vol. 5 (1966), pp. 120-123, 124-130. These may be compared with the L. Power setting included in this volume, No. 24b.

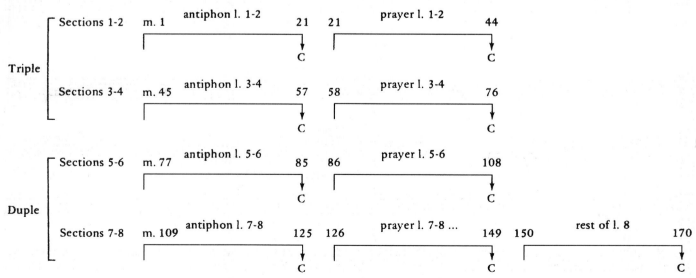

**Figure 3.** Design of Dufay's *Ave regina caelorum* [III] (No. 28).

Dufay paraphrases the antiphon melody in the motet, lengthening and ornamenting its component phrases so that they blend subtly with the newly composed music (see No. 7a). The tenor voice derives completely from the borrowed melody, which it states in its entirety. The long passages of silence in the tenor both reflect its dependence on the borrowed melody and help define sections and phrases within the polyphony. The tenor always presents at least one chant phrase while the other voices sing Dufay's prayer, but the resulting polytextuality has more of a symbolic than an overtly musical effect. When the tenor is silent, other voices (usually the highest-sounding part) sometimes paraphrase the chant. This is particularly conspicuous in the first section where superius and contratenor successively paraphrase the first two chant phrases. Chant references in the upper voices subsequently decline in frequency, but do occur consistently at the start of sections with antiphon text.

The C-centered chant melody makes its mark on the motet, every section of which cadences on C. Dufay twice underscores his own plea for mercy by a poignant modal inflection that puts a minor third over the C (mm. 21, 86). Both times the E-flat is isolated in the highest voice for maximum expressive effect. These inflections also articulate the first prayer section within each main division and preface the appearance of Dufay's own name in the text. In contrast to the more "objective" settings of the Mass Ordinary, this motet manifests a tendency toward personal expressivity that was to reach a peak in the motets of the late sixteenth century.

# 29. JOHANNES OCKEGHEM (1410/20-1497)
## Agnus Dei
### from Missa Mi-mi

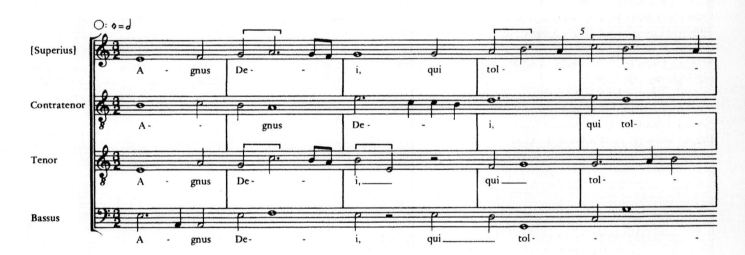

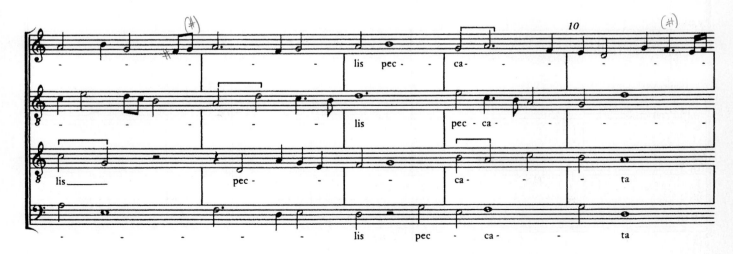

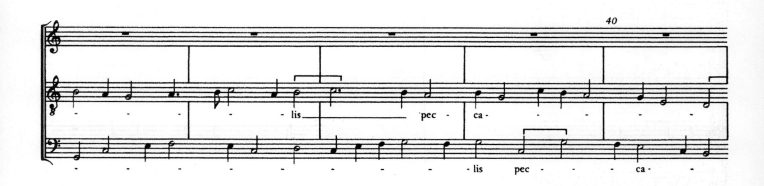

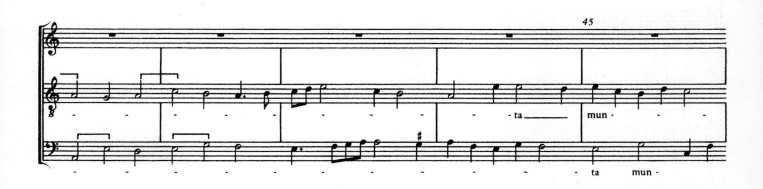

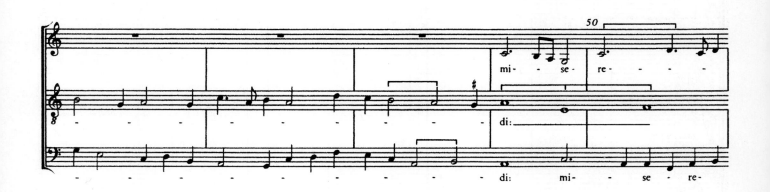

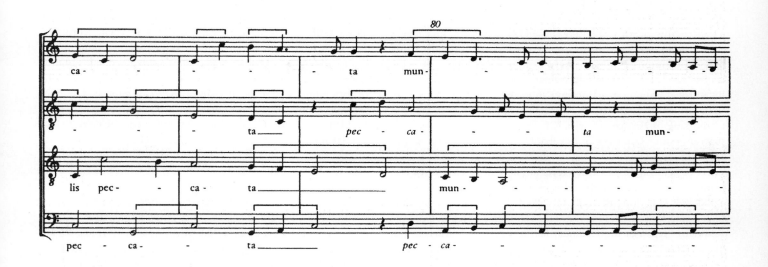

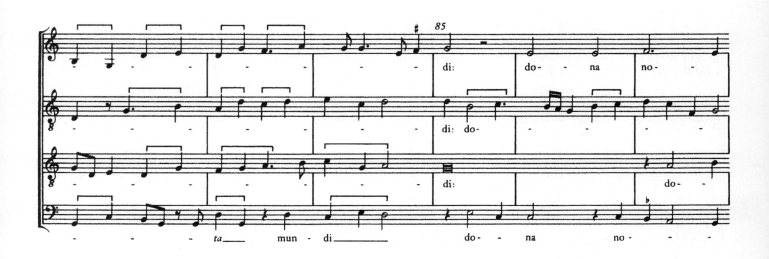

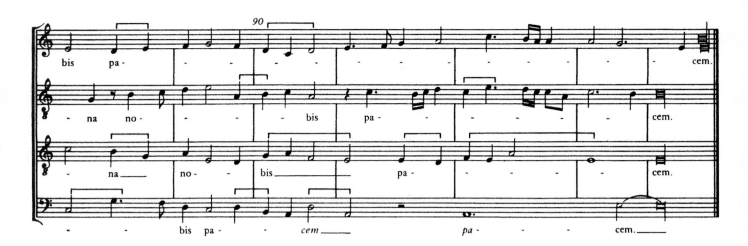

For translation of No. 29, see No. 1k.

After the death of Dufay in 1474, Johannes Ockeghem (c. 1410/20-1497) was widely recognized as the foremost living master of composition in northern Europe. Ockeghem's early life is obscure, but he was probably a native of Flanders and received his musical training in a Burgundian environment, perhaps from Gilles Binchois. In the 1450s, Ockeghem appears as first chaplain to the king of France, Charles VII. He retained that prestigious position under Louis XI and probably Charles VIII. Contemporary observers extolled Ockeghem both as a singer and as a composer of genius. He possessed a remarkable deep bass voice and favored the bass range in his Masses and motets.

Masses constitute the bulk of Ockeghem's extant works: thirteen cyclic Mass Ordinaries (not all complete) and a polyphonic Requiem. Seven of the Ordinary settings are tenor Masses, but others incorporate no borrowed material and are unified by other properties. In the *Missa Mi-mi*, the cyclic element is a bass motive of three notes, E-A-E. This motive acts as a motto at the beginning of each movement, but is not uniform in rhythm or in contrapuntal context as Dufay's mottos are. Comparison of the beginnings of the three Agnus Dei sections (mm. 1, 25, 66) shows how varied surfaces somewhat veil the motto. The E-A-E motive determines the Mass name, which derives from the bass solmization syllables: The low E is *mi* in the hexachord starting on C, the A is *mi* in that on F.

Just as the cyclic basis of Ockeghem's *Missa Mi-mi* is less obvious than that of Dufay's *Missa Se la face ay pale*, so too the musical syntax is less transparent, as comparison of the two Agnus Dei movements reveals. Ockeghem, for example, less frequently shapes a musical passage through changes in vocal scoring. A dense four-voice texture prevails in both outer sections of the *Missa Mi-mi* Agnus. The number of voices is reduced in the middle section, but range and vocal color remain more uniform than in the corresponding section of the *Missa Se la face ay pale*. The lines themselves tend not to focus consistently on complementary pairs of fourths and fifths. The result is a shifting harmonic field, elusive in tonal focus. Unlike Dufay, Ockeghem seldom adopts clearly chiseled rhythmic motives but subordinates individual rhythmic detail to a blended effect of intertwining voices. The blurring of detail extends even to phrase endings, where Ockeghem shows himself a master of avoiding cadential articulation. In the first Agnus, potential cadences are thwarted consistently by entrance of a new voice (m. 15), by an unexpected turn of sonority (mm. 10-11, 16-17), by phrase continuation (mm. 19-20). Even the final cadence of this section is metrically and harmonically unsettled.

Ockeghem's extraordinary achievement is a polyphony of the whole that works as an integrated complex of sound rather than as a combination of distinct, individual lines. No one voice predominates melodically, motivically or structurally; rather, a complex of homogeneous lines blends in one integral sound image. Historically, Ockeghem should be recognized as the first composer to abandon definitively the "heterogeneous" polyphony inherited from the fourteenth century (a polyphony of distinctly differentiated parts) and to achieve a truly "homogeneous" polyphony of equal and interdependent voices.

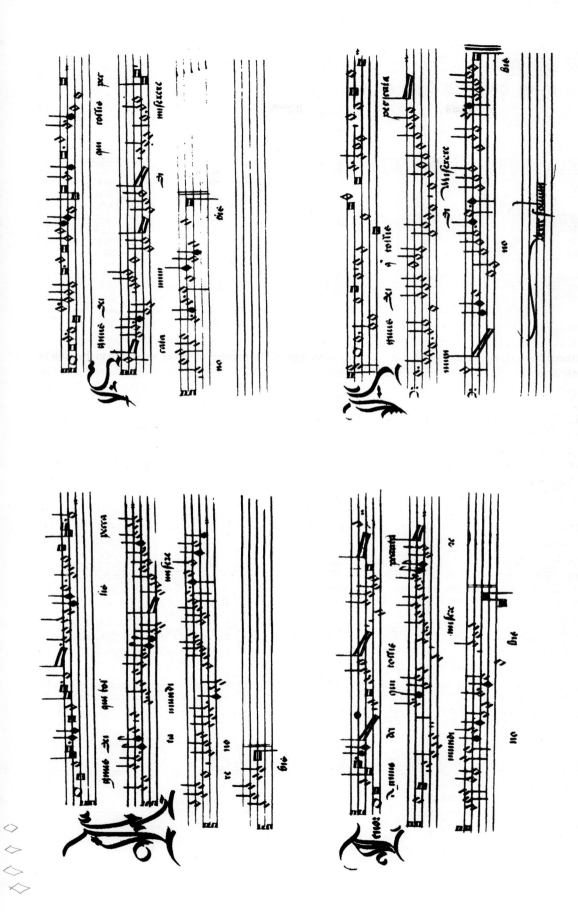

**Plate 3.** Rome, Biblioteca Apostolica Vaticana, Chigi Codex C VIII.234, ff. 13ᵛ-14. Agnus Dei from *Missa Mi-mi* (No. 29), by Johannes Ockeghem.

**30.** GUILLAUME DUFAY

**30a. Ce moys de may soyons lies et joyeux**

Rondeau

(*Refrain*)
1. Ce moys de may soyons lies et joyeux
   Et de nos cuers ostons merancolye.

2. Chantons dansons et menons chiere lye
   Por despiter ces felons envieux.

3. Plus c'onques mais chascuns soit curieux
   De bien servir sa maistresse jolye.

(*Half-Refrain*)
4. Ce moys de may soyons lies et joyeux
   Et de nos cuers ostons merancolye.

5. Car la saison semont tous amoureux
   A ce faire pourtant n'y fallons mye.

6. Carissimi! Dufay vous en prye
   Et Perinet dira de mieux en mieux.

(*Refrain*)
7. Ce moys de may soyons lies et joyeux
   Et de nos cuers ostons merancolye.

8. Chantons, dansons et menons chiere lye
   Por despiter ces felons envieux.

(*Refrain*)
1. *This month of May let us be glad and joyous*
   *and banish melancholy from our hearts.*

2. *Let's sing and dance, and make merry*
   *to spite those jealous fellows.*

3. *More than ever, let everyone strive*
   *to serve his pretty mistress well.*

(*Half-Refrain*)
4. *This month of May let us be glad and joyous*
   *and banish melancholy from our hearts.*

5. *For the season invites all lovers*
   *to do this, so do not fail in the least.*

6. *Dear ones! Dufay entreats you*
   *and Perinet will say it better and better:*

(*Refrain*)
7. *This month of May let us be glad and joyous*
   *and banish melancholy from our hearts.*

8. *Let's sing and dance, and make merry*
   *to spite those jealous fellows.*

# 30b. Adieu m'amour, adieu ma joye

Rondeau

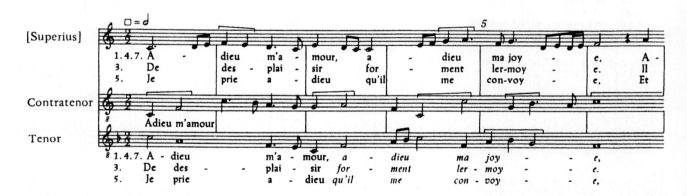

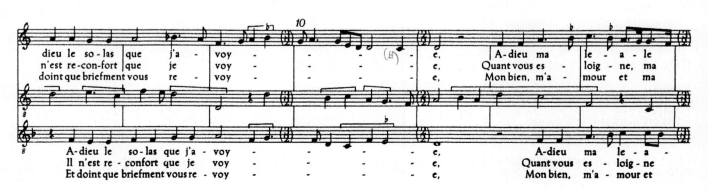

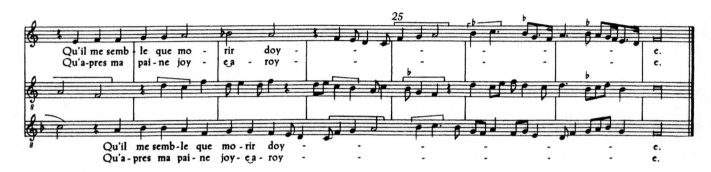

(Refrain)
1. Adieu m'amour, adieu ma joye,
   Adieu le solas que j'avoye,
   Adieu ma leale mastresse!

2. Le dire adieu tant forte me blesse
   Qu'il me semble que morir doye.

3. De desplaisir forment lermoye
   Il n'est reconfort que je voye
   Quant vous eloigne ma princesse.

(Half-Refrain)
4. Adieu m'amour, adieu ma joye,
   Adieu le solas que j'avoye,
   Adieu ma leale mastresse!

5. Je prie a Dieu qu'il me convoye
   Et doint que briefment vous revoye,
   Mon bien, m'amour et ma deesse!

6. Car l'adquis m'est de ce que laisse
   Qu'apres ma payne joye aroye.

(Refrain)
7. Adieu m'amour, adieu ma joye,
   Adieu le solas que j'avoye,
   Adieu ma leale mastresse!

8. Le dire adieu tant forte me blesse
   Qu'il me semble que morir doye.

(Refrain)
1. *Farewell my love, farewell my joy,*
   *farewell consolation that I had,*
   *farewell my loyal mistress.*

2. *To say "farewell" so deeply wounds me*
   *I feel I should die.*

3. *From chagrin I weep bitterly*
   *I see no comfort for myself*
   *when I depart from you, my princess.*

(Half-Refrain)
4. *Farewell my love, farewell my joy,*
   *farewell consolation that I had,*
   *farewell my loyal mistress.*

5. *I pray to God that he accompany me,*
   *and grant me a reunion with you soon,*
   *my good, my love, and my goddess.*

6. *For I am aware of what I am leaving*
   *and that after my pain joy will come.*

(Refrain)
7. *Farewell my love, farewell my joy,*
   *farewell consolation that I had,*
   *farewell my loyal mistress.*

8. *To say "farewell" so deeply wounds me*
   *I feel I should die.*

The fifteenth-century chanson continues fourteenth-century chanson tradition in its three-voiced texture and structural tenor-discant duet. The texts remain in fixed forms, although the rondeau replaces the ballade as the preferred poetic type. Yet in outward aspect, the fifteenth-century chanson differs conspicuously from its fourteenth-century predecessor. Rhythms are smoother, melody and counterpoint are more triadic in orientation, and text setting is more even, with melismas chiefly being relegated to the end of text lines. The three voices, too, become more homogeneous. Texting of tenor and even contratenor in some songs increases their prominence to the degree that the piece is heard not as a solo with subsidiary accompaniment, but as a true ensemble of interacting partners. Rondeau refrains become longer, expanding to four or five text verses (*rondeau quatrain, rondeau cinquain* respectively) in comparison with the two or three verses usual in fourteenth-century refrains.

**30a.** *Ce moys de May* is representative of Dufay's earlier songs in its definite metric pulse and fluctuations between what in modern terminology are $\frac{3}{4}$ and $\frac{6}{8}$ groupings. A *rondeau quatrain*, it conforms musically to the standard rondeau pattern: *ABaAabAB* (see No. 18b). As usual, the *A* section ends with an open cadence, the *B* with a closed. A moment of imitation marks the beginning of the *B* section and reinstates the initial tonal center. Precadential

melismas define phrase endings and contribute to the clear sense of shape in the song. Some have asserted such melismas to be instrumental in character, but this claim has not been confirmed by convincing evidence. In the sort of personal gesture that is a hallmark of Renaissance culture, Dufay includes his own name in the rondeau verse, and bids all to rejoice on May day.

**30b.** *Adieu m'amour,* a *rondeau cinquain,* is probably the best known and most admired of Dufay's late chansons. Imitation abounds, articulating all phrase beginnings except the first and imparting keen melodic definition to the cantus-tenor duet. The work has little sense of metric pulse. The lines unfold in irregular and unsynchronized rhythmic groupings, and seem to float suspended between cadences. Stable tonal definition is secured by emphasis on F and C as focal points in each line.[1] The combination of metric freedom with tonal clarity, the careful control of melodic contour, and the gently melancholy cast of the text combine to give a special character to this song.[2]

[1]Note that the so-called mixed signatures of this song and *Ce moys de may* relate to range and hexachord solmization and do not signify independent tonal realms.

[2]For a detailed discussion of text setting in this song see D. M. Randel, "Dufay the Reader," in *Studies in the History of Music,* vol. 1, *Music and Language* (New York: Broude Brothers, Ltd., 1983), pp. 38-78.

# 31. HAYNE VAN GHIZEGHEM  (c. 1445-before 1497)
## De tous biens plaine
Rondeau

(Refrain)

1. De tous biens plaine est ma maistresse
   Chascun luy doibt tribut d'honneur,

2. Car assouvye est en valeur
   Autant que jamais fut déesse.

3. En la voiant j'ay tel léesse
   Que c'est paradis en mon cueur.

(Half-Refrain)

4. De tous biens plaine est ma maistresse
   Chascun luy doibt tribut d'honneur.

5. Je n'ay cure d'aultre richesse
   Si non d'estre son serviteur.

6. Et pour ce qu'il n'est chois meilleur
   En mon mot porteray sans cesse:

(Refrain)

1. My mistress is full of all virtue,
   everyone must honor her,

2. for she is perfect in worth
   as much as any goddess ever was.

3. In seeing her I feel such joy
   that it is paradise in my heart.

(Half-Refrain)

4. My mistress is full of all virtue,
   everyone must honor her.

5. I am indifferent toward any other riches
   than in being her servant,

6. and because there is no higher calling
   in my words I will declare ceaselessly:

(*Refrain*)

7. De tous biens plaine est ma maistresse
   Chascun luy doibt tribut d'honneur,

8 Car assouvye est en valeur
   Autant que jamais fut déesse.

(*Refrain*)

7. *My mistress is full of all virtue,*
   *everyone must honor her,*

8. *for she is perfect in worth*
   *as much as any goddess ever was.*

Throughout the middle of the fifteenth century (c. 1419-1477), the court of Burgundy was the premier cultural center of northern Europe. The Burgundian dukes enhanced their political prestige and embellished their daily lives through patronage of music and visual arts. Because many chanson composers either came from towns in or near the Burgundian realm or were attached to the Burgundian court, the term "Burgundian chanson" has sometimes been applied wholesale to the courtly chanson tradition of the fifteenth century.

The late maturity of this tradition is admirably represented by *De tous biens plaine*, a rondeau included in most late fifteenth-century *chansonniers*. The composer, Hayne van Ghizeghem (c. 1445-before 1497), was in the service of Duke Charles the Bold of Burgundy, as was another expert songwriter of the epoch, Antoine Busnois (c. 1430-1492). Though generically similar to late Dufay chansons, *De tous biens plaine* possesses characteristics of a distinctly separate mode of composition. A dominant melody is supported by two untexted, less active parts, which possibly were intended for instruments. The contratenor lies mainly below the structural cantus-tenor duet and explores the lower register of the gamut.

The contratenor's position below the tenor produces significantly new cadence types, all of them based on the traditional major-sixth-to-octave progression between cantus and tenor. One is the "octave-leap" cadence in which the contratenor ascends to supply the fifth within the cantus-tenor octave (mm. 27-28, 46-47). Another is the "double-octave" cadence in which the contratenor falls a fifth to the octave below the tenor (mm. 59-60). A third type might be designated a "deflected" cadence, for in it the contratenor supplies a new pitch below the cantus-tenor octave, turning the phrase from the expected tonal goal (mm. 14-15, 40-41). This type occurs within the principal rondeau sections and bridges phrases so that no sharp break occurs between them. The first two types produce the $\hat{5}$-$\hat{1}$ succession in the lowest-sounding part that became established as the standard cadential bass movement in four-voiced music. Other characteristics of late Burgundian chanson style apparent in *De tous biens plaine* are a highly consonant sound quality and a pliant, continuous rhythmic flow.

An arrangement of this work made by Josquin Desprez reveals a much more animated musical sensibility.[1] Josquin preserves Hayne's cantus and tenor voices but replaces the contratenor with a lively pair of basses who chase each other in canon at the distance of a quarter note. These energetic parts even disregard the medial caesura of the rondeau, creating the impression of a single through-composed musical stanza.

[1]Printed in *Werken van Josquin Des Prés Wereldlijke Werken*, IV, ed. M. Antonowycz and W. Elders (1965), pp. 31-33.

**32.** JOSQUIN DESPREZ (c.1440-1521)

## Ave Maria gratia plena . . . virgo serena

Motet

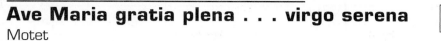

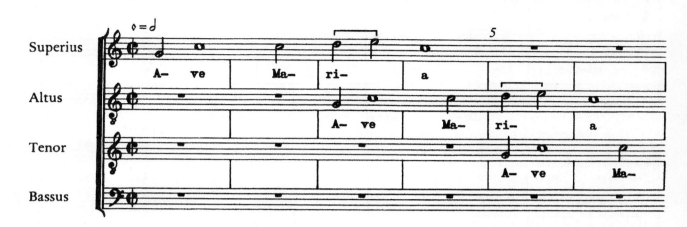

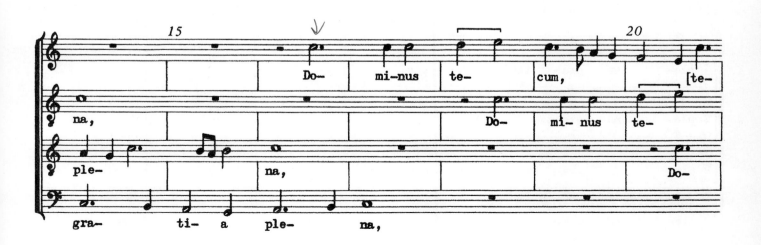

[1]For the "diatonic *musica ficta*" with which measures 43-53 might be sung appropriately, see M. Bent, "Diatonic *Ficta*," *Early Music History* IV (1984), pp. 29-34.

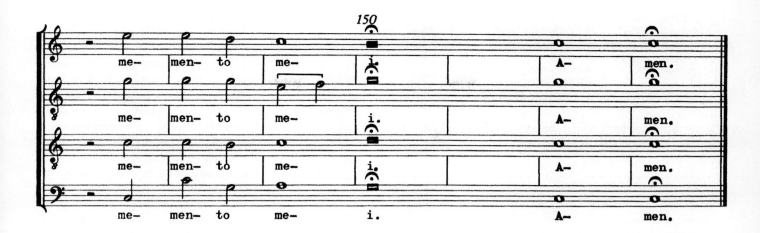

a. Ave Maria gratia plena
   Dominus tecum virgo serena

   1. Ave coelorum Domina[1]
      Maria plena gratia
      coelestia terrestria
      mundum replens laetitia.

   2. Ave cujus nativitas
      Nostra fuit solemnitas,
      Ut lucifer lux oriens
      Verum solem praeveniens.

   3. Ave pia humilitas
      Sine viro foecunditas
      Cujus annunciatio
      Nostra fuit salvatio.

   4. Ave vera virginitas
      Immaculata castitas
      Cujus purificatio
      Nostra fuit purgatio.

   5. Ave praeclara omnibus
      Angelicis virtutibus,
      Cuius fuit assumptio
      Nostra fuit glorificatio.

b. O mater dei
   Memento mei.
   Amen.

*a. Hail Mary, full of grace*
*the Lord be with you, fair virgin*

*1. Hail, Queen of the heavens*
*Mary full of grace,*
*filling the world*
*with heavenly and earthly joy.*

*2. Hail to her whose Nativity*
*was our solemn feast,*
*the morning star bringing forth light*
*preceding the true sun [i.e., Christ].*

*3. Hail holy humility,*
*fruitful without man,*
*whose annunciation*
*was our salvation.*

*4. Hail true virginity*
*undefiled chastity*
*whose purification*
*purged our sins.*

*5. Hail, admirable*
*in all angelic virtues,*
*whose assumption*
*was our glorification.*

*b. O mother of God*
*remember me.*
*Amen.*

[1]There are two different main readings of the first full verse. That printed by Glareanus and shown above is shared by five other sources, including the 1502 Petrucci print. That adopted in the modern edition, given below, appears in five other sources. It seems probable that this one, which completes the references to the cycle of Marian feasts, was substituted for the other more neutral verse.

        Ave cujus conceptio
        Solemni plena gaudio
        Caelestia terrestria
        Nova replet laetitia.

        *Hail to her whose conception*
        *full of solemn rejoicing*
        *fills heavenly and earthly beings*
        *with new joy.*

Among composers of polyphony and within the great crowd of talented people, . . . Josquin Desprez stands out for invention, attention to detail, and industry. . . . His genius was so versatile in all things, so equipped with natural acumen and mental power that there was nothing in this field [of music] he could not do.

—Heinrich Glareanus, *Dodecachordon*,
Bk. III, Ch. XXIV (1547)

Josquin is the master of the notes, which must do as he wishes. Other composers must do what the notes dictate.

—Martin Luther, reported by J. Mathesius in 1540

The dominant figure among composers in the early sixteenth century was Josquin Desprez (c. 1440-1521). Born probably in Franco-Flemish territory, he first established a career in Italy and was associated with the cathedral and the Sforza family of Milan (1459-1480s), with the papal chapel in Rome (1486-1490s) and with the Este family in Ferrara (1503-04). In the 1490s he also sojourned in France and wrote some music for the court of Louis XII. His last decades were spent as an ecclesiastical official in Condé-sur-l'Escaut, a town in the border region of present-day France and Belgium. Josquin was a master of craft and expression and is recognized for his adoption of imitation as a fundamental means of contrapuntal cohesion. He was relatively prolific, and extant sources preserve some 18 Masses, 87 motets, and 72 secular works of his composition.

Josquin's Marian motet *Ave Maria gratia plena . . . virgo serena* (written around 1497?) circulated widely in the sixteenth century. Although the opening derives textually and musically from a liturgical sequence,[1] the rest of the work is independently

conceived. The text refers successively to the five (or in one version, four) principal feasts of the Virgin and so would be appropriate to any one of them.

Musically, *Ave Maria* is a model of structural and tonal clarity, an extraordinary monument of hierarchical organization. Four prominent cadences on C divide the piece into four sections (beginning mm. 1, 54, 78, 111). Each major section is further subdivided by changes in texture and musical motive that coincide with integral text segments. The first section, for example, falls into four main subdivisions: two parallel points of imitation (mm. 1-16, 16-31), a set of paired duets (mm. 31-39), a broad chordal passage that is miraculously transmuted into a closely spaced sequential imitation before the cadence is achieved (mm. 40-54). This sort of energetic, directed, "drive to the cadence" is a hallmark of Josquin's mature style. The segmentation within sections is offset by similarities among musical motives,[2] and by cohesion about the tonal center C. Glareanus considered this to be an excellent example of his Hypoionian mode (*Dodecachordon, Book* III, Ch. XXIII).

Josquin's clever craftsmanship is perhaps most apparent in the triple-meter passage that concludes the third section (mm. 94-110). The texture at first seems chordal, but the attentive listener will perceive a closely spaced canon at the fifth between cantus and tenor. Such hidden artifices won Josquin the admiration not only of his contemporaries but of succeeding generations as well. Variety of textures, contrast between high and low duets, effortless canons, and energetic cadential approaches all contribute to the traditional image of a quintessential Josquin style.

---

[1] *Ave Maria gratia plena* printed in *The Utrecht Prosarium*, ed. N. de Goede, Monumenta Musica Neerlandica VI (1965), pp. 63-64. Only the initial textual and musical couplet is borrowed in the motet.

[2] Compare, for example, the motives on *Ave Maria; Dominus tecum; Ave cuius nativitas; verian solem; nostra fuit.*

# 33. JOSQUIN DESPREZ
## Agnus Dei II
### from Missa L'homme armé super voces musicales

| 2 | Track 8 |

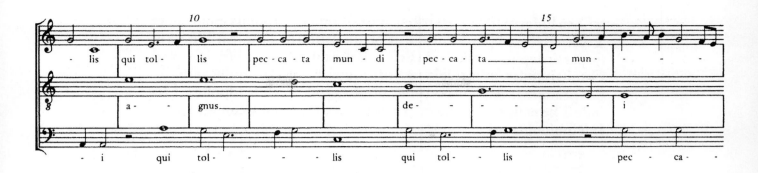

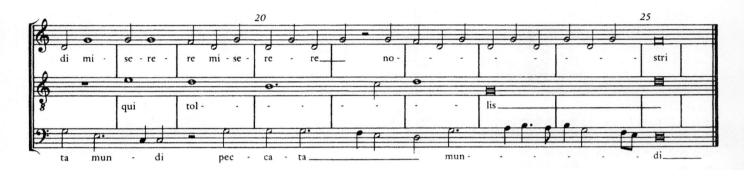

For translation of No. 33, see No. 1k.

Composers of the later fifteenth century delighted in canons. Literally, in its musical application, a canon was a special rule for realizing a notated musical part. Because the most common rule produced two lines identical in rhythm and intervals (as in No. 35a, contratenor and *quinta pars*), the term *canon* has come to signify absolutely strict imitation between two or more parts. Josquin was a master of canonic art, incorporating canons and canonic imitations in a multitude of his compositions, both sacred and secular (see No. 32, mm. 94-106; No. 34b, part II; No. 35a). The second Agnus Dei of his *Missa l'homme armé super voces musicales* (that is, upon solmization syllables) is a famous instance of his craft and exemplifies an especially challenging technical feat, the mensuration canon. Josquin wrote but one line (see Plate 4), which is to be sung simultaneously by three singers at three different pitch levels (D, a, and d), and in three different meters or mensurations: a very slow duple, a moderate duple, and a relatively animated triple (hence the name *mensuration canon*). The result is a complex, dense polyphonic fabric, rather similar in sound to Ockeghem's music. Ockeghem, whose death Josquin commemorated in a moving lament, is renowned for having written an entire Mass based on this principle, the *Missa Prolationum*.

IDem Iodocus treis uoces tribus diuerfis fignis præpofitis ex una uoce eliciendas exemplo docuit ubi ualor notularum in Tenore, fi Thema infpicias fit duplus ad notulas in Bafi.   Bafeos uero notulæ fefquialteræ ad Cantus notulas, Ita ut duplæ rationi fefquiplam mixtam intelligamus. Sed primum exemplum ponamus, ut ipfe ex eodem Miffa adpofuit. Deinde Thematis refolutionem in treis uoces cum propria cuiufque uocis fede fubiungamus.

Ex una uoce tres, ex eiufdē Io
doci Miffa Lhome arme fuper uoces muficales.

Agnus Dei qui tollis peccata mundi miserere nostri.

Sequitur refolutio.

Cantus

**Plate 4.** Agnus Dei II from *Missa L'homme armé super voces musicales* (No. 33), by Josquin Desprez. Printed in H. Glareanus, *Dodecachordon* (1547), p. 442.

## 34. JOSQUIN DESPREZ
### 34a. Kyrie

from **Missa Pange lingua**

See No. 7c.

2  Track 9

For translation of No. 34a, see No. 1c.

## 34b. **Agnus Dei**
### from **Missa Pange lingua**

For translation of No. 34b, see No. 1k.

Between 1502 and 1514, the pioneer Venetian music publisher Ottaviano Petrucci published three collections of Masses by Josquin—an honor granted no other composer. The fact that the *Missa Pange lingua* appears in none of Petrucci's volumes prompts the hypothesis that it is a late work, composed within the last seven years of Josquin's life.

Modern historians classify the *Missa Pange lingua* as a *paraphrase Mass*, a type that became increasingly prominent in the sixteenth century. Broadly speaking, a paraphrase differs from a cantus firmus approach in two primary respects: (1) the borrowed melody is not monopolized by one voice; and (2) the melody is considerably elaborated, not quoted directly.[1] The trend toward paraphrase in Masses follows directly from the adoption of imitation as a primary contrapuntal device. The borrowed melody serves more as a source of motives for imitation than as a structural scaffolding and permeates all voices equally.

Josquin's *Missa Pange lingua* is based on a hymn tune, a familiar melody sung at the feast of Corpus Christi (see No. 7c). In the Kyrie, Josquin treats the borrowed melody systematically, distributing the six chant phrases evenly: phrases 1 and 2 in Kyrie 1, 3 and 4 in the Christe, 5 and 6 in Kyrie II. Each phrase, except the sixth, is exposed in a set of imitations or imitative duets in which its opening contour and pitch qualities are pre-served. When he comes to the sixth and last chant phrase, Josquin abstracts its prominent falling third and with it launches a dramatic and energetic drive to the final cadence.

[1]No rigid line can, or should, be drawn between the two general types. Some Masses of Josquin and his contemporaries have characteristics of both cantus firmus and paraphrase treatment.

Josquin's specific techniques of elaboration sometimes create musical relationships not apparent in the given material. For instance, rhythmic and melodic similarities associate the two principal motives of Kyrie I in a direct way not expected from the chant. Similarly, the opening material of Kyrie II, based on phrase 5 of the chant, echoes the contour of the first motive of Kyrie I, producing a connection between the two sections even though the background chant phrases are quite different in nature.

Besides furnishing melodic material, the chant also sets the tonal framework of the Kyrie. The three cadences that end sections fall on the final tones of each pair of chant phrases: G, D, and E. The imitations begin either on the initial pitches of the relevant chant phrases or on cognate tones a fifth away.

The plainsong model is treated somewhat more freely in subsequent movements of the Mass, but the imitative treatment of phrase 1 at the beginning of each does unite the movements with an associative "motto" effect. Both Gloria and Credo resume the chant opening midway through, a recurrence prompted by the length of their texts. Comparison between the Kyrie and the first two Agnus Dei sections shows Josquin's versatility at remolding the given material and placing it within a fresh contrapuntal context. Agnus Dei I treats phrases 1 and 2 of the hymn in imitation. The third motive (m. 17, *"miserere"*) may echo the beginning of phrase 5, and recalls the beginning of Kyrie II melodically. Agnus Dei II is a tightly regulated canonic duet. After the opening motive, the chant recedes from the surface, but its second and third phrases may have inspired the descending-third motive of measure 48 and the rising-fourth figure of measure 65 respectively. The tight distance between voices creates an excited effect as from measure 42 on the second voice echoes the first on the very next beat.

## 35a. JOSQUIN DESPREZ
### Faulte d'argent
Chanson a 5

[1]*Faulte d'argent par nature* (that is, in the natural hexachord)

[2]*Faulte d'argent par ♭ mollis* (that is, in the soft [♭] hexachord)

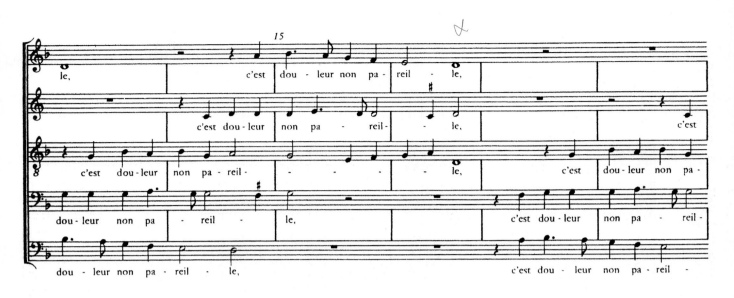

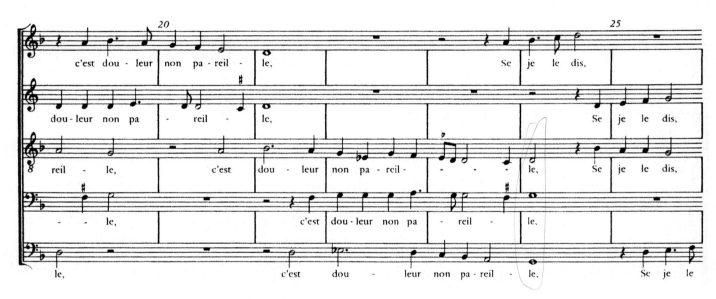

argent _____ se _____ re - sveil - - - - le. _____

sveil - - le. _____

pour _____ ar - gent _____ se _____ re - sveil - le. _____

le, _____ pour ar - gent _____ se - re - sveil - le. _____

le, _____ pour ar - gent se - re - sveil - le. _____

**35b.** ANTOINE DE FÉVIN   (c. 1470-1511/12)
## Faulte d'argent
Chanson a 3

SUPERIUS

TENOR

FAUL - TE   D'AR - GENT _____ C'EST DOU-LEUR NON|

BASS

_____ PA- -REIL-LE,   SY JE LE DIS, LAS,   JE SCAY _____ BIEN   POURQUOY

1. Faulte d'argent
   C'est douleur non pareille.
   Se je le dis,
   Las, je scay bien pourquoy
   Sans de quibus,
   Il se faut tenir quoy,
   Femme qui dort
   Pour argent se reveille.[1]

1. Lack of money
   *is painful beyond measure.*
   *If I say so*
   *alas, I only too well know why.*
   *Without "the necessary"*
   *one has to give up,*
   *a sleeping woman*
   *awakes for money.*

[1]In the Févin version, the last two lines read:
   Madame doit pour argent
   on l'esveille.

2[2]. Je suis aymé  
    D'une fille si belle  
    Je l'ayme bien  
    Aussi fait elle moy  
    Marri je suis  
    Quant point je ne la voy  
    En ce pays  
    N'en y a point d'autelle.

3. Mes compaignons  
    A tous je vous conseille  
    Ne prenez femme  
    S'elle n'a bien de quoy  
    Et la raison  
    Las, je vous diray  
    Quant elle dort  
    Pour l'argent on l'esveille.

(three stanzas of seven)

2. *I am beloved*  
    *by such a beautiful girl.*  
    *I love her well*  
    *and she loves me.*  
    *I am afflicted*  
    *when I do not see her.*  
    *In this country*  
    *there is no one like her.*

3. *My friends,*  
    *I counsel you all,*  
    *Don't take a wife*  
    *if she has no dowry*  
    *and the reason*  
    *alas, I will tell you,*  
    *when she sleeps*  
    *she'll waken for money.*

[2]Subsequent verses apply only to the Févin setting.

In the 1490s, the chanson enters on a new phase that is best observed in the mature works of Josquin Desprez. As in sacred music, a vocal ensemble of cantus, altus, tenor, and bass becomes the norm, sometimes augmented by a fifth voice (*quinta pars*). The structural cantus-tenor duet of the fifteenth century dissolves and is replaced as a principle of control by imitation, and sometimes strict canon. The fixed forms gradually evaporate. In their place are found courtly lyrics of a single stanza, which resemble isolated rondeau refrains. A new type of chanson appears, the *chanson rustique*, which imitates and often directly appropriates popular texts and tunes.

**35a.** Josquin's *Faulte d'argent* demonstrates the artistic heights attainable in a popular song setting. The unpretentious text, a complaint about money, is set in elaborate imitative polyphony. The borrowed tune appears in canon at the fifth between contratenor and quinta pars, but as these voices are the last to enter and are embedded within the middle of the texture, they do not stand out from the rest. Rather, they function as a hidden, two-voice, structural scaffolding, their rigorous contrapuntal relationship substituting for the consonant progressions of the old cantus-tenor duet. The substance of the borrowed tune is manifest to the ear in the principal motives of imitation. The multiple reiteration of short musical motives (e.g., "*c'est douleur non pareille,*" "*se je le dis*") produces extensive text repetition, another departure from the manner of the fifteenth-century courtly

chanson. The overlapping of voices is so intense that but one cadence stems the exuberant flow of notes. This occurs just before the fourth text line (m. 43), where the opening musical phrase returns. In this case, the return is built into the borrowed melody, but some pattern of musical repetition is usual in Josquin's chansons, whether they are courtly or popular in nature. Repetitions of phrases and motives replace the large-scale sectional patterns of the fixed forms. The long final cadence of *Faulte d'argent*, in which the activity gradually winds down around a held pedal, is entirely characteristic of Josquin.

**35b.** Josquin's eminently artful approach to *Faulte d'argent* stands in sharp contrast to a setting by his younger Parisian contemporary, Antoine de Févin (c. 1470-1511/12). Févin's simpler setting is for three high and relatively equal voices. The tune is stated forthrightly in the tenor, each phrase once through in order. The other voices adopt motives from the tenor but do not challenge its centrality. This modest setting is a good vehicle for the six additional stanzas that are found in chanson text collections of the early sixteenth century.[1] The textual discrepancy between the first stanzas of the Josquin and Févin settings is of the sort endemic to popular song.

[1]The additional strophes are printed in H. M. Brown, *Theatrical Chansons of the Fifteenth and Early Sixteenth Centuries* (Cambridge, Mass.: Harvard University Press, 1963), p. 69.

## 36. HEINRICH ISAAC (c. 1450-1517)
### La mi la sol
Instrumental work

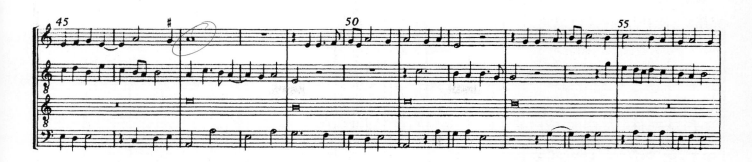

Secunda pars

Little is known about the origins of ensemble instrumental music in Europe. Medieval paintings show groups of instrumentalists, and ensembles improvised dance music in the days of Boccaccio and Chaucer, but not until the late fifteenth century did a repertory of pieces apparently conceived for instrumental ensembles appear in writing. The boundary between instrumental and vocal music in this period is avowedly imprecise, but characteristics such as short motivic cells, extensive sequence and repetition, and formulaic design are associated with an instrumental idiom. (Lack of text, another factor, cannot be taken as a determining criterion, because vocal pieces were often copied or printed without text.)

Heinrich Isaac's *La mi la sol* is a particularly ambitious ensemble work, conceived on the scale of a substantial motet. The piece dates from 1502, when Isaac was in the service of the Emperor Maximilian. It was reportedly composed in two days. In its solmization subject and schematic construction, this piece resembles such contemporary vocal works as Josquin's *Missa Hercules dux Ferrarie* and *Missa La sol fa re mi*.

The main subject is a four-note theme intoned on the hexachord syllables *la, mi, la,* and *sol* (E, B, E, and D in the hard hexachord). This subject is stated as an even-note cantus firmus in the tenor, first in prime order, then with the terminal intervals reversed (*la, sol, la, mi*). Successive statements decrease in duration from quadruple whole notes (in modern transcription), to double whole notes, to whole notes, to half notes, to quarter notes—a process that produces a built-in effect of acceleration. This rigid diminution scheme ceases midway through the second section, and the work concludes with sonorous chords built on motivic statements in the lowest voice.

Although the tenor cantus firmus constitutes the structural foundation of *La mi la sol*, the main motive also pervades the other voices. Isaac varies it in manifold ways, changing its rhythm and its position within the *tactus* or "measure," transposing it to different hexachords (especially the natural hexachord on C), stating it in isolation or extending it into a longer phrase, intensifying the rhythmic pace with closely overlapped imitations (mm. 23, 57). These protean transformations, along with varied rhythmic groupings in the three free lines, offset the stolid pace of the long-note tenor. The overall accumulation of rhythmic energy produces a stunning effect.

# 37. JUAN DEL ENCINA  (1468-1529/30)

## 37a. **Señora de hermosura**

Villancico

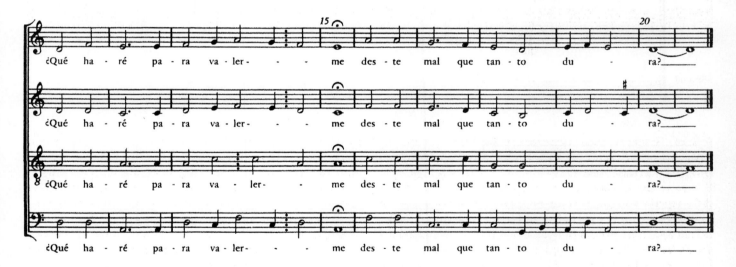

1. Señora de hermosura
   por quien yo espero perderme,
   ¿qué haré para valerme
   deste mal que tanto dura?

2. Vuestra vista me causó
   un dolor cual no pensáis,
   que, si no me remediáis,
   moriré cuitado yo.

3. Y si vuestra hermosura
   procura siempre perderme,
   no pienso poder valerme
   deste mal que tanto dura.

1. *Lady of loveliness*
   *for whom I hope to ruin me,*
   *what can I do to defend me*
   *from this suffering that lasts so long?*

2. *Your visit caused me*
   *a pain that you cannot imagine,*
   *and if you do not help me,*
   *I shall die of grief.*

3. *And if your loveliness*
   *tries always to ruin me*
   *I don't think I can defend me*
   *from this suffering that lasts so long.*

4. Yo creo que mejor fuera
   el morir cuando nací,
   que no que siempre dixera
   "Por venceros me vencí."

5. Que si vuestra hermosura
   del todo quiere perderme,
   no podré, triste, valerme
   deste mal que tanto dura.

4. *I think it were better*
   *to have died when I was born,*
   *than always to be saying*
   *"To conquer you I conquered me."*

5. *For if your loveliness*
   *wants to ruin me totally,*
   *I can't, poor me, defend me*
   *from this suffering that lasts so long.*
   —Translated by Elias Rivers

# 37b. Triste España

### Romance

2  Track 12

Triste España sin ventura,
todos te deven llorar.
Despoblada de alegría,
para nunca en ti tornar,
tormentos, penas, dolores
te vinieron a poblar.
Sembróte Dios de plazer
porque naciesse pesar;
hízote la más dichosa
para mas te lastimar.

*Sad Spain, unfortunate,*
*everyone should weep for you.*
*Uninhabited by joy,*
*that will never return to you,*
*torture, suffering, and pain*
*have come to inhabit you.*
*God sowed you with pleasure*
*for grief to be born;*
*He made you more fortunate*
*to make you grieve more.*

Tus vitorias y triunfos
ya se hovieron de pagar:
pues que tal pérdida pierdes,
dime en qué podrás ganar.
Pierdes la luz de tu gloria
y el gozo de tu gozar;
pierdes toda tu esperança,
no te queda qué esperar.
Pierdes Príncipe tan alto,
hijo de reyes sin par.
Llora, llora, pues perdiste
quien te havía de ensalçar.
En su tierna juventud
te lo quiso Dios llevar.
Llevóte todo tu bien,
dexóte su desear,
porque mueras, porque penes,
sin dar fin a tu penar.
De tan penosa tristura
no te esperes consolar.

*Your victories and triumphs*
*had to be paid for:*
*after such a loss*
*tell me how you can win.*
*You lose the light of your glory*
*and the enjoyment of your joy;*
*you lose all your hope,*
*you have nothing left to hope for.*
*You lose a Prince so lofty,*
*the son of peerless monarchs.*
*Weep, weep, for you have lost*
*him that would have raised you up.*
*In his tender youth*
*God's will took him away from you.*
*He took away all your treasure.*
*He left you only longing,*
*so that you die and suffer*
*without ending your suffering.*
*In such painful sadness*
*have no hope of consolation.*
—Translated by Elias Rivers

The early history of polyphonic secular song in Europe is dominated by the French chanson, but in the late fifteenth century diverse national polyphonic song idioms begin to surface. Italy produced the carnival song and *frottola*, Germany the three- and four-part *Tenorlied*, and Spain the *villancico* and the *romance*. These national genres are characterized not only by text in the local vernacular, but also by relatively simple musical language and a style well within the range of amateur singers.

The Spanish repertory is preserved in large collections such as the *Cancionero Musical del Palacio*, a manuscript that was copied late in the reign of Ferdinand II of Aragon (ruled 1479-1516). This *cancionero* preserves over three hundred villancicos and some forty romances. It includes many works by the poet, playwright, and musician Juan del Encina (1468-1529/30), a notable figure in the development of the polyphonic villancico.

**37a.** The villancico is a song type in which successive stanzas of poetry, sung to the same music, alternate with a recurring refrain. Some villancicos observe the format of the French virelai (*AbbaA*), but no one "fixed-form" pattern is standard. *Señora de hermosura* has a slightly unusual setting, akin to a strophic romance.[1] Its text is a thinly veiled seduction plea from an impatient lover. The music

observes the stock villancico manner: terse musical phrasing that faithfully follows the rhymed, stopped lines of text; homorhythmic texture; conjunct melodic motion (except in the bass); and simple harmonies built up in thirds, fifths, and octaves from the bass. This musical setting is, however, unusually repetitive harmonically, for Encina adheres to a conventional harmonic/melodic framework that became famous as the *folia*. From Spain, the *folia* spread to Italy, England, and France. It was still being used (especially as a basis for instrumental variations) late in the seventeenth century.[2] The bass pattern of intersecting fourths (D down to A, C up to F) gives *Señora de hermosura* a sparse, uniform harmonic quality. The harmonic uniformity is relieved somewhat by shifting rhythmic and accentual patterns, common phenomena in the villancico.

**37b.** Encina's romance *Triste España* was written for an occasion of national mourning, the death of Crown Prince Juan (4 October 1497), the only son of the great monarchs Ferdinand and Isabella of Spain. The musical setting is much like that of Encina's homophonic villancicos, except that rhythms are more sedate and modest ornamental extensions occur within phrases. As in *Señora de hermosura*, only the top voice has text in the source. The rhythmic homogeneity among the lines invites texting and vocal performance of all parts in both songs, but a solo voice accompanied by instruments is also conceivable. The musical source of *Triste España* gives only four text lines, but the rest of the poem can be sung to the same musical strophe.

[1]Alternative to a strophic solution, it would be possible to repeat the first two phrases for the first four lines of each verse and save the full strophe for the last group of lines. This can be represented as follows, where A = phrases 1 and 2 of music, B = phrases 3 and 4.

| Text: | 1-4 | 5-6 | 7-8 | 9-12 | 13-14 | 15-16 | 17-20 | 1-4 |
|-------|-----|-----|-----|------|-------|-------|-------|-----|
| Music: | AB | A | A | AB | A | A | AB | AB |

[2]For example, Corelli's Opus 5 violin sonatas (1700) include an extended set of variations on the *folia*.

# 38. Orsù orsù car'signori

Italian carnival song

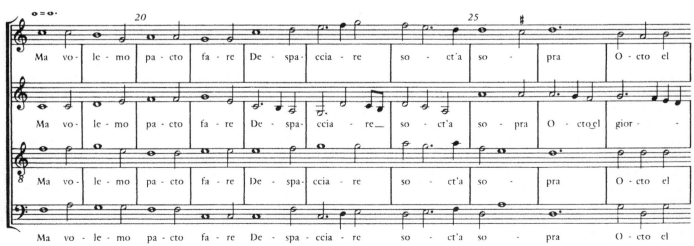

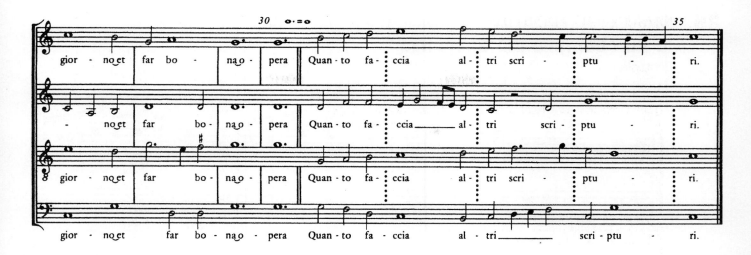

| Per Scriptores | For the Scribes |
|---|---|
| Orsù orsù car'signori | *Step up, step up, fine sirs,* |
| Chi soe bolle vol spedire | *whoever wants to send his bulls,*[1] |
| Venga ad nui che siam scripturi. | *come to us, who are scribes.* |
| Su signori se volete | *Come on, sirs, if you want* |
| Vostre bolle far spacciare | *to have your bulls dispatched* |
| Et se ad nui le manderete | *and if you will order them from us* |
| Novelle farem stentare. | *we will take the trouble to draw up new ones.* |
| Ma volemo pacto fare | *But we want to make an agreement* |
| Despacciare soct'a sopra | *to disperse all around* |
| Octo el giorno et far bona opera | *eight in a day and to do as good work* |
| Quanto faccia altri scripturi. | *as any other scribes.* |
| Ogni cosa in punto et bene | *We will keep everything precisely* |
| Et in ordine tenemo. | *as it should be and in good order.* |
| Per servire chi prima vene | *To serve whoever comes first* |
| Nostra penna in man piglemo | *we hold our pen ready in hand* |
| Nel calamaio la mectemo | *and dip it in the inkwell* |
| Et cacciamo for' l'ingiostro. | *and perhaps capture a bit of ink.* |
| Se provate el servir nostro | *If you try our services* |
| Non vorrete altri scripturi. | *you'll not want any other scribes.* |
| Orsù orsù car'signori | *Step up, step up, fine sirs,* |
| Chi soe bolle vol spedire | *whoever wants to send his bulls,* |
| Venga ad nui che siam scripturi. | *come to us who are scribes.* |

[1] A *bull* is an official papal document. The comic intent is to elevate ordinary (love) letters to the status of authoritative bulls.

During the Renaissance, the pre-Lenten carnival season and the month of May were celebrated with parades and masquerades in many major Italian cities. The *canti carnascialeschi* (carnival songs) that graced the festivities in Florence, Naples, and Venice began to be preserved in writing toward the end of the fifteenth century. Their texts often comment humorously on a guild, a social group, or a local custom. Their music is light in character, simple in style, and direct in effect.

*Orsù orsù car'signori,* an anonymous Neapolitan carnival song from about 1480, is an inflated sales pitch for the scribes (a very necessary profession in a society where reading and writing were not very common skills). Like many others of its genre, *Orsù orsù* is strophic with a refrain. Except for a slight imitative flourish in the last phrase of the refrain (m. 5), the musical is chordal in conception. The open fifths at beginnings and ends of phrases contrast with the fuller triadic sounds within phrases. The several shifts in mensuration and occasional syncopations impart an attractive lilt to the song and nicely alter the pacing of the text. Carnival songs continued to be created into the sixteenth century, but were succeeded in popularity by other light vernacular genres such as the *villanella* (1530s) and the *balletto* (1590s).

## 39. MARCHETTO CARA  (c. 1470-c. 1525)

### Io non compro più speranza

Frottola

Introductory Recercare by Franciscus Bossinensis

[1]The score reproduces the mechanical barring of the original print. Editorial notations above the staff interpret metric changes in the voice part.

²Readings from the four-part vocal version adopted here.

1. Io non compro più speranza
   Ché gli è falsa mercancia.
   A dar sol attendo via
   Quella poca che m'avanza.
   Io non compro più speranza
   Ché gli è falsa mercancia.

2. Cara un tempo la comprai,
   Hor la vendo a bon mercato.
   E consiglio ben che mai
   Non ne compri un sventurato
   Ma più presto nel suo stato
   Se ne resti con costanza.
   Io non compro più speranza
   Ché gli è falsa mercancia.

1. *I am no longer buying hope*
   *for it is false merchandise.*
   *I'm only waiting for a way to get rid*
   *of the little that I have left.*
   *I am no longer buying hope*
   *for it is false merchandise.*

2. *At one time I paid dearly for it,*
   *now I'm selling it cheaply.*
   *Good advice is that a poor wretch*
   *should never buy it*
   *but rather remain willingly in his condition*
   *with patient endurance*
   *I am no longer buying hope*
   *for it is false merchandise.*

3. El sperare è come el sogno
   Che per più riesce in nulla.
   El sperar'e proprio il bisogno
   De chi al vento si trastulla.
   El sperare sovente anulla
   Chi continua la sua danza.
   Io non compro più speranza
   Ché gli è falsa mercancia.

3. *Hope is like a dream*
   *that mainly comes to nothing.*
   *Hope is really only necessary*
   *to someone who drifts idly about in the wind.*
   *Hope often annihilates*
   *the person who keeps on with the dance she directs.*
   *I am no longer buying hope*
   *for it is false merchandise.*

In the early sixteenth century, a native Italian song tradition reasserts itself in the *frottola*. Rooted in an earlier unwritten custom of singing poetry to lute accompaniment, the frottola became a favorite mode of entertainment at the north Italian courts, particularly in Mantua and Ferrara. The Venetian music publisher Petrucci responded to the demand for frottole by publishing no less than eleven books of them between 1504 and 1514.

Generically speaking, the term *frottola* embraces musical settings of a broad range of poetic types: *strambotto, ode, canzona,* and *barzelletta* (the "true" frottola). All have in common a simple strophic musical setting with considerable repetition of phrases or phrase groups, and routine correspondence between text lines and musical phrases.

The singer-composer Marchetto (Marco) Cara (c. 1470-c. 1525) was among the leading creators of frottole. A contemporary observer characterized his manner of singing as "serene and full of plaintive sweetness" in comparison to another's "quick, vehement, and impassioned" mode of delivery.[1] Frottole might be performed as solos with instrumental accompaniment or as four-part vocal pieces. Cara's *Io non compro più speranza* appears in Petrucci's *First Book of Frottole* (1504) in a version for four voices (with full text only in the top part) as well as in a later collection (1509) of arrangements for solo voice and lute by Franciscus Bossinensis. The latter version is presented here.[2] It is a fairly straightforward transcription of the original, with the expendable alto voice omitted. The arranger contributed only some stereotyped instrumental ricercare that were doubtless strummed before the song to capture the audience's attention and to set the mode and tonal center for the singer. One of the three ricercare suggested for *Io non compro* is printed here.

Frottola poetry is not noted for literary aspirations and is often dismissed as mere *poesia per musica* (poetry for music). The text of *Io non compro*, a barzelletta in form, is an amusing diatribe against the false allurements of hope. Although a vein of bitterness colors the words, the poem does not approach the depth of personal expression attained in some later madrigal verse. The repetitive strophic setting blocks a specific musical response to the feeling of the text. The harsh sentiments of the third stanza are sung to the same music as the careless first stanza. Like most other national song idioms of the period, the music is essentially homophonic. It is, however, enlivened with rhythmic shifts in the main melodic line (indicated above the score) and with an unexpected melismatic flourish in the recurring refrain. The accompaniment acts as a harmonic support and rhythmic foil to the voice.

[1]B. Castiglione, *The Book of the Courtier*, trans. C. S. Singleton, (New York: Anchor Books, 1959), p. 60.

[2]The four-part version appears in *Ottaviano Petrucci Frottole Buch I und IV*, ed. R. Schwartz, Publikationen Älterer Musik VIII, (Leipzig: 1935; reprinted Hildesheim: 1967), p. 6.

## 40. Aus tiefer Not

Lutheran chorale

### 40a. MARTIN LUTHER (1483-1546)

## Aus tiefer Not

Chorale melody (1524)

Aus tie-fer Not schrei ich zu dir Herr Gott er-hör mein Ru-fen,
Dein gnä-dig Oh-ren kehr zu mir und mei-ner Bitt sie öf-fen,

Denn so du willst das se-hen an Wie man-che Sünd' ich hab ge-tan, Wer kann Herr vor dir blei-ben?

1. Aus tiefer Not schrei ich zu dir[1]
Herr Gott erhör mein Rufen.
Dein gnädig Ohren kehr zu mir
Und meiner Bitt sie öffen;
Denn so du willst das sehen an
Was Sünd und Unrecht ist getan,[2]
Wer kann, Herr, vor dir bleiben?

2. Bei dir gilt nichts denn Gnad und Gunst
Die Sünde zu vergeben.
Es ist doch unser Tun umsonst
Auch in dem besten Leben.
Vor dir niemand sich rühmen kann,
Des muss dich fürchten jedermann
Und deiner Gnade leben.

5. Ob bei uns ist der Sünden viel
Bei Gott ist viel mehr Gnade.
Sein Hand zu helfen hat kein Ziel
Wie gross auch sei der Schade.
Er ist allein der gute Hirt,
Der Israel erlösen wird
Aus seinen Sünden allen.

—Martin Luther

1. *Out of the depths I call upon thee*
*Lord God hear my cry.*
*Turn your gracious ear to me,*
*Open it to my prayer.*
*Then, as thou wilt, regard*
*What sin and injustice are there.*
*Who can stand before thee, Lord?*

2. *Before thee, grace and favor avail not*
*For the remission of sins.*
*For that, our deeds are worthless*
*Even in the best-led life.*
*Before thee no one can exalt himself,*
*Everyone must revere thee*
*And live in thy grace.*

5. *Although our sins are great*
*God's mercy is greater by far.*
*His helping hand observes no limit*
*No matter how great the injury.*
*He alone is the good Shepherd*
*Who will redeem Israel*
*From all its sins.*

(stanzas 1, 2, and 5 of six)

[1]The archaic spellings of Luther's version have been altered to conform with modern German.

[2]In the Erfurt edition:

Wie manche Sünd ich hab getan          How many sins I have done

## 40b. JOHANN WALTER (1496-1570)
## Aus tiefer Not
Four-part setting (1524)

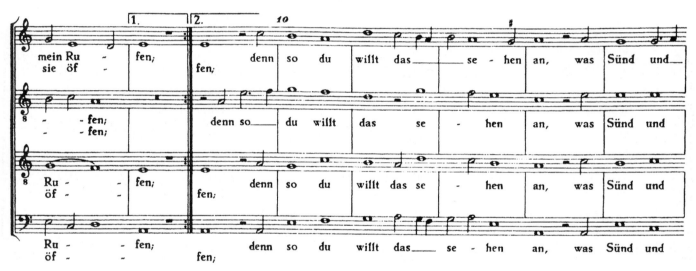

## 40c. ARNOLD VON BRUCK   (c. 1500-1554)
### Aus tiefer Not
Four-part setting (1544)

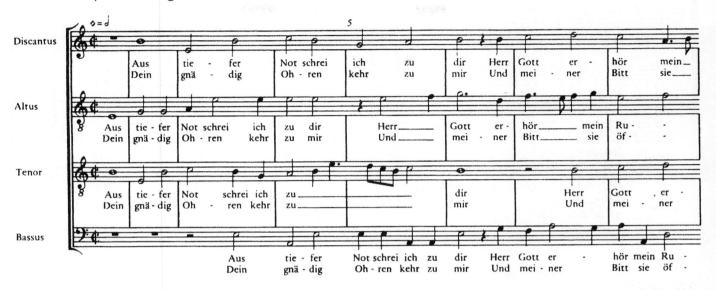

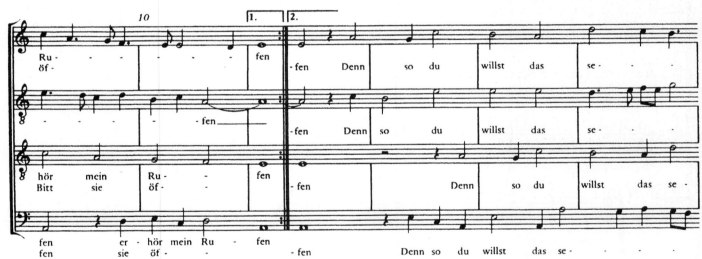

tan   Wer kann Herr vor dir blei - - - - - - ben?

Wer kann Herr vor _ dir _ blei - - - - - - ben?

tan   Wer kann Herr vor dir blei - - ben? 

Wer kann Herr vor dir blei - ben   Wer kann Herr vor _ dir blei - - - ben?

## 40d. JOHANN SEBASTIAN BACH (1685-1750)

**2  Track 14**

## Aus tiefer Not[1]

Four-part setting   (1724)

1. Aus tie - fer Noth schrei ich zu dir, Herr Gott er - höhr' mein Ru - fen! Denn so du
Dein gnä - dig Ohr'n neig' her zu mir und mei - ner Bitt sie öff - ne.

[1]In Cantata no. 38, the chorale is sung to the fifth text stanza, p. 213.

In 1517, the Roman Catholic Church was shaken by the ninety-five reform theses promulgated by Martin Luther (1483-1546), an Augustinian monk living in Wittenberg (a town in Saxony situated about halfway between Berlin and Leipzig). By 1522, Luther had been excommunicated, and his reform movement was fully launched. Luther, himself an able singer and informed musician, accorded a central place to music within the worship of the Reformation church. Spiritual songs, known now as *chorales*, served to spread the gospel and to unite the congregation in worship.[1]

From 1523 on, Luther himself took an active role in producing a corpus of spiritual songs in German. He also enlisted composers such as Johann Walter (1496-1570) in this effort. Both texts and melodies of the early chorales were frequently based on prior models. Texts were drawn from the Bible (especially the psalms), from the Roman liturgy, and from earlier vernacular sacred song. Melodies were adapted from plainsong, from earlier German sacred song, and from secular art and popular song. Even the newly composed melodies tended to imitate familiar melodic types.

In keeping with an ideal of practical use and memorability, the chorales favor rhymed, regular poetic texts, syllabic text setting, and repetitive strophic form. They were early (1524) published both as monophonic tunes and in four-part polyphonic settings. *Aus tiefer Not*, one of Luther's earliest chorales, is textually a rhymed adaptation of Psalm 130. The melody has no direct antecedent, but its *aab* structure (*Stollen-Abgesang*) follows a common *Meistersinger* pattern. The first three versions presented here typify the various guises in which Lutheran chorales first circulated. No. 40a, the earliest published appearance, is a monophonic version from the Erfurt *Enchiridion* ("Handbook") of 1524. No bar lines are drawn, but the time signature, the fairly even rhythmic values, and the text accent define a prevailing

duple measure. Syncopation in phrase 3 breaks the steady pace of the eight-syllable lines. The Phrygian mode of the melody underscores the plaintive quality of the text. The striking descending fifth at the beginning was probably inspired by the text ("from *deep* need"), but similar gestures occur in other songs of the period.

Version 40b is a chordal four-part setting from Johann Walter's *Geystliches gesangk Buchleyn* of 1524. Luther's tune, quoted exactly, appears in the tenor. Such placement of the main tune is typical of the contemporary German *Lied* and of course has antecedents in the cantus firmus practice of the fifteenth century. The other three voices surround the tenor with harmonic support and subtle rhythmic counterpoint. The bass, whose range lies a fifth below the tenor's, pulls the chorale harmonically toward A, but the first and final chords are on E, the final of the given tune.

Version 40c, by Arnold von Bruck (c. 1500-1554), is a more contrapuntal polyphonic setting, rather like a compact imitative motet. It dates from 1544. Tenor and soprano present the chorale tune in quite strict imitation, but neither states the original exactly. Phrase endings in particular are extended in one voice or the other (tenor, mm. 4-6; soprano, mm. 8-11). Alto and bass participate sporadically in the imitation (mm. 3-4, 11-12, 21). The bass often outlines harmonic movement by fourths and fifths and, as in Walter's setting, pulls the tonal center toward A.

The fourth version of *Aus tiefer Not* (40d), a setting by Johann Sebastian Bach from his Cantata no. 38 (1724), illustrates how four-part chorale settings had changed two hundred years after Luther's time. The melody is now in the topmost voice, and the texture is homophonic. Rhythms have been regularized. Now every phrase begins like the first with a prolonged opening note, and the syncopation of the third phrase has been suppressed. Despite the modal nature of the melody, Bach sets it with functionally tonal harmony. An A minor tonality is projected from the beginning with the resolution of the expressive initial dominant-seventh chord (in third inversion!). The final E major chord sounds in context like a dominant—it perhaps symbolizes the unresolved anguish in the text.

[1] See Luther's preface to the Wittenberg *Gesangbuch* edition of 1537, translated in O. Strunk, *Source Readings in Music History* (New York: Norton, 1950), pp. 341-342, and in paperback edition, *Source Readings in Music History: The Renaissance* (1965), pp. 151-152.

## 41. NICHOLAS GOMBERT (c. 1495-c. 1560)

### Ave regina caelorum

Motet

See No. 7a.

For translation of No. 41, see No. 7a.

One of the most prominent composers in the post-Josquin generation was Nicholas Gombert (c. 1495-1560), a Flemish singer who may have been a pupil of Josquin and who served in the chapel of the illustrious Holy Roman Emperor Charles V. Gombert may be said to have fused Josquin's imitative technique with Ockeghem's aesthetic of sustained continuity, forging a coherent, smooth texture that established itself, with some refinements, as the "international sacred style" of the sixteenth century.

In keeping with contemporary devotional practices, a large number of Gombert's motets are Marian in nature. His five-voice *Ave regina caelorum* (published 1541) adopts the text and paraphrases the melody of the traditional Marian antiphon (see No. 7a). Successive phrases of the chant provide motives for imitation, but once entries are made the lines depart freely from the chant model. The principle of pervasive imitation prevails, and nearly every text line is divided into two separate imitative points. Because cadences are constantly bridged by the start of a new series of imitations (e.g., m. 21, m. 46), the motet unfolds in a single uninterrupted trajectory from beginning to end. In comparison with Josquin's *Ave Maria . . . virgo serena* (No. 32), Gombert's *Ave regina caelorum* evidences a greater amount of text repetition and relatively little contrast between textures and registers. Junctions between sections are more blurred, and linear momentum is more constantly sustained. These characteristics—especially the renunciation of contrasts in favor of a homogeneous linear flow—typify the direction of sacred music for Roman Catholic worship in the second quarter of the sixteenth century.

## 42. GIOVANNI PIERLUIGI DA PALESTRINA (1525/6-1594)

### 42a. Veni sponsa Christi

Motet

2  Track 16

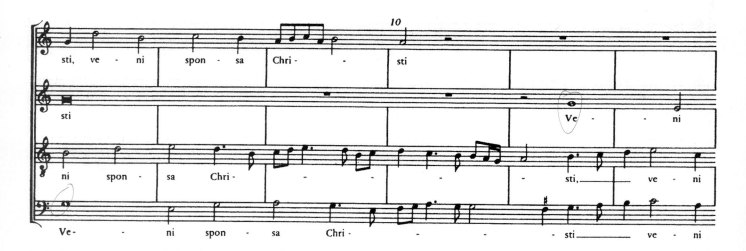

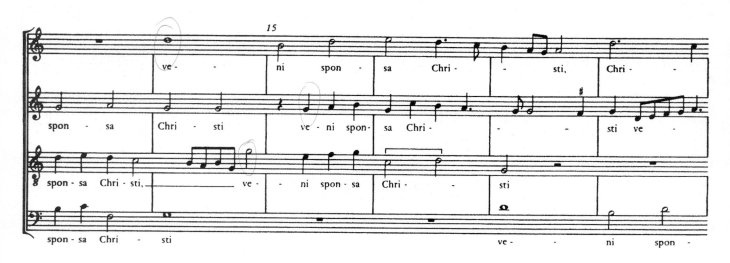

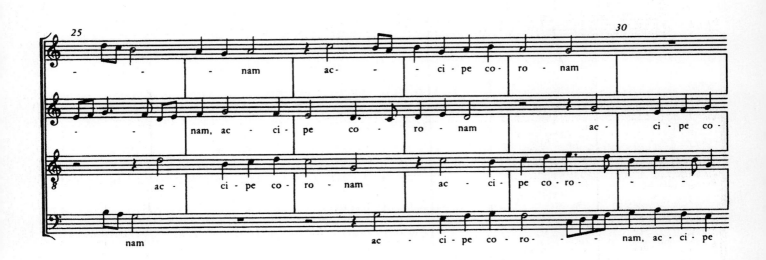

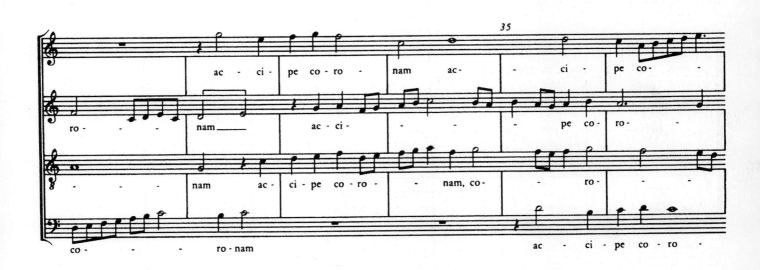

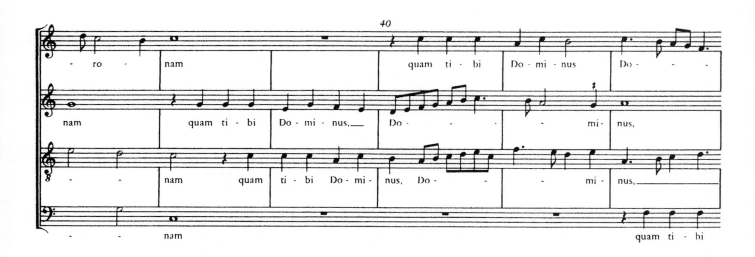

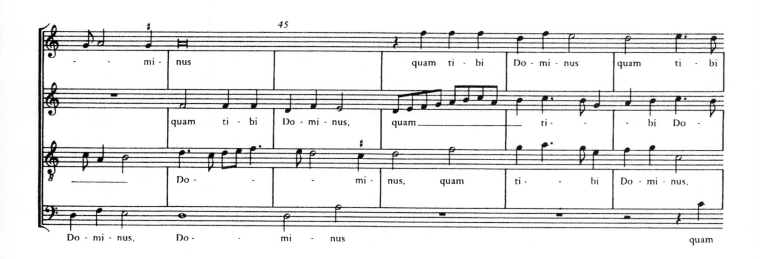

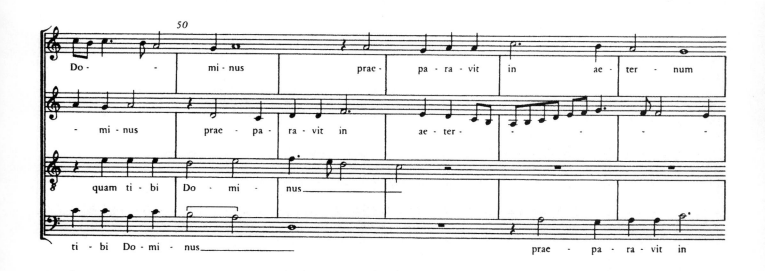

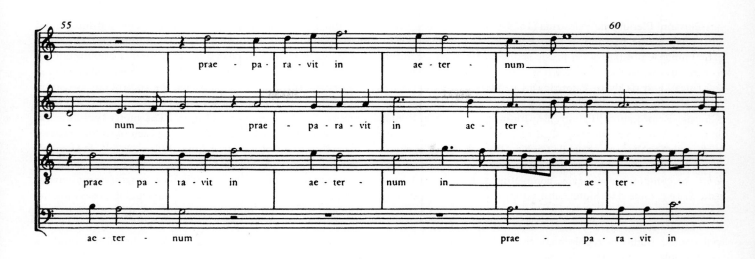

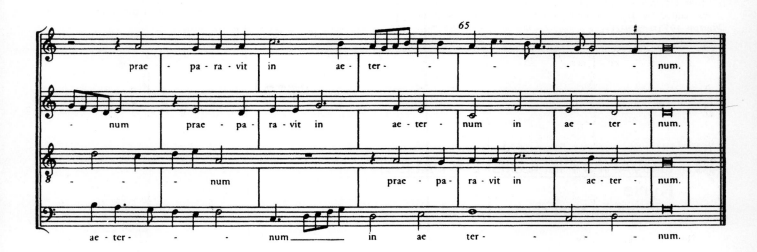

Veni sponsa Christi
accipe coronam
quam tibi Dominus
preparavit in aeternum.

*canonic mass – cantus*
*firmus*

*parody Mass*

*Come bride of Christ,*
*accept the crown*
*that the Lord prepared*
*for thee eternally.*

## 42b. Veni sponsa Christi
### Antiphon

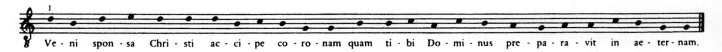

Ve - ni spon - sa Chri - sti ac - ci - pe co - ro - nam quam ti - bi Do - mi - nus pre - pa - ra - vit in ae - ter - nam.

[1]This is the standardized version from the *Antiphonale Monasticum* (Paris, Tournai, Rome: 1934). p. 682. In the tune Palestrina knew, the third phrase (*quam tibi*) evidently began with three repeated C's.

Giovanni Pierluigi da Palestrina (1525-6-1594) has long been enshrined as the paragon of high Renaissance polyphonic art. The immense prestige of his music is due partly to its technical control and stylistic consistency (easily translated into pedagogical rules), and partly to Palestrina's legendary association with musical reforms in the Roman Catholic Church during the Counter-Reformation.[1] Palestrina spent most of his life in Rome and served in several distinguished religious institutions of that city, including the papal Capella Giulia. Although duties as choir master and singing teacher must have preempted much of his time, he composed prolifically, completing at least 104 Masses and writing some 450 motets and settings of liturgical texts for service use.

The "Palestrina style" is a refinement of the Franco-Flemish polyphonic tradition represented by such earlier composers as Nicholas Gombert (see No. 41) and Adrian Willaert

[1] For documents concerning the reforms, see *Palestrina Pope Marcellus Mass,* edited by L. Lockwood, Norton Critical Scores (New York: Norton, 1975), pp. 6-27.

(c. 1490-1562). Palestrina's balanced contrapuntal lines, fluid phrase connections, graduated rhythmic motion, and controlled dissonance placement project a finely calibrated equilibrium derived from the sixteenth-century aesthetic of Gregorian plainsong.

Concrete integration of plainsong and polyphony occurs in many Palestrina works, as in his motet on *Veni sponsa Christi,* an antiphon for the Common of Virgins. The motet (published in 1563) paraphrases the antiphon, treating each of its four phrases in turn as a point of imitation (mm. 1, 19, 38, 50). Palestrina's general procedure is to start each phrase with a direct chant reference and to continue it freely with quicker rhythmic movement. A single cadence (m. 38) bisects the motet, and imposes on it the bipartite verbal and musical structure of the antiphon (two clauses set in two main phrases). The cadential closures of the two lesser phrases are covered by fresh imitative entrances (mm. 19-20, 50-51). The tonal character of the mode 7 antiphon is preserved in the choice of G final and in the pitches on which imitative entries occur. However, the motet's chief medial cadence falls on C, the controlling pitch of the following imitation, rather than on G as in the antiphon.

# 43. GIOVANNI PIERLUIGI DA PALESTRINA
## Kyrie
from **Missa Veni sponsa Christi**

2  Track 17

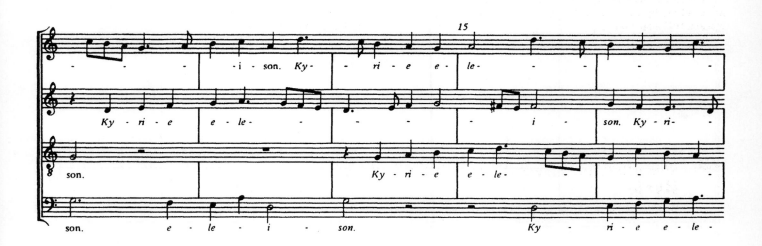

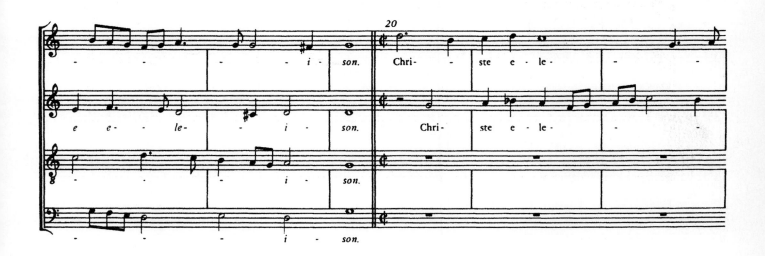

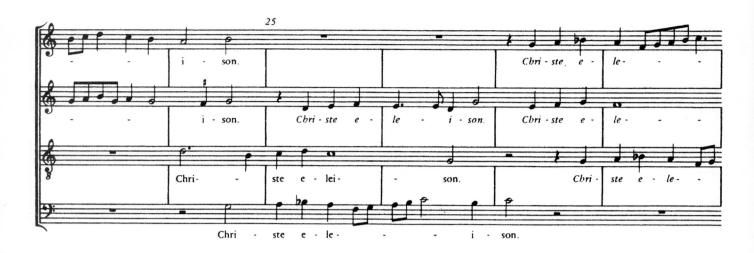

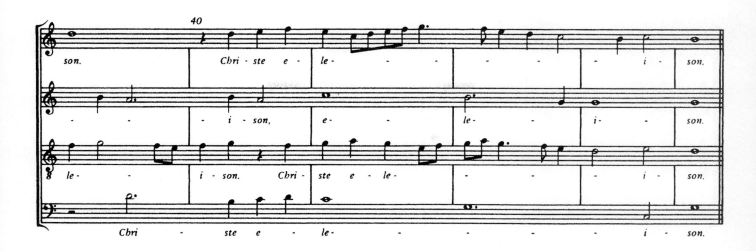

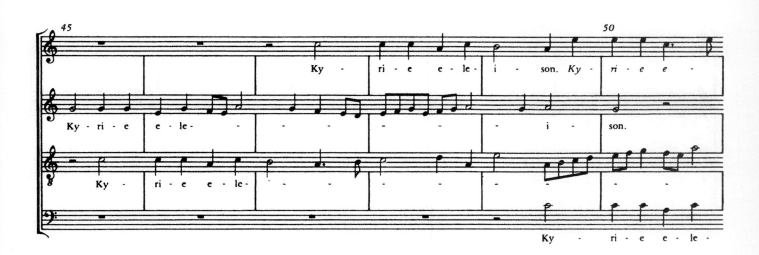

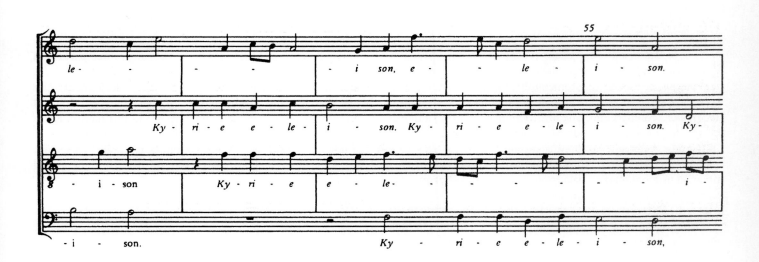

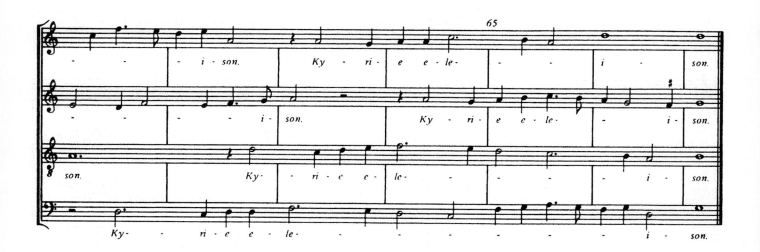

For translation of No. 43, see No. 1c.

Half of Palestrina's Masses are of a type called the *parody,* or, more properly, *imitation Mass.* Such Masses are based on preexistent *polyphonic* models (predominantly motets, sometimes chansons or madrigals) and incorporate substantial cross-sections of the model's counterpoint. The *Missa Veni sponsa Christi,* although always described as a parody Mass, actually combines elements of parody (reference to preexistent polyphony, in this case, Palestrina's own motet, No. 42a) and paraphrase (reference to a preexistent monophonic melody, in this case, the Gregorian antiphon, No. 42b). As is usually the case in a parody/imitation Mass, the Kyrie relates quite closely to the polyphonic model, although it is by no means a straightforward *contrafactum.* The main changes may be traced to the exigencies of framing a motet model composed in two main sections to the obligatory three-part Kyrie scheme. Kyrie I quotes the motet's first point of imitation (to about m. 11) and then departs upon a neutral scale figure. The Christe adopts the second motive of the motet (m. 20) but concentrates on its own new counterpoint to this motive. Kyrie II, which adheres most closely to the model, quotes the opening of the motet's second section and continues to parallel its second part. Later movements depart even further from the motet model.[1]

[1]The entire Mass is printed in *Il Libro nono delle messe (1599),* ed. L. Bianchi, *Le Opere Complete di Giovanni Pierluigi da Palestrina,* vol. 25 (1958), pp. 30-53.

**44.** ORLANDE DE LASSUS  (1532-1594)  

2  Track 18

**Tristis est anima mea**

Motet

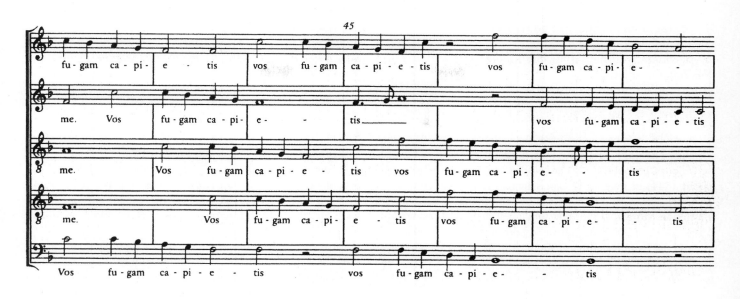

| | |
|---|---|
| Tristis est anima mea usque ad mortem. | *My soul is deathly sorrowful.* |
| Sustinete hic et vigilate mecum. | *Support me here, and watch with me.* |
| Nunc videbitis turbam quae circumdabit me. | *Soon you will see a crowd, which will surround me.* |
| Vos fugam capietis, | *You will take flight,* |
| et ego vadam immolari pro vobis. | *and I will go to be sacrificed for you.* |

A more international figure than the Roman Palestrina, Orlande (Roland) de Lassus was born in the Franco-Flemish province of Hainaut (1532) and spent his formative years (from about 1544) in Italy. After experiencing the musical cultures of Mantua, Naples, and Rome, he joined the chapel of the Duke of Bavaria in Munich (1556) and remained there until his death in 1594. As a composer, he cultivated both sacred and secular genres and made important contributions in Mass, motet, chanson, madrigal and *Lied*.

In his own day, Lassus was especially renowned for his subtle and vivid musical rhetoric. In a famous appreciation of Lassus's *Penetential Psalms*, a Munich colleague praised the composer's power of "expressing the force of the individual affections" and "placing the object almost alive before the eyes."[1] Lassus's keen sense of text and its appropriate musical expression results in more surface differentiation and contrast than is usual in Palestrina's sacred polyphony, and rather blurs the boundary between sacred and secular styles observed by many of his contemporaries.

The text of the motet *Tristis est anima mea* dramatizes one of the most poignant episodes in the New Testament, Christ's vigil with the apostles in the garden of Gethsemane before his arrest and condemnation.[2] The musical setting of the words resembles a dramatic reading, with each text segment specially colored in presentation. Some of the musical rhetoric might be categorized as word painting (see page 265): the broad, sustained idea for "*sustinete hic*"; a pronounced point of imitation, or *fuga* in sixteenth-century parlance, for "*vos fugam capietis.*" Some of the musical rhetoric is more generally expressive or symbolic in nature: the isolated, high first entry of the cantus (m. 5) paralleling the isolation of the speaker from his friends; the open fifth on "*mortem*" (m. 14) symbolizing the emptiness of death; the unusual turn of cadence (mm. 2728) projecting a mental shift as the speaker realizes the uselessness of his plea for support and turns suddenly to foretell the approaching betrayal; the emphatic repetitions of "I shall go to be sacrificed" (with the pointed "for you" withheld until the very end). The several sections of the motet are held together both by the integrity and dramatic unity of the text and by a strong tonal focus on F and its cognate C.

[1]Translated and quoted by A. Dunning, "Musica reservata," in *The New Grove Dictionary of Music and Musicians,* vol. 12 (1980), p. 825.

[2]The Gospel according to Saint Luke, Chapter 22. The motet text is liturgical, a respond from Matins of Holy Thursday, but its plainchant is not involved in Lassus's setting.

# 45.   ORLANDE DE LASSUS
## In teneris annis
## Sibylla Cimmeria
### Section IV of **Prophetiae Sibyllarum**

2  Track 19

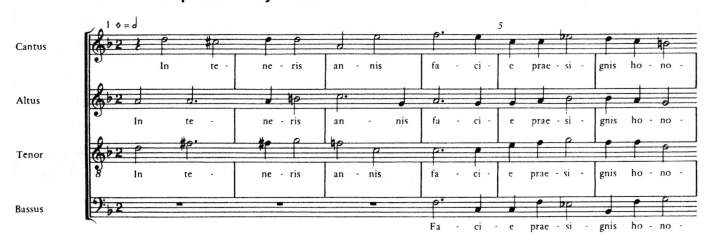

[1]Ordinary bars between staves correspond with the *tactus,* or measure of time, here groups of two or three (m. 12-17) half notes. Broken bars show rhythmic groupings that cut across the *tactus.* In these passages, short strokes ( | ) above the top staff indicate the location of the *tactus.*

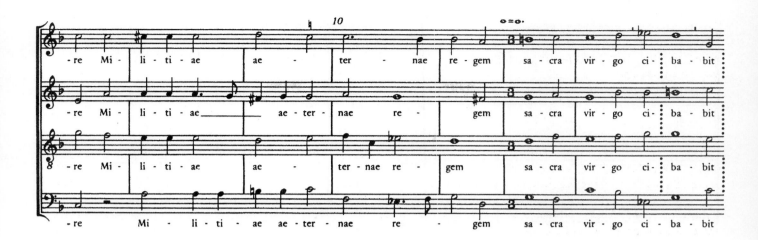

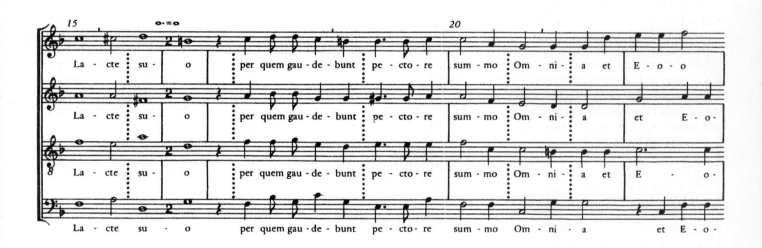

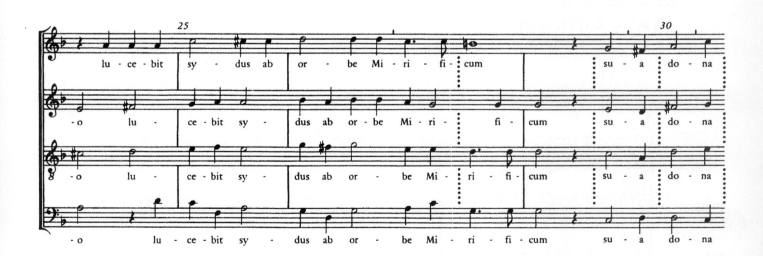

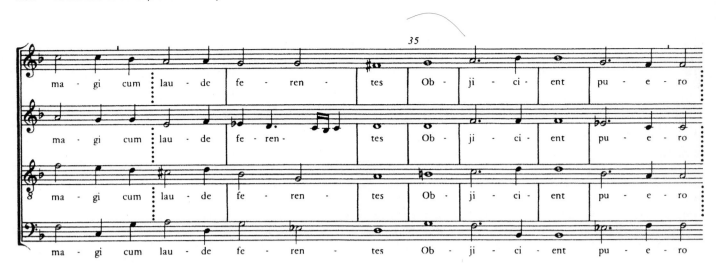

*Sibylla Cimmeria*

In teneris annis facie praesignis honore

Militiae aeternae regem sacra virgo cibabit

Lacte suo; per quem gaudebunt pectore summo
Omnia, et Eoo lucebit sydus ab orbe

Mirificum: sua dona Magi cum laude ferentes,
Obiicient puero myrrham, aurum, thura Sabaea.[1]

**The Thracian Sibyl**

*In tender years, the holy virgin, distinguished with*
*    beautiful*
*countenance, will feed the king of the eternal*
*    heavenly host*
*with her milk. Through him, all things will rejoice*
*wholeheartedly and a wonderful star shall shine forth*
*    from the land*
*of the dawn. Wise men, bearing their gifts with praise,*
*shall bring to the boy myrrh, gold, and Arabian incense.*

[1]Text from P. Bergquist, "The Poems of Orlando di Lasso's *Prophetiae Sibyllarum* and Their Sources," *Journal of the American Musicological Society* XXXII (1979), p. 532.

Lassus's *Prophetiae Sibyllarum* ("Prophecies of the Sibyls"), although atypical of his work as a whole, belongs within a significant experimental current in sixteenth-century music. This current, which involved chromatic inflection and unusual harmonic progressions, arose from two sources: one Franco-Flemish, in which far-reaching chains of hexachords led to distant tonal realms; the other Italian, in which humanistic studies of Greek musical theory led to revivals of Greek chromatic and enharmonic genera.[1]

The *Prophetiae Sibyllarum* is a cycle of twelve motets with prologue, all set in chromatic style. The Latin texts, translated from the Greek, are prophecies of the legendary Sibyls who, in popular Christian tradition, were credited with foretelling the Christ. Lassus's prologue announces the settings as "chromatic songs which you hear in a modulated manner in which the secrets of our salvation were sung long ago by the twelve Sibyls." The exotic texts inspire the unusual harmonic world of the music, which, in

turn, was doubtless intended to evoke a strange and antique song. This cycle was probably composed around 1558 and may have constituted part of the Duke of Bavaria's *musica reservata*, exceptional music reserved for an inner circle of connoisseurs.

The fourth motet in the cycle, the prophecy of the Thracian Sibyl, *In teneris annis,* achieves its strange sound quality through linear chromatic movement and a mix of third-related and fifth-related progressions. The climax of harmonic tension is carefully situated just before the end. As the extraordinary gifts of the Magi are enumerated, a dizzying series of chromatically inflected chords unfolds:

$$\begin{array}{cccccc} \text{3rd} & \text{3rd} & \text{4th} & \text{3rd} & \text{2nd} & \text{3rd} \\ \text{F} - \text{D} - \text{B} - \text{E} - \text{g\#} - \text{a} - \text{F} \end{array}$$

Despite the constant harmonic flux within phrases, the piece has some sense of primary tonal focus, for cadential points at major phrase endings are restricted to the final and its two flanking fifths (C-G-D). Even though *In teneris annis* is chordal in nature, a wonderful rhythmic vitality is achieved from shifts in synchronization among voices and from fluctuations in rate of declamation and in duple and triple groupings.

---

[1] Names associated with the former are Jacob Clemens "non Papa" and Hubert Waelrant; with the latter, Cipriano de Rore and Nicola Vicentino.

# 46a. WILLIAM BYRD (1543-1623)
## Miserere mihi, Domine
Motet from **Cantiones Sacrae** (1575)

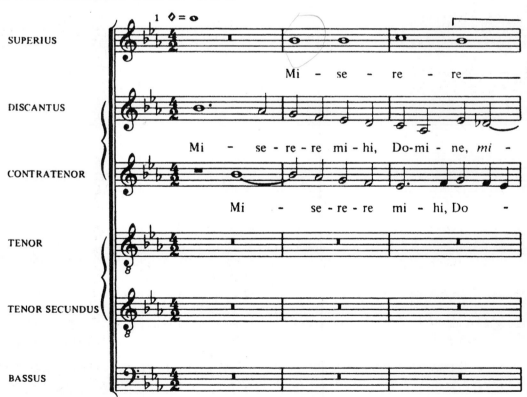

---

[1] Byrd's original notation has been moved a minor third higher to indicate the approximate pitch, by present-day standards, at which this motet would have been performed. The original has no key signature in any voice and ends on a G major triad.

2'CANON quator partes in duabus, cum duabus alijs ad placitum.'

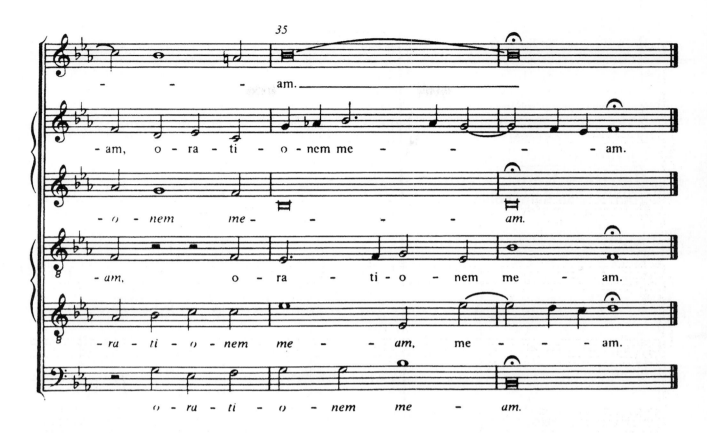

## 46b. **Miserere mihi, Domine**
Antiphon
Melody of Sarum (Salisbury, England) tradition

*Have mercy on me, O Lord, and hear my prayer with favor.*

In 1575, the seventeenth year of the reign of Queen Elizabeth I, William Byrd (1543-1623) and Thomas Tallis (c. 1505-1585) dedicated to the queen their first published collection of motets, the *Cantiones Sacrae*. Both were at that time members of the queen's musical establishment, the Chapel Royal, and each contributed seventeen motets to the collection, in homage to the extended span of her reign. Byrd's motets exhibit the combined mastery of contrapuntal art and expressive intensity that were to establish his fame in subsequent generations. Both qualities are apparent in *Miserere mihi,* a highly skillful essay in cantus firmus and canonic technique and a directly affective reading of the text.

Byrd's source material is a brief Compline antiphon of two phrases, a humble prayer for God's mercy and attention. The plainsong melody is little more than an elaborated recitation around the tone G. The only striking event is a leap of a minor third to C on "*hear* me." Byrd expands this material to a motet of substantial dimensions, first treating the melody as a cantus firmus (mm. 1-20), then paraphrasing it within a double canon (mm. 20-36). Although the bass has the principal cantus firmus statement, both superius and first tenor partially state the plainsong in extended note values. The relatively immobile cantus firmus stands in effective contrast to the mobile contrapuntal figures—strong descending scale motives at first, ascending disjunct figures for the second phrase of text. The motive on "*et exaudi*" (mm. 11 ff.) stresses the expressive minor third from the plainsong. This third is also brought to the fore in the canonic section both in the discantus-superius canon, which directly paraphrases the plainsong, and in the second tenor-bass canon, which is newly conceived.

Byrd's contrapuntal fabric, like Palestrina's, is nearly seamless. Only one internal cadence breaks the rhythmic momentum, and that but slightly. It occurs just at the juncture between cantus firmus and canonic sections (m. 21), but is bridged by continuing motion in four of the six voices. The final cadence is deliberately masked (m. 35), which gives a subdued and tentative tone to the end of the prayer. Sensitivity to register and sound quality is apparent throughout the motet, particularly in the unison opening, with the three top voices gradually expanding out from the tonal center, and in the superius entrance of measure 14, its extraordinarily deliberate, elongated motivic statement ("and hear") conspicuous above the other voices.

## 47. GIOVANNI GABRIELI  (1553/6-1612)
### Canzona Septimi Toni a 8
from **Sacrae Symphoniae** (1597)

2  Track 20

The earliest instrumental works called *canzone*, which appeared in the 1520s, were arrangements of French chansons. Not until the last quarter of the sixteenth century did freely composed ensemble and solo canzonas, independent of vocal models, become commonplace. Although conceived specifically for instruments, the late sixteenth-century ensemble canzona still retained traces of its vocal heritage, notably in its sectionalization and in the familiar chanson rhythm (♩ ♩ ♪) with which it frequently began (see No. 48).

The canzonas of Giovanni Gabrieli (c. 1553/6-1612) represent the culmination of the sixteenth-century canzona tradition, both in their extended scope and in their imaginative treatment of texture, form, and thematic material. They are written for as few as four and as many as fifteen parts, but canzonas *à 8* and *à 10* predominate. The ensemble for which they were intended chiefly comprised cornetts (a resonant soprano instrument usually made of wood) and sackbuts (a family of relatively low-range brass instruments, ancestors of the trombone), but stringed instruments and organ continuo were also available. The parts were usually not specifically labeled for one instrument or another.

The mature canzonas published in 1597 and in 1615 (posthumously) are mostly for two or three choirs of instruments, scorings inspired by the multiple galleries of Saint Mark's Cathedral in Venice, where Gabrieli was organist.[1] In the seventh-mode canzona presented here (from *Sacrae Symphoniae*, 1597) Gabrieli interweaves the two balanced but spatially separated choirs with brilliant effect. The two groups sometimes alternate over extended spans of time (mm. 1-34), sometimes carry on a quick-paced dialogue (mm. 35-44), sometimes unite in an impressive burst of sound (mm. 45-51). Metric changes articulate no less than seven sections, four of them subdivided by changes in thematic material and scoring (as at m. 21, for example). The rather loose agglomeration of disparate ideas is held together by a refrain element that consists of a triple-meter section and the beginning of the next duple section (mm. 35-51, 78-94, 121-137). The varying sequels to the duple portion of the refrain are a source of continual interest. In addition to the refrain, cadential overlap (e.g., mm. 21-22, 34-35) and occasional motivic recurrences (mm. 108-110/mm. 137-139; mm. 28-32/mm. 95 ff.) offset the extreme sectionalization of the piece. Traces of the virtuoso Venetian instrumental tradition[2] surface in the quick divisions (ornamental figures) of the fifth section. These are handled with particularly fine effect in measures 95-106, where the second choir states a sequential descending phrase with divisions in the soprano, the first choir restates it with divisions in the bass, and both then alternately burst forth with a quick rising scale in tenths between soprano and bass. The sequential design of these passages and others (e.g., mm. 24-32) foreshadows the central importance of sequence in melodic writing of the mature baroque style.

[1]For a picture of the interior of Saint Mark's, see the frontispiece of Denis Arnold, *Giovanni Gabrieli and the Music of the Venetian High Renaissance* (London: 1979).

[2]Virtuoso technique is particularly associated with the cornettists Giovanni Bassano and Girolamo della Casa, both of whom were at Saint Mark's and published treatises on diminution.

## 48. CLÉMENT JANEQUIN (c. 1485-1558)

### Ou mettra l'on ung baiser

Parisian chanson

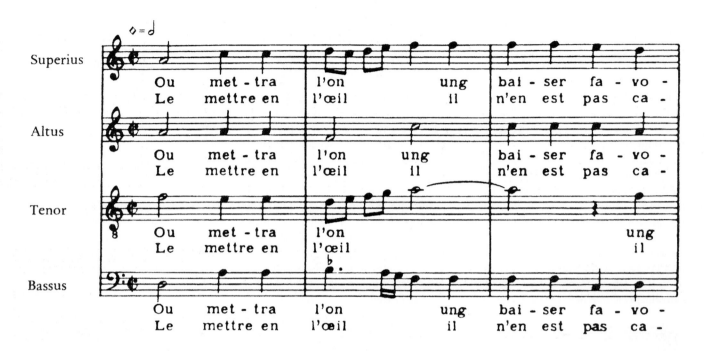

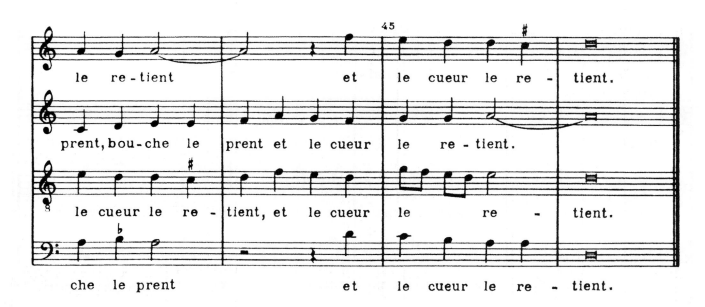

| | |
|---|---|
| Ou mettra l'on ung baiser favorable | *Where does one put a kind kiss* |
| Q'on m'a donné pour seurement tenir? | *that someone gave me for safekeeping?* |
| Le mettre en l'oeil il n'en est pas capable, | *Impossible to put it in the eye,* |
| La main n'y peult toucher ny advenir. | *the hand can neither receive nor keep it.* |
| La bouche en prent ce qu'en peult retenir | *The mouth takes what it can retain* |
| Et n'en retient qu'autant que le bien dure. | *but keeps it only as long as the kiss lasts.* |
| C'est donc au coeur l'effaict et garde seure | *It is therefore the heart—the effect and sure* |
| De ce présent a aultre n'appartient. | *guard of this gift belong to no other.* |
| O doulx baiser, estrange est ta nature. | *O sweet kiss, strange is your nature.* |
| Bouche le prent et le cueur le retient. | *The mouth takes it and the heart retains it.* |

All secular songs with French text are generically *chansons,* but music historians employ the label *French chanson* or *Parisian chanson* for a distinctive kind of chanson that emerged in the late 1520s in Paris. In contrast to the rather involved contrapuntal chansons of Josquin and his contemporaries, the sixteenth-century Parisian chanson featured a dominant treble melody with focused harmonic support. The voices largely declaim the text in synchrony; the textual line controls the musical phrase. Neither text nor music observes fixed forms, but the poetic rhyme scheme usually engenders some repetition pattern in the music, typically a direct repeat of opening phrases or a return of the opening at the end. The rhythm ♩ ♩ ♩ so often begins these songs that it has become known as *the* French chanson rhythm.

Clément Janequin (c. 1485-1558) was among the most successful composers of Parisian chansons, to judge from the prominent exposure of his works by the enterprising music publisher Pierre Attaingnant. Janequin's *Ou mettra l'on ung baiser* sets a charming ten-line poem about custody of a kiss.

The musical design is characteristically lucid, with the initial two phrases repeated immediately and also restated at the very end; a pattern of *a a* 〰〰〰 *a'*. The change in the final statement artistically blurs the blunt beginning of the phrase and achieves an ending on the tonal center, D. The clear tonal focus of the music follows the usual pattern for D-mode Parisian chansons, with emphasis on D, A, and F chords (in descending order of prominence). Fragments of imitation decorate the beginnings of internal phrases without, however, altering the basically homophonic character of the music.

In addition to lyrical chansons of this sort, Janequin also wrote narrative and descriptive chansons such as *Le chant des oiseaux* (*Réveillez-vous cueurs endormis*),[1] a delightful and virtuosic celebration of bird songs that recalls the fourteenth-century naturalistic virelai in spirit.

[1]Published in *Clément Janequin Chansons Polyphoniques,* ed. A. T. Merritt and F. Lesure, vol. 1 (Monaco: Éditions de l'Oiseau-Lyre, 1965), pp. 5-22.

# 49a. LUIS DE MILÁN   (c. 1500-c.1561)
## Pavan 1
in Tones I and II
### from El maestro

## 49b. DIEGO ORTIZ   (c. 1510-c. 1570)

### Recercada settima

from **Tratado de glosas**

Music for solo instruments suddenly burgeoned in the sixteenth century. The instrumental repertory was quite varied in nature, but can be roughly classified in three main categories: (1) music based on borrowed material—elaborations of sacred or secular melodies, arrangements of polyphonic vocal works; (2) pieces based on some fixed, abstract pattern—an established dance type or a formal procedure such as variation; (3) freely invented compositions—a contrapuntal type based primarily on imitation, and a rhapsodic type featuring idiomatic, often virtuosic, writing for the instrument. These categories are not mutually exclusive; for instance, dance pieces might be modeled on a chanson, or a rhapsodic piece might incorporate some aspects of variation (No. 49b). Publication of solo instrumental music encouraged the spread of instrumental idioms from one region to another. The composers of music for lute, guitar, viola da gamba, recorder, or keyboard were usually distinguished performers on the instrument for which they published. Spanish instrumentalist-composers such as Luis de Milán (c. 1500-c. 1561) and Diego Ortiz (c. 1510-c. 1570) made a particularly rich contribution to developing instrumental idioms.

**49a.** Luis de Milán's collection of music for Spanish guitar, *Libro de musica de vihuela da mano . . . El maestro* (1536), includes all three main categories of instrumental composition. Milán characterizes his pavans as "similar in their spirit and composition to the very pavans that are played in Italy,"[1] a bow to the Italian provenance of this courtly duple-meter dance. Pavan No. 1

[1]*Luis de Milán El Maestro*, ed. C. Jacobs (University Park and London: The Pennsylvania State University Press, 1971), p. 301.

combines qualities of both dance and variation. As in a dance, the phrases are paired and each (save the fourth) has just the right number of beats for a complete set of dance steps. Each phrase ends with two decisive repeated chords, a clear signal of the end of a choreographic unit. As in a variation, however, phrases are decorated and modified on repetition (compare phrases 2, 3, and 7; 4 and 5). Milán was one of the first composers to print tempo markings and to indicate the mode of a polyphonic piece not based on chant.

**49b.** Many instrumental collections were also instruction manuals. Luis de Milán's *El maestro* includes a preface addressed to beginners on the vihuela, and Diego Ortiz's *Tratado de glosas* (1553) for the *violone* (viola da gamba) systematically sets forth ornamentation patterns and methods for producing viola da gamba music with keyboard accompaniment. One kind of composition he illustrates is the *recercada* (from *ricercare*, "to search for," "to explore") on what he calls an "Italian tenor" or standard bass pattern (see No. 37a for a vocal example). The seventh *recercada* is based on the famous *romanesca* tenor, a basic framework of two fifth-related motions: B♭ -F, G-D-G. The solo gamba line starts with a formal motivic sequence, but soon dissolves into a free rhapsodic invention on various figures. Its rhythmic and melodic units are cleverly placed so as to cut across the even harmonic pace of the accompaniment and to obscure the end of the tenor pattern (m. 25, m. 48). Although the cembalo part is written in block chords, the performer doubtless animated it with some decorative flourishes. The *recercada* reaches a climax with its final sweeping two-octave descent, a magnification of many previous scale motives.

**50.** JACQUES ARCADELT (c.1505-1568)

3  Track 1

# Il bianco e dolce cigno
Madrigal

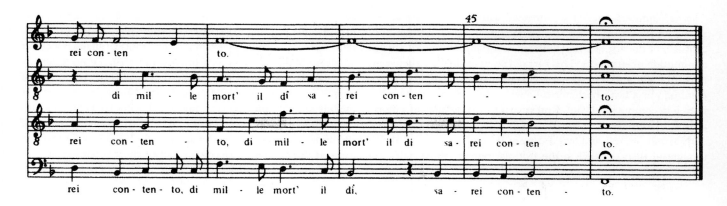

## Verse Structure

| | | |
|---|---|---|
| 7a | Il bianco e dolce cigno | *The white and gentle swan* |
| 7a | cantando more et io | *dies singing, and I,* |
| 11a | piangendo giung' al fin del viver mio. | *weeping, approach the end of my life.* |
| 7b | Stran' e diversa sorte, | *Strange and diverse fates,* |
| 7c | ch'ei more sconsolato | *that he dies disconsolate* |
| 7c | et io moro beato. | *and I die happy.* |
| 7d | Morte che nel morire | *Death, that in the [act of] dying* |
| 11d | m'empie di gioia tutt' e di desire. | *fills me wholly with joy and desire.* |
| 11e | Se nel morir' altro dolor non sento | *If in dying I feel no other pain* |
| 11e | di mille mort' il dì sarei contento. | *I would be content to die a thousand times a day.* |

About the time the Parisian chanson appeared in France, in the 1520s, a new kind of secular song emerged in northern Italy—the *madrigal*. The new genre took its name from a verse type in which seven- and eleven-syllable lines, arranged and rhymed in any fashion, were intermixed.[1] Broad literary and cultural currents, especially a resurgence of interest in the poetry of Francesco Petrarca (Petrarch, 1304-1374), and a desire to promote serious literary expression in Italian, fostered the rise of the madrigal. A new standard of poetic diction and purpose required a new level of musical craft and expressivity to achieve heightened artistic effects. Most remarkably, the aspirations linked with the early madrigal sparked extraordinary musical developments that were eventually to burst the bounds of accepted Renaissance style.

Compared with frottola verse, madrigal poetry was relatively elevated in tone and diction. The composers who set it were generally attentive to correct text accentuation and to individuality of words and feeling. They shunned wholesale strophic repetitions and usually dealt with only one strophe of text. The music of the early madrigalists tends similarly to be more carefully crafted than that of the frottolists. Melodic lines have more individual contour, textures are more diverse, and phrases are more varied rhythmically and harmonically.

The three acknowledged early masters of the Italian madrigal are (in order of birth) Philippe Verdelot (1470/80-1530/52), Costanzo Festa (c. 1490-1545), and Jacques Arcadelt (c. 1505-1568). All three were highly regarded church musicians, all three were well trained in the Josquin tradition of polyphony, and all three had Florentine connections (particularly strong for Verdelot and Festa). Festa was the only native-born Italian, but both Verdelot and Arcadelt, like Dufay and Josquin before them, first established their careers in northern Italy.

Arcadelt's *Il bianco e dolce cigno*, from his *First Book of Four-Voice Madrigals* (1539), was particularly well known and widely circulated in the sixteenth century. The text plays elegantly with a fairly elaborate paradox, which becomes comprehensible in the measure that one understands "death" not just in its literal sense, but also as a sixteenth-century poetic code word for sexual union. The composer prizes the sense of the text over its formal units. Rather than setting the first two poetic lines in separate phrases, he joins them in one as the meaning dictates, but splits line 2 so its last two words start the next phrase. This preserves the syntactic sense, but totally obscures the poetic rhyme.[2] In contrast to the frottola, individual elements of text receive special treatment that enhances their expressive force. "*Piangendo*" ("weeping") is underscored with an unexpected harmonic turn. The words "*more*" (mm. 4-5), "*sconsolato*" (mm. 18-19) and

---

[1]Not all madrigals have texts in madrigal verse. As in the case of the frottola, the name of a characteristic verse type was extended to the entire genre.

[2]The poetic device in which the sense and syntax cut across the formal line divisions is called *enjambment*.

"*morire*" (mm. 25-26, 31) are inflected with half steps in the exposed top voice. Most obviously, the "*mille morte*" ("thousand deaths") of the last line is elaborated in a point of imitation with a multitude of entrances. This sort of concrete analogue between musical event and textual sense is known as *word painting*. Word painting was a favorite rhetorical device of the madrigalists, who used it in combination with expressive musical gestures of a more abstract nature.

Not only are text and text setting in *Il bianco e dolce cigno* more thoughtful than is usual in the frottola, but the music is more subtly written. Rhythmic groupings within phrases are delightfully flexible, shifting in accord with short text modules (see notation above phrase 1, for example). The musical shape is a clever amalgam of direct phrase repetition (mm. 5/10, 35/39) and indirect association. Phrase 3 (mm. 15-17) echoes the beginning of phrase 1; phrases 4 (m. 24) and 5 (m. 30) begin with similar melody and rhythm; the bass of phrase 3 (mm. 16-17) anticipates the concluding imitative motive. The final extended point of imitation is not only textually apt but also serves as a satisfying musical climax to the preceding series of chordal phrases.

## 51. CIPRIANO DE RORE (1516-1565)
### Da le belle contrade d'oriente
Madrigal

3 Track 2

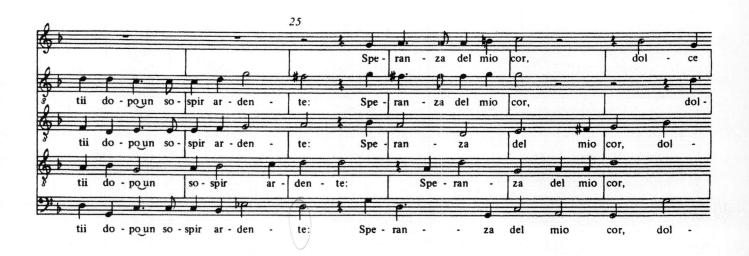

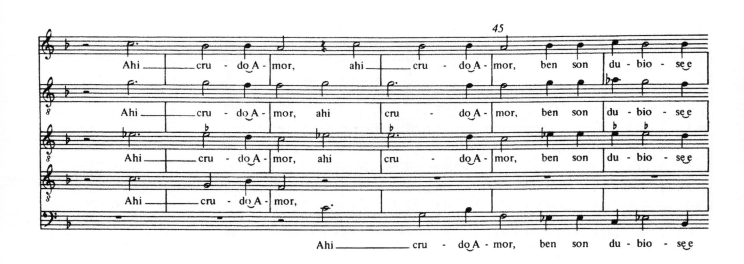

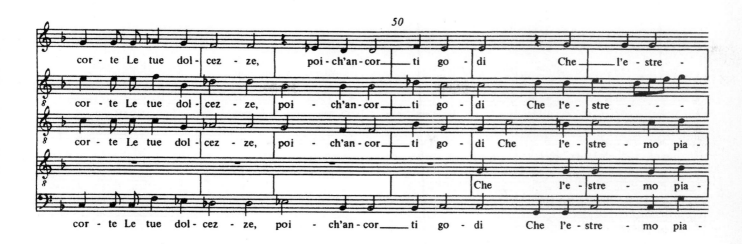

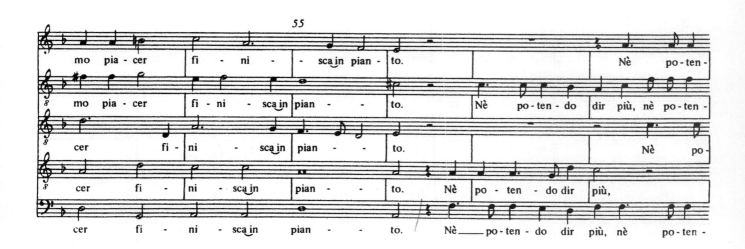

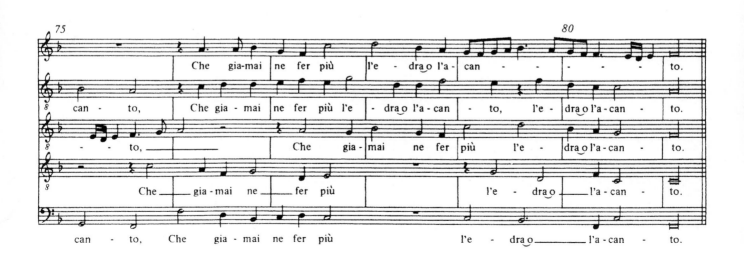

1. Da le belle contrade d'oriente
2. Chiara e lieta s'ergea Ciprigna et io
3. Fruiva in braccio al divin idol mio
4. Quel piacer che non cape humana mente,
5. Quando sentii dopo un sospir ardente:
6. "Speranza del mio cor, dolce desio,
7. Te'n vai, haime, sola mi lasci, adio.
8. Che sarà qui de me scura e dolente?
9. Ahi crudo Amor, ben son dubiose e corte
10. Le tue dolcezze, poi ch'ancor ti godi
11. Che l'estremo piacer finisca in pianto."
12. Nè potendo dir più cinseme forte
13. Iterando gl'amplessi in tanti nodi
14. Che giamai ne fer più l'edra o l'acanto.

1. *From the fair region of the East*
2. *bright and joyful arose the morning star, and I*
3. *in the embrace of my divine idol enjoyed*
4. *that pleasure which surpasses human understanding*
5. *when I heard, after an ardent sigh,*
6. *"Hope of my heart, sweet desire,*
7. *You go, alas! You leave me alone! Farewell!*
8. *What will become of me here, gloomy and sad?*
9. *Alas, cruel love, how false and brief*
10. *are your pleasures, for while I yet enjoy you,*
11. *the ecstasy ends in tears."*
12. *Unable to say more, she embraced me tightly,*
13. *repeating her embraces in more entwinings*
14. *than ever ivy or acanthus made.*

The madrigals of Cipriano de Rore (1516-1565) exemplify a second stage in the development of the madrigal, a stage marked by complexity of musical technique and extensive exploration of expressive means. De Rore, a Fleming by birth, was active at the court of Ferrara, where new ideas in literature, art, and music were encouraged. In line with contemporary literary trends, the text of de Rore's late madrigal *Da le belle contrade* (published 1566) is strongly charged in feeling. Within the confines of conventional sonnet form, the poet recreates a dramatic early-morning parting of two lovers, which pierces the woman with fear of abandonment.[1] The three phases of the compact drama are clearly differentiated in the musical setting. Long phrases and normal harmonic successions accompany the opening description of the scene. Short, exclamatory phrases, broken textures, disorienting harmonic shifts convey the woman's impassioned outburst. Complex imitative texture and renewed harmonic stability signal reconciliation and a return to the initial state of pleasure. As in *Il bianco e dolce cigno*, the numerous repetitions in the final section both mirror text meaning and produce an appropriate musical climax and formal balance.

The musical rhetoric in *Da le belle contrade* is more extreme than in the early madrigal, as is evident from the sobbing rests and broken texture at "*te'n vai haime*" (mm. 30-32), the isolation of the soprano at "*sola mi lasci*" (m. 33), the harmonic disjunctions after "*adio*" (mm. 35-36) and "*dolente*" (mm. 40-41). In addition, the five-part counterpoint is more intricate, the rhythmic movement more varied. Although earlier madrigalists were sensitive to text, it was the vivid expressive conjunction between text and music achieved by de Rore that earned him the enduring admiration of later masters like Claudio Monteverdi, who praised de Rore for madrigals "whose harmony obeys their words exactly."[2] Yet despite his attention to verbal nuance, de Rore still maintains a firm equilibrium between illuminating detail and overall musical coherence.

[1] A similar situation is treated at much greater length in Monteverdi's opera *L'incoronazione di Poppea* (see No. 64).

[2] Forward to *Il quinto libro de' madrigali*, translated in O. Strunk, *Source Readings in Music History* (New York: Norton, 1950), p. 407, and in paperback edition, *Source Readings in Music History: The Baroque Era* (1965), p. 47.

## 52.  LUCA MARENZIO    (1553/4-1599)
### Scaldava il sol
Madrigal

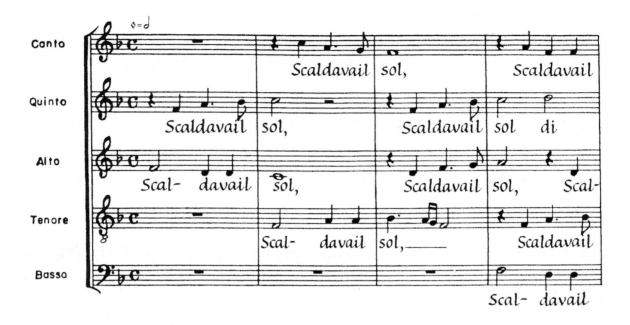

Scaldava il sol di mezo giorno l'arco
Nel dorso del Leon suo albergo caro.
Sotto'l boschetto più di frondi carco
Dormia'l pastor con le sue greggi a paro.
Giaceva il villanel de l'opra scarco
Vie più di posa che di spighe avaro.
Gl'augei, le fere, ogn'huom s'asconde e tace.
Sol la cicala non si sente in pace.
                                        —Luigi Alamanni

*The midday sun burned upon the arc*
*on the back of the Lion, its beloved mansion.*[1]
*Beneath a bush laden with leaves*
*slept the shepherd with his flock beside him.*
*The peasant, freed from work, lay outstretched,*
*much more covetous of rest than of food.*
*The birds, the beasts, all people hide and are silent.*
*The cicada alone does not feel at peace.*

[1]This is an astrological reference that would seem to place the scene in late July.

As madrigal texts became increasingly concrete in imagery and intense in feeling, conflicting claims between textual interpretation and musical continuity became ever more apparent in madrigal composition. The rhetorical approach to madrigal writing reaches an extreme in *Scaldava il sol* by Luca Marenzio (1553/4-1599). The text describes the blistering midday of an Italian summer in direct, pictorial images. Marenzio loses no opportunity to interpret the words in graphic musical metaphors. Among the most obvious of his rhetorical gestures are a five-note melodic arch on "*arco*" (mm. 8-10), a quick, repeated motif for the notion of many leaves (mm. 19-20), abrupt cessation of rhythmic activity for the sleep of the shepherd (mm. 23-26) and the prostration of the peasant lad (mm. 29-30), reduction from five voices to one to convey silence and the word "*sol*"

(mm. 51-53), an insistent dotted figure for the cicada's relentless chirr. Less obvious to the listener, but amusing to the singers, is Marenzio's pun on "*sol*" ("alone"), which each voice (save the tenor) sings on a note solmized as *sol* in either the natural or the soft hexachord (mm. 53-54).

Successful as a *tour de force* of word painting and aural mimicry of the poem, this madrigal is musically rather diffuse, even arbitrary in structure. Many individual events arrest the attention, but no underlying expressive mood or musical plan relates them in a coherent whole. Such descriptive madrigals were more popular in Rome, with its cultivated amateur singers, than at the north Italian courts of Mantua and Ferrara, where perceptive patrons and skilled professional singers offered an ideal environment for bold and challenging musical experimentation.

## 53. CLAUDIO MONTEVERDI (1567-1643)
### Cruda Amarilli
Madrigal
See No. 56.

Track 3

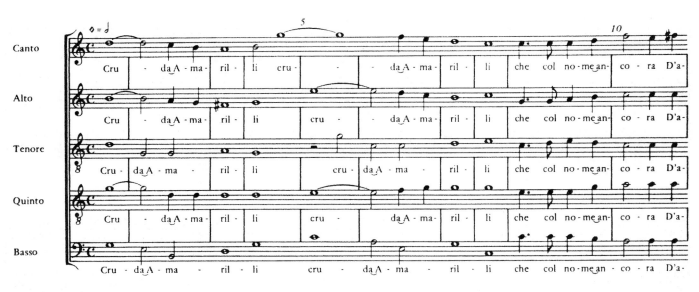

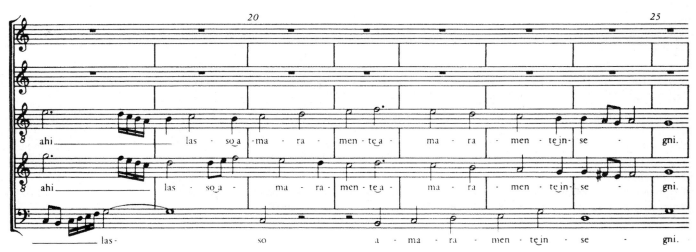

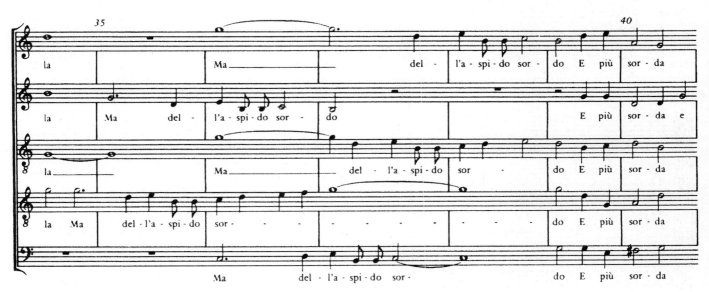

Cruda Amarilli, che col nome ancora
d'amar, ahi lasso, amaramente insegni!
Amarilli, del candido ligustro
più candida e più bella,
ma del'aspido sordo
e più sorda e più fera e più fugace,
Poi che col dir t'offendo,
I' mi morro tacendo.
    —G. B. Guarini, *Il pastor fido*, Act 1, scene 2

*Cruel Amaryllis, who even with that name,*
*Alas, teaches a bitter lesson of love!*[1]
*Amaryllis, whiter and more beautiful*
*Than the white-flowering privet,*
*But than the stealthy adder*
*Stealthier, and wilder, and more elusive.*
*Then if in speaking I offend you*
*I shall die in silence.*

A seventeenth-century version in rhymed couplets from the celebrated *Pastor fido* translation of Sir Richard Fanshawe (1648):

*O Amarillis, Authresse of my flame,*
*(Within my mouth how sweet now is thy name!*
*But in my heart how bitter!) Amarillis*
*Fairer and whiter than the whitest Lillies,*
*But crueller than cruell Adders far,*
*Which having stung (least they should pitie) bar*
*Their ears, and flie: If then by speaking I*
*Offend thee, I will hold my peace and die.*[2]

[1]The poet's word play among *amare* ("to love"), *amara* ("bitter"), and Amarilli (a lilylike flower and also a woman's name) cannot be duplicated in English.

[2]*Battista Guarini Il pastor fido*, Edinburgh Bilingual Library (II), ed. J. H. Whitfield (1976), p. 71.

Undoubtedly the most significant musical figure in the half-century from 1590 to 1640 was Claudio Monteverdi (1567-1643). A master of traditional sixteenth-century polyphonic technique, endowed with an inventive musical mind and keen psychological insight, Monteverdi was instrumental in exploring and promoting a radical new manner of writing that launched a new musical epoch, the baroque.

The first signs of a new musical language are already apparent in Monteverdi's five-voice madrigals, especially those of his Fourth and Fifth Books (published 1603 and 1605, but individual madrigals composed a decade or more earlier). A fierce attack on his compositions by the Bolognese musician Giovanni Maria Artusi (c. 1540-1613) forced Monteverdi to defend his unorthodox musical language and to articulate a doctrine of two separate and equally worthy "practices" in composition. Monteverdi's *prima pratica* was orthodox sixteenth-century style as perfected by Adrian Willaert and codified as theory by Gioseffo Zarlino in 1558. His *seconda pratica* was a more recent mode of composition, less circumscribed by rules, adopted by such distinguished madrigalists as Cipriano de Rore, Giaches de Wert, and Monteverdi himself. Its guiding principle was "to make the words the mistress of the harmony and not the servant."[1]

[1]Foreword to *Il quinto libro de'madrigali*, trans. O. Strunk, *Source Readings in Music History* (New York: Norton, 1950), p. 406; paperback edition, Part III, *The Baroque Era*, p. 46. The two major documents in

*Cruda Amarilli*, the opening piece in Monteverdi's Book V, is criticized by Artusi as confused, arbitrary, and harsh in sound. Artusi especially deplored the many dissonances introduced without proper preparation, left unresolved, or even coexistent with their own resolutions (e.g., mm. 13, 36, 54). Monteverdi justified such transgressions of contrapuntal propriety as being textually motivated, and indeed the music marvelously projects the bitter, wounded tone of the speaker. The cultured sixteenth-century listener would have recognized the poem as a famous speech from G. B. Guarini's popular drama *Il pastor fido* ("The Faithful Shepherd"), and would have supplied the dramatic context mentally. Monteverdi's expressive art goes well beyond a heightened dissonance level, and extends to a piercing range of the soprano voice, sudden melodic disjunctions (e.g., soprano, m. 4, mm. 53-54), and abrupt changes in rhythmic movement (mm. 41-43), in texture (mm. 9-14), and in vocal scoring (mm. 25-26, 34-35). Although some of the gestures are descriptive (e.g., the sweeping sighs on "*Ahi*," the quick movement to silence on "*fugace*"), most are generally expressive in character. Taken together, they create a consistent emotional tone in the musical setting.

the Artusi-Monteverdi controversy are translated in Strunk, *Source Readings*, pp. 393-415; paperback edition, *The Baroque Era*, pp. 33-55. Monteverdi's defense in the foreword to the Fifth Book of madrigals appears under the name of his brother, but the sentiments expressed are plainly his own.

Monteverdi ensures the musical coherence of the work by judicious repetition of appropriate phrases. He especially favors varied repetitions that alter, and usually intensify, the feeling.[2]

[2]For example, the opening anguished exclamation is reiterated at a higher pitch level (mm. 1-8); the dejected sigh recurs in the lower voices only and has a new, highly dissonant, continuation (mm. 9-26).

The main disjunctions in the piece (mm. 25-26, 43-44) articulate three relatively balanced main sections, each focused on G. The double point of imitation in the last section provides a suitably expansive musical closure appropriate to the speaker's exaggerated emotional state. Chief among the late madrigalists, Monteverdi understood how to satisfy the rival claims of expression and coherence, and this accounts in part for his place in the pantheon of major Western composers.

# 54. CARLO GESUALDO  (c. 1561-1613)
## Moro, lasso, al mio duolo
Madrigal

3  Track 4

[1]The bar lines are from an edition in score published in 1613 in Genoa.

| Moro, lasso, al mio duolo | *I shall die, miserable, in my suffering,* |
|---|---|
| E chi mi può dar vita, | *and the one who could give me life,* |
| Ahi, che m'ancide e non vuol darmi aita! | *alas, kills me and is unwilling to give me aid.* |
| O dolorosa sorte, | *O painful fate!* |
| Chi dar vita mi può, ahi, mi dà morte! | *The one who could give me life, alas, gives me death.* |

The mature madrigals of Carlo Gesualdo, Prince of Venosa and Count of Conza (c. 1561-1613), manifest a particularly individual, not to say eccentric, approach to the genre and reveal the far-reaching consequences of a textually dependent aesthetic. Inspired by the example of Luzzasco Luzzaschi of Ferrara, and doubtless by notions from Greek music theory, Gesualdo adopted a style of extreme contrasts and startling chromaticism. His chosen texts typically deal in abstract antitheses. That of *Moro, lasso* (Madrigals, Book 6, 1611) plays upon the paradoxical power of the beloved to kill or give life. The life/death antithesis in the text gives rise in the music to highly profiled contrasts in rhythmic flow, texture, and harmonic sound. The setting of the first line bemoaning death is homophonic, intensely chromatic, low in register, slow in pace with no definite rhythmic motive. That of the second line, which speaks of potential life, is imitative, diatonic, high in pitch, quick in movement with a clearly recognizable motive. In the sequel, similar contrasts persist, with tonally unsettled chromatic music always coloring text segments about death (line 3, end of line 5), stable diatonic music associated with life (line 5, beginning). The rather fragmented musical effect is offset by repetitions of phrase groups and individual phrases. The result is a collage held together by textual syntax and imagery.

Although other late madrigalists adopt a chromatic mode on specific occasions, Gesualdo alone takes chromaticism as a norm. Typical of his procedures are half step motion in individual lines, outlines of melodic tritones (alto, "*mio duolo*" m. 3; canto and basso, "*Ahi, chi m'ancide*" mm. 11-12), cross-relations, and strange harmonic successions that convey no consistent sense of tonal order. The opening four chords, although easily understood in terms of linear motion and consonance, use eleven different pitches and relate to no one tonal realm. The final cadence to A is a deliberate wrench from the preceding area colored by B-flats, E-flats, and G-naturals. Biting dissonances ("*sorte*," "*ahi mi da morte*") supplement the highly charged effect of the chromaticism. In music such as this, Gesualdo patently shunned Renaissance ideals of proportion and harmony and sought an expressive mode so flamboyant as sometimes to be labeled mannerist.

**55.** GIULIO CACCINI  (c. 1545-1618)

## Perfidissimo volto

Solo madrigal

from **Le nuove musiche**

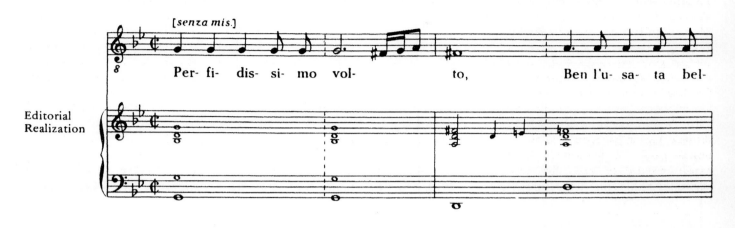

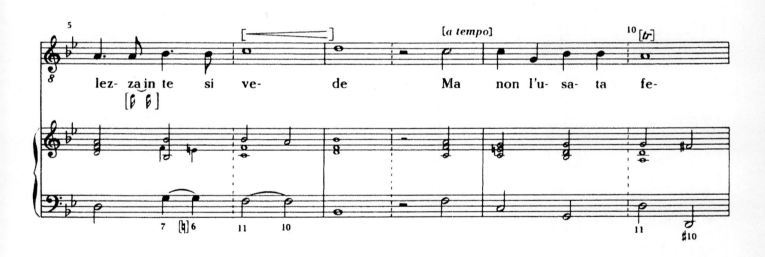

Perfidissimo volto,
Ben l'usata bellezza in te si vede
Ma non l'usata fede.
Già mi parevi dir: "Quest'amorose
Luci che dolcemente
Rivolgo à te, sì bell'e sì pietose
Prima vedrai tu spente,
Che sia spento il desio ch'à te le gira."
Ahi, che spento è'l desio
Ma non è spento quel per cui sospira
L'abbandonato core!
O volto troppo vago e troppo rio,
Perchè se perdi amore
Non perdi ancor'vaghezza?
O non hai pari alla beltà fermezza?
　　　　　　　—G. B. Guarini

*Most treacherous face,*
*Yes, the customary beauty appears in you*
*But not the customary fidelity.*
*Formerly you seemed to say to me: "These loving*
*Bright eyes that sweetly*
*I turn toward you, eyes so beautiful and so sympathic,*
*You will see them extinguished before*
*The desire they flash toward you is extinguished."*
*Alas, the desire is extinguished*
*But she for whom this abandoned heart sighs*
*Has not expired!*
*O face, too lovely and too cruel,*
*Why, if you lose love*
*Do you not also lose your loveliness,*
*Or do you not possess constancy equal to your beauty?*

Giulio Caccini's *Le nuove musiche* ("New Music," 1602) stands with Monteverdi's *Fifth Book of Madrigals* (1605) as a manifesto of a new musical sensibility. Caccini (c. 1545-1618) presents this collection of madrigals and airs for solo voice and instrumental bass as the product of his own acclaimed personal singing style. The medium itself was not entirely novel—a significant tradition of solo singing with lute accompaniment can be traced back to the late fifteenth century in Italy. What was new was Caccini's avowed attitude toward music and text—his desire to seem "to speak in musical sounds"—and his presentation of solo poetic settings as legitimate compositions, not just the fleeting products of performance. In the preface to *Le nuove musiche*, Caccini acknowledges the Camerata of Florence, led by Count Giovanni de' Bardi, as his guiding musical influence. They inculcated the Platonic ideal of music as speech, and encouraged him to conceive a music attuned to the sense and emotional substance of a text.

*Perfidissimo volto* is singled out by Caccini as one of the first works in which he tried to realize Camerata ideals. Its text, by the fashionable poet Giovanni Battista Guarini, is a passionate diatribe by a deceived lover. Caccini's setting paces the text as though it were a dramatic reading. The rhythms are irregular; the line now dwells on one note, now rises or sinks in register. The opening is recitativelike in character, but the numerous embellishments (*passaggi*) and overall melodic quality of the vocal line distinguish this style from the recitative of opera. Modern scholars often call it *monody*. The sense of an organized tune is

particularly strong toward the end in the music for the concluding sarcastic rhetorical question. The repetition of the final verses of text is appropriate to the poem, and is also Caccini's characteristic concluding gesture in his solo madrigals. More elaborate embellishments intensify the effect of the repeated words and music.

The score as published by Caccini does not provide all the essential information for performance. The instrumentalist must supply supporting harmonies above the bass notes,[1] while the singer must enhance the written melody with certain stylized vocal effects. Caccini explains and illustrates many of these effects in his preface—the trill, the tremolo, the *esclamazione*, various rhythmic alterations—but leaves it to the individual singer to decide where and how they may best be introduced (the modern editor has made some suggestions in this regard).[2] Effective performance of these solo madrigals depends on a complex tradition of vocal production that has not been fully reconstituted, although elements of it survive in vocal techniques of modern popular song.

[1] The keyboard realization for this song is supplied by the editor, H. W. Hitchcock, and represents only one among many possible modes of accompaniment. For some authentic early seventeenth-century realizations of basses to monodies see J. W. Hill, "Realized continuo accompaniments from Florence c. 1600," *Early Music* 11/2 (1983), pp. 194-208.

[2] Caccini's preface is published in *Giulio Caccini Le nuove musiche*, ed. H. W. Hitchcock, Recent Researches in the Music of the Baroque Era, vol. IX (1970), pp. 43-56.

**56.** SIGISMONDO D'INDIA (c. 1582-c. 1629)    Track 6

## Cruda Amarilli

Solo madrigal

See No. 53

¹T. = trill of Florentine type; repeat the pitch with gradual acceleration.

For translation of No. 56, see No. 53.

I then set myself to investigate some particular techniques for good solo singing, and I found that this could be effected in a true manner with unusual intervals, passing with the most novelty possible from one consonance to another, according to the varying sense of the words, and that by this means the songs would have greater effect and greater power to move the emotions [*affetti*] of the soul than those . . . composed with ordinary [melodic and harmonic] movement. . . . I myself sang some for Vittoria Archilei [a celebrated singer of contemporary music in Florence] who exhorted me to continue my way of making music [*maneria*], saying she had never heard a style of so much power that simultaneously interpreted the idea of the text with such diversity of pitch, variety of harmony, and such novel ornaments [*nova maneria di passeggiare*].[1]

So wrote Sigismondo d'India (c. 1582-c. 1629) in the preface to his first book of solo songs (1609).

[1]Preface to *Il primo libro di musiche da cantar solo*, edited by F. Mompellio, *Instituta et Monumenta*. Serie I, Monumenta No. 4 (Cremona: 1970), p. 24.

A Sicilian who established a career in northern Italy, d'India composed both ensemble madrigals (eight published books) and solo songs and duets with continuo accompaniment (five published collections). His monodic setting of *Cruda Amarilli*, a well-known soliloquy from G. B. Guarini's pastoral drama *Il pastor fido* (Act I, scene 2, lines 272-279) bears comparison with Monteverdi's five-voice madrigal on the same text (see No. 53) and illustrates aspects of the novel manner publicized in d'India's preface.

The music is clearly framed to the ideas and affect of the text. Pungent dissonances (mm. 1, 5, etc.) and chromatic inflections capture the bitter tone of the speaker. Irregular rhythms in both voice and bass and the varying rate of text declamation provide tension and a lively sense of dramatic recitation. The repeat of the last text line with an expanded musical phrase gives a sense of climax and formal closure. Tonally the piece seems deliberately unfocused (other d'India monodies begin and end on the same pitch center). A is the best candidate for a pitch center, but the piece starts on an F harmony and ends with a D cadence.

## 57. JOHN DOWLAND (1563-1626)

### 57a. **Flow my teares**

Lute song

Track 7

Lute[1]

Flow my teares, fall from your springs! Ex - ilde for ev - er, let mee morne; where
Downe vaine lights shine you no more! No nights are dark e - nough for those that

nights black bird hir sad in - fa - my sings, there let mee live for - lorne.
in dis - paire their lost for - tuns de - plore, light doth but shame dis - close.

Ne - ver may my woes be - re - liev - ed, since pit - tie is fled, and teares, and sighes,
From the high - est spire of con - tent - ment, my for - tune is throwne, and feare, and griefe,

and grones my wea - rie dayes, my wea - rie dayes, of all joyes have de - priv -
and paine for my de - serts, for my de - serts, are my hopes since hope is

[1]The accompaniment is a transcription of a lute tablature.

Harke you shad-owes that in darck - nesse dwell, learne to con-temne light,

Hap - pie, hap - pie they that in hell feele not the worlds de - spite.

*Lacrime.*[1]

Flow my teares fall from your springs,
Exilde for euer: Let mee morne
where nights black bird hir sad infamy sings,
there let mee liue forlorne.

Downe vaine lights shine you no more,
No nights are dark enough for those
that in dispaire their lost furtuns deplore,
light doth but shame disclose.

Neuer may my woes be relieued,
since pittie is fled,
and teares, and sighes, and grones my wearie dayes,
of all ioyes haue depriued.

From the highest spire of contentment,
my fortune is throwne,
and feare, and griefe, and paine for my deserts,
are my hopes since hope is gone.

Harke you shadowes that in darcknesse dwell,
learne to contemne light,
Happie, happie they that in hell
feele not the worlds despite.

[1]This version retains the archaic spellings of the first edition of 1600.

## 57b. **Lachrimae Gementes**
Instrumental pavane

**57a.** The English lute ayre flourished from about 1597 (the year Dowland's *First Booke of Songes or Ayres* was published) to the 1620s. The acknowledged master of the genre was John Dowland (1563-1626), an accomplished lutenist of European repute. His *Flow my teares* or *Lachrimae* from the *Second Booke of Songes* (1600) was easily the most famous ayre of the period, to judge from copies and editions as well as from frequent references in stage plays. The tone of the text, voicing sorrow, grief, and despair, resonates in numerous other Dowland songs. The music reflects the textual feeling with its affective intervals (minor sixth, diminished fourth) and cross-relations (often coupled with chord progressions by thirds). Dowland is keenly attentive to rhythm and text delivery. The word "fall" in the first line gains great weight from its duration and unexpectedly high melodic position. The catalogue of "tears and sighs and groans" assumes a breathless intensity from its short, off-beat rhythms. The sudden quickness of "learn to contemn light" reinforces its bitter sentiment. The lute provides a discreetly contrapuntal accompaniment and contributes to the textural and emotional climax in the second strain with its close imitation of the voice.

The poem, probably by Dowland himself, consists of five symmetrical quatrains. These are set with three strains of music that are asymmetric in phrasing. The repetition of each strain (the last with no change in text) produces an *aabbCC* pattern. The relatively balanced large form and the tuneful quality of this song ally it with the Italian Renaissance air, but the harmonic intensity and the sensitive text declamation concord with the aesthetic of the solo continuo madrigal.

**57b.** In 1604 Dowland published a set of seven instrumental pavanes on the *Lachrimae* tune. The print gives parts for a five-voice ensemble (characteristically, viols) as well as a full intabulation for solo lute. The first pavane of the series, the *Lachrimae Antiquae,* renders the song fairly closely, keeping its essential bass and cantus. Others have little direct connection with the song beyond sharing its tonal center and quoting the opening motif. The *Lachrimae Gementes* ("The Groaning Lachrimae"), third in the series, opens with a clear reference to the song but then deviates freely from it. More of the bass survives than of the melody. The pavane does preserve the tripartite form and the tonal outline of the song. The cadences of each section quote the song (note especially the distinctive plagal cadence ending the second strain), while the first and third sections start with the same sonority as their counterparts. One portion of the second strain (mm. 13-14) resembles a sequential passage in Josquin's *Déploration* on the death of Johannes Ockeghem.[1] The relationship is perhaps fortuitous—Dowland may have had in mind an inversion of the song motif in measures 23-25—but the association would have been apt in feeling. Among the factors contributing to the richly expressive quality of the pavane are prominent suspensions and melodic half steps, occasional cross-relations (mm. 5, 19-20) and the low tessitura. The fleeting references to the song effect a subtle meditation upon its gloomy sentiments.

[1] Josquin Desprez, *Weredlijke Werken* 1, p. 5, mm. 119-126.

## 58.  CLAUDIO MONTEVERDI
### Zefiro torna
Continuo madrigal
from **Scherzi musicali**

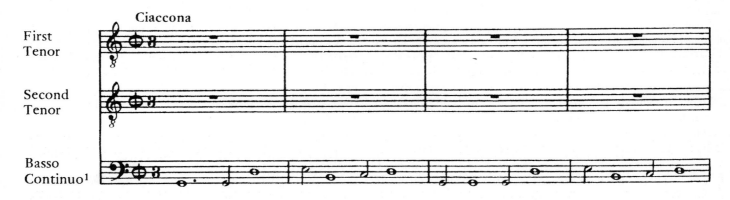

From THE COMPLETE WORKS OF CLAUDIO MONTEVERDI, edited by G. F. Malipiero. Used by permission of European American Music Distributors Corporation, sole U.S. agent for Universal Edition.

[1]A figured bass realization may be found in *Tutte le opere di Claudio Monteverdi*, vol. IX, edited by G. F. Malipiero (1929), pp. 9-20.

Zefiro torna e di soavi accenti
L'aer fa grato e'l piè discioglie a l'onde,
E mormorando tra le verdi fronde
Fa danzar al bel suon su'l prato i fiori,
Inghirlandato il crin Fillide e Clori
Note temprando amor care e gioconde
E da monti e da valli ime e profonde
Raddopian l'armonia gli antri canori.
Sorge più vaga in ciel l'aurora e'l sole
Sparge più luci d'or, più puro argento
Fregia di Teti il bel ceruleo manto.
Sol io per selve abbandonate e sole
L'ardor di due begli occhi e'l mio tormento.
Come vuol mia ventura hor piango, hor canto.

     —Ottavio Rinuccini

*The west wind returns and with soft accents*
*makes the air gentle and releases swift-footed waves,*
*and murmuring among the green branches*
*makes the flowers dance at its lovely sound*
*and curls round the hair of Phyllis and Clori,*
*love giving rise to fond and joyful song,*
*and from mountains and valleys, songs resound high and low,*
*and the sonorous caves reecho the music.*
*The dawn rises more lovely in the sky, and the sun*
*scatters more golden rays, and a purer silver*
*decorates Teti's beautiful sky blue coat.*
*Only I in the lonely, deserted forest—*
*the fire of two bright eyes is my torment.*
*As my fortune wills, I weep, then sing.*

The madrigal engaged Monteverdi's attention from his early twenties (*Book I,* published in 1587) through the end of his life (*Book VIII,* published in 1638; *Book IX,* published posthumously in 1651). From about 1615, Monteverdi turned definitively to the continuo madrigal, songs scored for solo voices with continuo or for mixed concertato forces. The duet with continuo accompaniment became his favorite medium. Although text expression remained central to his conception, several of his largest and most ambitious continuo madrigals are not governed solely by text, but are organized upon a repeated harmonic scheme. A celebrated composition of this type is this *ciaccona, Zefiro torna,* from *Scherzi musicali . . . con una ciaccona* of 1632.

The *chaconne* is a dance song of South American origin. It was imported to Spain, Italy, and France by Spanish adventurers about the turn of the sixteenth century and became popular as a basis for both instrumental and vocal works. Originally a reiterated harmonic pattern akin to familiar Renaissance basses (see commentary to 37a, 49b), the chaconne early became settled as a fixed melodic bass line or ground bass.

For most of its compass, *Zefiro torna* is a ground bass variation. The vocal lines first conform to the invariant four-beat bass module (mm. 5-13), then increasingly disregard it. The interplay between the rigid bass and the free vocal phrasing is one of the delights of the music. The descriptive sonnet by the Florentine poet Ottavio Rinuccini (1562-1621)—famous as an early opera

librettist: *Dafne, Euridice, Arianna*—offers ample opportunity for word painting. Monteverdi's musical rhetoric resembles that in earlier madrigals such as *Ecco mormorar l'onde* (*Book II,* 1590). The waves well up through rolling melismas, the wind murmurs in static, muttered figures, mountains rise by precipitous melodic ascent, valleys are carved out in sudden descent. The cheerful, predictable musical atmosphere is abruptly shattered, however, at line 12, where the speaker unexpectedly divulges his tormented state of mind (m. 114). The ground bass breaks off and is replaced by a seemingly random sequence of pitches, indeterminate in tonal allegiance. The regular triple meter dissolves. Recitativelike declamation replaces tuneful regulated melody. The musical disintegration brilliantly matches the psychological disorientation described in the text. The poet provides impetus for the reconciliation of these two very disparate sound worlds in the protagonist's final state of uncertainty: "I weep, then sing." With the apprehensive weeping, the declamatory manner, spiked with dissonance, reigns; with the optimistic singing, the stable ground bass returns with its attendant tuneful idiom. The glorious soaring melisma on "*canto*" that ends the piece mediates between the two states and recalls the affective virtuoso idiom promoted by Caccini.

Monteverdi's *Zefiro* bass was used by Heinrich Schütz in a sacred motet *Es steh Gott auf* (*Symphoniae Sacrae* II).

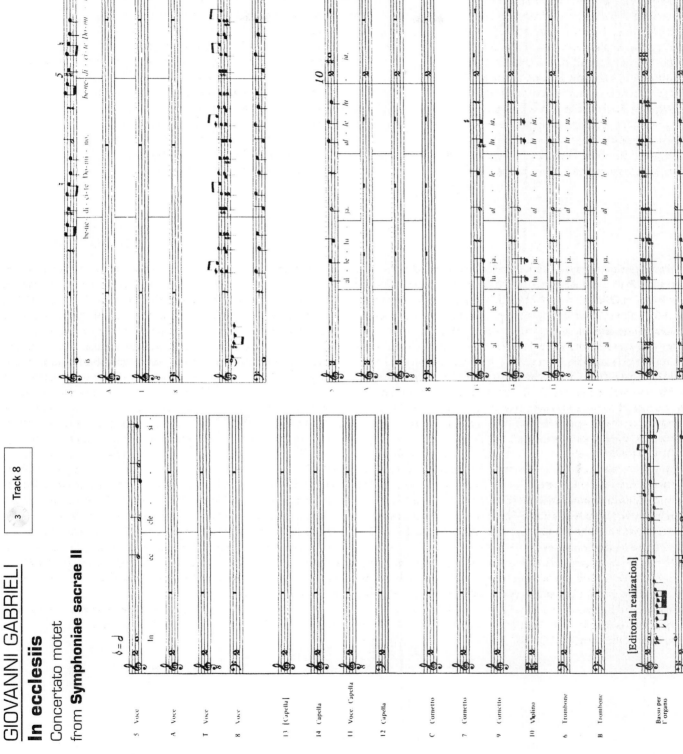

**59.** GIOVANNI GABRIELI
**In ecclesiis**
Concertato motet
from **Symphoniae sacrae II**

Track 8

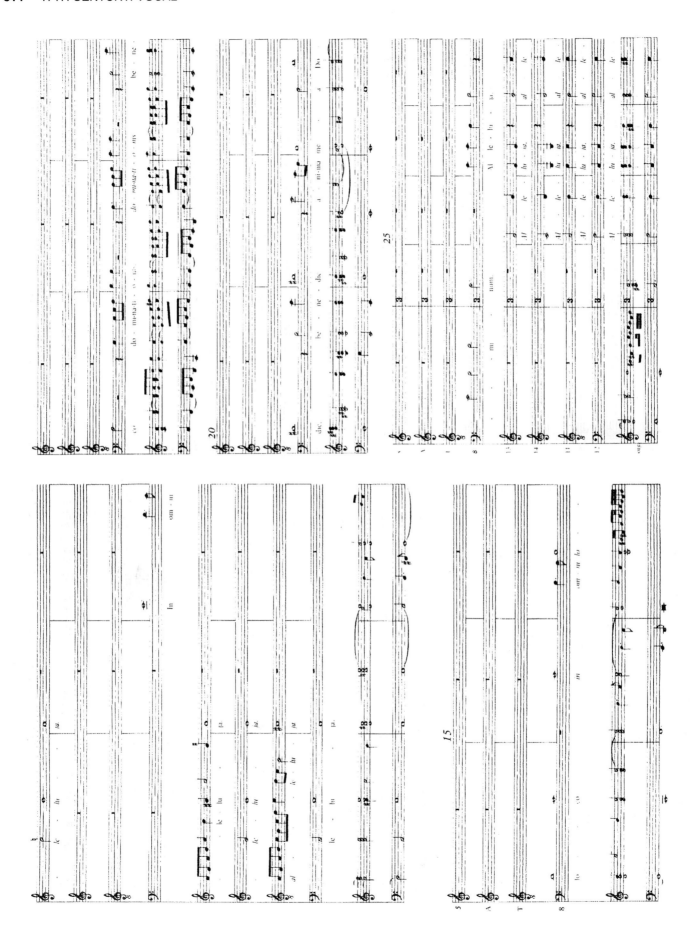

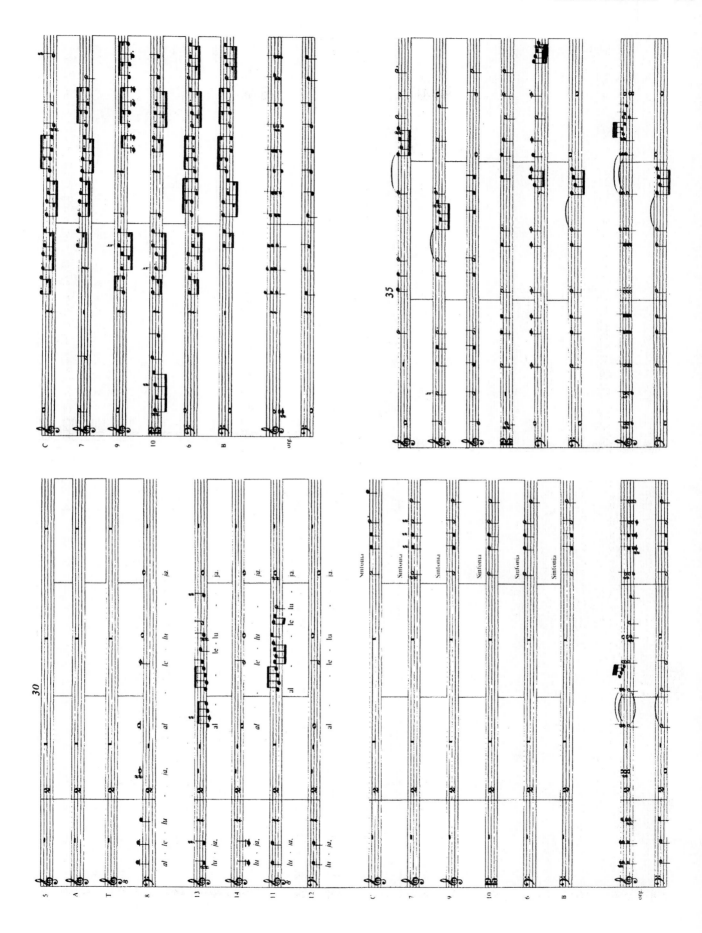

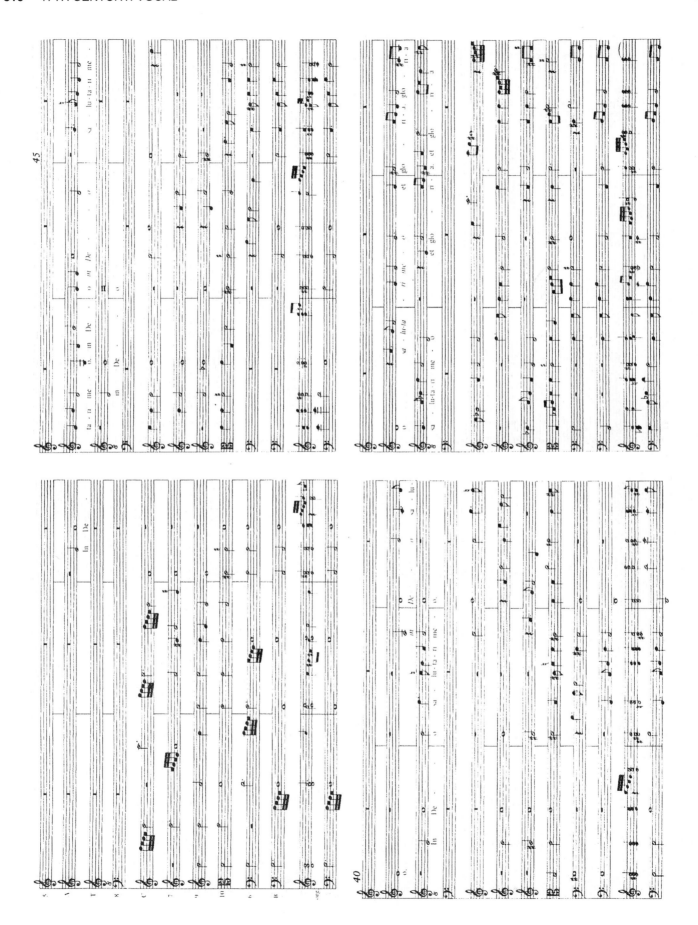

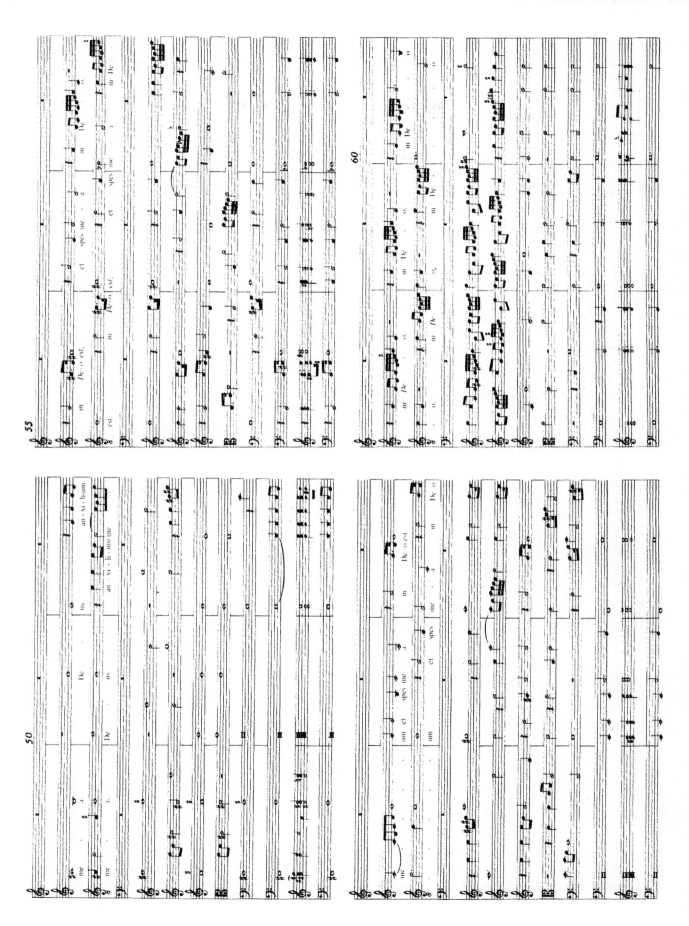

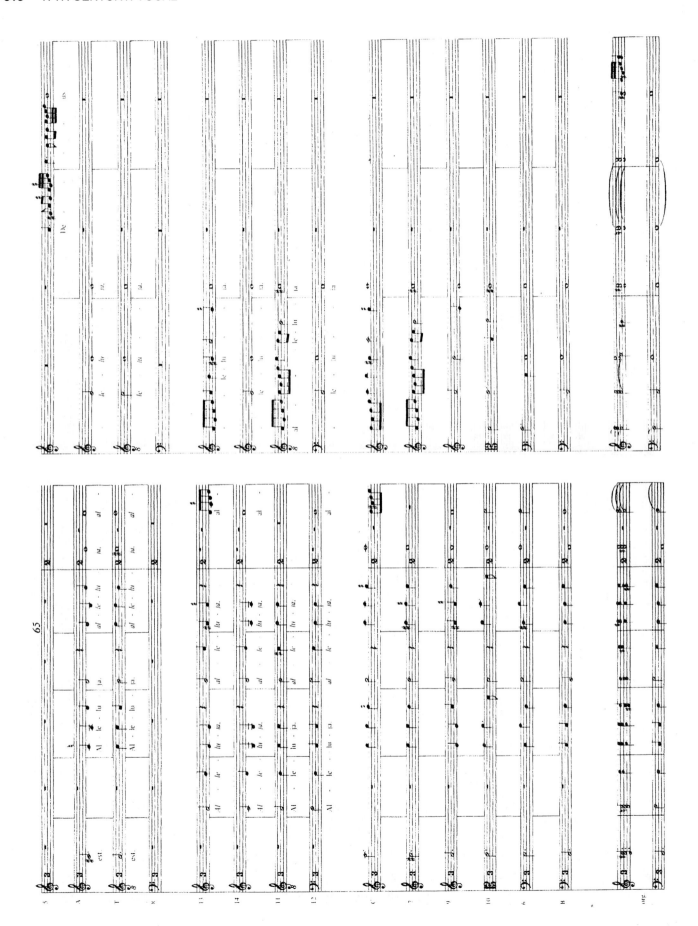

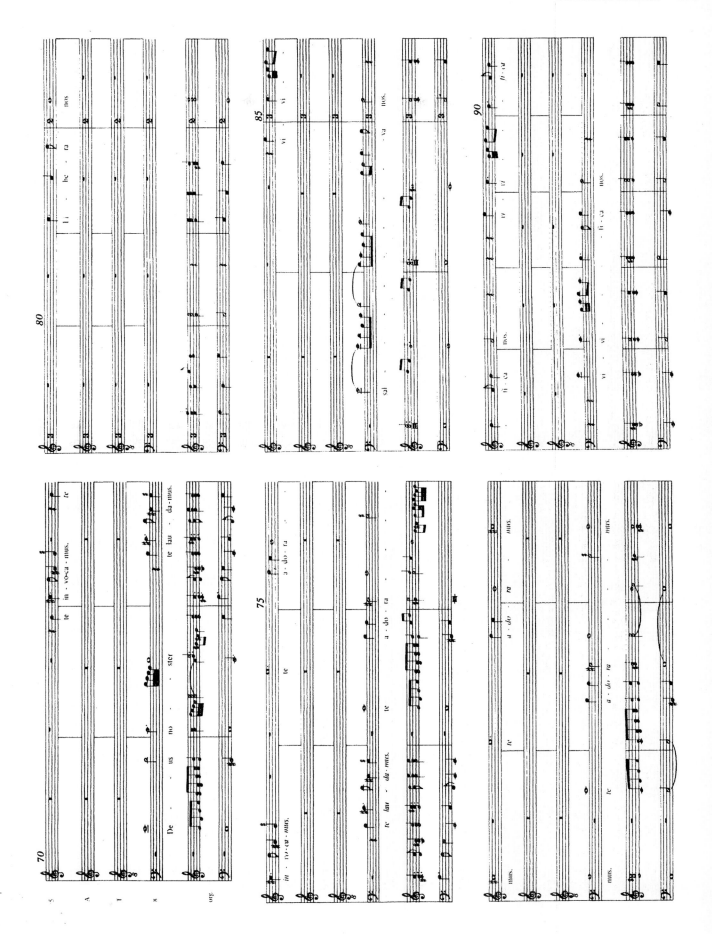

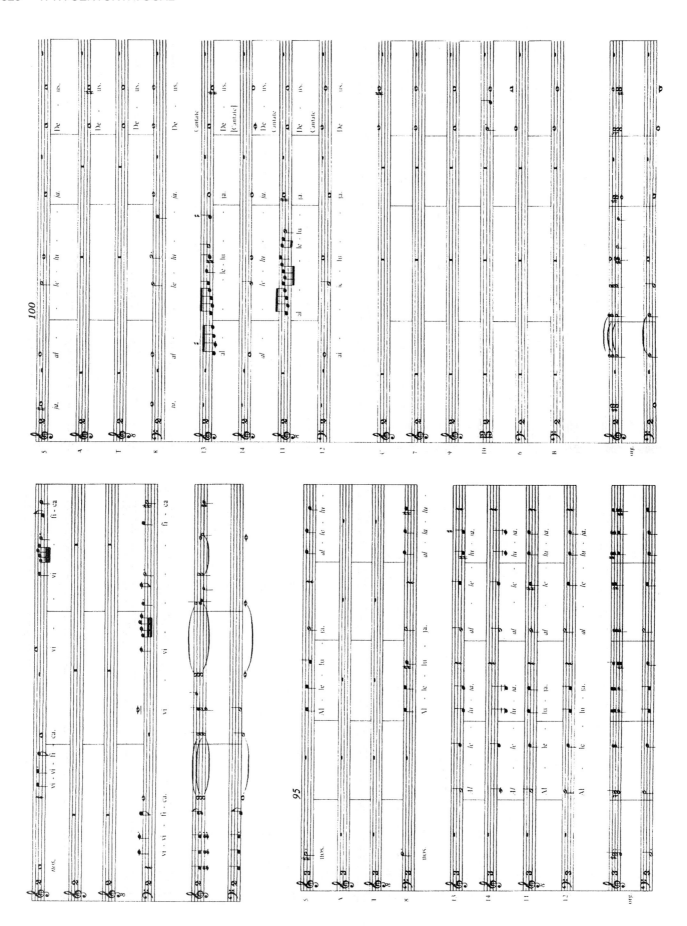

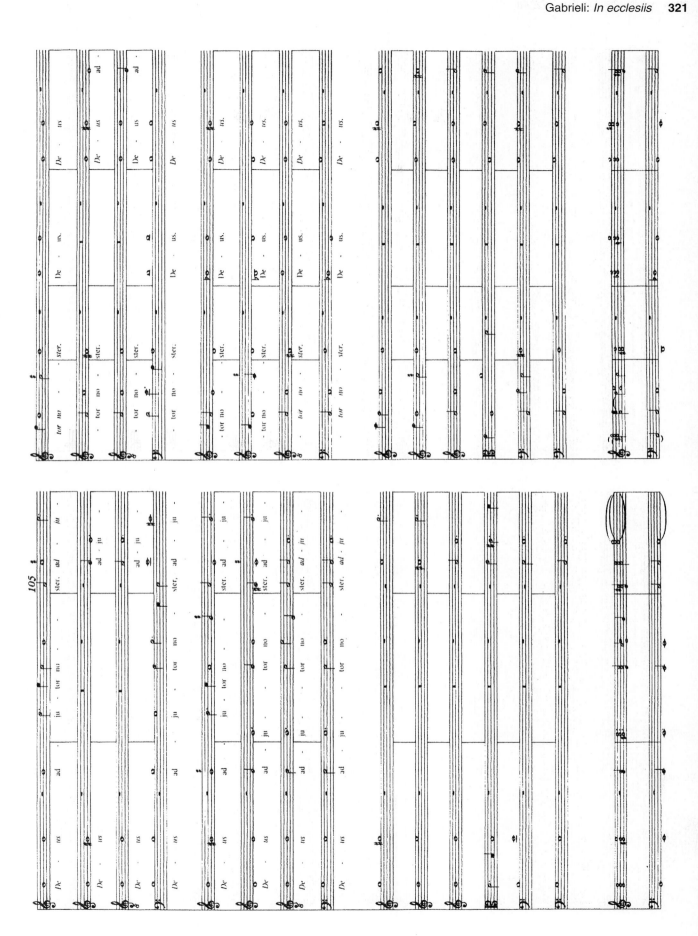

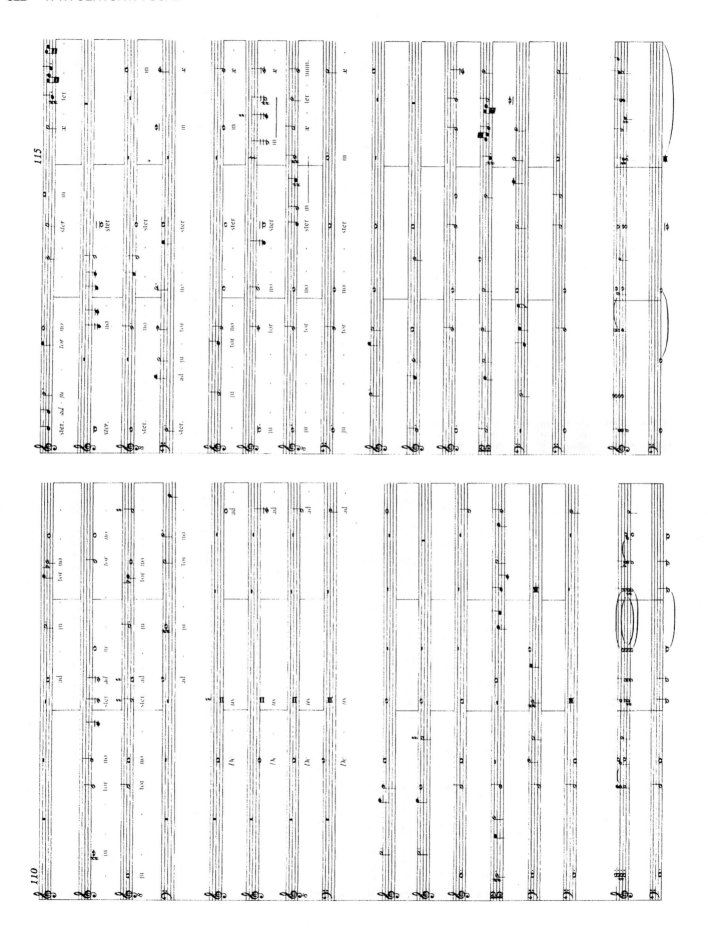

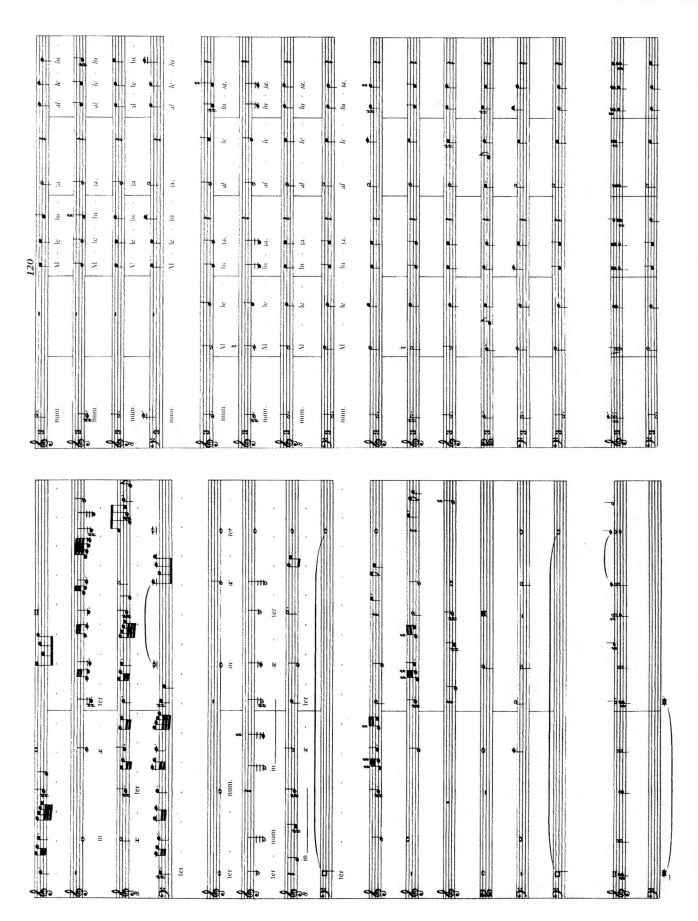

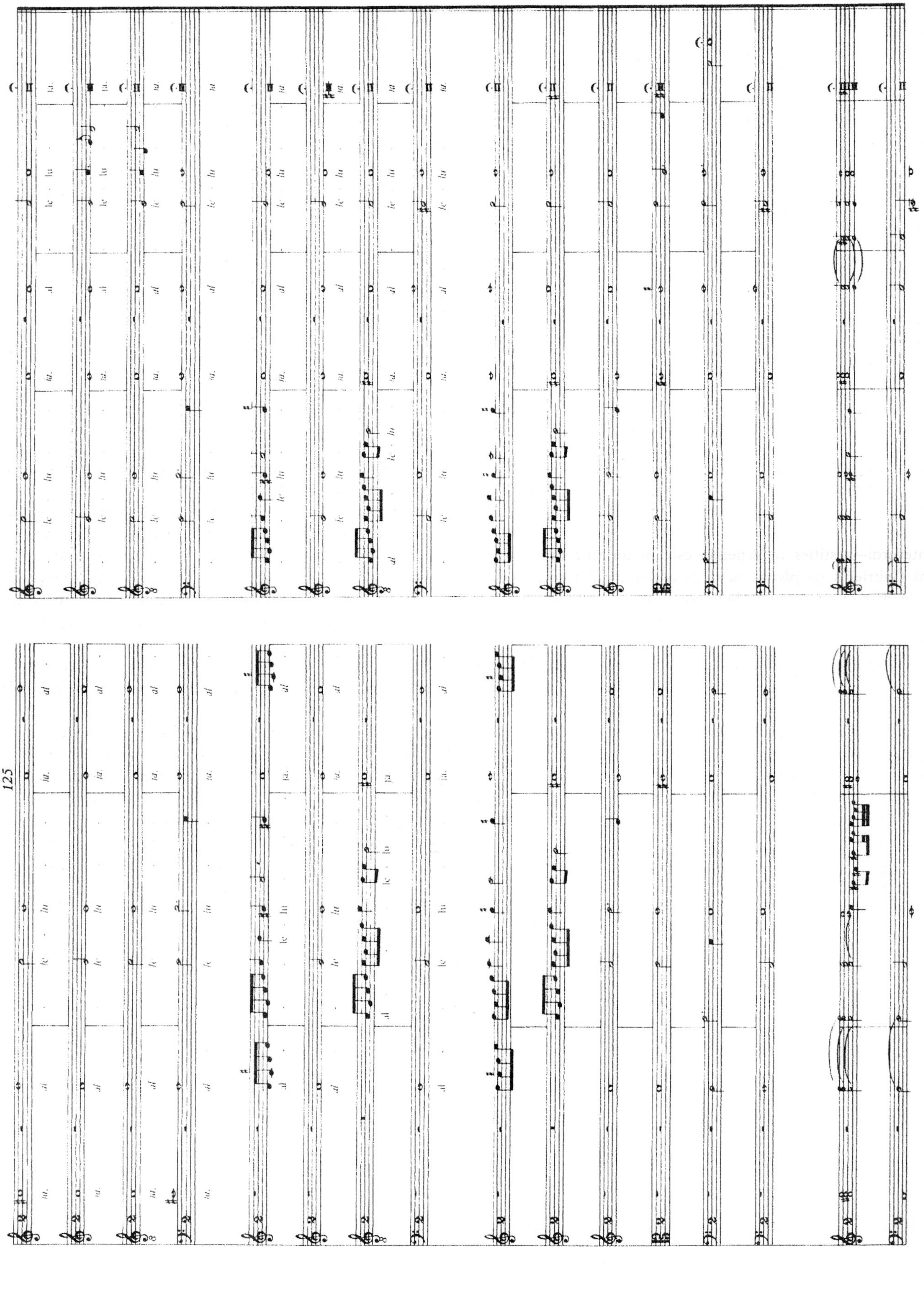
125

| | |
|---|---|
| In ecclesiis benedicite Domino. | *Bless the Lord in the congregations.* |
| Alleluia! | *Alleluia!* |
| In omni loco dominationis | *In every place of his power,* |
| benedic anima mea Dominum. | *bless the Lord, my soul.* |
| Alleluia! | *Alleluia!* |
| In Deo salutari meo et gloria mea. | *In God is my salvation and my glory.* |
| Deus auxilium meum | *God is my help* |
| et spes mea in Deo est. | *and my hope is in God.* |
| Alleluia! | *Alleluia!* |
| Deus noster te invocamus | *Our God, we call upon thee,* |
| te laudamus | *we praise thee,* |
| te adoramus. | *we worship thee.* |
| Libera nos. | *Deliver us.* |
| Salva nos. | *Save us.* |
| Vivifica nos. | *Invigorate us.* |
| Alleluia! | *Alleluia!* |
| Deus adjutor noster in aeternum. | *God our support forever.* |
| Alleluia! | *Alleluia!* |

The unique spatial qualities of St. Mark's Cathedral in Venice inspired sacred ceremonial music of special grandeur. The sequence of illustrious composers at St. Mark's from 1527 on—Adrian Willaert, Andrea Gabrieli, Giovanni Gabrieli, Claudio Monteverdi—testifies to Venetian esteem for fine music. Giovanni Gabrieli's *symphonia sacra In ecclesiis,* published posthumously in 1615, represents a high point in the development of the Venetian festival motet. It is scored for three *cori spezzati* (divided choirs)—two of voices and one of instruments.[1] The concertato effect of soloists, choirs, and instrumental ensembles became much cultivated in seventeenth-century sacred music, and was especially admired in Germany.

*In ecclesiis* is designed according to a ritornello principle and has a recurring choral refrain on the word *alleluia.* The sections between refrains are scored for small groups of voices or instruments and mainly feature florid soloistic writing. The whole is a wonderful study in contrasts of timbre, texture, and meter. The phrases within sections are so short as to be hardly more than motives. The frequent changes and contrasts in musical ideas distinguish this style both from the fluidity of mid-sixteenth-century sacred writing and from the broad sequential paragraphs of later baroque manner.

Despite the fragmentary nature of individual musical gestures, Gabrieli has conceived this motet on a sweeping dramatic plan. The passages between *alleluias* gradually grow longer and thicken in texture until the final intense supplication to God. This outcry achieves special poignancy from its chromatic inflections and ponderous rhythms. Its subdued quality imparts special jubilance to the fully scored, strongly metrical *alleluia* that follows.

[1]After the first four conventional designations (C, A, T, B), the voices are simply numbered in order from 5 to 14. The distribution of parts among the three groups is as follows, with ranges given in parentheses after Gabrieli's numbers: (1) soloists—5 (S), A, T, 8 (B); (2) *capella* (i.e., vocal choir)—13 (S), 14 (A), 11 (T), 12 (B); (3) instrumental ensemble—three cornetti—C, 7, 9 (all S range); violino (viola) 10 (A range); two sackbuts—6 (baritone range), B. The organ bass is continuous throughout and accompanies all the groups.

**60.** HEINRICH SCHÜTZ  (1585-1672)

# O quam tu pulchra es

from **Symphoniae sacrae I**

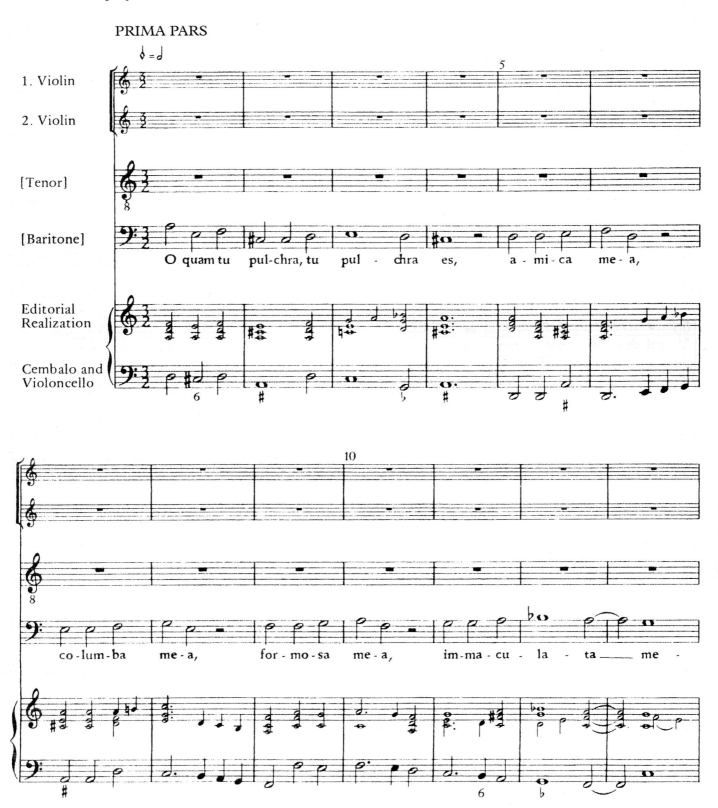

**Section**

| | |
|---|---|
| 1. O quam tu pulchra es<br>amica mea, columba mea,<br>formosa mea, immaculata mea<br>O quam tu pulchra es. | 1. *O how beautiful thou art*<br>*my friend, my dove,*<br>*my beauty, my purity,*<br>*O how beautiful thou art.* |
| 2. *Sinfonia* | 2. [Instrumental interlude, based on preceding musical material] |
| 3. O quam tu pulchra es. | 3. *O how beautiful thou art.* |
| 4. Oculi tui, oculi columbarum | 4. *Thine eyes—the eyes of doves* |
| 5. O quam tu pulchra es. | 5. *O how beautiful thou art.* |
| 6. Capilli tui sicut greges caprarum | 6. *Thy hair, like herds of goats* |
| 7. O quam tu pulchra es. | 7. *O how beautiful thou art.* |
| 8. Dentos tui sicut greges tonsarum | 8. *Thy teeth, like droves of shorn sheep* |
| 9. O quam tu pulchra es. | 9. *O how beautiful thou art.* |
| 10. Sicut vitta coccinea labia tua | 10. *Like a scarlet ribbon, thy lips* |
| 11. O quam tu pulchra es. | 11. *O how beautiful thou art.* |
| 12. Sicut turris David collum tuum | 12. *Like the tower of David thy neck* |
| 13. O quam tu pulchra es. | 13. *O how beautiful thou art.* |
| 14. Duo ubera tua<br>sicut duo hinnuli capreae gemelli | 14. *Thy two breasts*<br>*like the twin kids of a goat.* |
| 15. O quam tu pulchra es. | 15. *O how beautiful thou art.* |

—Text arranged after the Song of Songs, Chapter 4, verses 1-5

Among numerous excellent German composers of the seventeenth century, Heinrich Schütz (1585-1672) stands out for his assimilation of new Italian styles, mastery of compelling musical rhetoric, and clarity of mind. Trained as a choirboy at the court of the Landgrave of Hesse-Cassel (a central-western region of present-day West Germany), Schütz undertook two trips to Venice to study the latest Italian idioms: concertato and continuo textures, monody and recitative. During his first sojourn (1609-12) he studied composition and organ playing with the eminent Giovanni Gabrieli. During his second, undertaken when he was a mature musician in his early forties (1628-29), he learned from Monteverdi (then *maestro di capella* at Saint Mark's) the flexible melodic style of contemporary opera and continuo madrigal. Schütz spent most of his life in Dresden as *Kapellmeister* to Johann Georg I, Elector of Saxony, a post that was not without its vicissitudes, especially during the deprivations of the Thirty Years' War (1618-48). Schütz's works are almost entirely sacred. After 1630 he set mostly German texts, a reflection of the German Protestant milieu in which he worked.

On returning from his second Venetian study period, Schütz brought as a "votive gift" to his patron's heir his *Symphoniae sacrae* I (1629), twenty settings of biblical texts in Latin for diverse combinations of instruments and solo voices. By implication, these pieces illustrate the new "theory of composing melodies" and "fresh devices" which, according to his dedicatory remarks, he had just encountered in Italy.[1] The preface to the *Symphoniae sacrae* II (1647), settings of German texts, elaborates further upon the modern Italian manner, which was insufficiently understood by German musicians. Schütz especially stresses the necessity of adopting proper tempos and taking into account the "notes of lesser value." In addition to a newly modulated rhythmic style, dissonance treatment and affective rhetorical figures also betray a modern Italian spirit in the *Symphoniae sacrae* I.[2] Schütz does not mention the very cohesive motivic and tonal organization of these works, but in view of the "high baroque" idiom to come and the thematic diffuseness of much early seventeenth-century music, this too deserves special attention.

[1]The dedication to *Symphoniae sacrae* I is translated and printed in O. Strunk, *Source Readings in Music History* (New York: Norton, 1950), pp. 432-434; paperback edition, Part III, *The Baroque Era* (New York: 1965), pp. 72-74. The prefatory material to *Symphoniae sacrae* II, mentioned below, is also published in the *Source Readings,* pp. 434-438 and 74-78 in the respective editions.

[2]For a discussion of some of these aspects in *O quam tu pulchra es* see C. Palisca, *Baroque Music,* second edition, Prentice Hall History of Music Series (Englewood Cliffs, N. J.: 1981), pp. 103-107.

*O quam tu pulchra es* (SWV 265),[3] the *prima pars* of a two-part work,[4] seems on the surface to be a typical "fragmented" early baroque work with its fourteen (or more) subdivisions. Yet text, thematic treatment, and pitch relationships all contribute to a strong inner cohesion. The obsessive repetition of *O quam tu pulchra es*, an "improvement" by Schütz on the biblical source, both conveys overwhelming, sensuous adoration, and projects a clear cyclic design (despite its changing musical setting). The formalized motivic treatment of melody is apparent from the first paragraph of the baritone (mm. 1-19). The central melodic gesture is generated sequentially from a motive within the first phrase. The closure (mm. 15-19) repeats the first phrase but replaces its unstable, expectant ending with a stable arrival. The adoration continues with an intensified repetition of this material in two voices and on a different tonal plane. Instead of closing with the introductory phrase, as before, this statement is unexpectedly extended by a solo instrumental section in which the violins concertize on the familiar motives. The clear sense of sequential melodic "logic," and the equilibrium between order and diversity apparent here and throughout Schütz's subsequent work are unparalleled by any other German composers of his generation. Although the initial text phrase recurs with the same (or similar) rhythmic cast, the motive to which it is first bound returns only in the final section of this part as a signal of completion. (It recurs also in condensed form to close the *secunda pars*.)

The specific attributes singled out for praise are set in contrasting meter, and with a very different style of melody. In these sections Schütz generally abandons the tuneful aria style for a more speechlike idiom, or an expressive ornate manner (mm. 63-65; 93-95). The last of these subsections (mm. 100ff.) is the only one to be expanded musically through techniques of motivic sequence and repetition.

Tonally, O *quam tu pulchra* evidences careful planning with a minor triad on D as center and fifth-related areas extending to either side: C ← G ← $\boxed{\text{d}}$ → A. Additional color comes from passing cadences on F and E, and from modal shifts between adjacent chords (mm. 52-53; 81-32). The harmonically pointed bass line and the frequent, sharply articulated cadences (sometimes brought into relief by hemiola rhythm, mm. 12-14, 31-33) serve to define tonal areas. The harmonic successions, however, are not such that one can speak of "keys" or functional tonality. The presence of the *secunda pars* explains the closure on A rather than on the starting point, D.

---

[3]Schütz's compositions are commonly identified by order number in the standard catalogue of his works, the *Schütz-Werke-Verzeichnis, Kleine Ausgabe*, ed. W. Bittinger (Kassel and Basel: Bärenreiter Verlag, 1960).

[4]The second part, *Veni de Libano*, may be found in *Symphoniae sacrae* I, ed. R. Gerber, Heinrich Schütz neue Ausgabe sämtlicher Werke, vol. 13 (Kassel and Basel: Bärenreiter Verlag, 1957), pp. 88–95.

## 61. HEINRICH SCHÜTZ
# Saul, Saul was verfolgst du mich?
from **Symphoniarum sacrarum tertia pars**

Track 9

Saul, Saul was verfolgst du mich?
Es wird dir schwer werden wider den Stachel zu lökken.

*Saul, Saul, why dost thou persecute me?*
*It will be hard for thee to defy these goads.*[1]

(Acts 26:14)

[1]Literally, "to kick against the pricks," a Greek saying that can be traced back to the fifth century B.C. The general idea is that Saul cannot maintain his stubborn resistance to the Christian message.

In the third part of his *Symphoniae sacrae,* published in 1650, Schütz returns to the polychoral splendors of such earlier works as his *Psalms of David* (1619). His concertato motet *Saul, Saul was verfolgst du mich?* (SWV 415) resembles Gabrieli's *In ecclesiis* (No. 59) in its contrast of soloists and full choirs and its ritornello structure, but it is a far more compact and integrated work.

The text stems from one of the most powerful episodes in the New Testament, the miraculous conversion of Saul as he hastened to persecute the Christians in Damascus. The event is described three times in the Acts of the Apostles (Chapter 9, verses 1-8; Chapter 22, verses 6-11; and Chapter 26, verses 12-18). Schütz draws his text from the third account, Saul's report before King Agrippa:

> At midday, O King, I saw in the way a light from heaven, above the brightness of the sun, shining round about me and them which journeyed with me.
> And when we were all fallen to the earth, I heard a voice speaking unto me, and saying in the Hebrew tongue, Saul, Saul, why persecutest thou me? it is hard for thee to kick against the pricks.
> Acts 26:13-14 (King James version)

Schütz sets only the words of Christ—the audience would have known the dramatic context.

At the opening, Schütz aptly suggests Saul's dawning consciousness of the insistent heavenly voice through scoring and register. The words surge up from the lowest register in faint solo voices, then impose themselves in a forceful scoring of double chorus, soloists and instruments. This material recurs twice more, once in a compact form (m. 34) and later in a much expanded, climactic version (m. 63) in which an interior voice solemnly intones Saul's name over and over.

The contrasting setting of the second sentence is treated in a similar developmental way. Its first appearance is very compact, but the second is contrapuntally elaborated in a way that suggests a bewildering buzz in the mind of Saul. Here the development of musical materials and the realization of textual drama are perfectly coordinated.

Aspects of harmony and dissonance treatment also contribute to the power of the text setting in *Saul, Saul.* The exposed seconds and upper-voice leaps from dissonance to dissonance in the initial questions (mm. 3-4, 7-8, 11-12, etc.) give a harsh tone to the word *persecute.* Cross-relations and harmonic jolts (mm. 48-49, 57) convey Saul's pain and the difficulty of resistance. The succession of different harmonic goals in the first section (d in m. 5, a in m. 9, F in m. 13, D in m. 17, and G in m. 23) produces an effect of dislocation. The tonal wrenches become more brutal in the last section where the motivic material is displaced from F to G to a within a short span of time (mm. 64ff.) The return to the initial tonal sphere (d) along with the reduction of voices brings Saul's disturbing vision to an end.

Schütz's address to the "gracious reader" prefacing *Symphoniae sacrae* III specifies the organ as the continuo instrument and offers advice on possible ways of performance.[1]

[1]Printed in O. Strunk, *Source Readings in Music History* (New York: Norton, 1950), pp. 440-441; paperback edition, Part III, *The Baroque Era* (New York: 1965), pp. 80-81.

**Plate 5.** "Non piango e non sospiro" from *Euridice* (No. 62), by Jacopo Peri (Florence: 1600), page 17.

## 62. JACOPO PERI (1561-1633)
### Euridice
Excerpt from scene 2

**Per quel vago boschetto** through **Non piango e non sospiro**

[1]The edition preserves Peri's note values and irregular barring. The main unit of time is represented by two whole notes (semibreves), but the notated durations are presumably intended more as guides to fluid declamation than as signs of exact value.

[2]A figured bass realization may be found in *Le nuove musiche per l'Euridice*, edited by V. Frazzi (Florence: 1970), pp. 40–47.

DAFNE:

Per quel vago boschetto
ove rigando i fiori
lento trascorre il fonte degl'allori
prendea dolce diletto
con le compagne sue la bella sposa.
Chi violetta, o rosa
per far ghirland'al crine
togliea dal prato, o dall'acute spine,
e qual posand' il fianco
su la fiorita sponda
dolce cantava, al mormorar dell'onda;
Ma la bella Euridice
movea danzando il piè su'l verde prato,
quand'ahi! ria sorte acerba!
angue crudo, e spietato,
che celato giacea tra' fiori, e l'erba,
punsele il piè con si maligno dente,
ch'impalidì repente
come raggio di Sol che nube adombri,
e dal profondo core
con un sospir mortale
si spaventoso ohimè! sospinse fuore,
che, quasi havesse l'ale,
giunse ogni Ninfa al doloroso suono,
et ella in abbandono
tutta lasciossi all'or nell'altrui braccia.

DAPHNE:

*By that pretty little woods*
*through which, irrigating the flowers,*
*the laurel stream slowly flows,*
*the beautiful bride took sweet delight*
*with her companions, who,*
*to make garlands for their hair,*
*picked violets or roses*
*from the meadow, or from among sharp thorns,*
*and one, leaning over*
*the flowered bank*
*sang sweetly to the murmuring of the stream;*
*but beautiful Euridice*
*danced upon the green meadow*
*when, alas! bitter and evil fate!*
*a cruel and merciless viper*
*who lay hidden among flowers and grass*
*punctured her foot with so malignant a fang*
*that she suddenly paled*
*like a ray of sunlight shaded by clouds*
*and from the depths of her heart*
*a deathly sigh burst forth*
*so terrifying, alas,*
*that, as if endowed with wings,*
*every Nymph rushed toward that grevious sound*
*and she collapsing*
*fell directly into their arms.*

Spargea il bel volto, e le dorate chiome
un sudor viè più fredd'assai che ghiaccio
indi s'udio'l tuo nome
tra le labbra sonar fredd'e tremanti,
e, volti gl'occhi al cielo,
scolorito il bel volto, e bei sembianti,
restò tanta bellezza immobil gielo.

ARCETRO:
Che narri, ohimè! che sento?
Misera Ninfa, e più misero amante,
spettacol di miseria e di tormento.

ORFEO:
Non piango e non sospiro,
O mia cara Euridice,
che sospirar, che lacrimar non posso.
Cadavero infelice,
O mio core, o mio speme, o pace, o vita!
Ohimè! chi mi t'ha tolto,
chi mi t'ha tolto, ohimè! dove sei gita?
Tosto vedrai ch'in vano
non chiamasti morendo il tuo consorte.
Non son, non son lontano:
io vengo, o cara vita, o cara morte.

*Sweat colder than ice*
*poured from her beautiful face and golden hair;*
*then your name was heard,*
*sounding from cold and trembling lips,*
*and, eyes turned toward heaven,*
*colorless, look blank,*
*so much beauty froze into immobility.*

ARCETRUS:
*What do you say! what do I hear!*
*Unhappy nymph, and more unhappy lover,*
*a spectacle of misery and torment!*

ORPHEUS:
*I weep not, and sigh not,*
*O my dear Euridice,*
*for whom I cannot sigh or weep.*
*Unfortunate corpse,*
*O my heart, O my hope, O peace, O life!*
*Alas! who has taken you from me?*
*who has taken you from me, alas! where have you gone?*
*Soon you will see that, dying,*
*you did not call your husband in vain.*
*I am not far away,*
*I come, O dear life, O dear death.*

European opera had its genesis in northern Italy, its ancestry in two central cultural elements of the 1580s and 1590s: the elaborate festal entertainments and *intermedi* of northern Italian courts (particularly the Medici establishment at Florence and that of the Gonzagas at Mantua), and the speculative studies of Italian humanists (men such as Girolamo Mei, Count Giovanni de'Bardi and Vincenzo Galilei, to mention only some within the Florentine circle). Inspired by the writings of Plato and by vivid reports of ancient Greek theatrical productions, the humanists pleaded for revival, or regeneration, of a music capable of profound emotional impact.

The first offspring of this union were plays set entirely in music, which appeared around 1600. Emilio de'Cavalieri, Giulio Caccini, and Jacopo Peri all jostled for the prestige of being first to develop a new genre. *Dafne*, with text by Ottavio Rinuccini and music by Peri, is often cited as the "first" opera (first performance at Florence, 1598). Their *Euridice,* on which Caccini also collaborated, is the first opera whose music survives intact. This musical entertainment on a classic Greek fable of ardent conjugal love graced the marriage festivities of Maria de'Medici and King Henry IV of France (6 October 1600).

The hallmark of the new genre was the *stile rappresentativo*[1] or *stile recitativo*—a new mode of solo singing intended to duplicate the accent and capture the emotional power of passionate speech. With more subdued coloring, it also served for narrative passages. Besides recitative, the earliest operas incorporated ensemble canzonettas and madrigals, tuneful solo songs and lively instrumental ritornelli, in the manner of the festal *intermedi*.

Jacopo Peri (1561-1633), himself a skilled singer and organist, probably sang Orfeo in the first production of *Euridice*. Although the rudimentary notation of Peri's printed score (Plate 5) conveys neither the richness of accompaniment nor the nuance of vocal production heard in the Florentine performance,[2] something of the expressive capacity of the recitative can be gleaned from the passage in which the nymph Dafne describes the circumstances of Euridice's death. Her narration of the happy start of the day is tonally stable, consonant, and rhythmically fairly even. But as she describes the disaster (mm. 22 ff.) the tonal sphere shifts to a tenser, "sharper" realm, declamation becomes faster and rhythmically more irregular, and pronounced dissonances and shifts in mode portray deep agitation. An immovable bass and static melodic line communicate the stunned first reaction of Orpheus—a "spectacle of misery," too shocked to weep or sigh (m. 64). Grating dissonances (mm. 68, 78), untoward harmonic progressions (mm. 73-74, 76), and wider-ranging melody suggest a gradually reawakening consciousness. A slight measure of optimism even emerges when the soliloquy coalesces into a tuneful, tonally stable phrase (mm. 84-88) as Orfeo's resolution to seek out Euridice takes shape.

The flexibility of this mode of expression, described by Peri in his preface as intermediate between song and speech, recommended it as a means to effective representation of feelings in the theater. Monteverdi's setting of the parallel passage in *Orfeo* (No. 63) adopts the rhetorical style pioneered by Peri and Caccini in Florence and realizes it with even keener musical sensibility.

[1]On the Florentine *stile rappresentativo*, see Pietro de'Bardi's "Letter to G. B. Doni," translated in O. Strunk, *Source Readings in Music History* (New York: Norton, 1950), pp. 363-366; paperback edition, Part III, *The Baroque Era*, pp. 3-6.

[2]Aspects of this performance are described by Peri in his preface to *Euridice,* translated in O. Strunk, *op. cit.,* pp. 373-376; paperback edition, pp. 13-16.

# 63. CLAUDIO MONTEVERDI
## **Orfeo**

Track 10

Excerpts from Act II

63a. **Vi ricordi** through **Ahi caso acerbo**

Fu sonato questo ritornello di dentro da cinque viole da braccio, un contrabassso, due Clavicembali e tre chitaroni.[1]

[1]This ritornello was played backstage by five violins or violas, one contrabass, two harpsichords and three chitarrones.

[2]Figured bass realizations may be found in: *Tutte le opere di Claudio Monteverdi,* vol. XI, edited by G. F. Malipiero (1930), pp. 48-59 and 62-64; in *L'Orfeo,* edited by A. Wenzinger (Kassel, Basel et al.: 1958), pp. 30-33 and 36-40; in *L'Orfeo,* edited by E. H. Tarr (Paris: 1974), pp. 39-43 and 45-49; and in *L'Orfeo Favola in musica,* edited by Denis Stevens (Borough Green and London: 1968), pp. 47-53 and 56-61.

[3]Repeat to the beginning of the ritornello.

[4]An organ with wooden pipes and a chitarrone.

[5]A harpsichord, chitarrone, and *viola da braccio*. The alternation of continuo instruments presumably continues throughtout this passage.

ORFEO:
Vi ricorda o boschi ombrosi
de'miei lunghi aspri tormenti,
quando i sassi ai miei lamenti
rispondean fatti pietosi?

Dite allor' non vi sembrai
più d'ogni altro sconsolato?
Or Fortuna ha stil cangiato
ed ha volto in festa i guai.

Vissi gia mesto e dolente,
or gioisco e quegli affanni
che sofferti ho per tant' anni
fan più caro il ben presente.

Sol per te, bella Euridice,
benedico il mio tormento.
Dopo il duol si è più contento,
dopo il mal si è più felice.

PASTORE:
Mira, deh mira Orfeo, che d'ogni intorno
ride il bosco e ride il prato.
Segui pur col plettro aurato
d'addolcir l'aria in si beato giorno.

LA MESSAGGIERA:
Ahi caso acerbo! Ahi fato empio e crudele!
Ahi stelle ingiuriose! Ahi ciel avaro!

PASTORE:
Qual suon dolente il lieto dì perturba?

LA MESSAGGIERA:
Lasso, dunque debb'io
mentre Orfeo con sue note il ciel consola
con le parole miei passargli il core?

PASTORE:
Questa è Silvia gentile
dolcissima compagna de la bella Euridice.
O quanto è in vista dolorosa.
Hor che fia? Deh, sommi Dei,
non torcete da noi benigno il guardo.

LA MESSAGGIERA:
Pastor, lasciate il canto,
ch'ogni nostra allegrezza in doglia è volta.

ORFEO:
D'onde vieni? ove vai?
Ninfa, che porti?

ORPHEUS:
*You remember, O shady woods,*
*my long, bitter torments,*
*when the stones responded compassionately*
*to my laments?*

*Say, did I not seem then*
*more disconsolate than anyone else?*
*Now Fortune has changed her way*
*and turned woe into joy.*

*Then my life was sad and sorrowful,*
*now I rejoice and those sorrows*
*that I suffered for so many years*
*make the present joy more dear to me.*

*Only because of you, beautiful Euridice,*
*do I bless my torments.*
*After sorrow, there is more contentment,*
*after pain, more happiness.*

SHEPHERD:
*Look, O look, Orfeo, how on all sides*
*the woods and the fields laugh.*
*Continue on with your golden plectrum*
*to sweeten the air on such a blessed day.*

THE MESSENGER:
*Alas, bitter event! Alas, impious and cruel Fate!*
*Alas, injurious stars! Alas, covetous Heaven!*

SHEPHERD:
*What doleful sound disturbs this joyful day?*

THE MESSENGER:
*O misery, must I then,*
*while Orpheus consoles the heavens with his music,*
*pierce his heart with my words?*

SHEPHERD:
*This is gentle Sylvia,*
*sweetest companion of fair Euridice.*
*O how sad she looks.*
*What has happened? Ah, great Gods,*
*turn not your favorable regard from us.*

THE MESSENGER:
*Shepherd, cease your song,*
*for all our happiness has turned to sorrow.*

ORPHEUS:
*Where do you come from? where are you going?*
*Nymph, what is it you have to tell?*

LA MESSAGGIERA:
A te ne vengo, Orfeo,
messaggiera infelice
di caso più infelice e più funesto.
La tua bella Euridice . . .

THE MESSENGER:
*I come to you, Orpheus,*
*unhappy messenger*
*of an event more unhappy and more anguishing.*
*Your beautiful Euridice . . .*

ORFEO:
Ohimè, che odo?

ORPHEUS:
*Alas, what do I hear?*

LA MESSAGGIERA:
La tua diletta sposa è morta.

THE MESSENGER:
*Your cherished wife is dead.*

ORFEO:
Ohimè.

ORPHEUS:
*Oh, no . . .*

The messenger explains the circumstances of Euridice's death in a passage omitted from this excerpt.

## 63b. **A l'amara novella** through **Ahi caso acerbo**

ORFEO

15

20

¹An organ with wooden pipes and a chitaronne.

PASTORE:

A l'amara novella
rassembra l'infelice un muto sasso
che per troppo dolor non può dolersi.
Ahi, ben havrebbe un cor di Tigre o d'Orsa
chi non sentisse del tuo mal pietate
privo d'ogni tuo ben misero amante.

ORFEO:

Tu se'morta mia vita, ed io respiro?
Tu se'da me partita
per mai più non tornare, ed io rimango?
No! che se i versi alcuna cosa ponno
n'andro sicuro à più profondi abissi
e intenerito il cor del Re del' ombre
meco trarroti a riveder le stelle.
O se ciò negherammi empio destino
rimarrò teco in compagnia di morte.
A dio terra, a dio cielo, e sole, a dio.

CHORO:

Ahi caso acerbo! Ahi fato empio e crudele!
Ahi stelle ingiuriose! Ahi cielo avaro!
Non si fidi huom mortale
di ben caduco e frale
che tosto fugge e spesso
a gran fatica il precipizio è presso.

SHEPHERD:

*At this bitter news*
*the unhappy man stands like a mute stone;*
*in his excess of grief he cannot grieve.*
*Ah, only someone with the heart of a tiger or a bear*
*would not feel pity for your pain,*
*distressed lover, deprived of all your happiness.*

ORPHEUS:

*You are dead, my life, and I breathe?*
*You are gone from me*
*never to return, and I remain?*
*No! if I can do anything with my verses*
*I will definitely go to the deepest abysses*
*and, softening the heart of the King of the Shades,*
*will lead you back to view the stars again.*
*Or, if cruel destiny denies this to me,*
*I shall remain with you in company with death.*
*Farewell earth, farewell sky, and sun, farewell.*

CHORUS:

*Alas, bitter event! Alas, impious and cruel fate!*
*Alas, injurious stars! Alas, covetous Heaven!*
*Mortal man, do not trust*
*transient and fragile happiness*
*which soon evaporates and often,*
*after being gained with great exertion,*
*    takes you to the brink of disaster.*

As the subject for their first musical theater piece, Claudio Monteverdi and Alessandro Striggio (the younger) chose the Orpheus legend already treated by Jacopo Peri and Ottavio Rinuccini (see No. 62). *Orfeo* (Mantua, 1607) is the first opera whose theatrical impact and musical substance disclose the dramatic potential of this new type of stage work. Dramatically speaking, *Orfeo*, which was billed as a *favola in musica* (a tale set to music), belongs very much to the late Renaissance. It is pastoral in nature; it moves in static tableaux; it incorporates many musical elements of *intermedio* and ballet; its characters are more allegorical than earthly in nature (compare them with the sensuous reality of characters in Monteverdi's Venetian operas—see No. 64). But the very conception of a dramatic action projected entirely in music, as well as the resonating power of the monodic and recitative styles, mark *Orfeo* as the product of a new vision. The recent thinking of the Camerata is reflected even in the choice of text: a Greek fable that deals with the suprahuman power of music.

The basic dramatic plan of *Orfeo* is simple: Each of the five acts dramatizes a single step in the action. The musical climax is conspicuously and centrally located in Act III. There Orfeo sings the great solo *Possente spirto* that gains him access to Hades. This piece, a strophic variation in structure, is the pinnacle of vocal and instrumental virtuosity in the work. The second act centers on the brutal announcement of Euridice's sudden death. The moment is prepared with cogent irony. The bridegroom Orfeo and his friends merrily, confidently, rejoice in his happy union with Euridice when a messenger enters with the dreadful news. Here Monteverdi shifts musical style with stunning dramatic effect to underscore the reverse in emotional climate. Orfeo has been singing a bouncy strophic song that shifts teasingly between 3/4 and 6/8 accentuation. His companions doubtless dance to the bright ritornello preceding each strophe. The messenger's entrance brings a complete change in sonority and in vocal style. The *basso continuo* is colored by the hollow sound of the wood organ (specified by the composer). The tonal quality shifts from unclouded G major and C major to a chromatically inflected A minor. The regular rhythmic pulse ceases—the messenger speaks haltingly in irregular rhythms against a metrically amorphous bass. The melodic line becomes disjunct and the level of dissonance rises markedly (Messenger's recitative, m. 15 "*acerbo*," m. 16 "*empio*," etc.). This recitative style sustains the emotional tension of the interchange through the moment when the messenger reveals Euridice's death and Orpheus reacts with a single, stunned "Ohimè."

After a long narrative description in recitative of the circumstances of Euridice's death (omitted here), Orpheus collects himself enough to sing the superb lament in which he resolves to seek Euridice in Hades and bring her back, *Tu se' morta*. This moving passage amply reveals the emotional heights of which the *stile recitativo* was capable. Much of the musical rhetoric had already been employed by Monteverdi in the five-part madrigals of Books IV and V: the unprepared or unresolved dissonances, the declamatory manner of text delivery, the realistic word painting (sharp melodic descent to the abysses, m. 21, steep ascent to the stars, m. 25). But it is particularly intense here, and gains immeasurably in effect from the dramatic context and from performance by a solo singer, an individual character who lives the emotional response.[1] The broken delivery of the poetic text (*Tu se' morta . . . se' morta*) has a particularly poignant effect. The singer probably enhanced the written line with expressive vocal effects of the sort counseled by Caccini (see No. 55).

In accord with Greek tradition, the chorus breaks the tension of *Tu se' morta*, first echoing the messenger's initial outcry and then offering a generalized reflection on the transience of human happiness. In their *Ahi, caso acerbo* Monteverdi cleverly transmutes the original solo recitative into a somewhat more regular choral recitative. The statement of this outcry three times during the latter half of Act II is a conspicuous organizational device that also works dramatically to remind the audience of the messenger's shocking entry.

[1] A good description and comparison of this passage with a parallel passage in Peri's *Euridice* may be found in C. Palisca, *Baroque Music*, 2nd edition (Englewood Cliffs, N. J.: Prentice-Hall, 1981), pp. 40-42.

## 64.  CLAUDIO MONTEVERDI
# L'incoronazione di Poppea

Act I, scene 3

3  Track 12

[1]Figured bass realizations may be found in *Tutte le opere di Claudio Monteverdi,* vol. XIII, edited by G. F. Malipiero (1931), pp. 29-38; and in *L'incoronazione di Poppea,* edited by R. Leppard (London: 1977), pp. 30-41.

POPPEA:
Signor, signor, deh, non partire,
sostien che queste bracci
ti circondino il collo
come le tue bellezze
circondano il cor mio.

NERONE:
Poppea, lascia ch'io parto.

POPPEA:
Non partir, Signor,
deh, non partire.
Appena spunta l'alba
e tu che sei l'incarnato mio sole
la mia palpabil luce
e l'amoroso di de la mia vita
vuoi si repente far da me partita?
Deh, non dir di partir
che di voce si amara un solo accento
Ahi perir, ahi spirar quest'alma io sento.

NERONE:
La nobiltà de' nascimenti tuoi
non permette che Roma
sappia che siamo uniti
in fin ch'Ottavia . . .

POPPEA:
in fin che, in fin che . . .

NERONE:
In fin ch'Ottavia non rimane esclusa . . .

POPPEA:
Non rimane, non rimane . . .

NERONE:
In fin ch'Ottavia non rimane esclusa
col repudio da me.
Vanne vanne ben mio.
In un sospir che vien dal profondo del cor,
includo un bacio o cara et un a Dio.
Ci rivedrem ben tosto, sì, idolo mio.

POPPEA:
Signor, sempre me vedi
anzi mai non mi vedi.
Perchè s'è ver che nel tuo cor io sia
mentr'al tuo sen celata
non posso da' tuoi lumi esser mirata.

NERONE:
Adorati miei rai,
deh, restatemi homai.
Rimanti, o mia Poppea,
cor, vezzo, e luce mia.

POPPEA:
*My lord, my lord, ah! do not leave*
*allow these arms*
*to encircle your neck*
*just as your charms*
*encircle my heart.*

NERO:
*Poppea, do let me depart.*

POPPEA:
*Do not leave, my lord,*
*ah, do not leave.*
*Daybreak has hardly dawned*
*and you, who are my sun incarnate,*
*my palpable light*
*and the amorous day of my life,*
*you wish to abandon me so precipitately?*
*Ah, say nothing of leaving,*
*for at a single utterance of so bitter a word*
*Ah, I feel my soul perishing, ah, expiring!*

NERO:
*The nobility of your birth*
*prohibits Rome*
*from knowing that we are united*
*until Ottavia . . .*

POPPEA:
*Until, until . . .*

NERO:
*Until Ottavia is expelled forever . . .*

POPPEA:
*Forever, forever . . .*

NERO:
*Until Ottavia is expelled forever*
*through my repudiation.*
*Go, go my beloved.*
*In a sigh that comes from the depths of my heart*
*I include a kiss, dearest, and a farewell.*
*We will meet again soon, my idol.*

POPPEA:
*My lord, you see me always*
*yet never see me.*
*Because if it is true that I am within your heart*
*while hidden in your breast*
*I cannot be admired by your eyes.*

NERO:
*Eyes I adore,*
*Ah, stay forever with me.*
*Remain, O my Poppea,*
*my heart, my grace, and my light.*

POPPEA:
Deh, non dir di partire
che di voce si amara un solo accento
Ahi perir, ahi spirar quest'alma io sento.

NERONE:
Non temer tu stai meco a tutte l'hore,
splendor negl'occhi e deità nel core.

POPPEA:
Tornerai?

NERONE:
Se ben io vò pur teco io stò.

POPPEA:
Tornerai?

NERONE:
Il cor dalle tue stelle
mai mai non si disvelle.

POPPEA:
Tornerai?

NERONE:
Io non posso da te viver disgiunto
se non si smembra l'unità dal punto.

POPPEA:
Tornerai?

NERONE:
Tornerò.

POPPEA:
Quando?

NERONE:
Ben tosto.

POPPEA:
Ben tosto, me'l prometti?

NERONE:
Te'l giuro.

POPPEA:
E me l'osserverai?

NERONE:
E se a te non verrò, tu a me verrai.

POPPEA:
A Dio.

NERONE:
A Dio.

POPPEA:
*Ah , say nothing of leaving,*
*for at a single utterance of so bitter a word*
*Ah, I feel my soul perishing, ah, expiring!*

NERO:
*Do not fear, you are with me at every moment,*
*resplendent in my eyes, and divinity in my heart.*

POPPEA:
*Will you return?*

NERO:
*Although I leave, yet I remain with you.*

POPPEA:
*Will you return?*

NERO:
*My heart from your stars [eyes]*
*never, never can be separated.*

POPPEA:
*Will you return?*

NERO:
*I cannot live apart from you*
*any more than a unitary point can be divided.*

POPPEA:
*Will you return?*

NERO:
*I will return.*

POPPEA:
*When?*

NERO:
*Very soon.*

POPPEA:
*Very soon, you promise me?*

NERO:
*I swear it to you.*

POPPEA:
*And you will observe your oath?*

NERO:
*And if I do not come to you, you will come to me.*

POPPEA:
*Farewell.*

NERO:
*Farewell.*

POPPEA:
Nerone, Nerone, a Dio.

NERONE:
Poppea, Poppea, a Dio.

POPPEA:
A Dio, Nerone, a Dio.

NERONE:
A Dio, Poppea, a Dio.

POPPEA:
*Nero, Nero, farewell.*

NERO:
*Poppea, Poppea, farewell.*

POPPEA:
*Farewell, Nero, farewell.*

NERO:
*Farewell, Poppea, farewell.*

*L'incoronazione di Poppea* is one of only two late Monteverdi operas to survive. Composed on a text by the Venetian lawyer-poet G. F. Busenello, it was first performed in Venice in 1642. Mid-century Venetian opera differs from early *dramma per musica* in manifold respects, in social context as well as in musical style. It is written for public performance at commercial theaters, not for the private entertainment of an aristocratic circle. The drama is no longer pastoral but recreates familiar historical or legendary stories, full of incident and intrigue. The libretto is constructed to achieve a broad range of appeal. In *Poppea*, highly comic scenes (for example, III:6) mingle with scenes of profound seriousness (II:3, the death of Seneca; III:7, Ottavia's lament), angry confrontation (I:9), pointed eroticism (I:10), and sensational incident (II:14, the assassination attempt). The pastoral songs, instrumental dances, and choral scenes of *Orfeo* have disappeared. The emphasis is on individual characters who sing alone or in alternation. No set convention guides the musical expression, but characters sing more or less "tunefully" according to their words and the dramatic situation.

The story of *Poppea* (loosely based on Tacitus) focuses on the passionate love between the Roman emperor Nero and his mistress Poppea. The force of this love overcomes all obstacles, demolishing Poppea's former lover Ottone, Nero's sage advisor Seneca,[1] and his noble empress Ottavia. Concealed at first (because adulterous), their love is finally proclaimed publicly in the grand coronation scene that ends the opera. Act I, scene 3 depicts the long, drawn-out parting of Nero and Poppea after a night of illicit pleasure. Poppea, insecure about her conquest, tries to detain Nero. He gradually reassures her (and himself) of his ardor and promises to return soon. The exaggerated imagery of their language wonderfully captures their mutual self-conceit.

The musical expression is closely responsive to the text. It is possible to distinguish between recitative and aria styles (the latter often in pronounced triple meter), but Monteverdi roams freely through the entire continuum between these extremes. The free verse of the text facilitates easy passage along the continuum; the dramatic feeling determines Monteverdi's musical response. The informality of the recitative-aria relationship is plain, for example, in Nero's speech "*In un sospir*" (m. 69). This begins as a triple-meter "aria," but slips into recitative at moments when passion overcomes him. The "arias" vary greatly in manner. Some are merely short phrases (m. 53, "*Vanne ben mio*"). Others are substantial stanzas, set apart as integral units by internal phrase repetitions (m. 95, "*Signor, sempre mi vedi*"). Monteverdi and Busenello do not favor the strophic aria common in Venetian opera of the 1660s and later (see No. 66). The naturalistic flux of feeling they portray cannot be bound by formalistic regularity of text or musical structure.

Except for Seneca, a bass, all the leading roles in *Poppea* are for high voices. The part of Nero was written for a castrato, the preferred male voice in seventeenth- and eighteenth-century Italian opera. The castrato voice is described by contemporary observers as powerful, brilliant, clear, agile, and penetrating. In modern times, these parts are usually sung by countertenors or women. Only with the *opera buffa* of Mozart's day did the practice of writing for castrati fade.

---

[1]For an interpretation of the opera emphasizing Seneca's centrality see E. Rosand, "Seneca and the Interpretation of *L'incoronazione di Poppea*," *Journal of the American Musicological Society* xxxviii (1985), pp. 34-71.

## 65. GIACOMO CARISSIMI (1605-1674)
## Jephte
Oratorio

### 65a. **Cum autem victor** through **Cantate mecum**

vic - to - ri - am, vic - to - ri - am, vic - to - - - - ri - um.

HISTORICUS:
Cum autem victor Jephte in domum suam
reverteretur occurrens ei unigenita filia sua cum
tympanis et choris praecinebat:

FILIA:
Incipite in tympanis
et psallite in cymbalis.
Hymnum cantemus Domino
et modulemur canticum.
Laudemus regem coelitum,
laudemus belli principem,
qui filiorum Israel
victorem ducem reddidit.

DUO:
Hymnum cantemus Domino
et modulemur canticum,
qui dedit nobis gloriam
et Israel victoriam.

FILIA:
Cantate mecum Domino,
cantate omnes populi,
laudate belli principem,
qui nobis dedit gloriam
et Israel victoriam.

NARRATOR:
*When, however, the victorious Jephthah returned to
his house, his only child, a daughter, came to meet
him with tambourines and dancing, and singing.*

DAUGHTER:
*Sound the tambourines
and sing praises with cymbals.
Let us sing hymns to the Lord
and raise our song.
Let us praise the king of heaven,
let us praise the prince of war,
who gave the victory
to the sons of Israel.*

DUET [companions of the daughter]:
*Let us sing hymns
and raise our song to the Lord,
who gave glory to us
and victory to Israel.*

DAUGHTER:
*Sing with me to the Lord,
sing all the people,
praise the prince of war,
who gave glory to us
and victory to Israel.*

[A six-part chorus with continuo accompaniment next restates a variant of this verse.]

## 65b. **Cum vidisset Jephte** through **Heu mihi! filia mea**

heu fi-li-a me-a, de-cep-ta es, de-cep-ta es.

HISTORICUS:
Cum vidisset Jephte qui votum Domino voverat, filiam
suam venientem in occursum, in dolore et lachrimis
scidit vestimenta sua et ait:

JEPHTE:
Heu, heu mihi! filia mea,
heu decepisti me, filia unigenita,
decepisti me,
et tu pariter, heu filia mea,
decepta es, decepta es.

FILIA:
Cur ego te pater decepi,
et cur ego filia tua unigenita decepta sum?

JEPHTE:
Aperui os meum ad Dominum,
ut quicumque primus de domo mea occurrerit mihi
offeram illum Domino in holocaustum.
Heu mihi! filia mea,
heu decepisti me, filia unigenita,
decepisti me,
et tu pariter, heu filia mea,
decepta es, decepta es.

NARRATOR:
*When Jephthah, who had made his vow to the Lord,*
*saw his daughter coming to meet him, he rent his*
*clothing in sorrow and in tears and said:*

JEPHTHAH:
*Woe, woe to me! my daughter,*
*woe, you have deceived me, my only child,*
*you have deceived me,*
*and you also, woe, my daughter,*
*you are deceived, you are deceived.*

DAUGHTER:
*How, father, have I deceived you,*
*and how am I, your only child, your daughter,*
*    deceived?*

JEPHTHAH:
*I opened my mouth to the Lord, and said*
*whoever would first issue from my house to meet me,*
*I would offer that one to the Lord as a burnt offering.*
*Woe to me! my daughter,*
*woe, you have deceived me, my only child,*
*you have deceived me,*
*and you also, woe, my daughter,*
*you are deceived, you are deceived.*

"Giacomo Carissimi. . . . surpasses all others in moving the minds of listeners to whatever affection he wishes."
—A. Kircher, *Musurgia Universalis* (Rome: 1650)[1]

Learning from the secular example provided in opera, seventeenth-century church musicians dramatized biblical stories in musical settings that came to be known as *oratorios,* after the prayer halls in which they were presented. Rome was the birthplace of the oratorio, and Giacomo Carissimi (1605-1674), *maestro di capella* at the Jesuit *Collegio Germanico,* was the composer who brought the new genre to maturity. Carissimi's *Jephte* ("Jephthah") won praise from Anasthasius Kircher in 1650 for its depth of expression and is still esteemed as a powerful and moving work. In an age when nuclear destruction threatens the children of those who wage war, its story and its music carry particular poignancy. As with most of Carissimi's oratorios, the story of Jephthah is drawn from the Old Testament (Judges, Chapter 11) and is compressed into a single span of action, undivided by acts or scenes. The action is not staged, but individual singers portray the characters of the drama.[2] Choruses, which are standard in oratorios, sometimes provide external commentary on the action, sometimes represent participants in the drama (soldiers, the Israelites in *Jephte*). Dramatic economy is achieved through a solo narrator or *historicus,* whose summaries of action link the episodes chosen for musical elaboration. The narrator is not an individual role, but in *Jephte* is sung variously by bass and alto voices.

*Jephte* is a story of crushing dramatic irony. Having sworn the rash vow that if victorious in war he will sacrifice to Jehovah the first living being to issue from his house on his return, the Israelite general Jephthah becomes obligated to kill his beloved daughter and only child. The buoyant elation first produced by his victory cedes to piercing misery as his daughter hastens to greet him with song and dance. Carissimi communicates the emotional change through imaginative control of vocal idiom. A multisectional aria sung by Jephthah's daughter and two companions crystallizes the initial joyous reaction (No. 65a). Major harmonies, consonant sounds, motivically designed melodies, regular rhythms, ordered phrase relationships, exuberant

vocalizations project a mood of confidence and cheer. Even the narrator who prepares the daughter's entrance is permitted a joyful *passaggio* (mm. 7-9). Jephthah's horrified realization of his insensate action brings a complete reversal of sound quality, beginning with minor chords and chromatic inflection in the narrator's detached statement (No. 65b, mm. 1-10). Jephthah's own outburst, "*Heu, heu mihi! filia mea*" achieves expressive heights through accented dissonance, affective intervals (e.g., diminished fourth), unexpected harmonic successions, and irregular declamation. This manner of heightened recitative continues early Monteverdi tradition (No. 63b, "*Tu se' morta*"). Recurrence of Jephthah's lament after his response to his daughter's puzzled query both concentrates the feeling and gives formal definition to the scene, as if it were a set piece.

In contrast to Monteverdi's *L'incoronazione di Poppea* (see No. 64), but in keeping with the structure of the libretto, the different styles of singing—from aria to simple recitative to elevated declamation—are sharply separated in *Jephte*. Textual factors encourage this, for the victory song of Jephthah's daughter is written in eight-syllable regulated verse, the narrator's statements and Jephthah's lament in prose. The more "ordered" music contains in it the germ of the mature baroque style. For example, the last section of the victory song "*Cantate mecum Domino*" exhibits on a small scale the patterned lines, directed harmonic movement and melody-bass coordination considered central to the language of Handel and J. S. Bach. The close relationship between thematic design and tonal plan is shown in the following diagram of "*Cantate mecum*" (mm. 63-76):

| thematic material | a a b b c(=cadence) | b b c━━━c extended |
|---|---|---|
| central pitch | G C G D a | C G (d)   G   G |

Fifth relationships predominate, but on the scale of the chord more than of the tonal area. Handel's art involves considerable temporal expansion of such tonal relationships. Handel knew *Jephte,* but when he drew directly upon its musical substance, he seems to have preferred its more expressive passages.[3]

[1]Translation quoted from C. Palisca, *Baroque Music,* Prentice-Hall History of Music Series (2nd edition, Englewood Cliffs, N.J.: 1981), p. 125. The passage quoted by Palisca includes the appreciation of *Jephte* mentioned below.

[2]For an early (1639) description of an oratorio performance, see C. Palisca, *Baroque Music* (2nd edition), p. 123.

[3]A passage in *Alexander's Feast* is modeled on Jephthah's lament, cited G. Massenkeil, "Carissimi, Giacomo," in *The New Grove Dictionary of Music and Musicians,* vol. 3 (London, Washington, D.C.: 1980), p. 789. "Hear Jacob's God" from *Sampson* is modeled on the chorus "*Plorate filiae,*" cited by W. Dean, *Handel's Dramatic Oratorios and Masques* (London: Oxford University Press, 1959), p. 644.

# 66. FRANCESCO CAVALLI (1602-1676)
## Scipione Africano
Act II, scene 8

Giardino (A garden)

SOFONISBA

Di mi-se-ra Re-gi-na stra-no des-tin! Di li-ber-tà di re-gno e di con-sor-te son ve-do-va e pri-va e se peg-gior non vo-glio ch'il mio fa-to di-ven-ti mu-ta con-vien ch'io vi-va Che sup-pri-mai la-men-ti che le per-di-te mie si-mu-li e ce-li ch'al ce-ne-re-in-fe-li-ce del' es-tin-to mio Rè pa-ce non pre-ghi E'l tri-bu-to del pian-to an - cor gli ne - ghi. Chi tan-to me-co o Stel-le à-in-cru-de-lir v'ha mos-so? Son in-fe-

SOFONISBA:

Di misera Regina strano destin!
Di libertà, di regno, e di consorte
Son vedova e priva,
E se peggior non voglio
Ch'il mio fato diventi,
Muta convien ch'io viva,
Che supprima i lamenti
Che le perdite mie simuli e celi
Ch'al cenere infelice
Del' estinto mio Rè pace non preghi
E'l tributo del pianto ancor gli neghi.

SOFONISBA:

*Strange fate of an unhappy Queen!*
*Of liberty, of a kingdom, and of a husband,*
*I am widowed and deprived,*
*And if I do not wish*
*My fate to become worse,*
*It behooves me to live a mute,*
*To suppress my laments*
*And make a secret of my losses*
*And not to pray to heaven for the unhappy ashes*
*Of my dead King,*
*And even deny him the tribute of tears.*

| | |
|---|---|
| Chi tanto meco, ò Stelle, | *Who has moved you, O Stars,* |
| À incrudelir v'ha mosso? | *To so much cruelty toward me?* |
| Son infelice, e sospirar non posso. | *I am unhappy, and cannot sigh.* |
| | |
| Deh pietosè | *Ah pitying* |
| Verdi herbette | *Little green grasses* |
| Ruggiadose | *Dewy* |
| Morbidette | *Tender* |
| S'io non posso dir ohimè | *If I cannot say "Alas,"* |
| Lagrimate voi per mè. | *Weep you for me.* |
| | |
| Zeffiretti | *Little breezes* |
| Deh sentite | *Ah, listen* |
| Pietositti | *Compassionately* |
| Qui venite | *Come here* |
| E s'io dir non posso ohimè | *And if I cannot say "Alas,"* |
| Lagrimate voi per mè.[1] | *Weep you for me.* |

[1]In the printed libretto the two aria stanzas do not have the same refrain; this line reads: "Deh piangete voi per mè."

After the death of Monteverdi, Francesco Cavalli (1602-1676) emerged as one of the chief composers for the public opera houses of Venice. He was so esteemed beyond Italy as to be invited to Paris in 1660 to compose an opera for the marriage of Louis XIV to the Infanta of Spain (France as yet had no indigenous operatic tradition). *Scipione Africano* was written on his return to Venice, and received its first performance in February 1664. The librettist, Count Nicolò Minato, was an established poet and impresario who preceded Metastasio in the prestigious position of poet to the imperial court in Vienna. The plot of *Scipione Africano* is drawn from Roman history, and is so involved as to defy any intelligible summary here.[1] Suffice it to say that in usual mid-century Venetian manner the action is animated by a complex web of political and amorous intrigues, concealments, mistaken identities, and fortuitous misunderstandings. Each of the customary three acts is fragmented into twenty short scenes, some serious, some comic. The leading female role is Sofonisba, whose royal husband Siface is thought to be dead (he is actually very much alive). Sofonisba has been disguised as a warrior and concealed from the Roman general Scipio by a Roman captain who wants her for himself.

Act II, scene 8 is an episode in which the disguised Sofonisba laments her situation. The composition of this scene illustrates the general tendency of post-Monteverdian Venetian opera toward longer, more formal arias and toward more defined differentiation between recitative and aria. This trend culminated in the emergence of the aria as the dominant expressive force in eighteenth-century Italian opera. Sofonisba's soliloquy begins in recitative characterized by much declamation on repeated notes. Cavalli is sensitive to the feeling of the text: The rising line that conveys the queen's increasing agitation cuts off abruptly in mid-sentence and drops a seventh as she reflects on the silence she must observe to preserve her life (mm. 10-11). The aria that coalesces her unhappiness materializes in two phases. The first is an adagio in triple meter that uses the final summarizing line of the recitative text. The second is in duple meter and faster tempo and sets a six-line poem of two stanzas. Each of these phases has a clear musical design. The first consists of two parallel phrases (*aa'*) that are tonally a fourth apart (D, G). The second has two identical strophes, each with the internal phrase pattern *bcc'*. The *c* and *c'* phrases stand in the same tonal relationship (D, G) as the two phrases of the adagio. The rhythmically regular "walking bass" of the main, duple-meter aria is common in Venetian arias of this period. A three-part instrumental ritornello closes off both strophes and provides a pathetic echo to the singer's thoughts (see No. 69 for a similar gesture). The use of instruments not to accompany the voice but to preface or conclude an aria is typical in this period.

[1]A synopsis may be found in *Scipione Africano, Italian Opera 1640-1770,* The Garland Series, ed. H. M. Brown (1978), p. [4-5].

**67.** ANTONIO CESTI (1623-1669)

# Alpi nevose e dure

Cantata

Al - pi ne - vo - se e du - re per cui la not - te e'l gior - no in trac - cia del suo co - re il

Basso Continuo

cor___ pas - seg - gia na - scon - de - te - mi, na - scon - de - te - mi pu - re quel sol ch'al sol fa scor - no,

e se_ go - der no'l___ pos - so al - men, al - men no'l___ veg - gia___ e se_ go - der no'l___

pos - so al - men, al - men no'l___ veg - gia.___ Val - li che di Fi - le - no ri - spon - de - ste so - ven - te ai

que - ru - li cor - do - gli, all' al - ta stri - da, hor nel ge - la - to se - no sep - pel - li - te il do - len - te, e s'un fo - co m'av-

| | | |
|---|---|---|
| R₁ | Alpi nevose e dure<br>per cui la notte e'l giorno<br>in traccia del suo core<br>il cor passeggia,<br>nascondetemi pure<br>quel sol ch'al sol fa scorno | *Alps, snowy and harsh,*<br>*through which night and day*<br>*tracking its heart*<br>*the heart roams,*<br>*hide then from me*<br>*that sun that shames the sun* |
| M₁ | e se goder no'l posso<br>almen no'l veggia. | *and if I cannot enjoy it*<br>*at least let me not see it.* |
| R₂ | Valli che di Fileno<br>rispondeste sovente<br>ai queruli cordogli<br>all'alta strida,<br>hor nel gelato seno<br>seppellite il dolente<br>e s'un foco m'avvampa<br>un gel m'uccida. | *Valleys who*<br>*often echoed Fileno*<br>*in his sorrowful laments,*<br>*in his loud cries,*<br>*now in your frozen breast*<br>*intomb this sorrower*<br>*and if a fire kindles me*<br>*let a frost kill me.* |
| M₂ | E voi dolci pensieri<br>ma troppo ambiziosi<br>che per alti sentieri<br>la mia pace involaste<br>e i miei riposi,<br><br>fermate, o dio, fermate.<br>Troppo vi lusingate<br>sperando nel mio sol<br>costanza e fede.<br><br>Ottener non desia<br>chi troppo chiede. | *And you, tender thoughts,*<br>*but too aspiring,*<br>*who, through lofty paths,*<br>*robbed me of my peace*<br>*and my repose,*<br>*stop, O god, stop.*<br>*You entice me too much*<br>*to hope for constancy and faith*<br>*from my sun.*<br><br>*He who asks for too much*<br>*will not obtain his desire.* |
| A₁ | Si si voglio morir<br>Nacque libero il mio cor<br>ma soggiace per amor<br>a tirannico martir. | *Yes, yes I want to die,*<br>*my heart was born free*<br>*but is subjected by love*<br>*to a tyrannical martyrdom.* |
| A₂ | O cara libertà<br>che vivo persi<br>e dalla morte spero<br>deh m'addita il sentiero<br>ond'a morir si va.<br>O cara libertà. | *O dear liberty,*<br>*that I lost while living*<br>*and hope for in death,*<br>*ah, show me the path*<br>*whence one can go to death.*<br>*O dear liberty.* |
| R₃<br>M₃ | E la via d'Acheronte a tutti aperta,<br>E chi morir non sa vita non merta. | *The way to Acheron [hell] is open to all,*<br>*and he who does not know how to die does not*<br>*    deserve life.* |
| A₁ | Si, si voglio morir . . .<br>    . . . martir. | *Yes, yes, I want to die . . .*<br>*    . . . martyrdom.* |

The Italian *cantata* evolved out of the solo song and was the principal type of vocal chamber music in Italy from the 1630s into the 1700s. The mid-century cantata is a substantial, multisectional work on a secular text cast in both irregular and strophic verse. The preferred scoring is for one voice with basso continuo, but duet cantatas are not unusual. The stylistic development of the cantata parallels that of opera, and in many respects cantatas are conceived as operatic scenes.

Cantatas did not have a standard format in the later seventeenth century; the music is formed according to the structure and syntax of each individual text. Although recitative and aria styles are quite clearly differentiated (as in opera of the time), they do not alternate regularly. The aria assumes the main expressive burden. As in mid-century instrumental music, the multisectional nature of the cantata challenges composers to create a coherent structure on large and small levels. This is achieved largely through repetition of phrases or sections, and, to some degree, through tonal relationships.

The cantata *Alpi nevose e dure* of Antonio Cesti (1623-1669), a successful composer of opera for the Venetian stage, shows a characteristically tight connection between text and music, and illustrates common formal patterns. The grandiloquent text is the lament of a rejected lover. Its musical setting falls into nine distinct sections defined by changes in meter and in melodic style. These numerous sections can be grouped into two larger units of four (2 + 2) and five (2 + 2 + 1) on the basis of textual and musical syntax. The first of these units comprises the speaker's apostrophe to the Alps, the valleys, and his own too-elevated thoughts. The second begins with his personal expression of longing for death and regret for lost liberty. This second unit is framed by the return of the initial section at the end.

Musically, the individual sections fall into three categories: (1) recitative (R); (2) aria (A); and (3) melodic sections (M) that possess the ordered meter and melody of aria but are allied textually to the preceding recitative. A diagram showing the types of sections and their internal phrase repetitions reveals multiple levels of organization in this cantata:

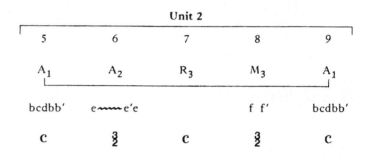

| | Unit 1 | | | | Unit 2 | | | | |
|---|---|---|---|---|---|---|---|---|---|
| **Section** | 1 | 2 | 3 | 4 | 5 | 6 | 7 | 8 | 9 |
| **Type** | $R_1$ | $M_1$ | $R_2$ | $M_2$ | $A_1$ | $A_2$ | $R_3$ | $M_3$ | $A_1$ |
| **Phrases** | | a a' | | | bcdbb' | e~~~e'e | | f f' | bcdbb' |
| **Meter** | C | $\frac{3}{2}$ | C | $\frac{3}{2}$ | C | $\frac{3}{2}$ | C | $\frac{3}{2}$ | C |

Cesti habitually sets the last line or couplet of recitative verse with two parallel phrases, the second a fourth above the first, as occurs here in sections 2 and 8 (see also No. 66, mm. 28-37). The fourth section is particularly complex. It begins with a conventional descending-fourth ground bass but drops it half-way through (just at the point where the text mentions constancy!). This section contains the most overt word painting of the cantata—a sinuous melisma on "*lusingate*" ("entice") and a long-held note on "*costanza*" ("constancy"). The two main aria sections share a common basic plan: An initial phrase returns at the end at two different tonal levels. On a small scale, this is akin to the idea of sectional return (evident in unit 2), which becomes the prevailing convention in the *da capo* aria of mature Italian baroque opera (see No. 82).

## 68. JEAN-BAPTISTE LULLY (1632-1687)
### Alceste
Act II, scenes 7-8

3  Track 13

**Scene 7**  *ALCESTE, CÉPHISE, PHÉRÈS*
(Alcestis, Cephise, Pheres)

[1]The ornament sign + normally signifies a mordent or a trill. Those in parentheses (+) come from the 1703 parts.

[2]¢ 𝅗𝅥 = 3 𝅘𝅥 throughout this scene.

[3]A figured bass realization may be found in *Oeuvres Complètes de J.-B. Lully Les Opéras*, vol. 2, edited by H. Prunières (c. 1937), pp. 163-171.

**Scene 8** *ADMÈTE blessé, CLÉANTE, ALCESTE, PHÉRÈS, CÉPHISE, SOLDATS*
(Admetus wounded, Cleanthus, Alcestis, Pheres, Cephise, soldiers)

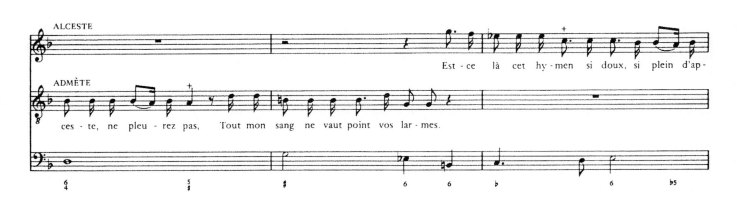

**Scene 7**

ALCESTE, CÉPHISE, PHÉRÈS:
Cherchons Admète promptement.

ALCESTE:
Peut-on chercher ce qu'on aime
Avec trop d'empressement!
Quand l'amour est extrême
Le moindre éloignement
Est un cruel tourment.

ALCESTE, CÉPHISE, PHÉRÈS:
Cherchons Admète promptement.

**Scene 8**

ALCESTE:
O Dieux! quel spectacle funeste?

CLÉANTE:
Le Chef des ennemis, mourant et terrassé
De sa rage expirante a ramassé le reste
Le Roy vient d'en être blessé.

ADMÈTE:
Je meurs, charmante Alceste:
Mon sort est assez doux
Puisque je meurs pour vous.

ALCESTE:
C'est pour vous voir mourir que le Ciel me délivre!

ADMÈTE:
Avec le nom de votre époux
J'eusse été trop heureux de vivre.
Mon sort est assez doux
Puisque je meurs pour vous.

ALCESTE:
Est-ce là cet hymen si doux, si plein d'appas,
Qui nous promettoit tant de charmes?
Falloit-il que si tôt l'aveugle sort des armes

Tranchât des noeuds si beaux par un affreux trépas?
Est-ce là cet hymen si doux si plein d'appas,
Qui nous promettoit tant de charmes?

ADMÈTE:
Belle Alceste, ne pleurez pas
Tout mon sang ne vaut point vos larmes.

ALCESTE:
Est-ce là cet hymen si doux, si plein d'appas,
Qui nous promettoit tant de charmes?

ADMÈTE:
Alceste, vous pleurez?

ALCESTIS, CEPHISE, PHERES:
*Let us find Admetus right away.*

ALCESTIS:
*Can one search for one's beloved
with too much ardor?
When love is excessive
the least separation
is a cruel torment.*

ALCESTIS, CEPHISE, PHERES:
*Let us find Admetus right away.*

ALCESTIS:
*O Gods! what dismal sight is this?*

CLEANTHUS:
*The enemy leader, dying and vanquished,
pulled together all his dying rage,
and has just wounded the king.*

ADMETUS:
*I die, charming Alcestis.
My fate is sweet enough
because I die for you.*

ALCESTIS:
*Did Heaven deliver me to see you die!*

ADMETUS:
*To be called your husband
would have made me too happy to live.
My fate is sweet enough,
because I die for you.*

ALCESTIS:
*Is this the marriage so sweet, so full of attractions,
that promised us so many delights?
Was it necessary that the blind destiny of war should so soon*

*Cut such a beautiful attachment by a dreadful death?
Is this the marriage so sweet, so full of attractions,
that promised us so many delights?*

ADMETUS:
*Beautiful Alcestis, do not weep.
All my blood is not worth your tears.*

ALCESTIS:
*Is this the marriage so sweet, so full of attractions,
that promised us so many delights?*

ADMETUS:
*Alcestis, you weep?*

ALCESTE:
Admète, vous mourez?

ALCESTE:
Se peut-il que le Ciel permette,
Que les coeurs d'Alceste et d'Admète
Soient ainsi séparés?

ADMÈTE:
Alceste, vous pleurez?

ALCESTE:
Admète, vous mourez?

ALCESTIS:
*Admetus, you die?*

ALCESTIS:
*How can Heaven permit
the hearts of Alcestis and Admetus
to be thus separated?*

ADMETUS:
*Alcestis, you weep?*

ALCESTIS:
*Admetus, you die?*

The figure of Jean-Baptiste Lully (1632-1687) dominates French music in the latter half of the seventeenth century. A Florentine by birth, Lully was brought to Paris at the age of fourteen and by his twentieth year had securely established himself under the patronage of Louis XIV, *le Roi-soleil*. Lully first concentrated his energies on composition and production of grandiose ballets (he was himself a distinguished dancer) but turned his attention in the 1670s to opera. To Lully and his librettist Philippe Quinault (1635-1688) goes the distinction of establishing an indigenous French opera, the *tragédie lyrique*. *Tragédie lyrique* fused music, drama, dance and spectacle in the closest approach to a "total artwork" before Richard Wagner. In contrast to contemporary Italian opera, it allotted a significant role to the chorus and to the ballets that ended each of the obligatory five acts. From Italian opera, it adopted recitative and aria as the two main modes of solo singing. The plots were drawn from Greek stories or from chivalric legend and were elaborated with subintrigues and (in early works) comic incident.

Lully and Quinault's *Alceste* was first produced under royal auspices in 1674.[1] The poet took considerable liberties with the model provided by Euripides. Instead of being an established married couple, Admetus and Alcestis are just celebrating their wedding. Admetus's fatal illness originates in a wound he receives as he rescues Alcestis from abduction by one of her rejected suitors. A comic subplot contrasts the faithful love of Admetus and

Alcestis with the casual attitude of Alcestis's attendant Cephise toward her suitors.

The segment printed here, scenes 7 and 8 of Act II, illustrates Lully's responsiveness to text and drama. In scene 7, Alcestis, who has just been liberated from her abductor, sets out happily with Cephise and Pheres (Admetus's father) to find her beloved. Their music is cheerful, metrically regular, and songlike. The shock of finding Admetus mortally wounded is first expressed in the instruments, which shift to the minor mode and state the descending stepwise bass that is the hallmark of the baroque lament (see No. 69). It is confirmed by Alcestis's shift to recitative style in an outcry that bursts from the top of her register. The recitative that predominates in this scene hovers between expressive declamation and an ordered melodic style. The frequent changes in written meter promote a flexible, speechlike effect. The exchange between Alcestis and Admetus eventually coalesces into a moving duet in which the singers gasp out short phrases against a chromatically inflected bass.

The recurring refrains in both scenes are Lully's characteristic method of imparting musical coherence to a segment of the drama. They may serve an expressive purpose as well, as when Alcestis's recurrent phrase "Est-ce là cet hymen . . ." projects her obsessive disappointment at being deprived of promised happiness. Lully's airs tend to be short, tonally coherent, and framed on a simple repetition scheme. For example, the opening phrase of Alcestis's scene 7 air is repeated (m. 7), while the last two phrases are melodically parallel though contrasted tonally. The entire brief song is framed by the compact trio.

Despite external changes in musical syntax, the Lully-Quinault *tragédie lyrique* remained the model for French serious opera through Rameau (see No. 83) and decisively influenced the operatic "reforms" of Gluck.

[1]A 1676 engraving of a scene from *Alceste* as performed in the *Cour de marbre* at Versailles may be found in the *Oeuvres Complètes de J.-B. Lully, Les Opéras*, vol. 2, ed. H. Prunières (Paris: c. 1937, reprint New York: 1966), facing p. 5.

## 69. HENRY PURCELL (1659-1695)
## Dido and Aeneas

Concluding scene

3  Track 14

DIDO

Thy hand, Be-lin - da; dark - ness shades me, On thy bo - som let me rest; More I would, but Death in - vades me; Death is now a wel - come guest. When I am laid,__ am laid _____ in earth, may my wrongs__ cre - ate No

Basso Continuo[1]

Violin I

Violin II

Viola

---

[1]Figured bass realizations may be found in *Dido and Aeneas,* edited by M. Laurie, The Works of Henry Purcell, vol. 3 (Borough Green: Novello, 1979), pp. 94-97; in *Dido and Aeneas,* edited by M. Laurie and T. Dart (Borough Green: Novello, 1974), pp. 70-73; and *Dido and Aeneas,* edited by B. Britten and I. Holst (London and New York: Boosey and Hawkes, 1961), pp. 104-108.

trou - ble, no trou-ble in\_\_\_\_\_ thy breast, When I am

Re - mem-ber me! re - mem-ber me! but

ah! _____ for-get my fate, re - mem-ber me! but ah! _____

scat - ter ro - ses, scat - ter, scat - ter_ ro - ses_ on_her tomb,

scat - ter ro - ses, scat - ter, scat - ter_ ro - ses on her tomb, Soft, soft____ and

And scat - ter, scat - ter_ ro - ses on her tomb, Soft, soft,_

And scat - ter_ ro - ses, scat - ter_ ro - ses on her tomb,

Soft,_ soft ____ and gen - tle, soft,_ soft,_ soft,_ soft ____ and

gen - tle as_her heart, gen - tle as her_heart, soft,_ soft ____ and gen - tle,

soft and gen - tle as her heart, soft,_ soft ____ and

Soft,_ soft ____ and gen - tle, soft,_ soft,_ soft,_ soft,_ soft ____ and

gen - tle as \_ her heart; Keep here, here your watch, keep here, here, keep here your watch, and

gen - tle \_ as her heart; Keep here, here \_ your watch, keep here, here, keep here your watch, and

gen - tle \_ as her heart; Keep here, here your watch, keep here, here, keep here your watch, and

gen - tle as her heart; Keep here, here your watch, keep here, here, keep here your watch, and

nev - er, nev - er, nev - er part, and nev - er, nev - er, nev - er, nev - er part. With droop - part.

nev - er, nev - er, nev - er part, and nev - er, nev - er, nev - er, nev - er part. part.

nev - er, nev - er, nev - er part, and nev - er, nev - er, nev - er, nev - er part. With part.

nev - er, nev - er, nev - er part, and nev - er, nev - er, nev - er, nev - er part. part.

DIDO:
*Thy hand, Belinda, darkness shades me*
*On thy bosom let me rest,*
*More I would but Death invades me,*
*Death is now a welcome guest.*

*When I am laid in earth may my wrongs create*
*No trouble in thy breast.*
*Remember me but, ah, forget my fate.*

CHORUS:
*With drooping wings we Cupids come*
*And scatter roses on her tomb,*
*Soft and gentle as her heart*
*Keep here your watch and never part.*

The outstanding English composer of the period from 1600 to 1750 was Henry Purcell (1659-1695). Trained in the Chapel Royal, he absorbed the contemporary musical idioms of France and Italy as well as native English traditions. In Purcell's time, opera had yet to be established in England. Purcell wrote for the theater, but, with one exception, his stage works consist of music (songs, choruses, dances, instrumental interludes) to be interpolated into a spoken drama. His one true opera is *Dido and Aeneas* (1689), written on a libretto by Nahum Tate and intended for performance in a London boarding school for "young gentlewomen." French influence predominates in this work, evidenced in the inclusion of choruses and dances and in the amount and expressive character of the recitative. Italian dramatic convention most touches the character of Dido, whose feelings are etched in two substantial and compelling ground-bass arias.

"When I am laid in earth," her parting elegy, is preceded by a deeply felt recitative whose vocal line descends slowly, with chromatic inflections, through a minor seventh. The ground bass, stated alone before the voice enters, picks up the chromatic motif. It consists of a descending chromatic tetrachord closed off by a cadence. The descending tetrachord bass had much earlier become associated with the lament genre in Italian circles (for example, Monteverdi's *Lamento della ninfa, Book VIII*, 1638 and Cavalli operas such as *Egisto* of 1643 and *Statira* of 1655). The lasting power of the association radiates in the *Crucifixus* of J. S. Bach's Mass in B minor. Purcell achieves great expressive impact through exposed voice-bass dissonances, simple monotone recitation ("Remember me"), irregular rhythms in the voice, and overlapping phrases between voice and bass. Dido speaks against the bass without heeding or yielding to its unalterably regular pace. The orchestral epilogue wordlessly intensifies the chromaticism and the sorrow as the spurned queen ascends her funeral pyre.

## 70. WILLIAM BYRD (1543-1623)

Track 1

### John come kiss me now
### from The Fitzwilliam Virginal Book

From *William Byrd Keyboard Music* II, ed. A. Brown, Musica Britannica 28 (London: Stainer and Bell, 1971), 121-215.

[1]The symbol ≈ indicates an ornament. The choice of embellishment in each case is left to the player's discretion.

The Fitzwilliam Virginal Book, with its repertory of nearly three hundred compositions, is a rich source of English keyboard music from the late sixteenth and early seventeenth centuries. The collection was compiled and copied sometime between 1609 and 1619 by the recusant Francis Tregian, who accomplished this task during the enforced leisure of imprisonment for his religious beliefs.

The many works of William Byrd collected by Tregian compass the chief keyboard genres of the time: fantasias (some on solmization themes), pavanes, galliards and other dances, pieces on a ground bass, and variations. The variation "John come kiss me now" would appear on stylistic grounds to be one of Byrd's late works, dating from the 1590s or the first decade of the

seventeenth century. The short melody (eight measures of modern transcription) is framed to the *passamezzo moderno* bass. The unyielding reiteration of harmonic progression and phrase structure, coupled with a set melodic outline, gives the piece a homogeneous, repetitive quality. Against this stable background, the inventive figuration produces an ever-varied, wonderfully decorative surface. The segmentation of the piece into distinct, short sections is offset by a gradual increase in rhythmic energy and textural density as the work progresses. The process culminates in the virtuosic display of section 14 and the dense counterpoint of section 15. Changes in figuration midway through some variations (nos. 3, 5, 6, and 9, for example) also help alleviate the impression of regular eight-measure units.

# 71a. SAMUEL SCHEIDT (1587-1654)

## Jesus Christus unser Heiland, der von uns

Psalmus sub communione

from **Tabulatura Nova, Part III**

1. Versus à 4 Voc.

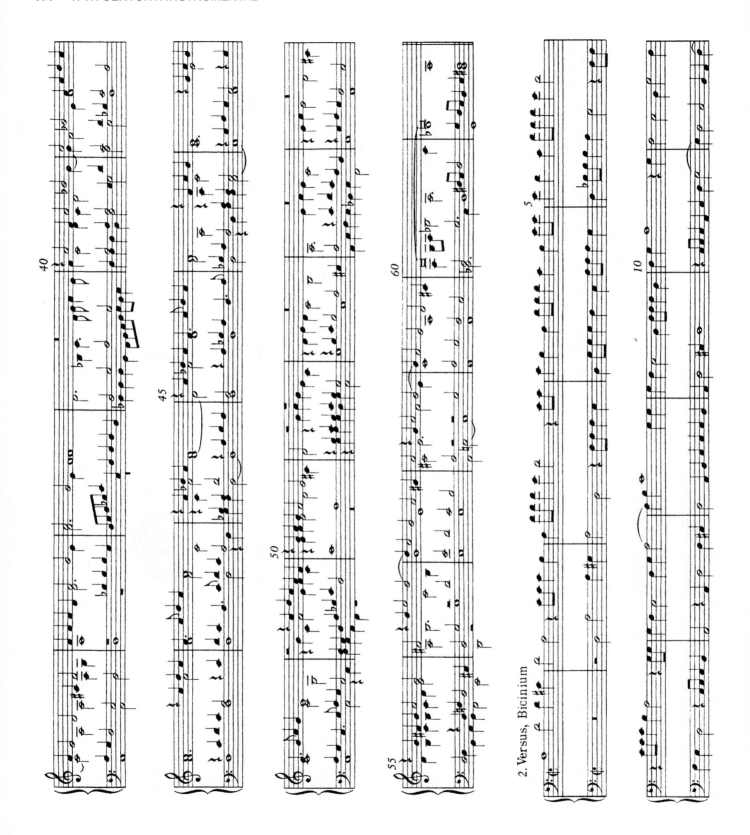

2. Versus, Bicinium

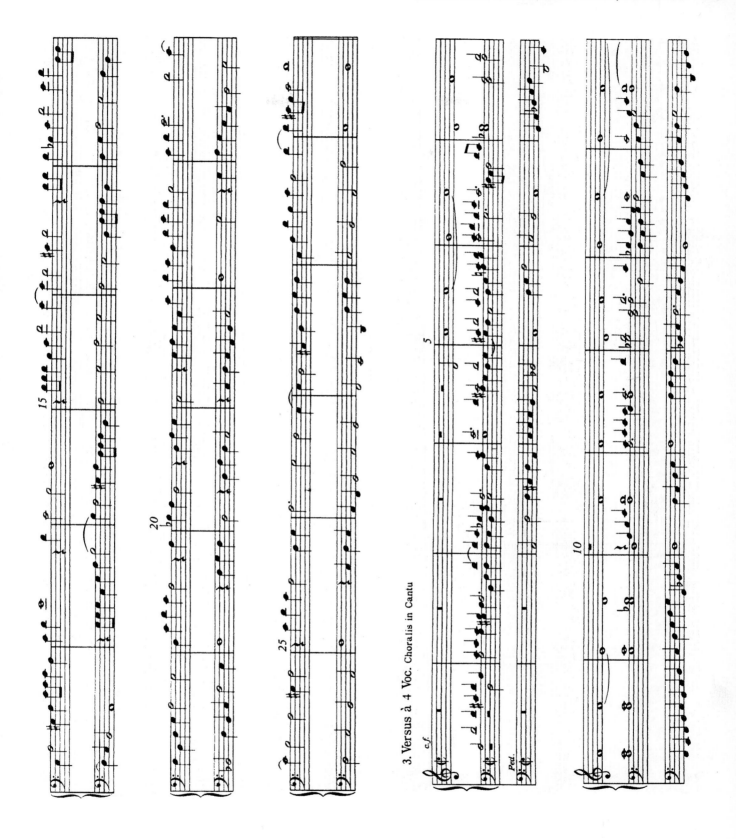

3. Versus à 4 Voc. Choralis in Cantu

4. Versus à 4 Voc. Choralis in Alto

¹Pedal sounds an otave higher than written.

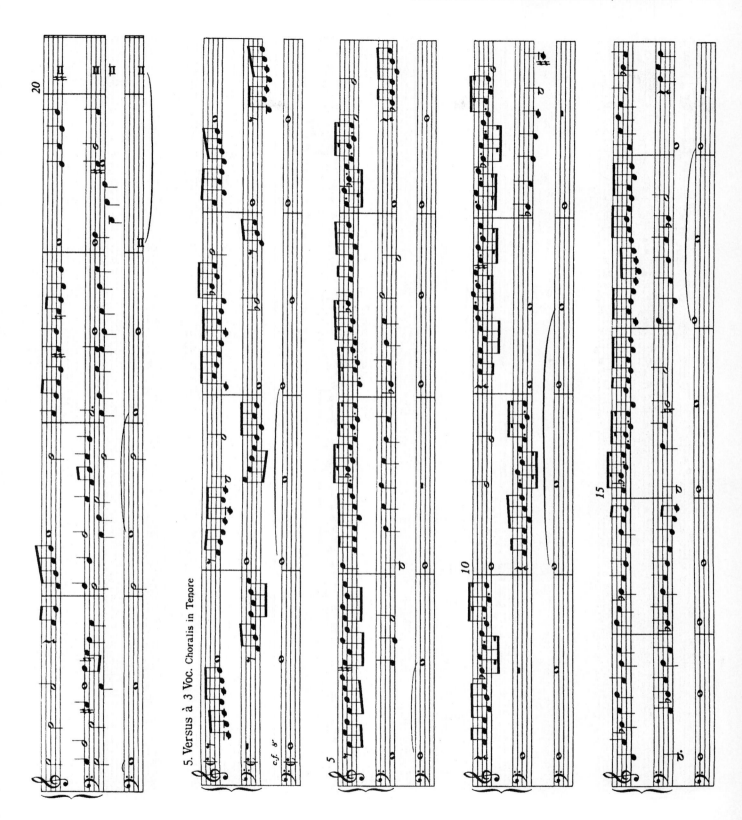

5. Versus à 3 Voc. Choralis in Tenore

6. Versus à 4 Voc. Choralis in *Tenore et Basso*

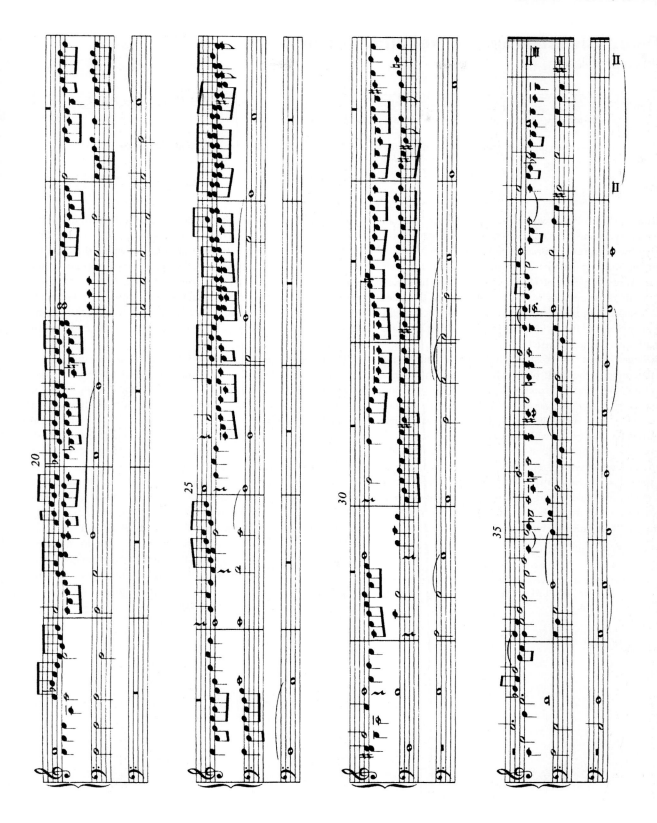

# 71b. Jesus Christus unser Heiland, der von uns

Chorale melody[1]

Je-sus Chri - stus, un-ser Hei - land, der von uns den Got-tes-zorn ___ wandt, durch das bit-tre Lei-den sein ___ half er uns aus der Höl - le Pein.

[1]Scheidt's version of the chorale differs in some melodic and rhythmic details from Luther's melody as first published in the Erfurt *Enchiridion* of 1524.

Samuel Scheidt (1587-1654) worked all his life in the German city of Halle, first as a church organist, then as court organist and *Kapellmeister* to the Margrave of Brandenburg, and later as director of music for the city when war disrupted the Margrave's establishment. After the peace of 1638 he returned to his court position. He studied for perhaps a year (c. 1609) with the celebrated Dutch organist Jan Pieterszoon Sweelinck, who is thought to have introduced him to the style of the English virginalists and possibly to have encouraged a taste for variation writing.

The *Tabulatura Nova* of 1624 is the central source for Scheidt's organ music, the bulk of which is based on chorale or plainsong melodies. Part III contains this chorale variation on *Jesus Christus unser Heiland, der von uns*, a chorale by Luther himself that often was sung during Communion. Although Luther's text has ten verses, Scheidt's setting has only six variations.[1] (There is no obvious influence of text on musical setting as is frequent in later chorale preludes of Buxtehude and J. S. Bach.) The verses/variations contrast with each other in manner of treating the chorale melody and in density of texture (verse 2 for two voices, verse 5 for three, the rest for four voices). The first two verses are in effect imitative ricercares in which each phrase

of the chorale is successively treated either as a point of imitation (verse 1, beginning) or as a source of motives (verse 1, m. 42). The last four verses are cantus firmus variations in which the chorale, in long note values, is systematically presented in soprano, alto, tenor, and bass. Although from the score the inner-voice statements of the cantus firmus might seem somewhat concealed, Scheidt instructs the organist to register them on a separate manual (keyboard) or pedal (with a four-foot stop) to make them sound forth plainly.

The influence of the chorale on the voices surrounding it fluctuates considerably during the course of the piece. In some passages, the figuration is directly derived from the chorale (verse 3, opening; verse 5, mm. 8-11) while in others it is freely invented (verse 5, opening). Verse 6 ends the series with a substantial double variation. Although identified as the "chorale in bassus" verse, this section in fact presents each chorale phrase twice: first in the tenor with soprano and alto accompaniment, then in the bass with tenor and alto accompaniment. The tenor states the melody on D, the pitch center of the entire variation; the bass states it on A. (Johann Walter's setting in the *Geistliches Gesangbüchlein* of 1551 provides a precedent for this.) To end the verse on D, Scheidt repeats the last phrase of the chorale in the bass, transposed to D (m. 33). The resumption of full four-part texture, the slowing of rhythmic motion, and the density of suspensions all call attention to this last phrase and impart a dignified sense of culmination to the final verse.

[1]Vocal renditions of some stanzas very likely alternated with the organ verses, a performance practice described in a late-sixteenth-century guide to liturgical practices at Halle.

**72.**  GIROLAMO FRESCOBALDI   (1583-1643)
# Toccata No. 8
from **Toccate e partite . . . libro primo**

Girolamo Frescobaldi (1583-1643) was born in Ferrara, one of the most progressive musical centers in Europe. He studied with Luzzasco Luzzaschi, a distinguished keyboard player and composer of madrigals. In 1608, Frescobaldi was elected to the prestigious post of organist at Saint Peter's, Rome. Except for occasional interruptions (the longest a sojourn as court organist in Florence, from 1628 to 1634), he retained this post for the rest of his life. Contemporary musicians praised him for his skill, his manual dexterity, and his new style of playing.

The toccatas (Book I, 1615; Book II, 1627) and the *Fiori Musicali* (1635) are not concert pieces but music for church services, intended to enhance the ritual. The *toccatas* (from the Italian verb *toccare*, "to touch"), with their inventive figurations and virtuoso passage work, exemplify Frescobaldi's bold manner of playing, which so impressed his contemporaries. The preface to the *First Book of Toccatas* is a highly important document of performance practice.[1] In it, Frescobaldi offers indispensable instructions on the execution of the music: (1) the toccatas should be played not with a fixed beat, but in the manner of modern madrigals where the beat is now languid, now quick, according to the emotion (affect) or the sense of the words; (2) individual sections can be played independently, and a player may begin or end according to his or her pleasure without having to play the whole toccata; (3) the openings should be arpeggiated and played in a leisurely manner: (4) the player should slow down toward the ends of sections, which are marked by the concurrence of both hands in consonance on a quarter note (or longer value).

The second comment quoted above—that the player may begin and end anywhere in the piece—offers the best guide to musical appreciation of the toccatas. They do not follow an ordered pattern of growth and development controlled by tonal or motivic relationships, but rather unfold in a rhapsodic way, with one musical idea yielding to another at the composer's fancy. (In this respect, they anticipate the "open" structures cultivated in some music after 1945.) Toccata 8, for example, moves casually from a sustained passage marked by affective suspensions and syncopations (mm. 18-22), to a dotted figure in imitation (mm. 22-24), to volatile thirty-second-note runs (mm. 24-26), to another series of short figures tossed between the hands (mm. 28-29). Frescobaldi handles this highly sectionalized composition with remarkable subtlety. Some sections are distinctly separated by a cadence and change in figuration (m. 11, m. 24). Others flow smoothly into the next through continuity of harmony (mm. 4-5) or rhythmic momentum (m. 31). Some sections cohere in larger units through some common musical idea. For example, the passage from measure 15 (last half note) to measure 24 (second half note), although subdivided into three units through changing figuration, is unified harmonically by persistent chains of dissonant suspensions. The passage is further marked as a unit by clear cadences at either end. The relaxed harmonic language of Toccata 8, whose diatonic progressions are largely free of functional tensions, stands in pronounced contrast to the tonally functional harmony that drives a work such as J. S. Bach's well-known toccata in D minor (BWV 565), composed some one hundred years later.

---

[1]The preface is published with English translation in *Girolamo Frescobaldi Orgel- und Klavierwerke,* edited by P. Pidoux, vol. 3 (Kassel, Basel: Bärenreiter Verlag, 1961), p. [1-2], and without translation in *Il primo libro di toccate,* edited by E. Darbellay, Girolamo Frescobaldi Opere Complete, Monumenti Musicali Italiani, vol. 4 (Milan: Edizioni Suvini Zerboni, 1977), pp. XXVI-XXVII.

**73.**  GIROLAMO FRESCOBALDI
**Canzona dopo l'epistola**
from **La Messa della Domenica,**
**Fiori musicale**

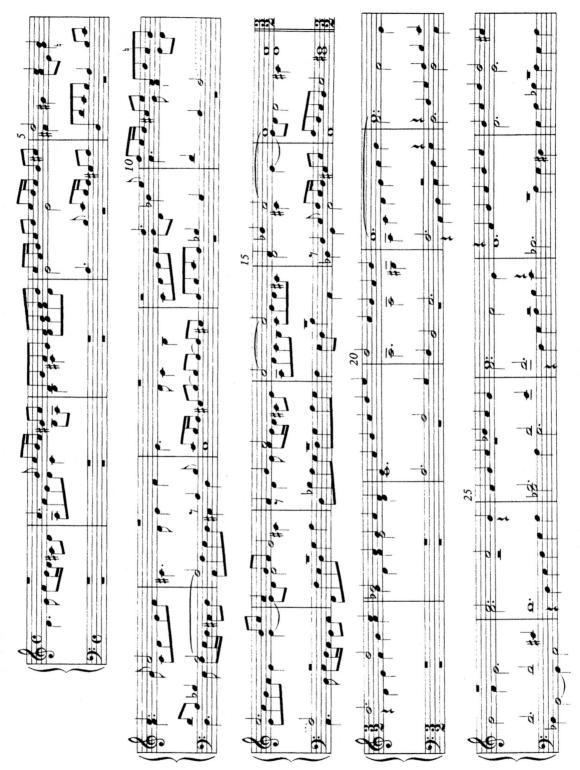

The *canzona* originated in the sixteenth century in intabulations and arrangements of vocal works, particularly chansons. By 1600, it had emerged as an independent instrumental piece in several contrasting sections (see No. 47). The canzona differs from the toccata in its imitative texture and fundamentally contrapuntal conception—legacies of its vocal heritage. It may be written for a soloist (lute, keyboard) or for an ensemble.

This organ canzona from the *Messa della Domenica* (Mass for Sundays) in Frescobaldi's liturgical collection *Fiori Musicali* (1635) was intended for performance during the Mass, after the reading of the Epistle. It is in four clearly defined sections, the third of which is a toccata-style link into the fourth. The other sections are all imitative. The second contrasts sharply with the first in its triple meter and double motive in invertible counterpoint. The first and last sections are alike in meter, in motivic contour, and in general rhythmic flow. Their similarity helps the cohesion of the piece. In its sectional construction, the canzona resembles other early seventeenth-century instrumental music. In its imitative idiom, it is a significant precursor of fugue, a preeminent instrumental genre of the early eighteenth century (see No. 87).

# 74. JOHANN JACOB FROBERGER (1616-1667)
## Suite VI

4  Track 2–5

Lamento sopra la dolorosa perdita della Real M<sup>stà</sup> di Ferdinando IV, Ré de Romani, etc.
[Allemande]

[1]The t is a general sign for an ornament. It most frequently designates a trill or a mordent.

Gigue

Courante

Sarabande

Johann Jacob Froberger (1616-1667) was the most renowned German keyboardist of his day. Son of the *Kapellmeister* at Stuttgart, he went to Vienna about 1634 and was eventually appointed court organist there. Froberger's native musical training was expanded through his travels to the principal musical centers of Europe: to Rome in the late 1630s (to study with Frescobaldi); to Rome, Florence, and Mantua about 1649; to Brussels, Paris, and London in the early 1650s. His keyboard works are usually separated into two categories: those showing Italian influence, specifically that of Frescobaldi (toccatas, ricercares, canzonas, etc.); and those showing French influence (suites for clavier).

Froberger's suites are among the first to incorporate a standard group of dances: allemande, gigue, courante, and sarabande. With the gigue moved to the end of the series (producing an alternation of relatively slow and fast tempos), this configuration became the "classic" baroque dance suite. In Suite VI,[1] the allemande is cast as a character piece, a lament on the death of the Emperor's infant son, Ferdinand IV, King of the Romans

(died 1654). All four movements are in binary form, a standard design comprising two sections, each of which is repeated. The first section characteristically modulates from the tonic to the fifth above (or the third above if the initial mode is minor). The second section starts in the new key and returns to the tonic. The repetition of each section, with improvised ornaments, produces fairly long movements.

The four dances differ in meter, tempo, and rhythm. The *allemande* is in slow duple meter and recalls the toccata in its volatile rhythmic figurations over a chordal background. The affective chromatic inflections and suspensions project the lament of the title. The final ascending scale is a curious detail, possibly meant to portray the ascent of the soul to heaven. (My inclination would be to play it only on the repeat of the section.) The *gigue* in this suite is a lively dance in compound meter (gigues can be in either duple or triple meter). The varied attack patterns of the inner voices create a fluctuating rhythmic surface quite different in nature from the rigid metric patterning of later baroque gigues. The *courante* is in triple meter and characteristically shifts between a 6/4 and a 3/2 division of the measure. It should be played in the French manner with *notes inégales*. The *sarabande* moves in a slow triple meter. As is usual in this type of dance, rhythm and harmonic motion accent the second beat of most measures.

[1]This suite is labeled Suite 12 in the Adler edition of 1899, a designation used in recent recordings. The 1979 edition by H. Schott, which follows Froberger's manuscript more closely, calls it Suite 6 in the 1656 book.

## 75. LOUIS COUPERIN   [c. 1626-1661]
### Prélude a l'imitation de M.ʳ Froberger
Unmeasured prelude

Track 6

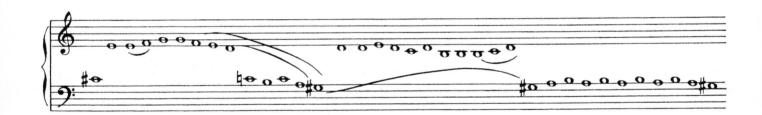

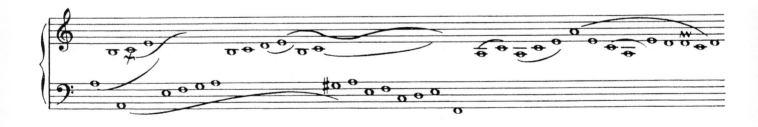

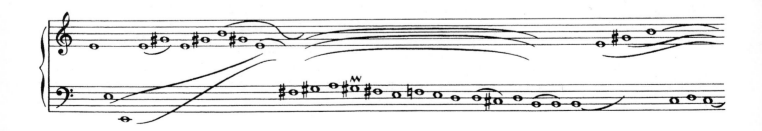

Changement de mouvement

Louis Couperin (c. 1626-1661) belonged to a family of professional musicians, records of whom extend from the mid-sixteenth to the mid-nineteenth century. Paris was the scene of his activities. He was appointed organist of St. Gervais in 1653 and also held an appointment as treble viol player in the Royal Chapel.

Louis Couperin seems to have been the first to adopt the unmeasured notation of the French lute prelude for toccatalike harpsichord preludes that the manuscripts label *préludes non mesurés*. The notation affords the performer considerable freedom in rhythmic interpretation (a freedom that was granted also in Italian toccatas despite their seemingly more precise notation— see comment on No. 72). The notated whole notes do not signify equal values but rather offer a neutral base upon which the player can impose his or her own rhythm and timing.[1] The slurs variously indicate: (1) the cohesion of several notes in one basic harmony; (2) an ornamental or melodic unit; or (3) harmonic structure and voice leading within a group of notes. The prelude shown here has three sections, the first and third unmeasured and chordal in nature, the middle one in set meter and contrapuntal in texture. The opening closely parallels the beginning of a Froberger organ toccata that was published in conventional notation.[2] The most complete manuscript source for Couperin's prelude acknowledges the homage to Froberger in its title. The *préludes non mesurés* sometimes may have been played independently, but could also introduce suites of dance movements.

Louis Couperin's illustrious nephew François Couperin acknowledged the special French tradition of preludizing in his *L'art de toucher le clavecin* of 1716/17. Even though the eight preludes included in his treatise are presented in measured notation, the younger Couperin specifies that they are to be played in "the usual fashion" ("*un goût d'usage*"), in a rhythmically free manner, unless expressly marked *mesuré*.

[1]Modes of realizing these unmeasured preludes are discussed in Richard Troeyer, "Metre in unmeasured preludes," *Early Music*, vol. 11/3 (1983), pp. 340-345, and in Davitt Moroney, "The performance of unmeasured harpsichord preludes," *Early Music*, vol. 4/2 (1976), pp. 143-151.

[2]Toccata 1, *J.-J. Froberger Oeuvres Complètes pour clavecin*, vol. 1, ed. H. Schott (Paris: Heugel, 1979), *Le Pupitre* No. 57.

# 76. SALAMONE ROSSI (1570-c.1630)
## Sonata in dialogo
"La Viena"

[1]Figured bass realizations can be found in *Salomone Rossi Trio Sonatas*, edited by A. Mann and F. Rikko, Documents of the Musical Past, no. 4 (New Brunswick, N.J.: Rutgers University Press, 1965), pp. 8-11; and in *Salomone Rossi Sonate*, edited by F. Piperno, Il Seicento Musicale Italiano 2 (Rome: Pro Musica Studium, 1980), pp. 56-60.

For his *Third Book* of "various sonatas, sinfonias, galliards, branles and correntes," the Mantuan composer and string player Salamone Rossi (1570-c. 1630) adopted a scoring that was to become standard for the later baroque trio sonata: two violins and a bass. The title page specifies *chitarrone* or "other similar instrument" for the bass. Rossi's sonatas are all multi-sectional, but they differ from the ensemble canzona (their immediate forebear) in not being thoroughly imitative in texture. The *Sonata in dialogo* actually combines elements of the solo and the trio sonatas, for the two melody parts "speak" alternately over the first four sections and only join together in the concluding one.

As implied by the title "*in dialogo,*" the overall shape of this sonata is dramatic—or at least textual—in inspiration. The piece finds its coherence not so much in motivic connections between sections (although these do exist) but in the process whereby the two melodic voices (the two performers) gradually achieve a common viewpoint. Their opening solo statements are vastly different. Canto I seems freely inspired with its sudden changes in motive and rhythmic movement. Canto II seems almost prosaic in its rhythmic evenness. Their next two statements are more akin in spirit and in motivic ideas. The melodies in both are spun out sequentially and are far more patterned than the initial solos. Canto I even picks up the ascending scale and dotted-rhythm motives from the preceding Canto II solo. The process of unification is completed when in the last section the two players concord in imitation, using figures that recall material from previous sections. The repetition of the very opening gesture of the piece at the beginning of this section gives a fleeting impression of return, but the dotted-rhythm motive first proposed by Canto II receives most emphasis. The tonal spheres of the two melodic voices also confirm their separateness. Canto I moves within G minor harmony, Canto II within D minor harmony. The two spheres are reconciled in the final section, which ends with a G cadence.

**77.** GIOVANNI BATTISTA VITALI   (1632-1692)
# Sonata a due Violini col suo basso continuo per l'organo

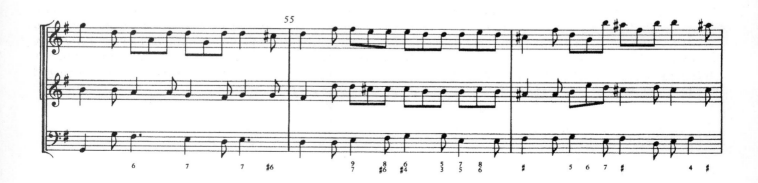

The north Italian city of Bologna was a leading center for instrumental music in the mid-seventeenth century, and Giovanni Battista Vitali (1632-1692) was arguably the city's most gifted composer at the time. During his lifetime, Vitali published four collections of ensemble sonatas and five of ensemble dances, observing a distinction that toward the end of the century was codified under the terms *sonata da chiesa* ("church sonata") and *sonata da camera* ("chamber sonata").

The foundations of later musical language are quite apparent in Vitali's compositions. Indeed, in a certain sense, the mature Italian and German baroque style can be considered an elaboration, expansion, and refinement of the basic language crystalized by Vitali and his contemporaries. Although a relatively early work (published 1667), this sonata for two violins and (organ) continuo anticipates Corelli and his successors in many respects. Each section is motivically unified; phrases are generated through harmonic and motivic sequence; the harmony is functional and focuses unequivocally on tonic and dominant; the counterpoint is permeated with (even subservient to) the harmonic background; the bass preserves a steady beat and occasionally assumes a motivic role. The general plan of the work anticipates the fully developed *sonata da chiesa* in which slow, chordally conceived movements alternate with fast, imitative ones.

In comparison with Corelli's sonatas (see nos. 78 and 80), this work seems modest in scope and limited tonally. The individual sections are differentiated enough in meter, tempo, and thematic ideas to have separate identities but are not independent enough in structure to be considered real movements. None could successfully be removed from its context and played alone. The internal organization of each is rather schematic and unimaginative. The second section, for example, consists of five parallel phrases. Each starts with the same figure in sequence and ends with an ornamented descending scale laced with suspensions. The modified "tonal" answer made when the first violin takes up the opening figure (m. 21) indicates a concern for tonal consistency that becomes standard in later fugal writing. Tonally, each section clings to the tonic, E minor. Cadences occur on a few other harmonies (on a G major triad in m. 8, on B minor triads in m. 25 and 33, etc.), but these are heard more as temporary stopping places than as actual excursions to new tonal areas. The tonal system appears here in a very simple and primitive stage.

# 78. ARCANGELO CORELLI (1653-1713)
## Sonata da camera a tre
Opus 4, No. 5

Preludio

[1]Editorial slurs are dotted lines. Figures and dynamics are from the early Dutch editor Estienne Roger.

## Allemanda

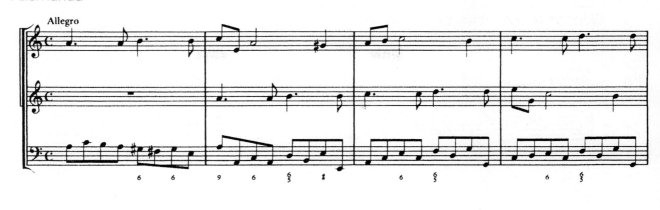

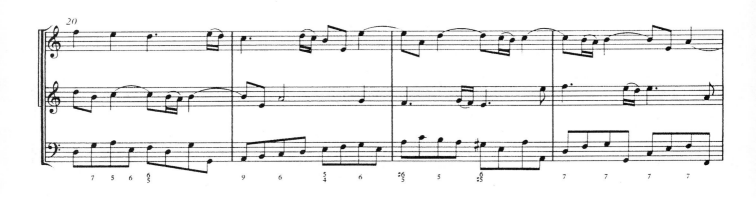

## Corrente

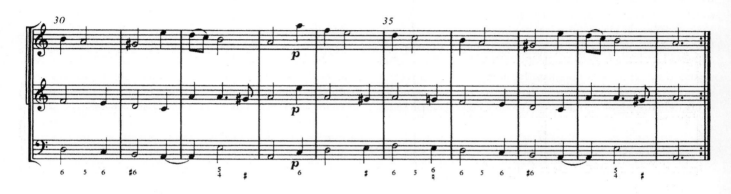

## Gavotta

Da Capo[2]

[2]Repeat *Gavotta* once through.

Arcangelo Corelli (1653-1713) was renowned in his own day as a violinist, composer, and teacher. The composer-pedagogue Francesco Gasparini extolled him as "a super-virtuoso [*virtuosissimo*] of the violin, the true Orpheus of our time."[1] His formative studies were in Bologna, where the art of violin playing was ardently cultivated, but his career flourished in Rome, where he settled in 1675. Corelli's devotion to the violin is manifested in his concentration on works for that instrument: solo and trio sonatas and concerti grossi. The many reprints of his published *opera*—not just in Italy but in northern Europe also—testify to their popularity and broad exposure.

The twelve sonatas of Opus 4 (the fourth of Corelli's trio sonata collections, 1694) are all *sonate da camera,* or chamber sonatas. Except for stately preludes, their movements are stylized dances in binary form (see comment on No. 74). Corelli handles this form with relative freedom in Sonata 5 of Opus 4. The first section of the allemande does not really modulate from A minor, but ends on a dominant harmony. Its second section starts abruptly in C major. The brief gavotte refrains from modulating until the middle of the second section, and even then slides

quickly over the C major cadence into a sequence headed back to A minor. The corrente is in rounded binary form. The entire first section is restated at the end of the second, modified so as to end in the tonic. From these examples it can be seen that binary form is not a fixed mold, but rather an abstract format that composers elaborated in quite varied fashions.

The appeal of the trio sonata resides largely in the interplay of two melodies over a supporting bass line. Corelli handles this texture differently in each movement of this sonata. In the allemande, the two violins imitate each other and delight in strings of suspensions. The bass provides a steady "walking" background to their dialogue. In the lively corrente, similar rhythms in all voices create an essentially homophonic texture. The texture of the gavotte is conditioned by the bass's insistent echo of the three-note violin rhythm.

The listener should note the distinctive rhythmic patterns of the corrente, especially the *hemiola* at cadential approaches (mm. 8-9, mm. 19-20, mm. 31-32, mm. 37-38). In hemiola, the rhythmic grouping shifts from two units of triple to three units of duple (or vice versa), producing a syncopated effect.

No really stylish recording of this work exists. The listener will have to imagine ornamentation in the prelude and on repeated strains of the dance movements (see No. 80).

[1]*L'armonico pratico al cembalo* (2nd edition, 1715), Ch. VII, p. 44.

# 79.    HEINRICH IGNAZ FRANZ VON BIBER    (1644-1704)
## Rosary Sonata X
(The Crucifixion of Christ)

[1]The diagram indicates a *scordatura* tuning, with the highest string of the violin lowered from the normal e to d. In order for the usual fingerings to produce the correct pitches, all notes located on the highest string must be notated a whole tone higher than they sound. This edition consistently shows the pitches as actually sounded, but a sample of Biber's original notation, which assumes the *scordatura*, is printed above the first five measures.

[2]A figured bass realization may be found in *Heinrich Franz Biber Sechzehn Violin Sonaten*, edited by E. Luntz, Denkmäler der Tonkunst in Österreich Jahrg. XII/2, vol. 25, pp. 44-48.

[Variatio II]

"Of all the violin players of the last century, Biber seems to have been the best, and his solos are the most difficult and the most fanciful of any Music I have seen of the same period." So wrote Charles Burney in the 1780s of Heinrich Ignaz Franz von Biber (1644-1704).[1] Biber, who worked at Salzburg, is particularly known for his exploration of new violin sonorities, his penchant for *scordatura*[2] and double stops, and for his technical audacity.

The sixteen Mystery (or Rosary) Sonatas for solo violin were grouped together about 1676. Fourteen different *scordatura*

[1]*A General History of Music* (London: 1789, reissue 1957), p. 462.

[2]Literally, "out-of-tune." As a formal device, *scordatura* involves deliberately tuning a stringed instrument in a specified unconventional way so as to produce sounds (especially chords) and tone quality not available under normal tuning.

tunings are employed in the set, each creating special qualities of sound and a special technical situation. Each sonata is associated with a specific incident in the life of Christ and many of them interpret their subjects programmatically. (The *Biblische Historien* keyboard sonatas of Johann Kuhnau, J. S. Bach's predecessor at Leipzig, constitute a slightly later chapter in the history of sacred programmatic music.) Sonata X relates to Christ's suffering on the cross. The earthquake (Matthew 27:51) is easily heard in the final section, and the insistent dotted triplets of the prelude have been likened to the hammering of nails. Apart from the introductory prelude, this sonata is a variation, a favorite form for Biber. This form allows Biber to become progressively virtuosic—and the piece builds in a spectacular way from the simple aria statement to the pyrotechnics of the final variation.

## 80. ARCANGELO CORELLI
## Sonata for violin and violone or cembalo
Opus 5, No. 1

4  Tracks 7–11

[1]A figured bass realization may be found in Arcangelo Corelli, *Zwölf Sonaten für Violine and Basso Continuo Opus 5*, edited by B. Paumgartner (Mainz: B. Schott, 1953), pp. 2-14.

[2]Bass note alone in accompaniment.

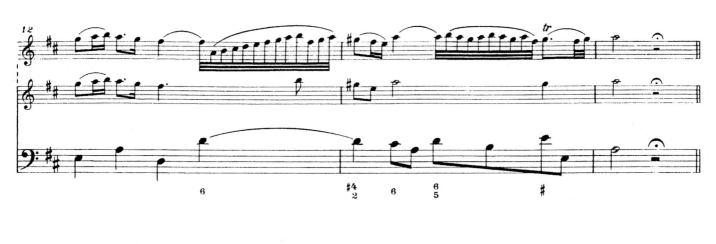

[3]Despite the indication, *Tasto solo*, the eighteenth-century editor gives figures for this passage.

With Corelli's violin works, as with much other seventeenth- and eighteenth-century music, the printed page does not represent the music as executed. Each performance was enlivened with extemporaneous embellishments, which tended to be particularly dense in slow movements. Corelli's solo sonatas Opus 5 were first issued (1700) in very plain versions, but the Brussels publisher Estienne Roger soon (1710) brought out a version with

ornamentation purportedly as played by Corelli himself. Both versions are shown in this edition. Although the ornamented line represents an authentic performance practice, the student should bear in mind that it illustrates only one of many ways in which a violinist of Corelli's day (or the composer himself) might have elaborated the given melodic outline. To a lesser extent, details are left open in the fast movements also, as when the player is instructed to arpeggiate block chords (second movement, mm. 66, 93).[1] Burney viewed the plainness of Corelli's lines as a virtue, for they could easily be modernized with the ornamentation currently in vogue: "The plainness and simplicity of Corelli have given longevity to his works, which can always be modernized by a judicious performer, with very few changes or embellishments."[2] The number of musical details left unspecified in scores of this epoch helps us to realize that the modern distinction between composers and performers (or composition and performance) should not be assumed for a time when composers themselves usually performed professionally, and when

performers were trained in techniques of ornamentation and improvisation.

This first sonata of Opus 5 observes the typical outline of a *sonata da chiesa* with its two fast fugal movements, each preceded by a slow movement. The opening slow movement is itself disrupted by quick, rhapsodic interjections. The middle slow movement, which is in B minor, provides the principal contrast of key and mode in this D major piece. Its ending on a dominant chord (after a proper cadence to the main tonic, m. 43) links this Adagio to the energetic fugal movement following. The sonata as a whole amply displays Corelli's fluent and idiomatic violin writing. In comparison with Vitali's works of mid-century (see No. 77), movements and phrases are greatly expanded in length and complexity. This results in large part from a more advanced handling of functional tonality: Harmonic progressions maintain their tension over a longer span of time; fresh tonal areas offer contrast to the tonic and give a sense of real motion and development.

[1]For a slightly later example of various modes of arpeggiation see the *Larghetto* movement of Vivaldi's concerto for four violins in G minor, Opus 3, No. 10 (1712) (Complete Works, vol. 415, p. 38). During this movement, four different arpeggiations occur simultaneously.

[2]Charles Burney, *A General History of Music* (London: 1789, reissued 1957), p. 444.

**81.** ALESSANDRO SCARLATTI   (1660-1725)          4   Track 12

## Su le sponde del Tebro

Cantata

Arias 3 and 4 and recitative

[1.] Di - te al - me - no, al - me - no, a - stri cru - de - li,
[2.] Dim mi o ciel, o ciel se de miei ma - li

quan - do mai, quan - do mai vi of - fe - se, vi of - fe - se il pet - to,
so - no an - cor, so - no an - cor sa tie le sfe - re, sa tie le sfe - re

che ri - cet - to voi lo fa - te di do - lo - re,
che si fie - re a pe - nar m'han de - sti - na - to,

che ri - cet - to voi lo fa - te di do - lo - re? Di - te al - me - no a - stri cru -
che si fie - re a pe - nar m'han de - sti - na - to. Dim mi o ciel se de mie i

de - li quan - do mai vi of - fe - se il pet - to che ri - cet - to voi lo fa -
ma - li so - no sa tie an - cor le sfe - re che si fie - re a pe - nar

[1] For a figured bass realization, see *Su le sponde del Tebro*, edited by B. Paumgartner (Heidelberg: 1956).

fi - ne,  che  nè  pian - ti,  nè  pre - ghi  sa - pe - va - no ad - dol - ci - re  un  cor  di  sas - so,

ri - so - lu - to e  co - stan - te  co - si  dis - se al  suo  cor  scher - ni - to,  scher - ni - to a - man - te:

**Aria [4]**

Tromba

Violino I

Violino II

[Canto]

Basso

[1.] Tra - la - scia  pur  di  pian - ge - re,    tra - la - scia  pur  di  pian - ge - re,
[2.] Non  ti  cu - rar  di  vi - ve - re,    non  ti  cu - rar  di  vi - ve - re

²Small notes indicate conventional cadence formulas.

pian - ge - re d'un in - fi - da, in - fi - da il suo ri - gor, d'un in - fi - da, in - fi - da il suo ri-
fin - ge - re e ne - gli oc - chi, ne - gli oc - chi il bel se - ren, e ne - gli oc - chi ne - gli oc - chi il bel se-

gor.
ren.

Tra - la - scia pur di pian - ge - re,        tra-
Non ti cu - rar di vi - ve - re,        non

**[Third Aria]**

1. Dite almeno astri crudeli
   Quando mai vi offese il petto
   Che ricetto voi lo fate di dolore?
   E già martire d'amore
   Nelle lagrime fedeli
   a sperar solo è costretto.

2. Dimmi o ciel se de miei mali
   Sono satie ancor le sfere[1]
   Che si fiere a penar m'han destinato.
   Crudo ciel perfido fato
   Con saette più mortali
   Del mio sen fatte l'arciere.

**[Recitative]**

All'aura, al cielo, ai venti pastorello
gentil così parlava, e pur l'aura crudel
fido adorava, ma conoscendo al fine, che
nè pianti, nè preghi sapevano ad dolcire
un cor di sasso, risoluto e costante cosi
disse al suo cor schernito, schernito
amante:

**[Fourth Aria]**

1. Tralascia pur di piangere
   Povero afflitto cor.
   Che spezzato dal tuo fato
   Non ti resta che compiangere
   D'un infida il suo rigor.

2. Non ti curar di vivere
   Misero nel mio sen
   Che spietata Clori
   Ingrata ha per uso
   saper fingere
   e negli occhi il bel seren.

[1]The scribe also writes this line: "*Sono ancor satie le sfere.*"

**[Third Aria]**

1. *Say at least, cruel stars,*
   *whenever did my heart offend you,*
   *causing you to expose it to so much sorrow?*
   *And now a martyr to love,*
   *it is constrained to hope only*
   *in tears of faithfulness.*

2. *Tell me, O heaven, if the spheres,*
   *which so cruelly have destined me to suffer,*
   *are yet satisfied with my miseries.*
   *Cruel heaven, perfidious fate,*
   *with more deadly darts*
   *you play the archer toward my heart.*

**[Recitative]**

*To the air, to the sky, to the winds, the*
*gentle shepherd spoke, and again,*
*faithful, he prayed to the cruel air. But*
*realizing finally that neither tears nor*
*prayers could soften a heart of stone, the*
*scorned lover resolutely and firmly spoke*
*to his heart:*

**[Fourth Aria]**

1. *Now put aside your weeping*
   *poor afflicted heart,*
   *for, despised by your fate,*
   *nothing remains for you but to pity*
   *the harshness of a faithless creature.*

2. *Take no more care for living,*
   *miserable heart in my breast,*
   *for cruel, spiteful Clori,*
   *that ingrate,*
   *is accustomed to feign*
   *a look of untroubled calm.*

The chief exponent of Neapolitan vocal style from the 1680s to the 1710s was Alessandro Scarlatti (1660-1725). Although he wrote a few purely instrumental works, he was most prolific in composing operas and cantatas. Charles Burney's opinion that Scarlatti was "the most voluminous and most original composer of cantatas that has ever existed" has never been pointedly challenged, but has sparked little real interest in the music (less than 1 percent of which has been published). Scarlatti's cantatas and operas are, historically, a significant link between mid-seventeenth-century secular vocal works with their multifarious approaches to text setting and early eighteenth-century cantata and opera with their stereotyped conventions of text setting. Prominent among the shifts in musical style is a pronounced differentiation between recitative and aria. In the last decades of the seventeenth century, recitative largely ceases to be expressive in nature and becomes a conventional manner of speech. The aria, distinguished as an individual entity by its coherent internal organization, memorable melodic material, and stable tonal focus, becomes the main vehicle of emotional expression. Cantatas and opera scenes settle into a predictable alternation of recitative and aria, which is programmed in the texts supplied by the poets. Recitative text—the words in which basic information about plot and situation is conveyed—is in irregular rhymed lines or in prose. Aria text—the words in which characters express their feelings—is regulated poetry. Both cantata and opera become aria (and solo singer) centered, for the arias are the main locus of musical interest.

Few of Scarlatti's cantatas can be dated reliably, but *Su le sponde del Tebro*, with its overt reference to the banks of the Tiber, was probably composed between 1703 and 1708, a period of particular cantata productivity for Scarlatti, when the composer was in Rome. The work is a dramatic *scena* portraying the lament of the shepherd Aminto over his betrayal by the faithless Clori. It was probably written for a castrato, for the voice part is in a soprano register, while the aria texts plainly belong to a man. Most cantatas by Scarlatti and his comtemporaries are accompanied by basso continuo alone, but this one has comparatively elaborate accompaniment forces of two violins, solo trumpet, and continuo.

Only the last three sections of *Su le sponde del Tebro* are printed here. The entire cantata consists of: (1) introductory *sinfonia* for instruments; (2) recitative in which Aminto is depicted on the banks of the Tiber, crying "I am betrayed"; (3) a *da capo* aria with instrumental introduction in which Aminto asks his faithful thoughts to guard his heart from the pain of his betrayal; (4) a recitative link that prepares (5) a slow aria where Aminto asks his eyes to vent his sorrow through weeping; (6) a third aria in which Aminto asks the stars what he has done to deserve such suffering, that closes with an instrumental ritornello; (7) a recitative reporting that the betrayed lover finally perceives the senselessness of such a show of grief; and (8) a fourth aria where Aminto instructs his heart to cease weeping.[1] All of the recitative texts are in the narrator's voice and describe the various phases of Aminto's reaction to his betrayal. All of the poetic aria texts are in Aminto's voice and directly express his successive mental states. A single singer serves as both narrator and protagonist; the two "voices" are distinguished by musical and textual style.

The two arias presented here exhibit two different formal patterns, both related in some degree to the *ABA da capo* aria that became standard in later Italian baroque opera (see No. 82). "*Dite almeno*" divides into three parts that correspond respectively to the first three text lines, the second three, and (returning) the first two text lines. The first part (mm. 1-43) is in A minor. The second (mm. 44-73) modulates and cadences in

E minor. The third (mm. 73-86) returns to A minor and quotes the end of part 1 (compare mm. 73-78 with mm. 32-37) before branching out to a different A minor cadence. The subsequent orchestral ritornello helps to restore balance after this short return. The consistency of motivic material between the middle and the two outer parts blurs distinctions, so that they are perceived more as subsections of a single strophe than as separate units. The D major aria, "*Tralascia pur dipiangere*," is a concise example of *da capo* form (so called because of the eighteenth-century convention of writing *da capo*, "from the beginning," at the end of a second section to indicate a complete repetition of the first). The first and third sections (mm. 1-15 beat 1, 20-34 respectively) are identical, while the middle one (mm. 15-20 beat 1) contrasts with them in key, melodic movement, and accompaniment forces. The text divides asymmetrically between the sections, two lines for the outer ones and three for the middle. Both arias are compact enough to be repeated entire with second stanzas of text provided in some manuscripts.[2] The recitative between the two arias is unstable tonally and free metrically except for the very end where the sixteenth-note continuo figure (mm. 14-15) prepares the approaching aria.

Scarlatti's arias share important fundamentals of language with those of Handel, chief among the next generation of opera and cantata composers. They use functional harmony as a formal and expressive resource, and have carefully molded melodic lines that gain character from repetition and sequential projection of distinctive motives. But Handel's arias are generally broader—even more massive—in scope. His melodic lines tend to trace longer arches and can rise to heights of breathtaking virtuosity. Handel also achieves greater control of large-scale harmonic and rhythmic motion (see No. 82). This is not to disparage Scarlatti's achievement, but only to point out that from a historical point of view his work may be seen more as a starting point than as the culmination of an artistic tradition.

---

[1] A performing edition of the complete cantata may be found in *Su le sponde del Tebro*, edited by B. Paumgartner (Heidelberg: 1956).

[2] That some manuscripts do not include the second stanzas is perhaps more a sign of scribal negligence than an indication that the repetition was optional.

## 82. GEORGE FRIDERIC HANDEL (1685-1759)
### Admeto

82a.  Act II, scenes 7 and 8

[1]Small notes indicate the conventional cadence formulas of eighteenth-century recitative.

## SCENA VIII.

ADMETO solo.

*Qui-vi trà que-sti so-li-ta-rii or-ro-ri, lon-tan dall'al-tre cu-re,*

*ven-go a sfo-gar gl'in-ter-ni miei do-lo-ri. Ad-me-to, e che fa-rai?      frà*

*l'om-bre del-le not-te, quando tut-to s'ob-li-a, per dop-pio fo-co l'al-ma tua s'af-fan-na;*

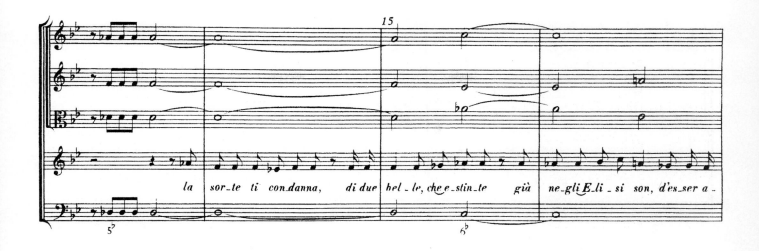

la sor_te ti con_danna, di due bel _ le, che e _ stin _ te già ne _ gli E _ li _ si son, d'es _ ser a _

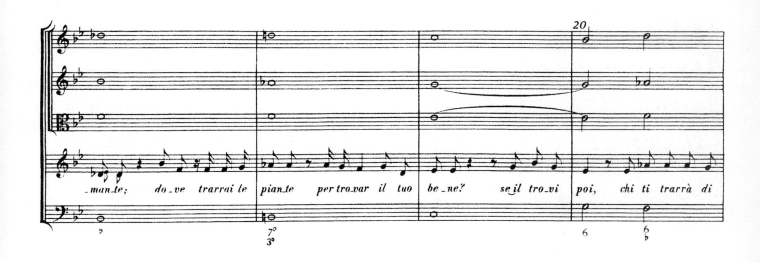

_ man _ te; do _ ve trar_rai le pian_te per tro_var il tuo be _ ne? se il tro _ vi poi, chi ti trarrà di

pe _ ne? Ah! che se ab _ brac_cio Al _ ce _ ste, An _ ti _ go _ na di_sprezzo, e al mio cor, ben _ chè a _ vez _ zo a pe _ nar

sem_pre,   un tal do_lo_re è   troppo.                 Giusti Nu_mi del ciel, se de_ste a i_ta    a

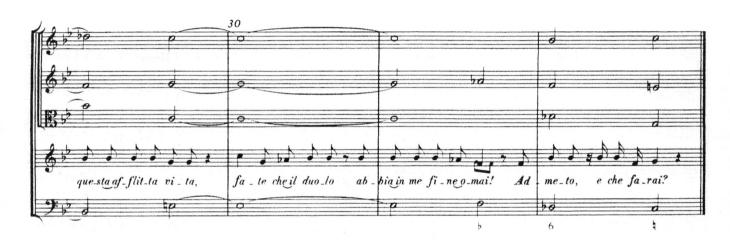

que_sta af_flit_ta vi_ta,   fa_te che il duo_lo   ab_bia in me fi_ne o_mai!   Ad_me_to,   e che fa_rai?

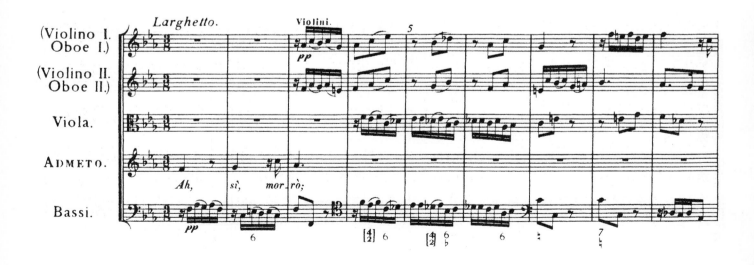

(Violino I.
Oboe I.)

(Violino II.
Oboe II.)

Viola.

ADMETO.

Bassi.

*Larghetto.*   Violini.

Ah,   sì,   mor_rò;

u _ na e l'altra bel_la ri_splendau_na fa_cel_la, ri_splendau_na fa _ cel _ la in doppio fo _ co, all' u_na e l'altra

bel_la, all' u_na e l'altra bel_la ri_splendau_na fa _ cel_la in dop_pio fo _ co, ri_splendau_na fa_cel_la in dop_

_pio fo _ co, all' u_na e l'altra bel_la ri_splendau_na fa_cel_la in dop_pio fo_ _co!

*Adagio.*

*Da Capo.*

### Act II    Scene 7
A wood. Hercules and Alcestis [dressed as a warrior].

**[Recitative]**

HERCULES:
*To what end, O Queen, do you disguise yourself as a warrior?*

ALCESTIS:
*Hercules, I will tell you the secrets of my heart. Know that jealousy has made me dress myself thus. You have seen whether I have adored my husband, and know it. Now thanks to your victorious right arm I have returned from the abyss [death] to the light. I want to discover if my husband's love for me is extinguished with my death.*

HERCULES:
*Believe me, he deplores your fate most sorrowfully, and utters your name hourly.*

ALCESTIS:
*If he mourns for me, I say that he is the first husband who, widowed, has been seen to weep for his wife with tormented longing.*

HERCULES:
*Ah, at your appearance, as soon as he sees you, joy will arise spontaneously in his heart, and a smile will appear on his sad lips.*

ALCESTIS:
*But please gratify me first, Alcides [Hercules]. Return to court and say that you scoured Hell in vain and did not find me.*

HERCULES:
*At this sad news, his excessive sorrow might kill him.*

ALCESTIS:
*I will be prompt to give aid and restore him to health.*

HERCULES:
*All right, if that pleases you, I go, Alcestis, to serve you.*                    [*Exit*]

ALCESTIS:
*I will be ready to follow you.*

**[Aria]**

| | |
|---|---|
| Gelosia spietata Aletto | *Jealousy, ruthless Fury,* |
| Meco uscisti dall'inferno | *You came out with me from Hell* |
| E m'entrasti a forza in petto | *And forcibly entered my heart* |
| Per affligger questo cor. | *In order to distress me.* |
| | |
| Ti vorrei scacciar dal seno | *I want to expel you from my breast* |
| Mà non ho vigore bastante. | *But I have insufficient strength.* |
| Chi non prova il tuo veleno | *Whoever has not felt your poison* |
| nò, non sà, che cosa è amor. | *Does not know what Love is.*    [*Exit*] |

### Scene 8
[Admetus, alone]

**[Recitative]**
*Here amid these solitary horrors
far from other cares,
I come to pour out my inner sorrows.*

*Admetus, what will you do?*
*Among the shadows of night, when all sleep,*
*your soul is troubled with double fire.*
*Fate condemns you to be the lover of two beautiful women,*
*who, dead, are already in Elysium.*
*Where would you guide your tears to find your beloved?*
*If you found her, what would resolve your difficulty?*
*Ah, if I embrace Alcestis, I scorn Antigona*
*and will always suffer for it in my heart.*
*Such grief is too much.*
*Just gods in heaven, give help to my afflicted life,*
*Make an end to my sorrow.*
*Admetus, what will you do?*

**[Aria]**

| | |
|---|---|
| Ah, sì, morrò | *Ah, yes, I shall die* |
| E allor potrò | *And then I will be able* |
| Dividere quel cor | *To divide this heart* |
| Che in vita è poco. | *Which in life is too slight.* |
| | |
| Così nel doppio amor | *Thus in a double love* |
| All'una, e l'altra bella | *To both one and the other beauty* |
| Risplenda una facella | *A light may shine* |
| In doppio foco. | *With double fire.*                [*Exit*] |

## 82b.   Act III, scene 6

**Act III, scene 6**
[Hercules has just liberated Alcestis—still in disguise—from the guards who were holding her.]

**[Recitative]**

ALCESTIS:
*Orindo did not recognize me in the garb of a warrior, but I could not discover the compelling reason that made them take me prisoner.*

HERCULES:
*Go, Alcestis, to court and, in amazement, see your husband changed in his affections.*

ALCESTIS:
*What?!*

HERCULES:
*If I am not mistaken, I fear you will find a new flame born in his heart, injurious to you.*

ALCESTIS:
*This news kills me. Oh, from what source flow my misfortunes?*

HERCULES:
*Come to court and find out.*

ALCESTIS:
*Ah, my heart has had cause to be tormented with jealousy, but, with righteous control, I will learn to mock jealousy, beloved Admetus.*

**[Aria]**

| | |
|---|---|
| Là dove gli occhi io giro | *There where I turn my eyes* |
| E l'erbe, e i fior rimiro | *And view grass and flowers* |
| Farsi più vaghi e belli | *They seem more lovely and beautiful* |
| Per chè il mio ben frà lor | *Because among them my beloved* |
| Mosse le piante. | *shed his tears.* |
| | |
| Ogn'aura e dolce vento | *Every breeze and mild wind* |
| A me porge contento | *Brings pleasure to me* |
| E il canto degli augelli | *And the song of the birds* |
| Per chè a me dica ogn'or: | *Seems to say to me each moment:* |
| Egli è costante. | *He is constant.*    [*Exit*] |

George Frideric Handel (1685-1759) was one of the most cosmopolitan figures of the early eighteenth century. Born and trained in Germany, he developed and polished his compositional skills in Italy (1706-10), and ultimately established himself in London (1712-59). Handel's London career breaks into two phases: a first when he composed principally Italian *opera seria* (1711-c. 1735), a second when he redirected his energies to oratorios with English text (mid-1730s-1750s). In his *opere serie*, Handel essentially followed Italian conventions as frozen in the libretti of Pietro Metastasio (though he himself rarely set a Metastasio text). The subjects are invariably heroic in nature and deal with themes of love, duty, and honor. The intrigue unfolds inprose, while outbursts of feeling take shape in poetry. The mainstay of musical expression is the solo *da capo* aria, a substantial piece in which a character responds emotionally to the situation of the moment. The musical style derives from Neapolitan and Roman traditions, for Handel's singers, imported from Italy, were thoroughly trained in Italian operatic style.

*Admeto, Rè di Tessaglia*, the last opera Handel wrote for the Royal Academy, was a signal success when first produced in January 1727. In setting the text, Handel was free to exploit the virtuosic Italian vocal tradition to its fullest, for his extraordinary cast included two celebrated prima donnas, Faustina Bordoni (Alceste) and Francesca Cuzzoni (Antigona) as well as the eminent *castrato* Senesino (Admeto). The plot derives from Greek tragedy, mediated and considerably complicated by eighteenth-century Italian operatic versions. It focuses not so much on the problem of marital sacrifice (as in Gluck's later treatment) but on the conflicting attractions of two loves, each of which has claims to legitimacy.[1] The conventional three acts neatly segment the action. In the first act, King Admetus revives from mortal illness when his wife Alcestis secretly sacrifices herself for him. In the second, Alcestis is retrieved from hell by the hero Hercules, but disguises herself as a warrior in order to discover whether her husband's love for her endures. Meanwhile, Admetus's former betrothed, Antigona, has arrived at court in disguise with the object of engaging the king's affections. Unknown to her, Admetus's brother, Trasimede, infatuated with her himself, deceitfully sabotaged her marriage with the king, whereupon Admetus wed Alcestis instead. In the third act, Admetus (unaware that Alcestis has been restored to life) and Antigona declare their love. Enraged at seeing his brother claim his own beloved, Trasimede tries to assassinate Admetus, but is prevented by an unknown warrior (Alcestis in disguise), who is standing by. Alcestis reveals her identity, and Antigona graciously yields in favor of the woman who has proved her love so selflessly and twice saved Admetus's life.

**82a.** The excerpts presented here have been chosen to illustrate some of the dramatic conventions of *opera seria* as well as modes of expression and musical style. In Act II, scene 7, Hercules and Alcestis carry on a conversation in simple recitative (or, in nineteenth-century parlance, *secco* recitative), the mode in which all the action of the plot and interchange between characters takes place. At the end of their discussion, Alcestis expresses her jealousy in a splendid heroic *da capo* aria that captures "the fierce singleness of [baroque] operatic passions."[2] The quick scale passages in the instruments and the singer's brilliant vocalizations and sudden wide leaps amply convey her fervor. The eight-line text is divided in half and treated in two sections of unequal length, conventionally called the *A* and the *B* sections. The *A* section is normally the longer of the two, and divides into two subsections. Here, in the first subsection, an instrumental ritornello introduces the first vocal statement, which modulates from G minor to B-flat major. A brief ritornello (mm. 32-34) confirms B-flat and punctuates the division between subsections. The second subsection begins and ends in G minor, and another ritornello rounds off the whole. The short *B* section (mm. 64-74) contrasts with *A* in motivic material and in key. It begins in B-flat and ends in the minor dominant. The lack of vocal pyrotechnics

gives this section a sense of inner meditation relative to *A*. The entrance of the opening ritornello (m. 75) signals the return of the *A* section. It is repeated in full (the initial ritornello somewhat abbreviated), hence the designation *da capo* for the entire *ABA* form. This aria is a characteristic example of the fully developed form. Singers were expected to vary the repeat and demonstrate their vocal prowess with embellishing ornaments. The conventional exit after the aria gives time for applause and tends to segment the opera into discrete separate units, each culminating in an aria.

With calculated dramatic effect, scene 8 shows Admetus indeed worrying over his attachment to two women. The depth of his emotion is immediately communicated by the adoption of *obbligato* (or accompanied) recitative to support his words. The rich harmony and unexpected harmonic disjunctions that accompany his soliloquy metaphorically express his distress and indecision. His F minor *da capo* aria, "Ah, sì, morrò," is in the pathetic vein, and contrasts pointedly in feeling with Alcestis's preceding *aria di bravura*. Handel aptly conveys Admetus's overflowing emotions by having him anticipate the aria before the formal ritornello. The motivic bass, which maintains a constant dialogue with the violins, is an unusual feature of the music. This special bass-melody relationship was doubtless inspired by the textual images of duality and a divided heart.

**82b.** The excerpt from Act III, scene 6 shows Alcestis's reaction to the confirmation of her fears. Instead of raging against Admetus, she dwells on the beauties of nature, which remind her of her beloved husband and persuade her of his constancy. This lovely aria makes rigorous demands on the singer's technique—Burney reports that in 1727 its performance was thought to be supernatural.[3] But the *fioritura* (which persists even in the *B* section) is not simply for display, but functions to convey Alcestis's successful effort at attaining inner serenity in this harsh moment. The *da capo* form of this aria is like that of the other two presented here, but the musical expression is as different from them as they are from each other. The dramatic effect of Handel's *opera seria*, which can be very powerful, rests on the cumulative effect of many such pieces, each of which reveals something about a particular character or a general human reaction to external forces.

Burney's *History* contains a valuable report and critical appreciation of the first run of *Admeto*.[4]

---

[1] The Lully-Quinault treatment (No. 68) gives yet another twist to the story.

[2] Joseph Kerman, *Opera as Drama* (New York: Alfred A. Knopf, 1952), p. 51.

[3] Charles Burney, *A General History of Music* (London: 1789, reissued 1957), p. 745.

[4] *Ibid.*, pp. 742-747.

## 83. JEAN-PHILIPPE RAMEAU (1683-1764)   treatise   1722
## Hippolyte et Aricie
Act I, scene 2

[1]Harmonizations of the bass may be found in *Hippolyte et Aricie,* edited by C. Saint-Saëns and V. d'Indy (Paris: A. Durand, 1900; reprinted Broude Brothers Ltd., 1968), pp. 56-63 and in the piano-vocal score edited by C. Poisot, Chefs-d'Oeuvre Classiques de l'Opéra Française 33 (Paris: T. Michaelis [n.d.]; reprinted Broude Brothers Ltd., 1971), pp. 47-56.

[2]In the recitative 2♩ = 3♩ = C♩

[3]+ indicates an ornament whose nature is not further specified. The kind chosen would depend in each case on the context and the singer's taste.

## Act I, scene 2

A temple dedicated to Diana, with an altar.

HIPPOLYTUS:

*Princess, what preparations surprise me in this temple?*

ARICIE:

*Diana presides in this place,*
*To consecrate my days to her is to follow your example.*

HIPPOLYTUS:
*No, you sacrifice this life that is so precious.*

ARICIE:
*I fulfill the supreme command of the king,*
*To Theseus, to his son, this life is hateful.*

HIPPOLYTUS:
*I hate you?—O Heaven—what an extreme injustice!*

ARICIE:
*Then I am not the object of your emnity?*

HIPPOLYTUS:
*I feel for you a pity*
*that is as tender as love itself.*

ARICIE:
*What! The proud Hippolytus . . .*

HIPPOLYTUS:
*Alas! I have said too much, but I do not repent my words.*
*If you have condescended to hear me*
*My confusion, my sighs, your misfortunes, your charms,*
*all announce to you a heart too susceptible and too tender.*

ARICIE:
*Ah! what have you just told me?*
*This settles all, my tranquillity is lost forever.*
*Perhaps your indifference would sooner or later have restored it [tranquillity] to me,*
*But your love now removes all hope of this.*
*This settles all, my tranquillity is lost forever.*

HIPPOLYTUS:
*What do I hear? What transport possesses my soul?*

ARICIE:
*Do you forget that we are being separated?*
*In this ominous temple, what will be my destiny?*

**[Air]**
*A loving Hippolytus will fill my thoughts constantly*
*And from the altars of the Goddess*
*I will feel my heart fly back to its beloved*
*And I shall there lament my happiness and his.*
*A loving Hippolytus will fill my thoughts constantly*
*And I shall lament my happiness and his.*

HIPPOLYTUS:
*I shall free you from such a cruel law!*

ARICIE:
*Phaedra has absolute power over her captive.*
*What matter that we love? We will never see each other again.*

HIPPOLYTUS:
*O Diana, protect so beautiful a flame of love!*

## [Duo]

(ARICIE and HIPPOLYTUS)
*You reign over our hearts as over our forests,*[1]
*You lend us the weapons to combat love,*
*But when virtue itself lets fly the arrows of Love,*
*Who can resist its attraction?*

[1]Diana was, of course, goddess of the hunt.

The *tragédie lyrique Hippolyte et Aricie,* with text by the playwright Simon-Joseph de Pellegrin and music by Jean-Philippe Rameau (1683-1764), was first performed in 1733. The work essentially conforms to the tradition established some sixty years earlier by Lully and Quinault (see No. 68). The eighteenth-century French *tragédie lyrique* is a genre of musical theater quite distinct from the Italian *opera seria.* Choruses and ballets are prominent in each act, a legacy from Greek drama. The entire text is in rhymed poetry, and so does not exhibit the sharp cleavage between prose and poetic passages characteristic of *opera seria* libretti. Because of the more fluid text structure, aria (*air*) and recitative are much less strongly differentiated than in *opera seria.* As in late Monteverdi, the recitative ranges over a broad spectrum from straightforward recitation to highly expressive song-speech. The airs are often not distinctly separated from the preceding and following music. For example, Aricie's "Peut-être votre indifférence," designated an air in the score, flows smoothly out of the preceding recitative (m. 33) with no framing instrumental ritornello to set it apart. After two phrases, the music reverts back to recitative, and continues so as Hippolytus breaks in. Her second venture at an air, "Hippolyte amoureux," is more expansive, but appears modest and relatively unfocused musically in comparison with a full-blown Handel *da capo* aria.

Because the ebb and flow of the music is so intimately bound up with the text in *tragédie lyrique,* an understanding of the words is particularly necessary in order to appreciate the work. Also, because much of the impact of the genre derived from spectacle—brilliant formal dances, marvelous sets (the second act of

*Hippolyte* takes place amid the fires of hell, for example), rich costumes—the *tragédie lyrique* suffers more than Italian *opera seria* in being divorced from the theater.

The plot of *Hippolyte et Aricie* goes back to Greek mythology, but Pellegrin's immediate models were the *Hippolytus* of Euripides and the *Phèdre* of Racine. The context for Act I, scene 2 is that Theseus has killed Pallas, King of Athens, and usurped his throne. To insure that no male heir will contest the new dynasty, Theseus has ordered Pallas's daughter Aricie to become a celibate priestess of Diana, goddess of the hunt. Scene 2 takes place in the solemn atmosphere of Diana's monumental temple. Hippolytus, son of Theseus, comes upon Aricie as she reluctantly prepares to take her vows. Stung by her assertion that her life is hateful to the usurpers, Hippolytus confesses his love for Aricie, whereupon she reveals her passion for him. This scene is crucial dramatically, for the rest of the plot turns upon the struggle of the lovers to stay together and the fierce opposition of Phaedra, Hippolytus's stepmother, to the union. Comparison between this scene and those from Handel's *Admeto* (No. 82) will reveal the strikingly different conventions and musical styles of the *opera seria* and the *tragédie lyrique.*

In addition to composing *tragédies lyriques, opéra-ballets,* and keyboard music, Jean-Philippe Rameau was a distinguished music theorist. His ideas on harmony and chord function, expressed in a series of publications initiated by the *Traité de l'harmonie* of 1722, were central to the development of tonal theory. The lucid harmonic movement of his compositions complements the interest in codifying basic principles of melody and harmony evident in his theoretical writings.

## 84. GIOVANNI BATTISTA PERGOLESI (1710–1736)
### La serva padrona
Intermezzo primo

5  Track 1

Aria: **Aspettare e non venire**

Edited by K. Geiringer. Used by permission of European American Music Distributors Corporation, sole U.S. agent for Philharmonia Scores.

[1]A figured bass realization may be found in G. B. Pergolesi, *La serva padrona,* edited by K. Geiringer (Vienna: Universal Edition A. G. Wien, n.d.), pp. 1–10.

mi-re e    non gra-di - re,    son tre co - se da   mo - ri - re,

da - mo - ri - - re!    A - spet - ta - re e    non ve-

ni - re,    sta - re a let - to e    non dor - mi-re,   ben ser-vi-re e    non gra-

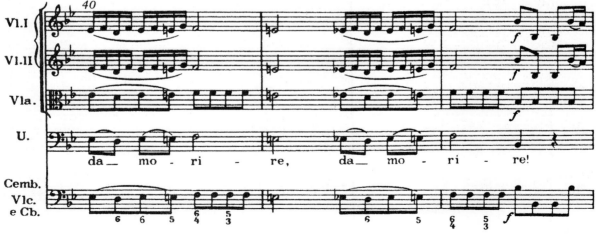

## Recitative: **Questa e per me disgrazia!**

²The conventional graces of eighteenth-century recitative are shown in small notes.

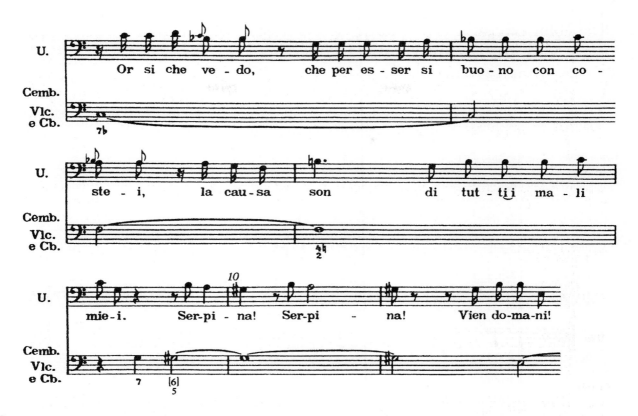

U. Or si che ve - do, che per es - ser si buo - no con co -

ste - i, la cau - sa son di tut - ti i ma - li

mie - i. Ser-pi - na! Ser-pi - na! Vien do-ma-ni!

**Aria**

Aspettare e non venire
Stare a letto e non dormire
Ben servire e non gradire
Son tre cose da morire.

*To wait, and no one comes,*
*To lie abed and not to sleep,*
*To be useful indeed and yet not give satisfaction,*
*These three things are enough to make you die.*

**Recitative**

Questa è per me disgrazia! Son tre ore ch'aspetto, e la mia serva portarmi il ciocolatte non fa grazia, ed io d'uscire ho fretta! O flemma benedetta! Or si che vedo, che per esser si buono con costei, la causa son di tutti i mali miei. Serpina! Serpina! Vien domani!

*This is disgraceful! I've waited three hours and my maidservant has not yet done me the favor of bringing my morning chocolate, and I am anxious to go out. What a blessed annoyance! Now I see that being so good to her is the cause of all my troubles. Serpina! Serpina! Coming tomorrow?*

*La serva padrona* ("The maid [as] mistress") by Giovanni Battista Pergolesi (1710-1736) is a comic intermezzo in two parts. It was originally written for performance between the acts of a serious opera. First presented in Naples on 28 August, 1733, this modest work for two singers and one mute actor soon achieved renown, spreading to other Italian cities, to Germany and to France, where it sparked the *querelle des bouffons*. In setting this amusing comedy about a well-to-do old bachelor, Uberto, who is tricked into marrying his young maidservant, Pergolesi adopted a tuneful, easily grasped musical idiom that is often characterized as *buffo* style. Common traits of *buffo* style are unison passages, repetition of concise, memorable melodic ideas, octave leaps and triadic outlines, and relatively slow harmonic rhythm. In its transparent simplicity, this style appealed to many and eventually contributed to a new mode of expression, which we designate the "classical style."

In contrast with serious opera of the day, the texts and situations of *La serva padrona* are unabashedly comic. The aria that opens the intermezzo is sung in bed by the old man Uberto, who is furious that his maid is three hours late in bringing his morning hot chocolate. His growing rage (and the simplistic parallel construction of the text) is expressed musically in the ascending sequence of his first three phrases and in the rhythmic acceleration of the last section of the aria (mm. 32-37). The chromaticism and abrupt drop in register on the words "*da morire*" (mm. 18, 40) provides an apt comic exaggeration and can be viewed as a parody of *seria* pathos. This aria does not follow conventional *da capo* format, but expresses Uberto's impotent impatience in its threefold repetition of the same words.

# 85. JOHANN SEBASTIAN BACH (1685-1750)

## Jesu, der du meine Seele, BWV 78[1]

Cantata for the 14th Sunday after Trinity

5 Tracks 2–8

[1]J. S. Bach's compositions are commonly identified by *BWV* number, their order number in the standard catalogue of his works by W. Schmieder, the *Thematisch-systematisches Verzeichnis der musikalischen Werke von Johann Sebastian Bach: Bach-Werke-Verzeichnis*, third edition (Leipzig: 1966).

[2]Piano reductions with some continuo realizations may be found in J. S. Bach, *Jesu, der du meïne Seele (Klavierauszug)*, edited by W. H. Bernstein (Kassel, Basel: Bärenreiter, 1970), and in J. S. Bach, *Kantate Nr. 78 (Klavierauszug)*, edited by G. Raphael (Wiesbaden: Breitkopf und Härtel, 1933/61).

## 2. Aria. Duetto

### 4. Aria

## 6. Aria

## 7. Choral

**1. [Chorus]**

Jesu, der du meine Seele
Hast durch deinen bittern Tod
Aus des Teufels finstern Höhle
Und der schweren Seelennot
Kräftiglich herausgerissen
Und mich solches lassen wissen
Durch dein angenehmes Wort,
Sei doch jetzt, O Gott, mein Hort!

**1. [Chorus]**

*Jesus, you who through your bitter death*
*Have forcefully torn my soul*
*From the devil's dark cave*
*And from grave distress of soul,*

*And have let me know of this*
*Through your comforting Word,*
*Be now, O God, my refuge!*

**2. Aria. Duet.**

Wir eilen mit schwachen, doch emsigen Schritten
O Jesu, o Meister, zu helfen zu dir.
Du suchest die Kranken und Irrenden treulich.
Ach höre, wie wir die Stimme erheben,
Um Hilfe zu bitten!
Es sei uns dein gnädiges Antlitz erfreulich!

**2. Aria. Duet.**

*We hasten with weak but persistent steps*
*O Jesus, O master, to you, for help.*
*You faithfully seek the sick and the wandering.*
*Ah, hear, how we raise our voices*
*To pray for help!*
*May your gracious countenance cheer us!*

**3. Recitative**

Ach! ich bin ein Kind der Sünden,
ach! ich irre weit und breit.
Der Sünden Aussatz, so an mir zu finden,
verlässt mich nicht in dieser Sterblichkeit.
Mein Wille trachtet nur nach Bösen.
Der Geist zwar spricht: ach! wer wird mich erlösen?
Aber Fleisch und Blut zu zwingen
und das Gute zu vollbringen,
ist über alle meine Kraft.
Will ich den Schaden nicht verhehlen,
so kann ich nicht, wie oft ich fehle, zählen.
Drum nehm ich nun der Sünden Schmerz und Pein
und meiner Sorgen Bürde,
so mir sonst unerträglich würde,
ich liefre sie dir, Jesu, seufzend ein.
Rechne nicht die Missetat,
die dich, Herr, erzürnet hat!

**3. Recitative**

*Ah! I am a child of sin!*
*Ah! I wander far and wide.*
*The leprosy of sin found on me*
*will not leave me in this lifetime.*
*My will inclines toward evil,*
*my spirit then says, "Ah! who will redeem me?"*
*But to compel flesh and blood,*
*and to accomplish good*
*is beyond all my strength.*
*Though I do not want to hide my misdeeds,*
*I cannot count how often I err.*
*Thus I now take the grief and pain of my sins*
*and the burden of my cares,*
*which would otherwise be unbearable to me,*
*I deliver them to you, Jesus, sighing.*
*Do not count the misdeeds*
*that angered you, O Lord!*

**4. Aria.**

Das Blut so meine Schuld durchstreicht,
Macht mir das Herze wieder leicht
Und spricht mich frei.

Ruft mich der Höllen Herr zum Streite,
So stehet Jesus mir zur Seite,
Dass ich beherzt und sieghaft sei.

**4. Aria**

*(Your) blood so cancels out my guilt,*
*That it makes my heart light again*
*And declares me free.*

*If the Lord of Hell summons me to battle*
*Then Jesus stands at my side*
*So I may take courage and be victorious.*

**5. Recitative**

Die Wunden, Nägel, Kron und Grab,
die Schläge, so man dort dem Heiland gab,
sind ihm nunmehro Siegeszeichen
und können mir verneute Krafte reichen.
Wenn ein erschreckliches Gericht
den Fluch vor die Verdammten spricht,
so kehrst du ihn in Segen.

**5. Recitative**

*The wounds, nails, crown and grave,*
*the blows they gave there to the savior,*
*are now tokens of victory to him*
*and can extend new strength to me.*
*When a horrifying judgment pronounces a curse*
   *on the damned,*
*you turn it into a blessing.*

Mich kann kein Schmerz und keine Pein bewegen,
weil sie mein Heiland kennt;
und da dein Herz vor mich in Liebe brennt,
so lege ich hinwieder
das mein vor dich nieder.
Dies mein Herz, mit Leid vermenget,
so dein teures Blut besprenget,
so am Kreuz vergossen ist,
geb ich dir, Herr Jesu Christ.

*No pain or grief can alter me,*
*when my savior knows them.*
*And since your heart burns in love before me,*
*so, in return,*
*I lay mine down before you.*
*This my heart, wrought with suffering,*
*sprinkled with your precious blood*
*shed on the Cross,*
*I give to you, Lord Jesus Christ.*

## 6. Aria

Nun du wirst mein Gewissen stillen,
So wider mich um Rache schreit;
Ja, deine Treue wirds erfüllen,
Weil mir dein Wort die Hoffnung beut.

Wenn Christen an dich glauben,
Wird sie kein Feind in Ewigkeit
Aus deinen Händen rauben.

## 6. Aria

*Now you will calm my conscience,*
*Which calls for vengeance against me;*
*Yes, your faith will fill it,*
*Because your Word offers me hope.*

*If Christians believe in you,*
*No enemy, through eternity,*
*Will steal them from your hands.*

## 7. Chorale

Herr, ich glaube, hilf mir Schwachen,
Lass mich ja verzagen nicht;
Du, du kannst mich stärker machen,
Wenn mich Sünd und Tod anficht.
Deiner Güte will ich trauen,
Bis ich frölich werde schauen
Dich, Herr Jesu, nach dem Streit
In der süssen Ewigkeit.

## 7. Chorale

*Lord, I believe, help my weakness*
*Do not let me despair;*
*You, you can make me stronger,*
*When sin and death trouble me.*
*I want to trust your goodness,*
*Until I shall joyfully look upon*
*You, Lord Jesus, after the battle*
*In sweet eternity.*

Johann Sebastian Bach (1685-1750) is the most illustrious member of a musical dynasty that has been traced back to the late sixteenth century. Trained as a church organist, J. S. Bach was especially esteemed in his own time as a virtuoso performer and judge of instruments. Yet the posts which he held—chief among them court organist at Weimar (1708), *Kapellmeister* at Cöthen (1717), *Kantor* at the *Thomaskirche* in Leipzig (1723)—all required him to create as well as to perform music. The modern catalogue of his works lists over one thousand extant compositions. A significant number of compositions (for instance, an estimated 40 percent of his cantatas) are lost. The bulk of Bach's works were destined to ornament the Lutheran liturgy: vocal cantatas, chorale preludes and preludes and fugues for organ. Pieces for harpsichord or clavichord, many written as study material for his family and students, comprise another large segment of his *oeuvre*.

Bach's earliest extant cantatas date from the first decade of the eighteenth century (1707/08), but his most prolific outpouring of cantatas came in the first two years of his Leipzig appointment. The cantata *Jesu, der du meine Seele* (BWV 78) belongs to the second cycle of Leipzig cantatas (1724-25), and was written for the fourteenth Sunday after Trinity (10 September 1724).[1] It is a chorale cantata, a type particularly favored by Bach in this period. The first and last movements adopt the text of an established mid-seventeenth-century chorale by Johann Rist. The middle movements have new text by an unknown poet who occasionally quotes or paraphrases middle stanzas of the chorale. The textual duality of the work reflects the duality of its musical heritage. The mature Bach cantata fuses German Lutheran traditions, particularly the chorale and choral singing, with Italian secular genres, particularly solo cantata and opera. As in many of Bach's Leipzig cantatas, the opening and concluding movements of *Jesu, der du meine Seele* are scored for chorus and incorporate the familiar chorale melody. The five middle movements alternate between aria and recitative and are freely composed.

The two-part design of all three aria texts points toward the *da capo* aria convention, but only the first (a duet) is actually cast in *da capo* form. In the tenor and bass arias, Bach's keen concern for textual imagery and interpretation overrides the built-in *da capo*

---

[1]Bach's cantata cycles commence not with the beginning of the church year in Advent but with the first Sunday after Trinity.

premise of the poem. Both arias concentrate on the second part of the text in their second halves, rather than treating it as a subsidiary interlude between two closed statements of the main thought as occurs in the typical Italian *da capo* aria (see No. 82). Bach's arias differ also from their Italian counterparts in scoring and texture. In both these arias the voice is paired with an *obbligato* instrument (transverse flute in No. 4, oboe in No. 6). The interplay of the two melodic lines produces a rich contrapuntal texture akin to the instrumental trio sonata.

The two recitatives in *Jesu, der du meine Seele* are deeply expressive with their disjunct melodic lines, exposed dissonances, and exceptional harmonic progressions. In spirit, they recall Monteverdi more than the usual recitative of contemporary Italian opera. The second of them, which speaks emphatically of Christ's passion, achieves special impact through its *obbligato* instrumental accompaniment. Both recitatives mutate toward the end into a melodious arioso as the speaker directly addresses the Lord.

The opening chorale movement of this cantata is a masterpiece of craft. Its complexity and chromaticism serve as a metaphor for the struggle with doubt that is the dominant theme of the entire cantata text. Bach here combines no fewer than four separate compositional devices: in the instruments, ritornello form and a chromatic ground bass; in the voices, a cantus firmus (the chorale melody) and fugal imitation on each text line. The treatment of the ground bass is especially noteworthy, for it migrates from the bass to other voices, modulates, and somehow manages to harmonize six different chorale phrases. The unadorned four-part setting of the chorale at the end of the cantata not only makes a satisfying formal closure (the return of the chorale melody and of the chorus), but also, in its stark simplicity, dramatizes the victory of the soul over doubt. Bach's attention to musical projection of the text extends from the large-scale conception of the work down to fine details. No listener can fail to notice how long notes highlight the idea of steadfast endurance on "*stehet*" ("stand") in the tenor aria (mm. 53-56) and on "*Ewigkeit*" ("eternity") in the bass aria (mm. 37-38). The steady motivic bass of the duet projects both the textual image of walking and the general tone of futility, for the insistently regular pulse does not "hasten" *("eilen")* at all. Consistent with the sense of trying but getting nowhere, the first section does not modulate (as is conventional in a *da capo* aria) but remains stuck in B-flat major.

An illuminating account of the dramatic nature of this cantata may be found in Joseph Kerman's *Opera as Drama* (New York: Alfred A. Knopf, 1952), pp. 64-70.

# EXPLICATION DES AGRÉMENTS ET DES SIGNES

**Plate 6.** "Explanation of Ornaments and Signs" from *Pièces de clavecin, Premier livre* (see No. 86), by François Couperin.

## 86. FRANÇOIS COUPERIN (1668-1733)
### Pièces de clavecin, Premier livre
Premier ordre

5 Tracks 9–11

Allemande l'Auguste

<sup>1</sup>*Reprise* indicates the starting point of a sectional repeat. *Petite reprise* marks the repetition of a short phrase, usually situated at the end of a binary movement.

Première Courante

[2]*Dessus plus orne sans changer la Basse.*

("More ornamented melody on the same bass.")

Sarabande la Majestueuse

³"The 'short reprise' of this Sarabande, more ornamented than the first one."

French music early in the era of Louis XIV (reigned 1643-1715) is epitomized by Lully (see No. 68), that in the last decades of the reign by François Couperin (1668-1733), scion of a family of musicians and nephew of the esteemed Louis Couperin (see No. 75). François Couperin's skills as a performer and gifts for musical invention were honored by prestigious court appointments, first as royal organist (1693) and later as harpsichordist among the king's chamber musicians (1717, reign of Louis XV).

Thoroughly schooled in the French tradition, François Couperin was open to the new Italian manner as manifested in the sonatas of Corelli. In his *Les goûts-réünis* (a set of chamber suites), he sought to achieve a union between French and Italian idioms. His four published books of harpsichord music and his manual of harpsichord playing *(L'art de toucher le clavecin,* 1716, revised 1717) crown a grand tradition of French harpsichord music. This tradition mingles with a distinctive seventeenth-century school of lute playing, with which it shares, among other features, a taste for expressive ornamentation and the *style brisé* ("broken style"), an arpeggiated texture of rhythmic finesse.[1]

A major problem addressed by Couperin was how to play expressively on so mechanical an instrument as the harpsichord (literally, as he phrases it in *L'art de toucher le clavecin,* how "to give soul to the instrument").[2] To vary the quality of attack and achieve nuance in tone color, Couperin advocated a combination of two opposite devices, cessation and suspension of sound. This approach is pervasive, but may be exemplified within the first four measures of the *Allemande l'Auguste,* where suspensions combined with registral breaks and variations in timing create a richly colored texture. François Couperin is known for regularizing the signs for traditional ornaments *(agréments)* and for careful notation of ornaments, which he considered to be essential to the spirit of a work. In the *Première Courante* and the *Sarabande* of his first *ordre* (suite) of pieces, he even shows how a repeat can be intensified with more lavish ornamentation. (See Plate VI for Couperin's explanations of his embellishments.)

The titles of the dance movements, such as *Allemande l'Auguste* and *Sarabande la Majestueuse,* direct the performer toward the desired character to be achieved. These are not mere abstract dance movements. In the preface to this first book of harpsichord pieces Couperin claims to have had an object in mind in composing each piece and to have conceived many of them as musical portraits—a view to which Schumann would have been sympathetic.

The three dances presented here are from the first *ordre* of François Couperin's *Pièces de clavecin, Premier livre* (1713), a group of eighteen movements on a G tonic (eleven in minor and seven in major mode). All three are in binary form, but the three realizations of this form differ subtly in tonal structure. In the *Allemande,* the first strain ends on a half cadence in G minor; a real modulation and cadence to the relative major, B-flat, is deferred until the fourth measure of the second strain (m. 13). In the *Première Courante,* the D-major chord ending the first strain is approached as a tonic, while in the *Sarabande* the first strain modulates directly to B-flat. All three dances differ in meter and in character. The *Allemande* is a stately duple-meter dance whose moderate tempo affords ample space for melodic embellishment. The *Courante* has a more transparent texture and shifts between 6/4 and 3/2 metric groupings *(hemiola;* compare measures 1 and 2, for example), as is characteristic of this dance type. The triple-meter *Sarabande* reinstates the grand style of the *Allemande* and is true to type in its rhythmic emphasis on the second beat of each measure. The expressive dissonance heralding the tonic return in the second strain (mm. 19 and 25) provides an acerbic touch in this majestic portrait.

J. S. Bach knew Couperin's music and imitated the French style in some of his keyboard suites and partitas. Compared with Couperin's dances, Bach's tend to be steadier in harmonic rhythm and more regularly patterned in figuration. The melodic surfaces are far less embroidered with ornamentation (though Bach may well have performed them with more embellishment than he notates). The keyboard works of Couperin's younger compatriot Rameau generally have less expressive detail but more precisely chiseled harmonic profiles.

---

[1] *Style brisé* is a modern term used to connote a spectrum of traits common in French lute music of the baroque period. See D. J. Buch, "*Style brisé, Style luthé,* and the *Choses luthées,*" *The Musical Quarterly* LXXI (1985), pp. 52-67.

[2] Edition of 1717, reprinted Broude Brothers Ltd., Monuments of Music and Music Literature in Facsimile, Second Series XXIII, p. 15. The designation "mechanical" is in contrast to the lute, where the performer's fingers are in direct contact with the strings, or to the violin, where a sound can swell or diminish while in progress.

**87.** JOHANN SEBASTIAN BACH
**Prelude and Fugue in D minor,** BWV 851-852
from **Das wohltemperirte Clavier I**

5   Track 12

[1] *c* in accordance with the sources; according to analogous bar 18 it should be *c♯*.

The two books of the *Well-Tempered Clavier* (*WTC*) are famous not only for their musical riches but also for Bach's systematic employment of all twenty-four major and minor keys. Bach drew attention to this novel feature in subtitling Book I "preludes and fugues on all tones and semitones." The use of all keys in what became entrenched as the functional tonal system depended on tuning the harpsichord (or clavichord) in a temperament compatible with any tonic pitch. In Bach's time, several such temperaments were advocated, including the system of equal temperament.[1]

Bach compiled the first book of the *WTC* at Cöthen in 1722. The twenty-four pairs of preludes and fugues are ordered according to the chromatic scale with major and minor modes on each tonic: C major, C minor, C-sharp major, C-sharp minor, etc.). The prelude and fugue pairing constitutes a rationalistic conjunction of opposites. *Preludes* typically are free figural pieces, fundamentally harmonic in conception, that trace their ancestry to the toccata (see No. 72). *Fugues* are strictly contrapuntal pieces that examine a single theme or subject in depth. They trace their ancestry to the ricercare and canzona (see Nos. 47 and 73). The

prelude and fugue in D minor (BWV 851-852) from Book I exemplify the basic difference between the genres. The prelude spins out an arpeggio figure in a varied and individualistic way. Its textural evenness is relieved by two striking events: a D pedal that temporarily arrests the quick pace of harmonic motion (mm. 15-21) and a chromatic "cadenza" of diminished chords that leads dramatically to a resonant chordal cadence. (In an earlier version, from his son Friedemann's *Klavierbüchlein*, the prelude ends at m. 15, before these climactic events.) The D minor fugue begins with a systematic statement of a clearly profiled subject in each of its three voices. After this section, called the *exposition* in conventional terminology, the piece alternates between statements of the subject and episodes in which the complete subject is not present. This fugue is one of the richest in the *WTC* in terms of the variety of procedures it incorporates within a short temporal span. Bach presents the subject in stretto (for example, mm. 17-18, 21-23) and also inverts it (for example, m. 22; inexactly, m. 14). Single statements of the subject are accompanied by a countersubject (mm. 2-5, 6-7, for example). Motives from the subject and countersubject supply the material for modulating episodes that link statements (mm. 9-12, 15-16, for example). The concentration on a limited stock of motives produces a tightly constructed work whose orderly surface is untouched by any extraneous flights of fancy.

[1] For a discussion of temperaments possibly used for the *WTC*, see John Barnes, "Bach's keyboard temperament: Internal evidence from the *Well-tempered Clavier*," *Early Music* 7:2 (1979), pp. 236-249.

## 88. DOMENICO SCARLATTI (1685-1757)

### 88a. Sonata in D minor
K. 120 (L. 215)

Track 13

Allegrissimo

[1]D = Right hand (*main droite*)
  G = Left hand (*main gauche*)

## 88b. **Sonata in D major**
K. 119 (L. 415)

5   Track 14

Alessandro Scarlatti is best known for operas and cantatas, but his son, Domenico (1685-1757), excelled in keyboard music. After leaving Italy in 1719 to join first the Royal Chapel at Lisbon, then the Spanish court at Madrid, Domenico Scarlatti composed over 550 single movements for keyboard solo. Because these movements are called simply "sonata," it is usual to identify each by its number either in the Kirkpatrick catalogue (*Domenico Scarlatti*, Princeton: Princeton University Press, revised edition, 1983) or in the Longo edition (*Opere Complete,* Milan: Ricordi, 1906-10). The Kirkpatrick numbers attempt to outline a chronological ordering, but there is little firm evidence on which to date any of the sonatas. Some of the sonatas are paired in manuscript collections, but opinions differ on whether such pairings were definitely intended by the composer or imposed by copyists. The sonatas in D minor, K. 120 (L. 215), and D major, K. 119 (L. 415), appear frequently enough in juxtaposition (in the order K. 120, K. 119) to be considered a valid unit.

The novelty of Scarlatti's keyboard writing is attested by the English music historian Charles Burney (1726-1814), who wrote that in the 1740s "Scarlatti's were not only the pieces with which every young performer displayed his powers of execution, but were the wonder and delight of every hearer who had a spark of enthusiasm about him, and could feel new and bold effects intrepidly produced by the breach of almost all the old and established rules of composition."[1]

The sonatas K. 120 and K. 119 display many of the intrepidly "new and bold effects" for which Scarlatti is still noted. Foremost among these are brilliant virtuosity and trenchant dissonance. Among the virtuoso effects in K. 119 are rapid repeated notes (m. 18 ff.) and sweeping passage work (mm. 7 ff., 31 ff.). K. 120 features fast figures doubled in thirds and sixths (mm. 4 ff., 46 ff.) and agile crossing of hands (mm. 13 ff., 37 ff.). Both sonatas are spiced with emphatic dissonances and incisive tone clusters

[1]Charles Burney, *A General History of Music* (London: 1789, reissued 1957), vol. 2, p. 1008.

(K. 119, mm. 61 ff., 97 ff., 163 ff.; K. 120, mm. 19 ff.). In both movements also, prodigal streams of diverse thematic ideas cloak a rather static and deliberate harmonic skeleton. The first twenty-seven measures of K. 119, for example, essentially prolong a tonic D-major chord as four distinct motivic ideas dance by. This combination of extravagant motivic invention and slow underlying harmonic rhythm points unmistakably toward a preclassical aesthetic and contrasts markedly with the thematic economy and harmonic flux of J. S. Bach's preludes and fugues (see No. 87).

Nearly all of Scarlatti's sonatas are in binary form, but their internal designs are quite individual, both thematically and tonally. In the first half of K. 120, a strong cadential arrival on the new tonic, A minor, is deferred until the closing measures (mm. 23-27), but the new key area is present from measure 11 on, when its dominant takes root. (The clever opening on the dominant chord of the tonic key D minor presents the same harmonic process within a much shorter time span.) By contrast, in the first half of the D major sonata, K. 119, the new tonic arrives relatively early—heralded by a prominent dominant preparation and miniature cadenza (mm. 28-35)—but its mode is an untoward minor. Not until the cadential figure of the first key area returns (m. 73) is the A tonic allowed to shine forth in major. The crucial tonic returns in the second halves are also differently handled. In K. 119, the tonic return has a strong dominant preparation parallel to that in the first section (mm. 137-142/mm. 28-35), and the rest of the piece closely follows the last two-thirds of the first half. The tonic return in the latter part of K. 120 is less closely allied with a clear thematic articulation, but from measure 43 on, the thematic pattern of the first section (mm. 6 ff.) is loosely recalled. In neither of these movements is the very opening material of the piece restated in the second half, but both adhere to the principle that thematic ideas originally presented in the second key area return in the tonic. Scarlatti's attention to coordination of broad key areas with specific sequences of thematic material allies him with sonata composers of the later eighteenth century, for whom such matters were a central concern.

**89.** ANTONIO VIVALDI  (1678-1741)
# Violin Concerto in G minor,
Opus 8, No. 8, RV 332[1]
from **Il cimento dell'armonia e dell'inventione**

[1]The works of Antonio Vivaldi are best identified by *RV* number, their order number in the recent catalogue of his works by P. Ryom, *Verzeichnis der Werke Antonio Vivaldis* (Leipzig: 1974).

[2]A figured bass realization may be found in *Concerto in sol minore per violino, archi e cembalo* Fanno I n. 16, Istituto Italiano di Antonio Vivaldi, vol. 65, edited by G. F. Malipiero (Milan: 1949).

Tasto solo [3]

[3]Bass note alone without keyboard realization.

For much of his life, the virtuoso violinist Antonio Vivaldi (1678-1741) trained students and directed concerts at the *Pio Ospedale delta Pietà* in Venice, a convent for orphaned or indigent girls. Vivaldi's European fame rested particularly on his concertos, which crystallized the brilliant Italian instrumental style of the early 1700s. Johann Sebastian Bach copied and arranged the concerti in his apprentice days. Johann Joachim Quantz, on becoming acquainted with them in 1714, was indelibly impressed with this "completely new kind of musical pieces" and found that their "splendid ritornellos served me as good models in future years."[1] Although many of Vivaldi's 450-odd concerti circulated only in manuscript, some were published in Amsterdam during the composer's lifetime. *Il cimento dell'armonia e dell'inventione,* Opus 8 (roughly, "A Test of Harmony and of Invention"), a collection of twelve solo concerti, was issued there about 1725.

The typical Vivaldi concerto pits an orchestra of strings and continuo (called the *tutti*) against a solo instrument or group of instruments (the *solo/i* or *concertino*). Its three or four movements alternate between slow and fast tempos, the latter usually coupled with a driving rhythmic pulse. The first fast movement (which often stands second in the piece, preceded by a slow introductory movement) is normally in ritornello form: Virtuosic solo passages alternate with restatements of opening material by the tutti. Key structure, textural changes, and thematic contrasts all contribute to this design.

Both the first and the last movements of the solo violin concerto in G minor, Opus 8, no. 8 observe a ritornello structure. The ritornello of the first movement (mm. 1-16) displays characteristic additive construction. It consists of several juxtaposed phrases, each sequential in nature. Because the phrases are not integrally connected, subsequent restatements of the ritornello can be only partial and still retain their musical sense and identity. Ritornello statements clearly define the principal key areas of the movement: G Minor (mm. 1-15), B-flat major (mm. 30-35), C minor (mm. 46-49), E-flat major (mm. 50-54), and G minor (mm. 75-85). The solo passages between them present fresh thematic material that ranges from routine arpeggios to individualistic figurations enlivened by abrupt shifts in rhythmic motion.

The middle *Largo* movement in B-flat major provides respite from the rhythmic momentum of the first movement and introduces an entirely different mood. Its exposed suspensions and chromatically inflected bass line produce a languishing, pathetic effect.

The vigorous last movement, *Allegro,* is somewhat more "modern" in tone than the first, due to its generally slower rate of harmonic motion and its tendency toward even measure groups in the ritornello. The long solo sections with their capricious shifts in figuration give a powerful sense of improvisatory fancy. The key scheme differs from that of the first movement, but the movement still modulates to keys closely related to G minor: first to D minor and then to B-flat major.

---

[1] J. J. Quantz, "*Lebenslauf,*" in F. W. Marpurg, *Historisch-kritische Beyträge zur Aufnahme der Musik,* vol. 1 (1754), p. 205.

## 90. JOHANN SEBASTIAN BACH
**Musikalisches Opfer,** BWV 1079

5  Track 18

Canones diversi super Thema Regium[1]

90a. Canon 1. a 2 cancrizans

Realization

[1]"Diverse Canons on the Royal Theme"

90b.   Canon 2. a 2 violini in unisono

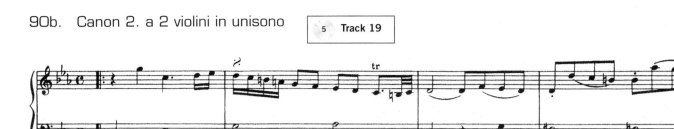

Realization

90c. Canon 3. a 2 per Motum contrarium

5 Track 20

Realization

90d.   Canon 4. a 2 per Augmentationem, contrario Motu
       Notulis crescentibus crescat Fortuna Regis[2]

5  Track 21

[2]"As the note values increase, so may the king's fortune increase."

90e.   Canon perpetuus

5   Track 22

In the last decade of his life, Johann Sebastian Bach probed deeply into the demanding contrapuntal techniques of canon and fugue. The *Musical Offering* (1747, BWV 1079) stands with the *Goldberg Variations* (1741-42) and *The Art of Fugue* (1745-50) as a pinnacle of contrapuntal art. The work had its genesis in a visit by Bach to the court of Frederick "the Great" of Prussia, where his son Carl Philipp Emanuel was employed. The elder Bach improvised upon a theme submitted by the king but upon returning home resolved "to work out this right Royal theme more fully and then make it known to the world" (dedicatory preface to the king).[1] The result was the *Musical Offering,* a collection of two ricercares (for three and for six voices), nine canons, a canonic fugue and a four-movement trio sonata, all of which incorporate the Royal Theme in one guise or another. Both the instrumentation and the ordering of the pieces have been matters of controversy, but it seems probable that Bach intended no definitive solution to either problem. Instrumentation is specified for only a few pieces (the canon for two violins and the trio sonata), and the others can all be played with some combination of flute, violin(s), and keyboard. (It is thought that Bach originally improvised the three-voice ricercare on a Silbermann pianoforte.) The question of order admits multiple solutions, as the *Offering* was doubtless intended not as an integral "work" to be played as an indissoluble unit, but rather as a *florilegium,* a carefully devised anthology from which individual elements could be drawn at will for performance and contemplation.

[1]The complete preface is published in translation in *The Bach Reader,* ed. H. T. David and A. Mendel (New York: Norton, 1945), p. 179.

The five canons shown here illustrate the broad range of Bach's canonic art as well as the ingenuity with which he treats the Royal Theme.

**90a.** Canon a 2 cancrizans ("Two-voice retrograde canon"). The melody begins as a statement of the Royal Theme, and continues in an apparently free way. Dual clefs (at the beginning and at the end of the line) supply the clue to the retrograde canon. One player states the entire melody in the conventional way, while the other starts at the end and plays it in reverse. The "free" eighth-note half of the melody turns out to be a flowing counterpoint to the Royal Theme.

**90b.** Canon a 2 violini in unisono ("Canon at the unison for two violins"). The Royal Theme is a bass to this compact and easily perceived canon at the unison. A sign shows that the second voice (*comes*) follows the first (*dux*) at a distance of four beats.

**90c.** Canon a 2 per motum contrarium ("Two-voice canon in inversion"). The Royal Theme functions as a cantus firmus in the soprano register. Its canonic counterpoint works in inversion, as indicated by the two clefs on the other staff.

**90d.** Canon a 2 per augmentationem, contrario motu ("Two-voice canon with augmentation and in inversion"). This canon is an astonishing contrapuntal feat as well as an elegant homage to the king: "As the notes increase [in length], so may the fortune of the king increase." A decorated version of the Royal Theme is the foundation about which the two canonic parts are fashioned. The *comes* answers the *dux* both in inversion (starting a fifth higher) and in doubled note values. The augmented voice of course takes twice as long to complete as its companion. However, the canon is so cleverly devised that the second half of the augmented line fits perfectly with a repetition of the entire *dux* and the Royal Theme (m. 9). This canon features the dotted rhythms and quick ornamental runs of grand French overture style, but its overall affect is rather melancholy.

**90e.** Canon perpetuus ("Perpetual canon"). This movement is cast in trio sonata texture and has two canonic upper voices supported by a bass that provides a steady rhythmic pulse and firm harmonic support. A paraphrased version of the Royal Theme starts the melody, and is answered in inversion from the fifth. The theme is later restated in the dominant (m. 18), this time with the *dux* proposing the inverted version and the *comes* answering in the normal direction. This canon has an air of effortless simplicity, its artifice hidden behind the facade of a graceful trio sonata movement.

Although a taste for the simple and artless was already ascendant when Bach wrote these intricate canons, some of his contemporaries would have agreed warmly with the theorist-critic-composer Friedrich Wilhelm Marpurg, who wrote in 1752 "no one has surpassed him [Bach] in thorough knowledge of the theory and practice of harmony, or, I may say, in the deep and thoughtful execution of unusual, ingenious ideas."[2]

---

[2]Preface to the 1752 edition of *The Art of the Fugue,* translated in H. David and A. Mendel, *The Bach Reader,* p. 267.

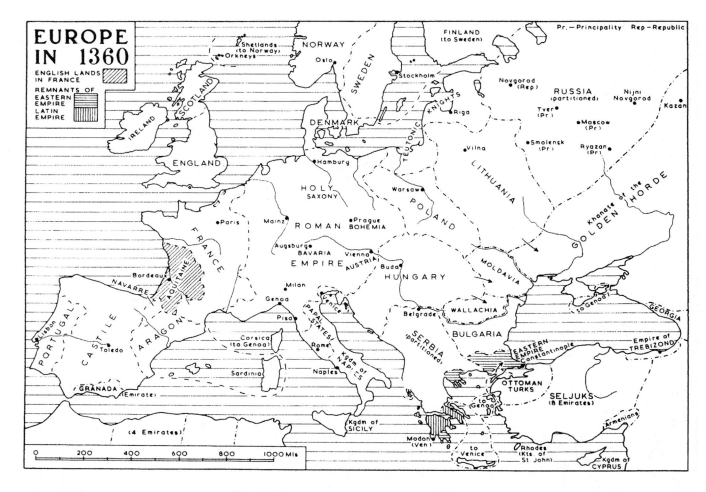

Map 1. Europe in the Mid-Fourteenth Century.

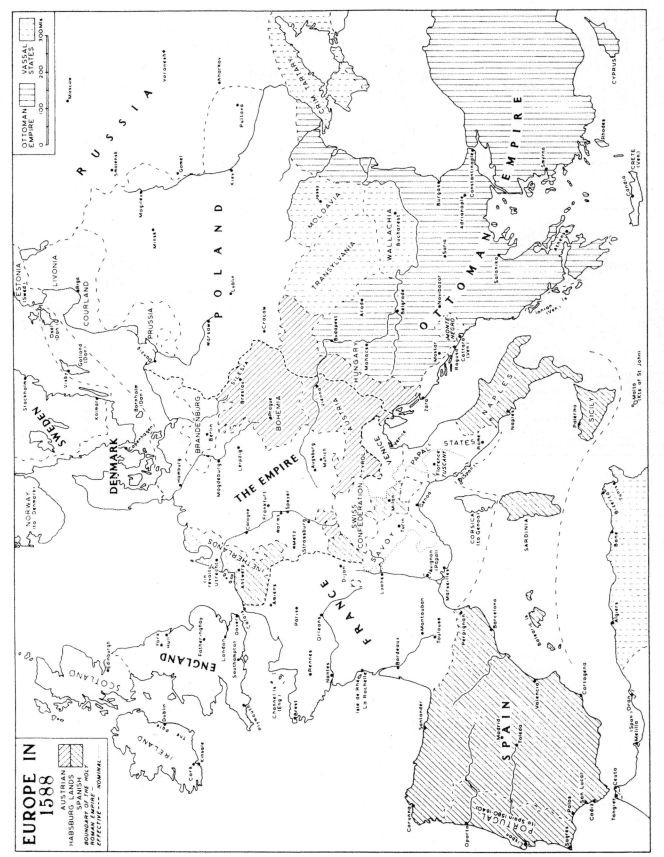

**Map 2.** Europe in the Late Sixteenth Century.

1. *Easter Mass Proper and Ordinary*
   **a.** (*Resurrexi*), **e.** (*Haec dies*), **f.** (Alleluia), **i.** (*Terra tremuit*), **l.** (*Pascha nostrum*)
   > *Missa in Tempore Paschalis,* Archiv 2533 131 or 2723 071 (6)
   > *Liturgia Paschalis,* Archiv 3088/90
   > *Masses for Christmas and Easter from the Laon Manuscript,* Nonesuch H 71348
   
   **c.** (melismatic Kyrie), **d.** (Gloria), **j.** (Sanctus), **k.** (Agnus Dei)
   > *Gregorianischer Choral: Weihnachtsmessen,* Archiv 410 658
   > *Visitatio Sepulchri: Missa in Domenica Resurrectionis,* Harmonia Mundi 1C 165 99 925/26
   > (with some tropes and polyphony)
   
   **c.** (Kyrie, melismatic and Latin versions)
   > *Dictionary of Medieval Music,* Harmonia Mundi HMU 441
   
   **b, g.** [tropes and prose (sequence)]
   > *Anglo-Saxon Easter,* Archiv 413 546-1
   
   **h.** (Credo)
   > *A Guide to Gregorian Chant,* Vanguard VSD 71217

For a reconstruction of an Easter Mass as it might have been performed in Paris about 1200, see *Visitatio Sepulchri: Missa in Domenica Resurrectionis,* cited above. For a performance of the Easter Propers in a recently developed singing style and in a new, non-Vatican edition, see *Gregorianischer Choral,* Archiv 2723 084, side 6. The Ordinary (cycle IV) is on side 1.

4. **Theorists' Examples** (polyphony)
   **a.** (*Rex caeli*), **b.** (*Sit gloria*)
   > *Medieval Music: Ars Antiqua Polyphony,* Peters International PLE 115
   
   **a.** (*Rex caeli*), **d.** (Kyrie *Cunctipotens genitor*)
   > *Chant Grégorien et Polyphonie Primitive,* Le Chant du Monde LDX 78 620
   
   **d.** (Kyrie *Cunctipotens genitor*)
   > *The Mass,* Opus Musicum, OM 201/03

5. **Wulfstan of Winchester,** *Alleluia te martyrum*
   > *Medieval Music: Ars Antiqua Polyphony,* Peters International PLE 115

7. **Liturgical chant** (12th century)
   **a.** (*Ave regina*)
   > *Chants for Feasts of Mary,* Archiv 2533 310
   
   **b.** (*Veni sancte spiritus*)
   > *Chants for Lent and Easter,* Turnabout TV 340 70
   > *Antiphons, Hymns and Responsories,* Philips 6580 061
   > *Hymns, Sequences, Responsories,* Telefunken SAWT 9493 (in measured rhythm)
   
   **c.** (*Pange lingua*)
   > *Maundy Thursday,* Archiv 2726 004 (2)
   
   **d.** (*Aeterna Christi munera*)
   > *History of European Music I,* Orpheus (Musical Heritage Society) OR 349

8. **Troubadour and Trouvère Songs**
   **a.** Bernart de Ventadorn, *Can vei la lauzeta mover*
   > *Chansons der Troubadours,* Telefunken SAWT 9567-B
   
   **b.** Peire Vidal, *Baros de mon dan covit*
   > *Chansons der Troubadours,* Telefunken SAWT 9567-B
   
   **c.** Gaucelm Faidit, *Fortz chausa es*
   > *Music of the Crusades,* Argo ZRG 673
   
   **d.** *Chevalier mult estes guariz*
   > *Music of the Crusades,* Argo ZRG 673

    **e.** Gace Brulé, *Biaus m'est estez*

        *Troubadours and Trouvères,* Telefunken 6.35519

        *Music of the Trouvères,* Telefunken AW 6.41275 or EX 6.35412 (4)

    **f.** Guillaume d'Amiens, *Prendes i garde*

        *The World of Adam de la Halle,* Turnabout TV-S 34439

**9. 12th-Century Polyphony**

    **a.** *Viderunt Emmanuel*

        *Dictionary of Medieval Music,* Harmonia Mundi HMU 442 (performed erroneously as a
            Gradual trope)

    **b.** Kyrie *Cunctipotens genitor* (from *Codex Calixtinus*)

        *The Mass,* Opus Musicum OM 201/03

**10a. Leonin, *Alleluia Pascha nostrum***

        *Music of the Gothic Era,* Archiv 2723 045

**10b. *Alleluia Pascha nostrum*** (revised version)

        *Ars Antiqua,* Telefunken SAWT 9530/31-B

**11. Perotin (?), *Alleluia Pascha nostrum***

        *Ars Antiqua,* Telefunken SAWT 9530/31

        *Visitatio Sepulchri: Missa in Domenica Resurrectionis,* Harmonia Mundi 1C 165 99 925/26

**12. Conductus**

    **a.** *Deus in adjutorium*

        *Ars Antiqua,* Telefunken SAWT 9530/31

    **b.** *O tocius Asie*

        *Music of the Crusades,* Argo ZRG 673

**13th-Century Motets** (to c. 1250)

**13b, c.** *Ad solitum vomitum/Regnat* and **13d.** *Depositum creditum/Ad solitum vomitum/Regnat*

        *Missa Tournai: Motets,* Telefunken SAWT 9517

**13f.** *L'autre jour/Au tens pascour/In seculum*

        *Secular Music ca. 1300,* Telefunken SAWT 9504

        *The Central Middle Ages: Chansons and Motets of the 13th Century,* Archiv ARC 3051

**14. "A certain Spaniard," *In seculum breve***

        *Music of the Gothic Era,* Archiv 2723 045 or 2565 051

**13th-Century Motets** (after c. 1250)

**15a.** *El mois de mai/De se debent bigami/Kyrie*

        *Music of the Gothic Era,* Archiv 2723 045 or 2565 051

**15b.** *On parole de batre/A Paris/Frese nouvele*

        *Music of the Gothic Era,* Archiv 2723 045 or 2565 051

        *Dictionary of Medieval Music,* Harmonia Mundi HMU 443

**15c.** *Alle psallite cum luya/Alle psallite cum luya/Alleluia*

        *Music of the Gothic Era,* Archiv 2723 045 or 2565 051

        *Dictionary of Medieval Music,* Harmonia Mundi HMU 443

        *Ars Antiqua,* Telefunken SAWT 9530/31

**15d.** Petrus de Cruce, *Aucun ont trouvé/Lonc tans/Annuntiantes*

        *Music of the Gothic Era,* Archiv 2723 045 or 2565 051

**16. Philippe de Vitry, *Tribum que/Quoniam secta/Merito hec patimur***

        *Missa Tournai: Motets circa 1320,* Telefunken SAWT 9517-A

17. **Guillaume de Machaut,** *Bone pastor Guillerme/Bone pastor qui pastores/Bone pastor*
    *Messe de Notre Dame und Motetten,* Telefunken SAWT 9566-B

18. **Guillaume de Machaut, secular songs**
    **a.** *Nes que on porroit*
      *Ah! sweet Lady,* Decca DL 9431
      *Guillaume de Machaut: 10 Secular Works,* Archiv 3032 (one stanza)
    **b.** *Quant j'ay l'espart*
      *The Art of Courtly Love,* Seraphim SIC 6092
    **c.** *Dame a vous sans retollir*
      *Guillaume de Machaut Chansons I,* Electrola Reflexe 1C 063 30 106
      *The Mirror of Narcissus,* Hyperion A 66087

19. **Jacopo da Bologna,** *Non al suo amante*
    *Jacopo da Bologna and the Trecento,* Electrola Reflexe 1C 063 30 111

20. **Gherardello da Firenze,** *Tosto che l'alba*
    *Music from the Time of Boccaccio's Decameron,* Philips 802 904 LY
      (also IMS 6747 004 [5])
    *The Early Renaissance Madrigale e Caccie from the Codex of Antonio Squarcialupi,*
      Archiv ARC 3003

21. **Francesco Landini,** *Questa fanciull'amor*
    *Landini,* Electrola Reflexe 1C 063 30 113

22. **Borlet (?),** *Ma trédol rosignol joly*
    *The Art of Courtly Love,* Seraphim SIC 6092
    *Frühe Musik in Italien, Frankreich und Burgund,* Telefunken SAWT 9466-B

23. **Johannes Ciconia,** *Sus un'fontayne*
    *Johannes Ciconia,* Electrola Reflexe 1C 063 30 102
    *Johannes Ciconia L'oeuvre intégral,* Musique en Wallonie MW 80040/44

24. **Leonel Power**
    **a.** Credo (*Opem nobis*)
      *Music in Honor of Saint Thomas of Canterbury,* Nonesuch H 71292
    **b.** *Ave regina caelorum*
      *Leonel Power: Messen und Motetten,* EMI Reflexe 1C 069 46 402

25. **John Dunstable,** *Beata mater*
    *Dufay-Dunstable: Motets,* Archiv 2533 291

26. **Guillaume Dufay,** *Christe redemptor omnium*
    *Guillaume Dufay: Adieu m'amour,* Electrola Reflexe 1C 063 30 124
      (This recording uses the hymn text for the Feast of All Saints, *Christe redemptor . . .*
      *conserva tuos.*)

27a. **Guillaume Dufay,** *Agnus Dei* **from** *Missa Se la face ay pale*
    *Music of Guillaume Dufay: Missa "Se la face ay pale,"* Seraphim S-60267
      (This recording also includes the chanson from which the Mass tenor is drawn.)

28. **Guillaume Dufay,** *Ave regina caelorum (III)*
    *Guillaume Dufay: Messensätze, Motetten und Hymnen,* Telefunken SAWT 9439

**29. Johannes Ockeghem,** *Agnus Dei* **from** *Missa Mi-mi*
   *Ockeghem Requiem, Missa "Mi-mi,"* EMI Angel DFO 38188
   *Johannes Ockeghem: Missa "Mi-mi,"* Archiv 198 406

**30. Guillaume Dufay, secular songs**
   **a.** *Ce moys de may soyons lies et joyeux*
      *Guillaume Dufay: Adieu m'amour,* Electrola Reflexe 1C 063 30 124
      *The Art of Courtly Love,* Seraphim SIC 6092
      *Guillaume Dufay Complete Secular Music,* L'Oiseau-Lyre 595001
   **b.** *Adieu m'amour, adieu ma joye*
      *Guillaume Dufay: Adieu m'amour,* Electrola Reflexe 1C 063 30 124
      *Guillaume Dufay Complete Secular Music,* L'Oiseau-Lyre 595001

**31. Hayne van Ghizeghem,** *De tous biens plaine*
   *Le Chansonnier Cordiforme,* L'Oiseau-Lyre D186 D4
   *The Art of the Netherlands,* Seraphim SIC 6104
      (This includes the Josquin Desprez arrangement, which also can be found in *Josquin Desprez Chansons, Frottole and Instrumental Pieces,* Nonesuch H-71261.)

**32. Josquin Desprez,** *Ave Maria gratia plena . . . virgo serena*
   *Josquin Desprez: Motets and Chansons,* Angel EMI S-38040
   *Josquin Desprez: Motetten,* Telefunken SAWT 9480-A

**33. Josquin Desprez,** *Agnus Dei* **II from** *Missa L'homme armé super voces musicales*
   *Josquin Desprez: Missa "L'homme armé super voces musicales,"* Archiv 2533 360

**34. Josquin Desprez**
   **a.** and **b.** *Kyrie* and *Agnus Dei* from *Missa Pange lingua*
      *Missa Pange Lingua,* Decca DL 9410 or 79410, Deutsche Grammophon Archiv 3159,
      and Telefunken Das Alte Werk SAWT 9595-A

**35a. Josquin Desprez,** *Faulte d'argent*
   *Josquin Des Prés: Musica Reservata,* Argo ZRG 793
   *Missa Pange Lingua/8 Secular Works,* Archiv ARC 3159

**35b. Antoine de Févin,** *Faulte d'argent*
   *Frühe Musik in Italien, Frankreich und Burgund,* Telefunken SAWT 9466-B

**36. Heinrich Isaac,** *La mi la sol*
   *Heinrich Isaac: Missa super "O praeclara,"* Telefunken SAWT 9544
      (This Mass also is on the *la mi la sol* theme.)

**37. Juan del Encina**
   **a.** *Señora de hermosura*
      (This work has not been recorded. *Si abrá en este baldrés,* a related Encina villancico on the *folia* bass, is performed on *Musica Iberica,* Telefunken SAWT 9620/21-B.)
   **b.** *Triste España*
      *Ceremonial Music of the Renaissance,* Telefunken SAWT 9524

**38.** *Orsù, orsù, car'signori*
   *A Florentine Festival,* Argo ZRG 602

**39. Marchetto Cara,** *Io non compro più speranza*
   *A Florentine Festival,* Argo ZRG 602

40. *Aus tiefer Not*
    c. (Arnold von Bruck)
    *Sacred Songs and Instrumental Music of Luther's Time,* Telefunken SAWT 9532
    d. (Johann Sebastian Bach)
    *J. S. Bach: Das Kantatenwerk,* Telefunken SKW 10/1-2 (with text of verse 5)

41. **Nicholas Gombert,** *Ave regina caelorum*
    *Gombert-Willaert: Ave Regina,* Archiv 2533 361

42a, b. **Giovanni Pierluigi da Palestrina,** *Veni sponsa Christi,* **and plainsong antiphon**
    *Palestrina: Veni Sponsa Christi,* Argo ZRG 578

43. **Giovanni Pierluigi da Palestrina,** *Kyrie* **from** *Missa Veni sponsa Christi*
    *Palestrina: Veni Sponsa Christi,* Argo ZRG 578

44. **Orlande de Lassus,** *Tristis est anima mea*
    *Orlandus Lassus: 8 Latin Motets,* Archiv ARC 3077

45. **Orlande de Lassus,** *In teneris annis* **(***Sibylla cimmeria***)**
    *Orlando di Lasso: Prophetiae Sibyllarum,* Nonesuch H 71053

46a. **William Byrd,** *Miserere mihi, Domine*
    *Tallis-Byrd: Cantiones Sacrae 1575,* L'Oiseau-Lyre SOL 311-3

47. **Giovanni Gabrieli,** *Canzona septimi toni a 8*
    *Giovanni Gabrieli: Canzoni e Sonate 1597-1615,* Archiv 2533 406

48. **Clément Janequin,** *Ou mettra l'on ung baiser*
    *Jannequin Choral Works,* Vox DL 710

49a. **Luis de Milán,** *Pavan 1*
    *Music of Spain: Lute,* vol. 1, RCA ARL 1-3435

49b. **Diego Ortiz,** *Recercada settima*
    *Die Instrumentalvariation in der Spanischen Renaissancemusik,*
    Electrola Reflexe 1C 063 30 116

50. **Jacques Arcadelt,** *Il bianco e dolce cigno*
    *Madrigal Masterpieces,* vol. 2, The Bach Guild BGS-5051
    *Early Italian Madrigals,* Pro Arte 2PAL-2021

51. **Cipriano de Rore,** *Da le belle contrade d'oriente*
    *Renaissance Vocal Music,* Nonesuch H 71097
    *Musicke of Sundrie Kindes,* L'Oiseau-Lyre DSLO 203-6

52. **Luca Marenzio,** *Scaldava il sol*
    *Luca Marenzio: 6 Madrigals,* Archiv 3073

53. **Claudio Monteverdi,** *Cruda Amarilli*
    *Claudio Monteverdi: Quinto Libro dei Madrigali 1605,* L'Oiseau-Lyre 410291
    *Claudio Monteverdi 7 Madrigals,* Archiv 3136

54. **Carlo Gesualdo,** *Moro, lasso, al mio duolo*
    *Carlo Gesualdo da Venosa: 6 Madrigali,* Archiv 3073

55.  **Giulio Caccini,** *Perfidissimo volto*
        *Canti Amorosi,* Archiv 2533 305

56.  **Sigismondo d'India,** *Cruda Amarilli*
        *Canti Amorosi,* Archiv 2533 305
        *Italienische Liebeslieder des Barok,* Telefunken 6.42226

57.  **John Dowland**
    **a.** *Flow my teares*
        *John Dowland: Second Booke of Songs, 1600,* L'Oiseau-Lyre DSLO 528/529
    **b.** *Lachrimae Gementes*
        *Dowland Lachrimae 1604,* L'Oiseau-Lyre DSLO 517

58.  **Claudio Monteverdi,** *Zefiro torna*
        *The Origins of 17th-Century Venetian Opera,* Angel S-36431 (also issued as *Music
           of Love and Lamentation,* Vanguard VCS 10 024)
        *Monteverdi Madrigali Libri 8-9-10,* Philips 6799 006

59.  **Giovanni Gabrieli,** *In ecclesiis*
        *Symphoniae Sacrae II (1615),* L'Oiseau-Lyre DSLO 537

60.  **Heinrich Schütz,** *O quam tu pulchra es*
        *Heinrich Schütz: Symphoniae Sacrae,* Nonesuch H 71160

61.  **Heinrich Schütz,** *Saul, Saul, was verfolgst du mich?*
        *Heinrich Schütz: Deutsches Magnificat; Saul, Saul, was verfolgst du mich; Psalm 2 Warum
           toben die Heiden,* Nonesuch H71134
        *Heinrich Schütz: Motets and Psalms,* Musical Heritage Society MHS 4082

62.  **Jacopo Peri,** *Euridice* (excerpt from Scene 2)
        *Jacopo Peri: Euridice,* Orpheus OR 344/345 or Telefunken 6.35014

63.  **Claudio Monteverdi,** *Orfeo* (excerpts from Act II)
        *Monteverdi: L'Orfeo,* Angel DSBX-3964 (Rogers and Medlam)
        *Monteverdi: l'Orfeo,* Telefunken Das Alte Werk 6.35020 (Harnoncourt)

64.  **Claudio Monteverdi,** *L'incoronazione di Poppea* (Act I, Scene 3)
        *Monteverdi: L'incoronazione di Poppea,* Telefunken Das Alte Werk 6.35247

65.  **Giacomo Carissimi,** *Jephte* (excerpts)
        *The Italian Seicento,* Series B, Archiv ARC 3005
        *Carissimi: Jephte,* Turnabout TV 34089

66.  **Francesco Cavalli,** *Scipione Africano* (Act II, Scene 8)
        *The Origins of 17th Century Venetian Opera,* Angel S-36431 (also issued as *Music of Love
           and Lamentation,* Vanguard VCS 10 124)

68.  **Jean-Baptiste Lully,** *Alceste* (Act II, Scenes 7 and 8)
        *Lully: Alceste,* Columbia M3-34580 or CBS 79301 (Malgoire)

69.  **Henry Purcell,** *Dido and Aeneas* (concluding scene)
        *Dido and Aeneas,* Chandos ABRD 1034 (Parrott)
        *Dido and Aeneas,* Archiv 198 424 (Mackerras)
        *Dido and Aeneas,* Harmonia Mundi 10067 (Cohen)

70. **William Byrd,** *John come kiss me now*
    *The Fitzwilliam Virginal Book,* L'Oiseau-Lyre D261 D2

71a. **Samuel Scheidt,** *Jesus Christus unser Heiland, der von uns*
    *Orgelmeister vor Bach,* Archiv 2565 087

72. **Girolamo Frescobaldi,** *Toccata No. 8*
    *Girolamo Frescobaldi: Selections from the First Book of Toccatas,* Musical Heritage
        Society MHS 3245
    *Toccatas for Harpsichord Books 1 and 2,* L'Oiseau-Lyre D260 D2

73. **Girolamo Frescobaldi,** *Canzona dopo l'epistola*
    *Buxtehude, Prelude and Fugue in D major; Frescobaldi, Canzona dopo l'Epistola et al.,*
        Telefunken AW6-42164

74. **Johann Jacob Froberger,** *Suite VI*
    *Suittes de Clavessin,* Telefunken Das Alte Werk 6.42125 (Verlet)
    *Johann Jacob Froberger Cembalo- und Orgelwerke,* Telefunken SAWT 9569 (Leonhardt)
    *Johann Jacob Froberger Works for Harpsichord,* Archiv 2533 419 (Gilbert)

75. **Louis Couperin,** *Prélude a l'imitation de M.ͬ Froberger*
    *Louis Couperin: Pièces de Clavecin,* Deutsche Grammophon ARC 2533325

76. **Salamone Rossi,** *Sonata in dialogo,* **"La Viena"**
    *17th-Century Italian Virtuoso Violin Music,* Telefunken SAWT 9542

77. **Giovanni Battista Vitali,** *Sonata a due violini . . .*
    *History of Music in Sound,* vol. VI, RCA LM 6031-2

78. **Arcangelo Corelli,** *Sonata da camera a tre,* Opus 4, No. 5
    *Corelli Twelve Trio Sonatas,* Odyssey 32 360006
    *Corelli Trio Sonatas,* Vox VBX 36

79. **Heinrich Ignaz Franz von Biber,** *Rosary Sonata X*
    *Rosenkranz-Sonaten,* Archiv 198 422/23

80. **Arcangelo Corelli,** *Sonata for violin and violone or cembalo,* Opus 5, No. 1
    *Corelli Violin Sonatas Op. 5,* Archiv ARC 2533 132

81. **Alessandro Scarlatti,** *Su le sponde del Tebro* (arias 3 and 4 and recitative)
    *The Italian Settecento Series B: The Neapolitan Group, Alessandro Scarlatti Su le
        sponde del Tebro,* Archiv ARC 3008
    *Alessandro Scarlatti, Su le sponde del Tebro; George Frideric Handel, Aires and Arias,*
        Columbia M 34518

82. **George Frideric Handel,** *Admeto* (Act II, Scenes 7-8, Act III, Scene 6)
    *Admeto,* Electrola Reflexe 1C 163 30 808/12

83. **Jean-Philippe Rameau,** *Hippolyte et Aricie* (Act I, Scene 2)
    *Rameau: Hippolyte et Aricie,* Columbia 79314

84. **Giovanni Battista Pergolesi,** *La serva padrona* (intermezzo primo)
    *La Serva Padrona,* Nonesuch H 71043, Archive 3039, or Musical Heritage Society
        MHS 3105

85. **Johann Sebastian Bach,** *Jesu, der du meine Seele,* BWV 78
    *Jesu, der du meine Seele, Das Kantatenwerk* vol. 20, Telefunken 6.35362

86. **François Couperin,** *Pièces de Clavecin, Premier livre* (*Premier ordre,* excerpts)
    *François Couperin,* Vox SVBX 5448

87. **Johann Sebastian Bach,** *Prelude and Fugue in D minor,* BWV 851-852 (from *Das wohltem-perirte Clavier I*)
    *Das Wohltemperirte Clavier,* Harmonia Mundi HM 20309/13 or IC 153-99752/6
      (Leonhardt)
    *The Well-Tempered Clavier Book I,* Archive ARC 3211/12 (Kirkpatrick)

88. **Domenico Scarlatti,** *Sonatas in D minor* (**K. 120**) *and D major* (K. 119)
    *Domenico Scarlatti: Sixty Sonatas,* Columbia SL-221

89. **Antonio Vivaldi,** *Violin Concerto in G minor,* Opus 8, No. 8, RV 332
    *Antonio Vivaldi II Cimento dell'Armonia e dell'Inventione,* Telefunken Das Alte
      Werk 6.35386

90. **Johann Sebastian Bach,** *selected canons* **from** *The Musical Offering*
    *Musikalisches Opfer,* ABC L-67007 (Leonhardt)
    *Das musikalische Opfer,* Archiv 25 33422 (Musica Antiqua, Köln)
    *Ein musikalisches Opfer,* Telefunken 4.41124 (Harnoncourt)

# SOURCES AND ACKNOWLEDGMENTS

Abbreviations used below:

CMM   Corpus Mensurabilis Musicae, general editor Armen Carapetyan, American Institute of Musicology (no place of publication given in most volumes).

F-Pn   France, Paris, Bibliothèque nationale. Specific manuscripts are cited according to category and shelf number.

## MUSIC

1. ***Easter Mass Proper and Ordinary***
    a. (*Resurrexi*), e. (*Haec dies*), f. (Alleluia), i. (*Terra tremuit*), l. (*Pascha nostrum*): Montpellier, Bibliothèque de l'École de Médecine, Ms H 159, facsimile in Paléographie Musicale, vol. 8 (Solesmes: 1906), p. 47 (a), 156 (e), 119 (f), 220 (i), 69 (l).
    c. (melismatic Kyrie), d. (Gloria), j. (Sanctus), k. (Agnus Dei), m. (Ite, missa est): F-Pn, fonds latin 803, ff. 295′-296′.
    c. (Latin Kyrie): F-Pn, fonds latin 1112, f. 105′.
    b. (*Quem queritis, Ecce pater*): F-Pn, fonds latin 1121, ff. 11′-12.
    g. (*Fulgens praeclara*): F-Pn, fonds latin 1119, f. 160′.
    h. (Credo): edited from *Graduale Romanum* (Paris, Tournai: 1961), p. 59★.

2. ***First Vespers on the Feast of the Nativity of the Lord*** (excerpts)
    a. (*Deus in adjutorium*), e. (*Benedicamus Domino*), psalm tone for **b** (Psalm 112): *Liber Usualis* (Tournai: 1961), p. 250 (a), 152 (b), 124 (e).
    b. (*Rex pacificus*), c. (*Magnificatus est*): Lucca, Biblioteca capitolare, Ms. 601, facsimile in Paléographie Musicale, vol. 9, pp. 30-31.
    d. (*Veni redemptor*): melody adapted from *Hymnen* I, ed. B. Stäbelin, Monumenta monodica medii aevi I (1956), p. 369; text, *Analecta Hymnica*, vol. 2, ed. G. M. Dreves (1888), p. 36.

3. **Modal Formulas**
    a. (9th Century): edited from *Commemoratio Brevis de Tonis et Psalmis Modulandis*, ed. T. Bailey (Ottawa: 1979), pp. 30, 34, 36, 38, 40, 42, 44.
    b. (12th Century): *Johannis Affligemensis De Musica*, ed. J. Smits van Waesberghe, Corpus Scriptorum de Musica I, p. 86. © Copyright 1950 by American Institute of Musicology/Hänssler-Verlag, Neuhausen-Stuttgart. Reprinted by permission.

4. **Theorists' Examples** (polyphony)
    a. (*Rex caeli*), b. (*Sit gloria*): edited from *Musica et Scolica Enchiriadis*, ed. H. Schmid, Bayersiche Akademie der Wissenschaften, Veröffentlichungen der Musikhistorischen Kommission, vol. 3 (Munich: 1981), pp. 49 and 51 (a), 42 (b).
    c. (*Ipsi soli*): edited from *Guidonis Aretini Micrologus*, ed. J. Smits van Waesberghe, Corpus Scriptorum de Musica IV (American Institute of Musicology: 1955), pp. 209-210.
    d. (Kyrie *Cunctipotens genitor*), e. (Alleluia): Milan, Biblioteca Ambrosiana, Ms M. 17. sup., f. 56 (d), 58 (e). Facsimile in *Ad organum faciendum*, ed. H. H. Eggebrecht and F. Zaminer, Neue Studien zur Musikwissenschaft III (Mainz: 1970), plates 1, 2 and 5.

5. **Wulfstan of Winchester (?),** ***Alleluia Te martyrum:*** Cambridge, Corpus Christi College, Ms 473, f. 3 (principal voice), f. 164 (organal voice).

6. ***Castitatis lilium:*** F-Pn, fonds latin 1139, f. 42.

7. **Liturgical chant** (12th Century)
    a. (*Ave regina*): F-Pn, fonds latin 12044, f.f 177′.
    b. (*Veni Sancte Spiritus*): *The Utrecht Prosarium*, ed. N. de Goede, Monumenta Musica Neerlandica (Amsterdam: 1965), pp. 43-44. Reprinted by permission of the Vereniging voor Nederlandse Muziekgeschiedenis.
    c. (*Pange lingua*): melody adapted from *Hymnen* I, ed. B. Stablein, Monumenta monodica medii aevi I (Kassel and Basel: 1956), pp. 33-34; text, *Analecta Hymnica*, vol. 50, ed. C. Blume and G. M. Dreves (1907), p. 5.
    d. (*Aeterna Christi*): as for 4a, p. 193.

8. **Troubadour and Trouvère Songs**
    a. Bernart de Ventadorn, *Can vei la lauzeta:* music, Milan, Biblioteca Ambrosiana, Ms. R 71 sup., f. 10; text, *Anthology of Troubadour Lyric Poetry*, ed. A. R. Press, Edinburgh Bilingual Library (3) (Austin, Texas: 1971), pp. 76-78. Reprinted by permission of Edinburgh University Press.
    b. Peire Vidal, *Baros de mon dan:* music, F-Pn, fonds français 22543, f. 65; text and translation as for text of 8a, pp. 198-200. Reprinted by permission of Edinburgh University Press.
    c. Gaucelm Faidit, *Fortz chausa es:* music as for music of 8a, f. 29; text, Les Poèmes de Gaucelm Faidit, ed.

**c.** Gaucelm Faidit, *Fortz chausa es:* music as for music of 8a, f. 29; text, *Les Poèmes de Gaucelm Faidit,* ed. J. Mouzat, Les Classiques d'Oc (Paris: 1965), pp. 415-418. Reprinted by permission of the publisher, A. G. Nizet.

**d.** *Chevalier mult estes:* Erfurt, Wissenschaftliche Allgemeinbibliothek, Amploiana CA 8 °32, f. 88.

**e.** Gace Brulé, *Biaus m'est estez:* music, F-Pn, fonds français 846, f. 15´; text, *Gace Brulé Trouvère Champenois,* ed. H. P. Dyggve, Memoires de la Société Néophilologique de Helsinki XVI (Helsinki: 1951), pp. 220-221. Reprinted by permission of the Neuphilologischen Mitteilungen von Helsinki.

**f.** Guillaume d'Amiens, *Prendes i garde:* music and refrain text, F-Pn, fonds français 25566, f. 165; remainder of text, N. H. J. van den Boogaard, *Rondeaux et Refrains du XIIe siècle au début du XIVe* (Paris: 1969), p. 59.

**9. 12th-Century Polyphony**
   **a.** *Viderunt Emmanuel:* F-Pn, fonds latin 3549, f. 151´.
   **b.** Kyrie *Cunctipotens genitor,* Santiago de Compostela, Biblioteca de la Catedral, Codex Calixtinus, f. 190. Facsimile in J. López-Calo, *La musica medieval en Galica* (La Coruña, 1982), p. 51.

**10. Leonin, *Alleluia Pascha nostrum***
   **a.** polyphony, Wolfenbüttel, Herzog-August-Bibliothek, Helmstedt 628, f. 27´ (old 31´); chant, F-Pn, fonds latin 1112, f. 105´ (transposed down a fifth to accord with the polyphony).
   **b.** (revised verse) polyphony, Florence, Biblioteca Medicea-Laurenziana, Plut. 29.1, f. 109; motet "Gaudeat devotio" as for polyphony of 10a, f. 98´ (old 107´); motet "Ave Maria," Wolfenbüttel, Herzog-August-Bibliothek, Helmstedt 1099, f. 156; chant as chant for 10a. For facsimile, see Plate 2.

**11. Perotin (?), *Alleluia Pascha nostrum:*** polyphony as for polyphony of l0b, f. 23; chant as for chant of 10a.

**12. Conductus**
   **a.** *Deus in adjutorium: The Montpellier Codex,* Pt. I, ed. H. Tischler, Recent Researches in the Music of the Middle Ages and Early Renaissance, vols. II and III, p. 1. © Copyright 1978 by A-R Editions, Inc., 315 West Gorham Street, Madison, Wisconsin 53703. Reprinted by permission.
   **b.** *O tocius Asie:* F-Pn, fonds latin, 15139; f. 266. Facsimile in E. Thurston, *The Music in the St. Victor Manuscript* (Toronto: 1959).

**13th-Century Motets** (to c. 1250)
   **13a.** Discant clausula: as for polyphony of 10b, f. 167.
   **13b, c.** *Ad solitum/Regnat:* as for 10b motet *Ave Maria,* f. 155´ (b), f. 128´ (c).
   **13d.** *Depositum/Ad solitum/Regnat: Compositions of the Bamberg Manuscript,* ed. G. A. Anderson, CMM 75, p. 11. © Copyright 1977 by American Institute of Musicology/Hänssler-Verlag, Neuhausen-Stuttgart. Reprinted by permission.
   **13e.** *Alleluia Hodie Maria:* F-Pn, fonds latin 1112, f. 188.
   **13f.** *L'autre jour/Au tens/In seculum:* as for 13d, p. 16, text translation by R. E. Smith, p. LXXX. © Copyright 1977 by American Institute of Musicology/Hänssler-Verlag, Neuhausen-Stuttgart. Reprinted by permission.

**14. *In seculum breve:*** as for 13d, p. 139. © Copyright 1977 by American Institute of Musicology/Hänssler-Verlag, Neuhausen-Stuttgart. Reprinted by permission.

**13th-Century Motets** (after c. 1250)
   **15a.** *El mois/De se debent/Kyrie:* as for 13d, p. 33, text translation by R. E. Smith, pp. LXXXVII-VIII. © Copyright 1977 by American Institute of Musicology/Hänssler-Verlag, Neuhausen-Stuttgart. Reprinted by permission.
   **15b.** *On parole/A Paris/Frese nouvele: Polyphonies du XIIIe Siècle,* vol. III, ed. Y. Rokseth, pp. 221-222. © Copyright 1936 by Éditions de l'Oiseau-Lyre, Les Remparts, Monaco. Reprinted by permission.
   **15c.** *Alle-psallite/Alle psallite/Alleluia:* as for 12a, Pt. III, Recent Researches in the Music of the Middle Ages and Early Renaissance, vols. VI and VII, p. 223. © Copyright 1978 by A-R Editions, Inc., 315 West Gorham Street, Madison, Wisconsin 53703. Reprinted by permission.
   **15d.** *Aucun ont/Lonc tans/Annuntiantes:* Montpellier, Bibliothèque de l'Ecole de Médecine, Ms H 196, f. 273. Facsimile in *Polyphonies du XIIIe Siècle,* vol. II, ed. Y. Rokseth (Monaco: 1936).

**16. Philippe de Vitry, *Tribum que/Quoniam secta/Merito:*** *The Roman de Fauvel,* ed. L. Schrade, Polyphonic Music of the Fourteenth Century, vol. I, pp. 54-56. © Copyright 1956 by Éditions de l'Oiseau-Lyre, Les Remparts, Monaco. Reprinted by permission.

**17. Guillaume de Machaut, *Bone Pastor/Bone Pastor/Bone Pastor:*** *The Works of Guillaume de Machaut,* ed. L. Schrade, Polyphonic Music of the Fourteenth Century, vol. III, pp. 4-7. Tenor rebarred from m. 97 to end. © Copyright 1956 by Éditions de l'Oiseau-Lyre, Les Remparts, Monaco. Reprinted by permission.

**18. Guillaume de Machaut, secular songs**
   **a.** *Nes que on porroit,* **b.** *Quant j'ay l'espart:* as for No. 17, pp. 122 (a), 145 (b). © Copyright 1956 by Éditions de l'Oiseau-Lyre, Les Remparts, Monaco. Reprinted by permission.
   **c.** *Dame a vous:* F-Pn, fonds français 1586, f. 51.

**19. Jacopo da Bologna, *Non al suo amante:*** *The Music of Fourteenth-Century Italy,* vol. IV, ed. N. Pirrotta, CMM 8, pp. 15-16. © Copyright 1963 by Armen Carapetyan/Hänssler-Verlag, Neuhausen-Stuttgart. Reprinted by permission.

20. **Gherardello da Firenze,** *Tosto che l'alba: The Music of Fourteenth-Century Italy,* vol. I, ed. N. Pirrotta, CMM 8, pp. 74-77. © Copyright 1954 by Armen Carapetyan/Hänssler-Verlag, Neuhausen-Stuttgart. Reprinted by permission.

21. **Francesco Landini,** *Questa fanciull'amor: The Works of Francesco Landini,* ed. L. Schrade, Polyphonic Music of the Fourteenth Century, vol. IV, pp. 116-117. © Copyright 1958 by Éditions de l'Oiseau-Lyre, Les Remparts, Monaco. Reprinted by permission.

22. **Borlet (?),** *Ma trédol rosignol: French Secular Compositions of the Fourteenth Century,* vol. 1, ed. W. Apel, CMM 53, pp. 21-22. © Copyright 1970 by Armen Carapetyan/Hänssler-Verlag, Neuhausen-Stuttgart. Reprinted by permission.

23. **Johannes Ciconia,** *Sus un' fontayne:* as for No. 22, pp. 25-27. © Copyright 1970 by Armen Carapetyan/ Hänssler-Verlag, Neuhausen-Stuttgart. Reprinted by permission.

24. **Leonel Power**
    a. Credo: *The Old Hall Manuscript,* vol. I, pt. 2, ed. A. Hughes and M. Bent, CMM 46, pp. 264-269. © Copyright 1969 by Armen Carapetyan/Hänssler-Verlag, Neuhausen-Stuttgart. Reprinted by permission.
    b. *Ave regina:* as for No. 24a, vol. I, pt. 1, pp. 127-128. © Copyright 1969 by Armnen Carapetyan/Hänssler-Verlag, Neuhausen-Stuttgart. Reprinted by permission.
    c. plainsong *Ave regina: John Dunstable Complete Works,* ed. M. Bukofzer, 2nd revised edition, ed. M. Bent, I. Bent, B. Trowell, Musica Britannica. vol. VIII, p. 160. © Copyright 1970 by Stainer and Bell Ltd. Reprinted by permission.

25. **John Dunstable,** *Beata mater:* as for No. 24c, p. 110. © Copyright 1970 by Stainer and Bell Ltd. Reprinted by permission.

26. **Guillaume Dufay,** *Christe, redemptor omnium: Opera Omnia Guglielmi Dufay,* vol. 5, ed. H. Besseler, CMM 1, pp. 40-41. © Copyright 1966 by American Institute of Musicology/Hänssler-Verlag. Neuhausen-Stuttgart. Reprinted by permission.

27. **Guillaume Dufay**
    a. Agnus Dei from *Missa Se la face ay pale:* as for No. 26, vol. 3, pp. 28-32. © Copyright 1951 by American Institite of Musicology/Hänssler-Verlag, Neuhausen-Stuttgart. Reprinted by permission.
    b. tenor from *Se la face ay pale:* Oxford, Bodleian Library, Canonici misc. 213, f. 53´.

28. **Guillaume Dufay,** *Ave regina caelorum:* as for No. 26, vol. 5, pp. 124-130. © Copyright 1966 by American Institute of Musicology/Hänssler-Verlag, Neuhausen-Stuttgart. Reprinted by permission.

29. **Johannes Ockeghem,** *Agnus Dei* **from** *Missa Mi-mi:* Rome, Biblioteca Apostolica Vaticana, Chigi C VIII .234, ff. 13´-16. For facsimile see Plate 3.

30. **Guillaume Dufay, secular songs**
    a. *Ce moys de may,* b. *Adieu m'amour:* as for No. 26, vol. 6, pp. 59 (a), 91 (b). © Copyright 1964 by American Institute of Musicology/Hänssler-Verlag, Neuhausen-Stuttgart. Reprinted by permission.

31. **Hayne van Ghizeghem,** *De tous biens: Hayne van Ghizeghem Opera Omnia,* ed. B. Hudson, CMM 74, pp. 14-15. © Copyright 1977 by American Institute of Musicology/Hänssler-Verlag, Neuhausen-Stuttgart. Reprinted by permission.

32. **Josquin Desprez,** *Ave Maria: Heinrich Glarean Dodecachordon,* vol. 2, ed. C. A. Miller, Musicological Studies and Documents 6, pp. 436-442. © Copyright 1965 by American Institute of Musicology/Hänssler-Verlag, Neuhausen-Stuttgart. Reprinted by permission.

33. **Josquin Desprez,** *Agnus Dei* **II from** *Missa L'homme armé super voces musicales:* H. Glareanus. *Dodecachordon* (1547), p. 442. For facsimile see Plate 4.

34. **Josquin Desprez**
    a. Kyrie, b. Agnus Dei from *Missa Pange lingua: Werken van Josquin des Pres,* ed. A. Smijers, *Missen,* ser. 1, vol. 4, pp. 1-3 (a), 22-27 (b). © Copyright 1963 by G. Alsbach & Co. Reprinted by permission.

35a. **Josquin Desprez,** *Faulte d'argent: Le septiesme livre contenant vingt et quatre chansons . . . composees par Josquin des Pres,* Tylman Susato 1545, f. X.
35b. **Antoine-de Févin,** *Faulte d'argent:* H. M. Brown, *Theatrical Chansons of the Fifteenth and Early Sixteenth Centuries,* pp. 67-68. © Copyright 1963 by Harvard University Press. Reprinted by permission.

36. **Heinrich Isaac,** *La mi la sol: Ein Altes Spielbuch Liber Fridolini Sichery,* vol. 1, ed. F. J. Giesbert. © B. Schott's Soehne, Mainz, 1936. Copyright renewed. All rights reserved. Used by permission of European American Music Distributors Corporation, sole U. S. agents for B. Schott's Soehne.

37. **Juan del Encina**
    a. *Señora de hermosura,* b. *Triste España:* music, Madrid, Palacio real, Biblioteca, Ms. 1335 (*olim* 2-I-5), known as Cancionero de Palacio, f. 54´ (a), f. 55´ (b); texts, *Poesía Lírica y Cancionero Musical de Juan del Encina,* ed. R. O. Jones and C. R. Lee, Clasicos Castalia 62, p. 223 (a), pp. 212-213 (b). © Copyright 1975 by Editorial Castalia. Reprinted by permission.

**38.** *Orsù, orsù car'signori:* Edited from *Sing-und Spielmusik aus älterer Zeit,* ed. J. Wolf (2nd edition, 1931), pp. 49-51.

**39. Marchetto Cara, *Io non compro:*** *Le Frottole per canto e liuto intabulate da Franciscus Bossinensis,* ed. B. Disertori, Istituzioni e Monumenti dell'Arte Musicale Italiana, vol. III, pp. 390-391, 444. © Copyright 1964 by G. Ricordi & Co., s.p.a.. Reprinted by permission.

**40.** *Aus tiefer Not*
   **a.** (Martin Luther): *Eyn Enchiridon oder Handbüchlein* (Erfurt: 1524), Psalm 129 "De profundis," (unpaginated, end of B fascicle).
   **b.** (Johann Walter): *Geistliches Gesangbüchlein,* ed. O. Schröder, *Johann Walter Sämtliche Werke* I (Kassel and Basel: 1953), pp. 20-21. Reprinted by permission of Bärenreiter-Verlag.
   **c.** (Arnold von Bruck): edited from *Denkmäler Deutscher Tonkunst,* vol. 34, ed. J. Wolf (Leipzig: 1908), p. 104.
   **d.** (J. S. Bach): edited from Cantata No. 38, *Johann Sebastian Bach's Werke,* vol. 7, ed. W. Rust (Leipzig: c. 1858), p. 300.

**41. Nicholas Gombert, *Ave regina caelorum:*** *Nicholai Gombert Opera Omnia,* vol. 8, ed. J. Schmidt-Görg, CMM 6, pp. 36-41. © Copyright 1970 by Armen Carapetyan/Hänssler-Verlag, Neuhausen-Stuttgart. Reprinted by permission.

**42. Giovanni Pierluigi da Palestrina**
   **a.** *Veni sponsa Christi: Motecta festonrum totius anni cum communi sanctorum . . . quaternis vocibus . . . liber primus* (Venice: A. Gardano, 1564).
   **b.** antiphon *Veni sponsa Christi:* edited from *Antiphonale Monasticum* (Tournai: 1934), p. 682.

**43. Giovanni Pierluigi da Palestrina, *Kyrie* from *Missa Veni sponsa Christi:*** *Missarum cum quatuor, quinque, et sex vocibus, liber nonus* (Venice: heirs of Girolamo Scotto, 1599).

**44. Orlande de Lassus, *Tristis est anima mea:*** edited from *Orlando di Lasso Magnum Opus Musicum* III, ed. F. X. Haberl, *Sämtliche Werke,* vol. V (Leipzig: c. 1896), pp. 48-50.

**45. Orlande de Lassus, *In teneris annis:*** edited from *Orlando Lasso Prophetiae Sibyllarum,* ed. J. Therstappen, Das Chorwerk, vol. 48 (Kassel and Basel: c. 1937), pp. 12-13.

**46. William Byrd**
   **a.** *Miserere mihi, Domine: Cantiones Sacrae,* ed. C. Monson, The Byrd Edition, vol. 1, pp. 161-166. © Copyright 1977 by Stainer & Bell, Ltd. Used by permission of Galaxy Music Corporation, New York, N.Y., sole U. S. agent.
   **b.** antiphon *Miserere mihi:* edited from *Antiphonale Sarisburiense,* facsimile ed. W. H. Frere (London: 1901-1904), p. 6.

**47. Giovanni Gabrieli, *Canzona septimi toni:*** *Giovanni Gabrieli Symphoniae Sacrae (1597), Canzona Septimi Toni à 8,* ed. R. P. Block. © Copyright 1972 by Musica Rara, Le Traversier, Monteux, France. Reprinted by permission.

**48. Clément Janequin, *Ou mettra l'on:*** *Clément Janequin Chansons Polyphoniques,* vol. 3, ed. A. T. Merritt and F. Lesure, pp. 81-84. © Copyright 1967 by Éditions de l'Oiseau-Lyre, Les Remparts, Monaco. Used by permission.

**49a. Luis de Milán, *Pavan 1:*** edited from *Luis de Milán El Maestro,* ed. C. Jacobs (University Park, Pa.: The Pennsylvania State University Press, 1971), pp. 101-102.

**49b. Diego Ortiz, *Recercada settima:*** *Tratado de glosas,* ed. M. Schneider (Kassel and Basel: 1961), pp. 126-129. Reprinted by permission of Bärenreiter-Verlag.

**50. Jacques Arcadelt, *Il bianco e dolce cigno:*** *Jacobi Arcadelt Opera Omnia,* vol. 2, ed. A. Seay, CMM 31, pp. 38-40. © Copyright 1970 by Armen Carapetyan/Hänssler-Verlag, Neuhausen-Stuttgart. Reprinted by permission.

**51. Cipriano de Rore, *Da le belle contrade:*** *Cipriano de Rore Opera Omnia,* vol. 5, ed. B. Meier, CMM 14, pp. 96-99. © Copyright 1971 by Armen Carapetyan/Hänssler-Verlag, Neuhausen-Stuttgart. Reprinted by permission.

**52. Luca Marenzio, *Scaldava il sol:*** *The Art of Music,* B. Cannon, A. Johnson, W. Waite (New York: 1960), pp. 189-193. Used by permission of Harper & Row, Publishers, Inc.

**53. Claudio Monteverdi, *Cruda Amarilli:*** *Il quinto libro de madrigali a cinque voci di Claudio Monteverdi* (Venice, 1605).

**54. Carlo Gesualdo, *Moro, lasso:*** from *Sämtliche Madrigale von Carlo Gesualdo,* vol. 6, ed. W. Weismann, pp. 74-77. © Copyright 1957 VEB Deutscher Verlag für Musik, Leipzig. Reprinted by permission.

**55. Giulio Caccini, *Perfidissimo volto:*** *Giulio Caccini Le nuove musiche,* ed. H. W. Hitchcock, Recent Researches in the Music of the Baroque Era, vol. IX, pp. 77-80. © Copyright 1970 by A-R Editions, Inc., 315 West Gorham Street, Madison, Wisconsin 53703. Reprinted by permission.

56. **Sigismondo d'India,** *Cruda Amarilli: Il primo libro di Musiche da cantar solo 1609,* ed. F. Mompellio, Instituta et Monumenta, serie I, No. 4 (Cremona: 1970), pp. 82-84. Reprinted by permission.

57. **John Dowland**
   **a.** *Flow my teares: The Second Booke of Songs or Ayres . . . composed by John Dowland* (London: Thomas Este, 1600); text, *Lyrics from English Airs 1596-1622,* ed. E. Doughtic (Cambridge, Mass.: 1970), p. 101.
   **b.** *Lachrimae gementes: John Dowland Lachrimae,* ed. F. J. Giesbert, Nagels Musik-Archiv 173, pp. 6-7. © Copyright 1964 by Nagels Musik-Archiv, Kassel. Reprinted by permission.

58. **Claudio Monteverdi,** *Zefiro torna: Tutte le Opere di Claudio Monteverdi,* vol. 9, ed. G. F. Malipiero (1929), pp. 9-20; revised according to *Madrigali e Canzonette a due, e tre voci del Signor Claudio Monteverdi . . . Libro nono* (Venice: 1651). Used by permission of European American Music Distributors Corporation, sole U. S. agent for Universal Edition.

59. **Giovanni Gabrieli,** *In ecclesiis: Giovanni Gabrieli Opera Omnia,* vol. V, ed. D. Arnold, CMM 12, pp. 32-55. © Copyright 1969 by Armen Carapetyan/Hänssler-Verlag, Neuhausen-Stuttgart. Reprinted by permission.

60. **Heinrich Schütz,** *O quam tu pulchra es: Symphoniae Sacrae* I, ed. R. Gerber, Heinrich Schütz Neue Ausgabe Sämtlicher Werke, vol. 13, pp. 80-87. © Copyright 1957 by Bärenreiter-Verlag, Kassel and Basel. Reprinted by permission.

61. **Heinrich Schütz,** *Saul, Saul was verfolgst du mich?:* Stuttgarter Schützausgabe, ed. G. Graulich. © Copyright 1969 by Hänssler-Verlag, Neuhausen-Stuttgart. Reprinted by permission.

62. **Jacopo Peri,** *Euridice* ("Per quel vago" through "Non piango"): *Euridice,* ed. H. M. Brown, Recent Researches in the Music of the Baroque Era, vols. XXXVI-XXXVII, pp. 63-71. © Copyright 1981 by A-R Editions, Inc., 315 West Gorham Street, Madison, Wisconsin 53703. Reprinted by permission. For facsimile see Plate 5.

63. **Claudio Monteverdi,** *Orfeo* (excerpts from Act II): *L'Orfeo Favola in Musica* (Venice: 1615), facsimile reprinted 1972 by Gregg International Publishers Ltd., pp. 32-41.

64. **Claudio Monteverdi,** *L'incoronazione di Poppea* (Act I, scene 3): Venice, Biblioteca nazionale di San Marco, ms. Italiani cl. 4, no. 439, facsimile in *L'incoronazione di Poppea,* Biblioteca Musica Bononiensis, Sec. 4, No. 81 (Bologna: 1969), ff. 13´-17´.

65. **Giacomo Carissimi,** *Jephte* (excerpts): *Giacomo Carissimi Jephte,* ed. Janet Beat, pp. 11-15, 20-22. © Copyright 1974 by Novello and Company Limited. Reprinted by permission.

66. **Francesco Cavalli,** *Scipione Africano* (Act II, scene 8): Venice, Biblioteca nazionale Marciana Ms. It. IV, 371, facsimile in *Italian Opera 1640-1770,* ed. H. M. Brown, Garland Series (New York: Garland Publishers, 1978), ff. 70´-71´.

67. **Antonio Cesti,** *Alpi nevose: The Italian Cantata, I: Antonio Cesti,* ed. D. Burrows, The Wellesley Edition, No. 5 (Wellesley, Mass.: 1963), pp. 10-18. Used by permission.

68. **Jean-Baptiste Lully,** *Alceste* (Act II, scenes 7 and 8): *Alceste Tragedie mise en musique par feu Monsieur de Lully,* Première Édition (Paris: H. Baussen, 1708), with some readings from manuscript score F-Pn VM$^2$ .12 and parts Mus. Rés. F 1701, both dated 1703.

69. **Henry Purcell,** *Dido and Aeneas* (concluding scene): *Dido and Aeneas,* ed. Margaret Lauric, *The Works of Henry Purcell,* vol. 3, pp. 94-99. © Copyright 1979 by Novello and Company Limited. Reprinted by permission.

70. **William Byrd,** *John come kiss me now: William Byrd Keyboard Music* II, ed. A. Brown, Musica Britannica XXVIII (2nd rev. edition, 1976), pp. 121-125. © Copyright 1971 by Stainer & Bell Ltd. Reprinted by permission.

71. **Samuel Scheidt,** *Jesus Christus unser Heiland: Tabulatura Nova Teil III,* ed. Ch. Mahrenholz, Samuel Scheidt Werke, vol. 7 (Ugrino Verlag, 1966), pp. 10-17. © Copyright VEB Deutscher Verlag für Musik, Leipzig. Reprinted by permission.

72. **Girolamo Frescobaldi,** *Toccata No. 8: Girolamo Frescobaldi Opere Complete II,* ed. E. Darbellay, Monumenti Musicali Italiani, vol. IV (1977), pp. 29-32. Reprinted by permission of Edizioni Suvini Zerboni, Publisher and Copyright Owner, and Boosey & Hawkes, Inc., sole agents.

73. **Girolamo Frescobaldi,** *Canzona dopo l'epistola: Girolamo Frescobaldi Orgel- und Klavierwerke,* vol. 5. ed. P. Pidoux, pp. 13-15. © Copyright 1959 by Bärenreiter-Verlag, Kassel and Basel. Reprinted by permission.

74. **Johann Jacob Froberger,** *Suite VI:* from *J.-J. Froberger Oeuvres Complètes pour clavecin,* vol. I, ed. H. Schott, Le Pupitre 57, pp. 198-202. © Copyright 1979 by Heugel Editeur-Propriétaire. Reprinted by permission.

75. **Louis Couperin,** *Prélude a l'imitation de M! Froberger: L. Couperin Pièces de Clavecin,* ed. A. Curtis, Le Pupitre 18, pp. 1-8. © Copyright 1970 by Heugel Editeur-Propriétaire. Reprinted by permission.

76. **Salamone Rossi, *Sonata in dialogo:*** from *Salomone Rossi Trio Sonatas for two Violins and Basso Continuo,* ed. A. Mann and F. Rikko, Documents of the Musical Past, No. 4, pp. 8-11. © Copyright 1965 by the Trustees of Rutgers College in New Jersey. Reprinted by permission.

77. **Giovanni Battista Vitali, *Sonata a due violini:*** edited from *Anthology of Instrumental Music from the End of the Sixteenth to the End of the Seventeenth Century,* ed. J. W. von Wasielewski (1874; reprinted with notes by J. G. Suess, New York, Da Capo Press, 1974), p. 47.

78. **Arcangelo Corelli, *Sonata da Camera,* Op. 4, No. 5:** *Sonata da Camera à Tre . . . di Archangelo Corelli Opera Quarta Dernière Edition* (Amsterdam: E. Roger et M. C. Le Cene, c. 1715).

79. **Heinrich Biber, *Rosary Sonata X:*** Edited from *Heinrich Franz Biber Sechzehn Violinsonaten,* ed. E. Luntz, Denkmäler der Tonkunst in Österreich, Jahrg. XII/2, vol. 25 (Leipzig: 1905), pp. 44-48.

80. **Arcangelo Corelli, *Sonata for Violin* Op. 5, No. 1:** reprinted from *Zwölf Sonaten für Violine und Basso Continuo Opus 5,* ed. B. Paumgartner (Mainz: 1953), pp. 2-14; revised according to *Sonate a violino e violone o cimbalo di Arcangelo Corelli opera quinta, Troisième edition on l'on a joint les agréments des adagio de cet ouvrage composez par Mr. A. Corelli comme il les joue* (Amsterdam: E. Roger, c. 1712). © Copyright Schott and Co., Ltd., London 1953. Copyright renewed. All rights reserved. Used by permission of European American Music Distributors Corporation, sole U. S. agent for Schott and Co., Ltd.

81. **Alessandro Scarlatti, *Su le sponde del Tebro*** (excerpts): edited from Vienna, Gesellschaft der Musikfreunde Archiv, Ms VI 37178, and Florence, Conservatorio di Musica Luigi Cherubini Biblioteca, Ms D 2364.

82. **George Frideric Handel, *Admeto*** (Act II, scenes 7-8, Act III, scene 6): *Admeto,* ed. F. Chrysander, *G. F. Händel's Werke,* ser. LXXIII, Opern, vol. XIX (Leipzig: 1877), pp. 68-76, 102-104.

83. **Jean-Philippe Rameau, *Hippolyte et Aricie*** (Act I, scene 2): *Hippolite et Aricie Tragedie mise en musique par Mr. Rameau . . .* [Paris: (1733)], pp. 4-10.

84. **Giovanni Battista Pergolesi, "Aspettare e non venire" from *La serva padrona:*** from *La Serva Padrona,* ed. K. Geiringer (Vienna: c. 1953), pp. 1-10. Used by permission of European American Music Distributors Corporation, sole U. S. agent for Philharmonia scores.

85. **Johann Sebastian Bach, *Jesu, der du meine Seele:*** *Kantaten zum 13. und 14. Sonntag nach Trinitatis,* ed. W. Neumann, Johann Sebastian Bach Neue Ausgabe Sämtlicher Werke, Serie I, vol. 21 (Kassel and Basel: 1958), pp. 117-146. Reprinted by permission of Bärenreiter-Verlag.

86. **François Couperin, excerpts from *Pièces de clavecin, Premier livre:*** from *François Couperin Pièces de Clavecin Premier Livre,* ed. K. Gilbert, Le Pupitre 21, pp. 2-5, 8-9. © Copyright 1975 by Heugel Editeur-Propriétaire. Reprinted by permission. For facsimile see Plate 6.

87. **Johann Sebastian Bach, *Prelude and Fugue in D minor:*** from *DAS WOHLTEMPERIERTE CLAVIER,* Teil I, ed. O. von Irmer (Munich-Duisberg, 1950), pp. 28-31. © Copyright 1978 by G. Henle Verlag. Reprinted by permission.

88. **Domenico Scarlatti, *Sonatas in D minor* (K. 120) and *D major* (K. 119):** from *Domenico Scarlatti Sonates,* vol. 3, ed. K. Gilbert, Le Pupitre 33, pp. 78-81, 72-77. © Copyright 1979 by Heugel Editeur-Propriétaire. Reprinted by permission.

89. **Antonio Vivaldi, *Violin Concerto in G minor,* Op. 8, No. 8:** edited from *Concerto in sol minore per violino, archi e cembalo F. I n. 16,* ed. G. F. Malipiero, Istituto Italiano Antonio Vivaldi, vol. 65 (1949).

90. **Johann Sebastian Bach, selected canons from *The Musical Offering:*** *Kanons. Musikalisches Opfer,* ed. C. Wolff, Johann Sebastian Bach Neue Ausgabe Sämtlicher Werke, Series 8, vol. 1 (Kassel and Basel: 1974), pp. 48-49, 52-53, 70-71. Reprinted by permission of Bärenreiter-Verlag.

## PLATES

1. ***Resurrexi:*** Montpellier, Bibliothèque de l'École de Médecine, Ms. H 159, facsimile from Paléographie Musicale, vol. 8, p. 47. Reprinted by permission of the Librarian, Bibliothèque de la Faculté de Médecine de Montpellier.

2. **Leonin, Alleluia Pascha nostrum:** Florence, Biblioteca Medicea-Laurenziana, Pluteo 29.1, f. 109. Reproduced by permission of the Director, Biblioteca Medicea-Laurenziana.

3. **Johannes Ockeghem, *Agnus Dei* from Missa Mi-mi:** Rome, Biblioteca apostolica vaticana, Chigi Codex C VIII. 234, ff. 13´-14. Reproduced by permission of the Biblioteca apostolica vaticana.

4. **Josquin Desprez, *Agnus Dei* II from *Missa L'homme armé super voces musicales:*** H. Glareanus, *Dodecachordon* (1547), p. 442, facsimile reprinted in Monuments of Music and Music Literature in Facsimile-Second Series-Music Literature LXV (New York: Broude Brothers Ltd., 1967), p. 442. Reproduced by permission of the publisher.

5. **Jacopo Peri, *Non piango e non sospiro* from *Euridice:*** *Le Musiche sopra l'Euridice Florence: 1600,* facsimile reprinted in Monuments of Music and Music Literature in Facsimile-First Series-Music XXVIII (New York: Broude Brothers Ltd., 1973), p. 17. Reproduced by permission of the publisher.

6. **François Couperin, "Explication des Agréments et des Signes":** from *François Couperin Pièces de Clavecin Premier Livre,* ed. Kenneth Gilbert, Le Pupitre 21, p. III. Reproduced by permission of Heugel Editeur-Propriétaire.

**Maps 1 and 2:** from R. R. Sellman, *An Outline Atlas of World History,* pp. 30 (1) and 40 (2). © Copyright 1970 by R. R. Sellman. Reprinted with permission of St. Martin's Press, Inc., New York, N.Y.

Titles and incipits appear in italics, composer's names and genres in roman type. Boldface page numbers indicate the location of a composition, while roman page numbers refer to the written commentary. Composers who lived prior to the fourteenth century are cited by first name (e.g., Bernart de Ventadorn, *not* Ventadorn, Bernart de), as are a few later composers known commonly by their first names.

*Ach, ich bin ein Kind der Sünden,* **531,** 546
*Ad solitum vomitum/Regnat,* **78,** 85
*Adieu m'amour, adieu ma joye,* **169,** 171
*Admeto,* **481,** 497. See also *Alceste*
*Aeterna Christi munera,* **40,** 41
Agnus Dei
    plainsong, **19,** 23
    polyphony, **146** (*Missa Se la face ay pale,*
        Dufay), 152; **161** (*Missa Mi-mi,*
        Ockeghem), 166, **167** (Pl. 3); **182**
        (*Missa L'homme armé super voces
        musicales,* Desprez), 183, **184** (Pl. 4);
        **188** (*Missa Pange lingua,* Desprez),
        194
*Ah, si, morrò,* **488,** 498
*Ahi caso acerbo,* **356, 361,** 363
*Alceste,* **393** (Act II, scenes 7-8), 399.
        See also *Admeto*
*Alle psallite cum luya/Alle psallite cum
        luya/Alleluya,* **91,** 98
*Alleluia Hodie Maria virgo,* **82,** 85
*Alleluia Justus ut palma,* **34,** 35
*Alleluia Pascha nostrum*
    plainsong, **9,** 22
    polyphony, **57** (Pl. 2), **58** (Leonin),
        **60** (revision of Leonin setting), 66;
        **67** (Perotin?), 74
*Alleluia Te martyrum,* **35,** 36
Allemande, **428** (Froberger), 433; **451**
        (Corelli), 454; **548** (F. Couperin),
        554
*Alpi nevose e dure,* **388,** 392
"Anonymous IV," 66, 87
Antiphon, 38, 41, **140,** 141 (*Ave regina
        caelorum*); **141** (*Beata mater*), 143; **33**
        (*Ipsi soli*), 35; **26** (*Magnificatus est*),
        28; **245** (*Miserere mihi, Domine*), 245,
        **2** (*Resurrexi*), 21; **24** (*Rex pacificus*)
        28; **227** (*Veni sponsa Christi*), 228. See
        also *Ave regina caelorum*
Aquitanian polyphony, **54,** 56
Arcadelt, Jacques
    *Il bianco e dolce cigno,* **263,** 265
Aria, 372, 384, 387, 392, 406, 479. *See also*
        Da capo aria
*Ars antiqua,* 102
*Ars nova,* 99, 102, 115, 117, 127
*Ars subtilior,* 127
*Aspettare e non venire,* **507,** 513
*Aucun ont trouvé/Lonc tans/Annuntiantes,*
        **93,** 98
*Aus tiefer Not,* **213** (Luther), **214** (Walter),
        **215** (von Bruck), **216** (J. S. Bach), 217
*Ave Maria fons leticie,* **62,** 67
*Ave Maria gratia plena . . . virgo serena,*
        **175,** 182
*Ave regina caelorum*
    plainsong, **38,** 41, **140** (Sarum), 141
    polyphony, **138** (Power), 141; **153**
        (Dufay), 160; **218** (Gombert), 223

Bach, Johann Sebastian, 406, 554
    *Aus tiefer Not,* **216,** 217
    *Jesu, der du meine Seele,* **514,** 545
    *Prelude and Fugue in D minor,* **555,** 559
    *Musikalisches Opfer,* **593,** 598
Ballade, **109,** 115
Ballata, **122,** 124
*Baros de mon dan covit,* **44,** 52
*Beata mater,* **141,** 143
*Benedicamus Domino,* **28,** 28, 37
Bernart de Ventadorn
    *Can vei la lauzeta mover,* **42,** 52
*Biaus m'est estez,* **49,** 53
Biber, Heinrich Ignaz Franz von
    *Rosary Sonata X,* **454,** 458
Binary form, 433, 454, 554, 570
*Bone pastor Guillerme/Bone pastor qui
        pastores/Bone pastor,* **104,** 109
Borlet (?)
    *Ma trédol rosignol joly,* **125,** 127
Bossinensis, Franciscus. *See* Franciscus
        Bossinensis
Bruck, Arnold von
    *Aus tiefer Not,* **215,** 217
Brulé, Gace. *See* Gace Brulé
Burney, Charles, 458, 471, 479, 498, 570
Busenello, Giovanni Franceso, 372
Byrd, William
    *John come kiss me now,* **407,** 412
    *Miserere mihi, Domine,* **239,** 245

Caccia, **118,** 121
Caccini, Giulio, 354
    *Perfidissimo volto,* **287,** 291
Caserta, Philippus (Philipoctus) de, 131
Cadence
    double leading-tone, 109, 140
    double octave, 174
    octave leap, 174
    under-third, 141
*Can vei la lauzeta mover,* **42,** 52
Canon, 121, **182,** 183, 194, 201, 245, **593**
        (*Canones diversi super Thema Regium,*
        J. S. Bach), 598
Cantata, **388** (Cesti), 392; **472** (Scarlatti),
        479; **514** (J. S. Bach), 545
*Cantate mecum Domino,* **378,** 384
*Canti carnascialeschi. See* Carnival songs
Cantus firmus, 152, 160, 194, 245, 420
Canzona, **246** (Gabrieli), 253; **426**
        (Frescobaldi), 428; 559
Cara, Marchetto
    *Io non compro più speranza,* **210,** 212
Carissimi, Giacomo
    *Jephte* (excerpts), **373, 380,** 384
Carnival songs, 207, **208,** 209
*Castitatis lilium effloruit,* **37,** 37
Castrato voice, 372
Cavalli, Francesco
    *Scipione Africano* (Act II, scene 8),
        **385,** 387
*Ce moys de may soyons lies et joyeux,*
        **168,** 171
Cesti, Antonio
    *Alpi nevose e dure,* **388,** 392
Chaconne, 312. See also *ciaccona*
Chanson rustique, 201
*Chevalier mult estes guariz,* **47,** 53
Chorale, 213, 214, 215, 216, 217; **420;**
        **543** (J. S. Bach), 545
*Christe redemptor omnium,* **143,** 145

Ciaccona, **300,** 312
Ciconia, Johannes
    *Sus un' fontayne,* **128,** 131
Color (of motet), 103, 109
Communion, **20,** 23
Concertato motet. See motet, concertato
Concerto, **571,** 592
Conductus, 37, 56, **74** (*sine cauda*), **75**
        (*cum cauda*), 78
Conductus motet, **78, 85**
Copula, 66
Corelli, Arcangelo
    *Sonata da camera a tre* (Opus 4, No. 5),
        **450,** 454
    Sonata for violin and violone or cembalo
        (Opus 5, No. 1), **459,** 470
Corrente, **452,** 454. See also courante
Couperin, François, 441
    *Pièces de clavecin, Premier livre,* **547**
        (Pl. 6), **548** (*Premier ordre*), 554
Couperin, Louis, 554
    *Prélude a l'imitation de Mr. Froberger,*
        **434,** 441
Courante, **431** (Froberger), 433; **550**
        (F. Couperin), 554. See also corrente
Credo, **14,** 22; **132** (Power), 140
*Cruda Amarilli,* **278** (Monteverdi), 281; **292**
        (d'India), 294
Crusader's song, **47,** 53
*Cunctipotensgenitor. See* Kyrie

Da capo aria, 392, 480, 497, 506, 545
*Da le belle contrade d'oriente,* **266,** 271
*Dame a vous sans retollir,* **113,** 115
*Das Blut, so meine Schuld durchstreicht,*
        **532,** 545
*Das wohltemperirte Clavier,* **555,** 559
de Milán, Luis. See Luis de Milán
*De tous biens plaine,* **171,** 174
*Deh pietosè verdi herbette,* **386,** 387
del Encina, Juan. See Juan del Encina
*Depositum creditum/Ad solitum
        vomitum/Regnat,* **80,** 85
Desprez, Josquin, 174, 223
    *Agnus Dei* II from *Missa L'homme armé
        super voces musicales,* **182,** 183, **184**
        (Pl. 4)
    *Agnus Dei* from *Missa Pange lingua,*
        **188,** 194
    *Ave Maria gratia plena . . . virgo serena,*
        **175,** 182
    *Faulte d'argent,* **195,** 201
    *Kyrie* from *Missa Pange lingua,* **185,** 194
*Deus in adjutorium,* **23** (versicle), 28, **74**
        (conductus), 78
*Dido and Aeneas,* **400** (concluding scene),
        406
*Die Wunden, Nägel, Kron und Grab,*
        **535,** 546
Diminution, 98, 109
Discant clausula, 66, 74, 85
    *latus,* **59, 62,** 72
    *luya,* **63,** 69
    *nostrum,* **60,** 71
    *Regnat,* **78**
Discant motet. *See* Motet, discant
Discant style, 66
*Dite almeno, astri crudeli,* **472,** 479
Dowland, John
    *Flow my teares* (*Lachrimae*), **295,** 299
    *Lachrimae Gementes,* **297,** 299

Dufay, Guillaume
  *Adieu m'amour, adieu ma joye*, **169**, 171
  *Agnus Dei* from *Missa Se la face ay pale*,
    **146**, 152
  *Ave regina caelorum*, **153**, 160
  *Ce moys de may soyons lies et joyeux*,
    **168**, 171
  *Christe redemptor omnium*, **143**, 145
  *Se la face ay pale*, **151**, 152
Dunstable, John, 140, 152
  *Beata mater*, **141**,143

Easter Mass, **2**, 21
*Ecce pater cunctis*, **4**, 21
*El meastro. See* Luis de Milán
*El mois de mai/De se debent bigami/Kyrie*,
  **87**, 97
*Euridice*, **348** (Pl. 5), 349, 354
"Explanation of Ornaments and Signs," **547**
  (Pl. 6), 554

Faidit, Gaucelm. *See* Gaucelm Faidit
*Faulte d'argent*, **195** (Desprez), 201; **199**
  (Févin), 201
Fauxbourdon, **143**, 145
Févin, Antoine de
  *Faulte d'argent*, **199**, 201
*Fiori musicale*, 425, **426**, 428
*Fitzwilliam Virginal Book, The*, **407**, 412
*Flow my teares*, **295**, 299
*Fortz chausa es*, **45**, 53
Franciscus Bossinensis, **210**, 212
Frankish chant, 21
French chanson. *See* Parisian chanson
Frescobaldi, Girolamo
  *Canzona dopo l'epistola*, **426**, 428
  *Toccata No. 8* from *Toccate e partite . . .
    libro primo*, **421**, 425
Froberger, Johann Jacob, 441
  *Suite VI*, **428**, 433
Frottola, 207, **210**, 212, 265
Fugue, **557**, 559
*Fulgens praeclara*, **11**, 22

Gabrieli, Giovanni, 334
  *Canzona Septimi Toni a 8*, **246**, 253
  *In ecclesiis*, **313**, 325
Gace Brulé
  *Biaus m'est estez*, **49**, 53
Gaucelm Faidit
  *Fortz chausa es*, **45**, 53
*Gaudeat devotio fidelium*, **60**, 67
Gavotte, **453** (Corelli), 454
*Gelosia, spietata Aletto*, **482**, 498
Gesualdo, Carlo
  *Moro, lasso, al mio duolo*, **282**, 286
Gherardello da Firenze
  *Tosto che l'alba*, **118**, 121
Ghizeghem, Hayne van. *See* Hayne
  van Ghizeghem
Gigue, **430** (Froberger), 433
Glareanus, Heinrich, 182, 184
Gloria, **7**, 22
Gombert, Nicholas
  *Ave Regina caelorum*, **218**, 223
Gradual, **8**, 22
Gregorian chant, **2**, 21, **23**, 28
Ground bass, **260** (Ortiz), 262; **300**
  (Monteverdi, 312; **400** (Purcell), 406
Guarini, Giovanni Battista, 281, 291, 294
Guido of Arezzo
  *Ipsi soli*, **33**, 35
Guillaume d'Amiens, *Prendes i garde*, **51**, 53

*Haec dies* (Gradual), **8**, 22, 85
Handel, George Frideric, 384, 480
  *Admeto*, **481** (Act II, scenes 7 and 8),
    497, **493** (Act III, scene 6), 497
Hayne van Ghizeghem
  *De tous biens plaine*, **171**, 174
  *Herr, ich glaube*, **543**, 546
  *Heu, mihi! filia mea*, **380**, 384
  *Hippolyte amoureux*, **501**, 506
  *Hippolyte et Aricie*, **499** (Act I, scene 2), 506
Hocket, **86**, 87
Hymn
  plainsong, **40** (*Aeterna Christi munera*),
    **40** (*Pange lingua gloriosi corporis*), 41;
    **27** (*Veni redemptor gentium*), 29
  polyphony, **143** (*Christe, redemptor
    omnium*), 145

*Il bianco e dolce cigno*, **263**, 265
*Il cimento dell'armonia e dell'inventione*,
  **571**, 592
*In ecclesiis*, **313**, 325
*In seculum breve*, **86**, 87
*In teneris annis*, **236**, 239
India, Sigismondo d'
  *Cruda Amarilli*, **292**, 294
Intermezzo, **507**, 513
Introit, **2**, 21
Introit trope, **4**, 21
*Io non compro più speranza*, **210**, 212
*Ipsi soli*, **33**, 35
Isaac, Heinrich
  *La mi la sol*, **202**, 204
Isorhythm, 103, 109, 140
Isorhythmic motet, **99** (Vitry), 103; **104**
  (Machaut), 109, 160
Ite, missa est, **20**, 23

Jacopo da Bologna
  *Non al suo amante*, **116**, 117
Janequin, Clément
  *Ou mettra l'on ung baiser*, **254**, 258
*Jephte*, **373**, **380**, 384
*Jesu, der du meine Seele*, **514**, **543**, 545
*Jesus Christus unser Heiland, der von uns*,
  **413**, 420
*John come kiss me now*, **407**, 412
Josquin. *See* Desprez, Josquin
Juan del Encina
  *Señora de hermosura*, **205**, 207
  *Triste España*, **206**, 207
Jubilus, 22

Kyrie
  **5** (*Cunctipotens genitor*, plainsong), 21; **34**
    (organum *Cunctipotens genitor*), 35; **55**
    (*Cunctipotens genitor*, from *Codex
    Calixtinus*), 56; **185** (from *Missa Pange
    lingua*), 194; **228** (from *Missa Veni
    sponsa Christi*), 232

*Là dove gli occhi io giro*, **494**, 498
*La mi la sol*, **202**, 204
*La serva padrona*, **507**, 513
"*La Viena,*" **441**, 445
*Lachrimae*, **295** (song), **297** (instrumental
  pavane), 299
*Lamento sopra la dolorosa perdita della M*$^{st\grave{a}}$ *di
  Ferdinando IV*, **428**, 433
Landini, Francesco
  *Questa fanciull' amor*, **122**, 124
Lassus, Orlande de

*In teneris annis* (*Sibylla cimmeria*), **236**, 239
  *Tristis est anima mea*, **233**, 236
*L'autre jour/Au tens pascour/In seculum*, **83**, 85
*Le nuove musiche*, 291
Leonin
  Alleluia *Pascha nostrum*, **58**, 66
*L'incoronazione di Poppea*, **364** (Act I,
  scene 3), 372, 384
Luis de Milán
  *Pavan 1* from *El maestro*, **259**, 262
Lully, Jean-Baptiste, 506, 554
  *Alceste*, **393** (Act II, scenes 7-8), 399
Lute song, **295**, 299
Luther, Martin
  *Aus tiefer Not*, **213**, 217
  *Jesus Christus unser Heiland, der von uns*,
    **420**, 420

*Ma trédol rosignol joly*, **125**, 127
Machaut, Guillaume de
  *Bone pastor Guillerme/Bone pastor qui
    pastores/Bone pastor*, **104**, 109
  *Dame a vous sans retollir*, **113**, 115
  *Nes que on porroit*, **109**, 115
  *Quant j'ay l'espart*, **112**, 115
Madrigal, **262** (Arcadelt), 265; **266** (Rore),
  271; **272** (Marenzio), 277; **278**
  (Monteverdi), 281; **282** (Gesualdo),
  286; **287** (Caccini), 291; **292**
  (d'India), 294; **300** (Monteverdi), 312
Madrigale, **116** (Jacopo da Bologna), 117
*Magnificatus est*, **26**, 28
*Magnus liber organi*, 66, 74
Marenzio, Luca
  *Scaldava il sol*, **272**, 277
Marpurg, Friedrich Wilhelm, 599
Mass, 21
  cantus firmus, 152
  paraphrase, 194
  imitation, 232
  parody, 232
  See also *Missa* (various titles)
Melismatic organum, 66
*Miserere mihi, Domine*, **239** (Byrd), **245**
  (plainsong), 245
*Missa L'homme armé super voces musicales*,
  **182**, 183, **184** (Pl. 4)
*Missa Mi-mi*, **161**, 166 **167** (Pl. 3)
*Missa Pange lingua*, **185**, **188**, 194
*Missa Se la face ay pale*, **146**, 152, 166
*Missa Veni sponsa Christi*, **228**, 232
Modal formulas, **29**, 30
Mode, 21, 30
Monody, 291
Monteverdi, Claudio, 406
  *Cruda Amarilli*, **278**, 281
  *L'incoronazione di Poppea*, **364** (Act I,
    scene 3), 372
  *Orfeo* (excerpts), **355**, **359**, 363
  *Zefiro torna*, **300**, 312
*Moro, lasso, al mio duolo*, **282**, 286
Motet
  ars nova (isorhythmic), **99** (Vitry), 103;
    **104** (Machaut), 109
  cantus firmus, **153** (Dufay), 160
  concertato, **313** (Gabrieli), 325; **326**
    (Schütz), 334, **336** (Schütz), 347
  discant, **138** (Power), 141; **141**
    (Dunstable), 143
  homophonic, **236** (Lassus), 239
  imitative, **175** (Desprez), 182; **218**
    (Gombert), 223; **224** (Palestrina),

228; **233** (Lassus), 236; **239** (Byrd), 245
thirteenth century (two voices), **60, 62, 67; 78, 85**
thirteenth century (three voices), **78, 80, 83**, 85; **87, 89, 91, 93**, 97
*Musica Enchiriadis,* 32 (*Rex caeli Domine*), **33** (*Sit gloria Domini*), **35**
*Musical Offering, The.* See *Musikalisches Opfer*
*Musikalisches Opfer,* **593, 598**
Mystery Sonata. See *Rosary Sonata*

*Nes que on porroit,* **109,** 115
*Non al suo amante,* **116,** 117
*Non piango e non sospiro,* 348 (Pl. 5), **352,** 354
Notre Dame polyphony, 66
*Nun du wirst mein Gewissen stillen,* **537, 545**

*O quam tu pulchra es,* **326, 334**
*O tocius Asie,* **75,** 78
Ockeghem, Johannes, 183, 223
*Agnus Dei* from *Missa Mi-Mi,* **161,** 166, **167** (Pl. 3)
Offertory, **17,** 22
*On parole de batre/A Paris/Frese nouvele,* **89,** 97
Opera
seventeenth century, 349 (Peri), 354; **355, 359** (Monteverdi, *Orfeo*), 363; **364** (Monteverdi, *Poppea*), 372; **385** (Cavalli), 387; **393** (Lully), 399; **400** (Purcell), 406
eighteenth century, **481** (Handel), 497; **499** (Rameau), 506; **507** (Pergolesi), 513
Opera seria, 497, 506
Oratorio, **373, 380** (Carissimi), 384
Ordinary (of Mass), 21
*Orfeo,* **355, 359,** 363
Organum, 35 (*Alleluia Te martyrum*), 36; **33** (*Ipsi soli*), 32 (*Rex caeli Domine*), 35, 33 (*Sit gloria Domini*), 35
Organum duplum, **58** (*Alleluia Pascha nostrum*), **60** (revision), 66
Organum style, 66
Organum triplum, **67** (*Alleluia Pascha nostrum*), 74
*Orsù orsù car'signori,* **208,** 209
Ortiz, Diego
*Recercada settima* from *Tratado de glosas,* **260,** 262
*Ou mettra l'on ung baiser,* **254,** 258

Palestrina, Giovanni Pierluigi da
*Kyrie* from *Missa Veni sponsa Christi,* **228,** 232
*Veni sponsa Christi* (motet), **224,** 228
*Pange lingua gloriosi corporis,* **40,** 41, 194. See also *Missa Pange lingua*
Parisian chanson, **254,** 258; 265
*Pascha nostrum,* **20,** 23. See also *Alleluia Pascha nostrum*
Passamezzo moderno, 412. See also ground bass
Pavane, **259,** 262, **297,** 299
Peire Vidal
*Baros de mon dan covit,* **44,** 52
Pellegrin, Simon-Joseph, 506
*Per quel vago boschetto,* **349,** 354
*Perfidissimo volto,* **287,** 291
Pergolesi, Giovanni Battista
*La serva padrona,* **507,** 513

Peri, Jacopo
*Euridice* (excerpts), **348** (Pl. 5), **349,** 354
Perotin, 66
*Alleluia Pascha nostrum,* **67,** 74.
Petrarch, Francesco, 117, 265
Petrucci, Ottaviano, 194, 212
Petrus de Cruce
*Aucun ont trouvé/Lonc tans/Annuntiantes,* **93, 98**
*Pièces de clavecin, Premier livre,* **547** (Pl. 6), **548** (*Premier ordre*), 554
Power, Leonel, 152
Credo *Opem nobis,* **132,** 140
*Ave regina caelorum,* **138,** 141
Prelude, **434** (unmeasured, L. Couperin), 441; **450** (Corelli), 454; **454** (Biber), 458; **555** (J. S. Bach), 559
*Prélude a l'imitation de Mr. Froberger,* **434, 441**
*Prendes i garde,* **51,** 53
Proper (of Mass), 21
*Prophetiae Sibyllarum,* **236,** 239
Prose, **11,** 22, **38,** 41
Psalm tone, **24, 26,** 28, 33
Purcell, Henry
*Dido and Aeneas,* **400** (concluding scene), 406

*Quant j'ay l'espart,* **112,** 115
*Quem queritis in sepulchro,* **3,** 21
*Questa fanciull' amor,* **122,** 124
Quinault, Philippe, 399, 506
*Quivi trà questi solitarii orrori,* **486,** 498

Rameau, Jean-Phillippe
*Hippolyte et Aricie,* **499** (Act I, scene 2), 506
*Recercada settima* (Ortiz), **260,** 262
Recercare. See Ricercare
Recitative, 372, 384, 387, 392, 479, 498, 506, 546. See also *Stile recitativo*
*Resurrexi,* **1** (Pl. 1), **2,** 21
*Rex caeli Domine,* **32,** 35
*Rex pacificus,* **24,** 28
Rhythmic modes, 66, 74, 85
Ricercare, **210,** 212; **260,** 262; 420, 559
Rinuccini, Ottavio, 312, 354
Ritornello, 325, 347, 355, 480, 498, 592
Roger, Estienne, 470
Romance, **205,** 207
Romanesca, **260,** 262. See also Variation, Ground bass
Rondeau, 51 (Guillaume d'Amiens), 53; **112** (Machaut), 115; **168, 169** (Dufay), 171; **171** (Hayne von Ghizeghem), 174
Rore, Cipriano de
*Da le belle contrade d'oriente,* **266,** 271
*Rosary Sonata X,* **454,** 458
Rossi, Salamone
*Sonata in dialogo* ("LaViena"), **441, 445**

Sanctus, **19,** 22
Sarabande, **432** (Froberger), 433; **552** (F. Couperin), 554
*Saul, Saul, was verfolgst du mich?,* **336,** 347
*Scaldava il sol,* **272,** 277
Scarlatti, Allesandro
*Su le sponde del Tebro,* **472,** 479
Scarlatti, Domenico
*Sonata in D major, K. 119 (L. 415),* **564,** 570
*Sonata in D minor, K. 120 (L. 215),* **560,** 570

*Scordatura,* 454, 458
Scheidt, Samuel
*Jesus Christus unser Heiland, der von us,* **413,** 420
Schütz, Heinrich
*O quam tu pulchra es,* **326,** 334
*Saul, Saul was verfolgst du mich?,* **336,** 347
*Scipione Africano,* **385,** 387
*Se la face ay pale,* **151,** 152
*Señora de hermosura,* **205,** 207
Sequence. See Prose
*Sit gloria Domini,* **33,** 35
Sonata, **441** (Rossi), 445; **454** (Biber), 458; **459** (Corelli), 470; **560** (D. Scarlatti, D minor), **564** (D. Scarlatti, D major), 570. See also Trio sonata
*Sonata a due Violini,* **446,** 449
Sonata da camera, 449, **450,** 454
Sonata da chiesa, 449, 471
*Sonata in dialogo* ("La Viena"), **441,** 445
Square notation, xv
St. Martial polyphony. See Aquitanian polyphony
*Stile rappresentativo,* 354
*Stile recitativo,* 354, 363. See also Recitative
Suite, **428** (Froberger), 433; **548** (F. Couperin), 554
*Su le sponde del Tebro,* **472,** 479
*Sus un' fontayne,* **128,** 131

*Tabulatura Nova,* **413,** 420
Talea, 103,109
*Terra tremuit,* **17,** 22
Toccata, **421, 425,** 559
*Tosto che l'alba,* **118,** 121
*Trágedie lyrique,* 399, 506
*Tralascia pur di piangere,* **475,** 480
*Tratado de glosas,* **260,** 262
Trecento song, 116, 117, 121, 124
*Tribum que/Quoniam secta/Merito hec patimur,* **99,** 103
Trio sonata, **441** (Rossi), 445; **446** (Vitali), 449; **450** (Corelli), 454
*Triste España,* **205,** 207
*Tristis est anima mea,* **233,** 236
Trope, **3** (*Quem queritis in sepulchro*), **4** (*Ecce pater cunctis*), 21
Troubadour song, **42,** 52
Trouvère song, **49,** 52
*Tu règne sur nos coeurs,* **503,** 506
*Tu se' morta,* **360,** 363

Variation, **260,** 262, **407, 412, 413, 420, 454,** 458. See also Ground bass
*Veni redemptor gentium,* **27,** 29
*Veni sancte spiritus,* **38,** 41
*Veni sponsa Christi*
plainsong, **227,** 228
Mass, **228,** 232
motet, **224,** 228
Ventadorn, Bernart de. See Bernart de Ventadorn
Versicle, **28** (*Benedicamus Domino*), **23** (*Deus in adjutorium meum*), 28, 78
Versus, **37,** 37, **54, 56,** 78
Vespers, Christmas, **23,** 28
Vidal, Peire. See Peire Vidal
*Viderunt Emmanuel,* **54,** 56
*Vi ricordi,* **355,** 363
*Violin concerto in G minor, Opus 8, No. 8* (Vivaldi), **571, 592**
Villancico, **205,** 207

Virelai, **113** (Machaut), 115; **125** (Borlet?), 127; **128** (Ciconia), 131
Vitali, Giovanni Battista, 471
  *Sonata a due Violini,* **446,** 449
Vitry, Philippe de
  *Tribum que/Quoniam secta/Merito hec patimur,* **99,** 102
Vivaldi, Antonio

*Violin Concerto in G minor,* Opus 8, No. 8 RV 332, **571,** 592
Voice exchange, 98

Walter, Johann
  *Aus tiefer Not,* **214,** 217
*Well-Tempered Clavier, The.* See *Das wohltemperirte Clavier*

*When I am laid in earth,* **400,** 406
*Wir eilen mit schwachen, doch emsigen Schritten,* **526,** 545
*With drooping wings ye Cupids come,* **403**
Word painting, 236, 265, 277
Wulfstan of Winchester
  *Alleluia Te martyrum,* **35,** 36

*Zefiro torna,* **300,** 312

## About the Author

**Sarah Fuller** is Associate Professor of Music at the State University of New York at Stony Brook where she teaches music history and literature. She received a B. A. *magna cum laude* in music from Radcliffe College and a Ph.D. in musicology from the University of California at Berkeley. Her publications delve into problems of early polyphony, medieval music theory, the *ars nova*, and the music of Guillaume de Machaut.